GESAMTKUNSTWERK

NEW ART FROM GERMANY

SAATCHI GALLERY DUKE OF YORK'S HQ LONDON

GESAMTKUNSTWERK

Introduction and texts by Lupe Núñez-Fernández

The word *Gesamtkunstwerk* can be translated as a total, ideal, or universal work of art, or as a synthesis of different art forms into one all-embracing unique genre. The term, first coined by the German philosopher K F E Trahndorff, was popularised in the nineteenth century by Richard Wagner, who used it in his 1849 essay entitled 'The Artwork of the Future' as a way of defining his own aesthetic ideals: integrating universal, archetypal themes found in folk legend into a single all-encompassing modern theatrical experience.

To Wagner the key to achieving this was to be found in music's expressive potential, epitomised by opera, in which individual artistic elements – composition, plot, libretto, costume and stage sets – are subordinated 'for the sake of achieving the overall purpose of them all'. As creative master of the *Gesamtkunstwerk*, the artist's ultimate power is to place the audience under a spell so that everyone experiencing the work is transported into a state of complete intoxication, as if in a mystical initiation, in which each individual becomes part of the artwork.

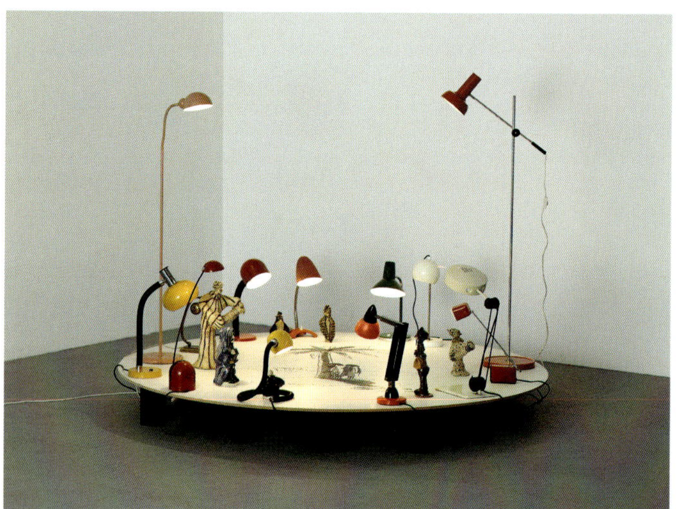

Friedrich Kunath, Untitled, 2007

The potential for the *Gesamtkunstwerk* to be read as a sinister, manipulative force became infamous through the Third Reich's ideological appropriation of Wagner's aesthetic vision, but the term's meaning has broadened since then and continues to be filtered into wider cultural discourse. It has been applied to the work of the architect, to design, to cinema and other audio, visual and sensory practices, which aim to fuse separate disciplinary elements into a single, significant whole.

It is hard not to keep the word in mind – both its original, myth-based roots and the way that, like a myth, it has come to inform our reading of multidisciplinary contemporary culture – when considering the work of the twenty-four artists from or based in Germany that are presented in this exhibition. Their art provokes a reassessment of thoughts associated with the unattainable nineteenth-century ideal, often pointing to the dramatic 'total, universal work of art', but also suggesting that it is something that defies interpretation.

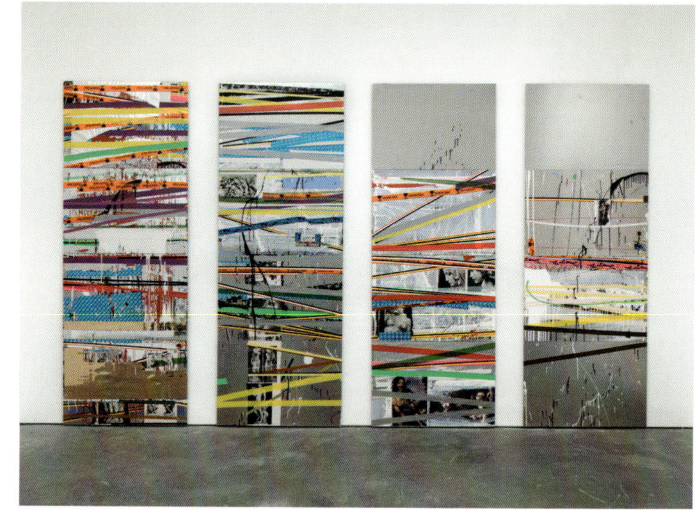

Isa Genzken, Kinder Filmen I, 2005

Much of the work in this exhibition asks us to think about the boundaries of art, in terms of our perception of it, its cultural specificity and its relationship to other disciplines. Running through the exhibition is an inherent reference to another, unconscious, quasi-*Gesamtkunstwerk*: the baggage of post-war German visual culture, and the work of earlier generations of German artists, from the Expressionists to Joseph Beuys, Anselm Kiefer, Martin Kippenberger, Rosemarie Trockel, Gerhard Richter and Franz West, with whom many of the artists in this exhibition seem to be in conversation.

Josephine Meckseper's vitrines, Isa Genzken's conceptual assemblages, Ida Ekblad's poetry-infused concrete paintings and Alexandra Bircken's unmonumental stretcher frames explore the boundaries between artistic practices and genres, as well as the associative potential between objects and the politics of globalisation, a theme that is also evident in Andro Wekua's graphic, oneiric tile and print installations.

Fusing a dual fascination with the past and the future, Markus Selg's intimately rendered figurative prints, sculptures and furniture refer to universal artistic motifs. His syncretic imagery, materials and blending of art and design into a single practice opens up the traditional physical demarcation around the artist's inner creative space of artifice and the truly *Gesamtkunstwerk* forces of nature, life and human society. This is raised as well through the conspiratorial, foreboding psychedelia permeating Thomas Zipp's 'museum installations', Zhivago Duncan's post-apocalyptic time-travel narratives and Kirstine Roepstorff's collaged deconstructions of twentieth-century society.

The *Gesamtkunstwerk's* associations with the synaesthetic are tapped into by works that provoke a physical reaction, or tease out transformative relationships between material and meaning. Jeppe Hein's unexpectedly experiential installations and Max Frisinger's crammed assemblages generate a sense of larger-than-life wonder, causing us to suspend our disbelief. Jutta Koether's loud abstractions resonate with allusion to sound and performance works, but also to the cultural hollowness and alienation explored in post-war German art. André Butzer's massive Abstract-Expressionst-via-Munch-and-Disney canvases and Stefan Kürten's riveting painted flora, with all their asphyxiating decorativeness, also engage with this subject matter. Thomas Kiesewetter's metal sculptures combine echoes of modernist art with the history of industrial and architectural form, highlighting the ongoing relationship between the past and the present.

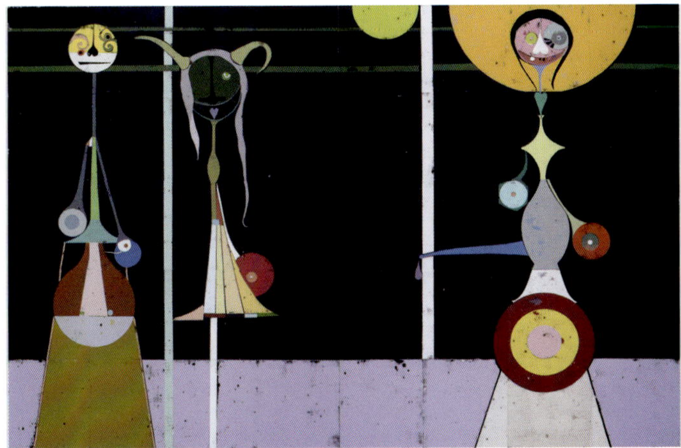

Gert and Uwe Tobias, Untitled, 2007

A blown-up and oversized – sometimes surreally operatic and grotesque – phantasmagoria permeates the work of this new generation of artists: consider Gert and Uwe Tobias's giant printed puppets, Dirk Bell's overwhelmingly sensual figuration, Volker Hueller's engulfing fragmented portraits and Friedrich Kunath's bittersweet reconsideration of the artist as sad clown.

Further flashes of a *Gesamtkunstwerk* made within the context of globalised culture can be seen in Julian Rosefeldt's iconology of soap opera characters, Corinne Wasmuht's painted information highway and Felix Gmelin's case study of modern iconoclasm, revealing the way art and history are constructed.

Choreographing traditional arts with the concerns of architecture, theatre, museology, urban studies, radical politics, poetry and more, the artists in this exhibition convey the ways in which art can be multidisciplinary and all-encompassing. It can involve aesthetic experimentation, lyricism, locally specific and universal social critique, as well as a globally aware and ongoing re-interpretation of its own historical boundaries. If their art points to a new kind of

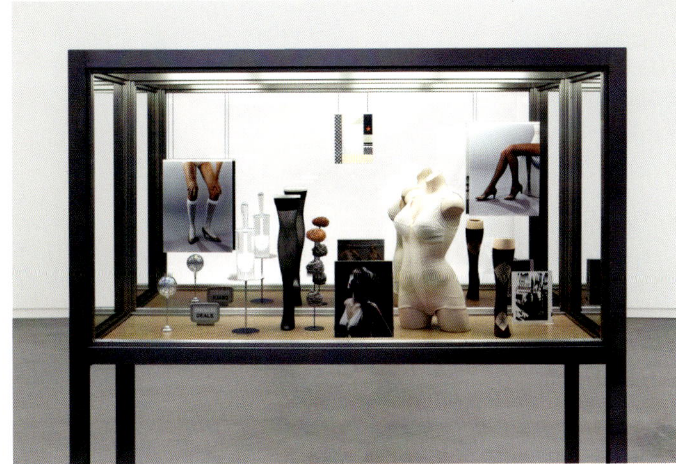

Josephine Meckseper, Blow Up (Michelli), 2006

Gesamtkunstwerk it is one in which high and low culture, the avant-garde and the historical, the everyday and everything in between can co-exist in a body of works which add up to much more than the sum of their parts.

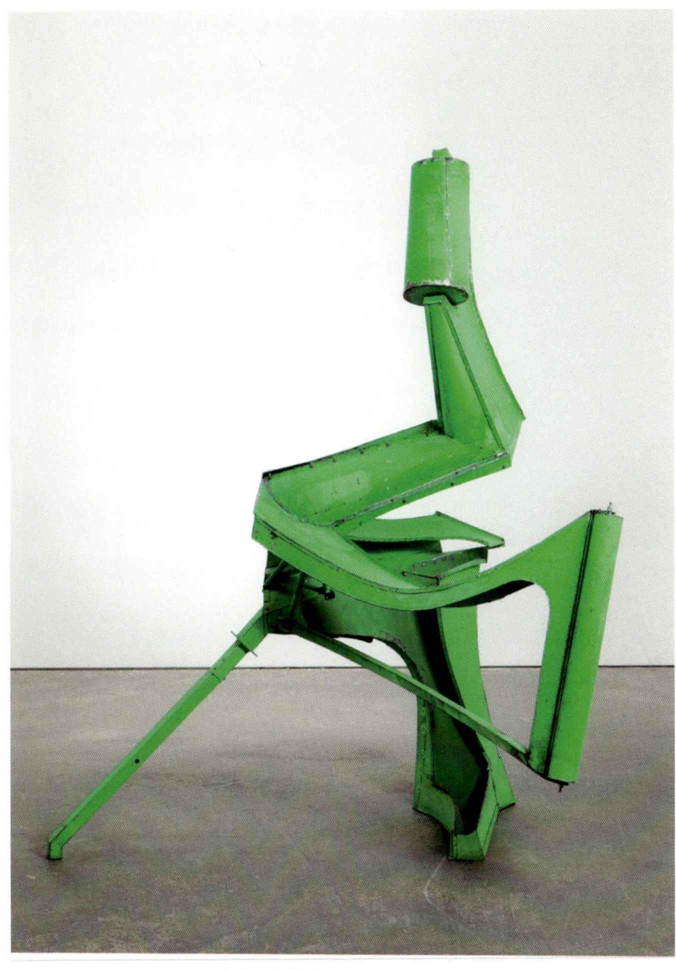

Thomas Kiesewetter, Untitled, 2004

DIRK BELL
Abgrund (Abyss) 2008
Mixed media on canvas, curtain, mirror pieces,
bones, wood, paint, neon lamp, electric cable
204.7 x 174.5 x 14.4 cm

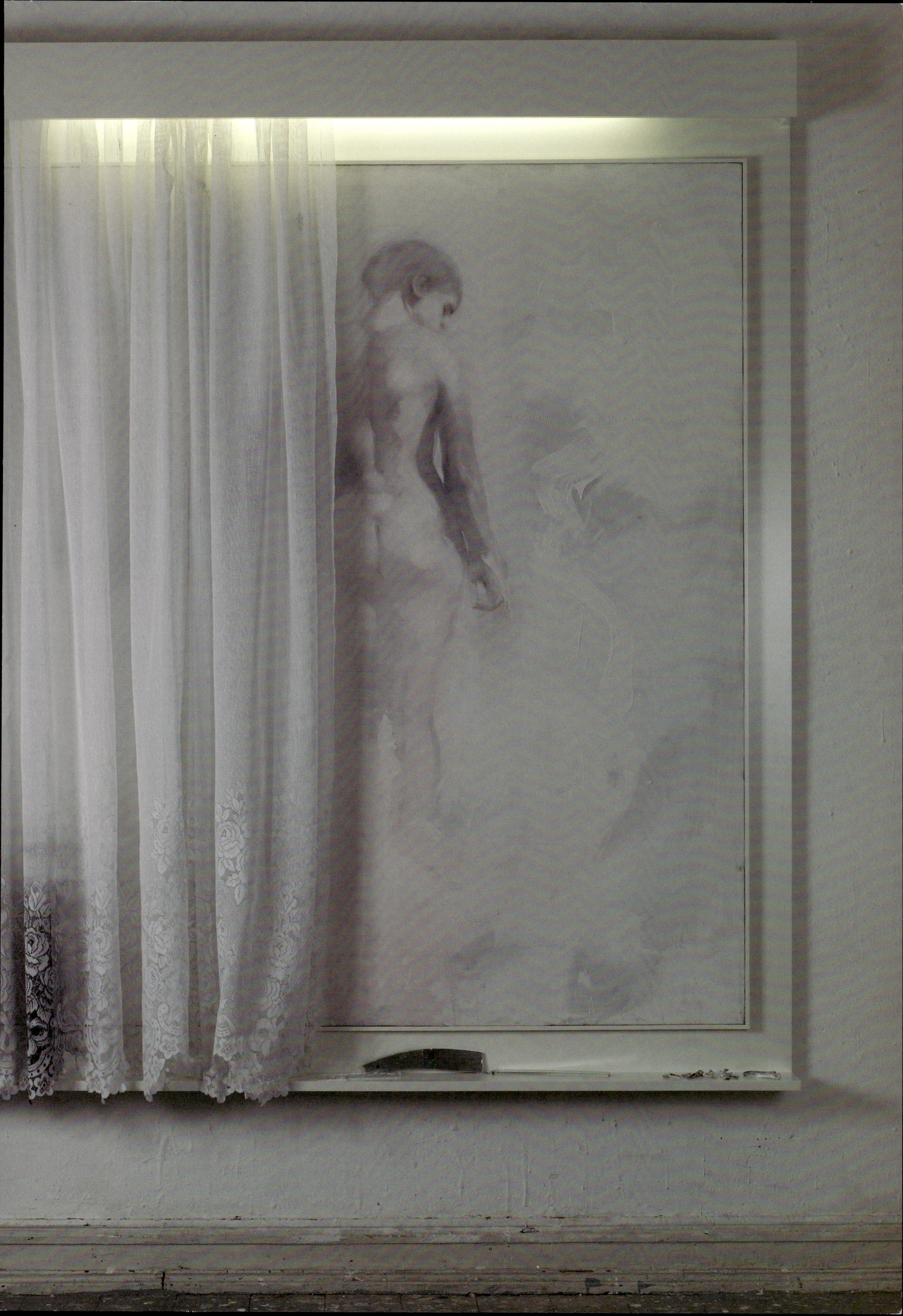

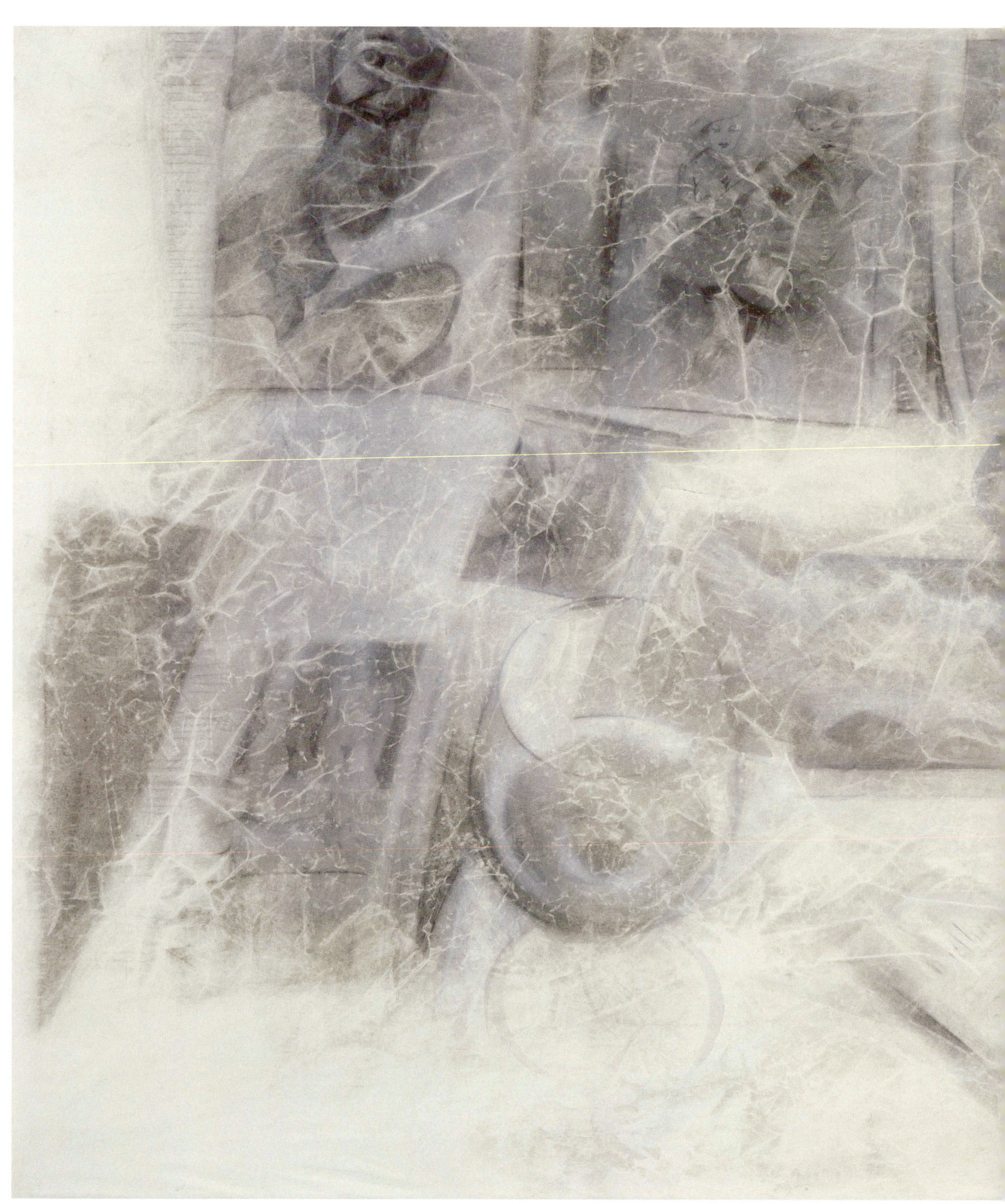

DIRK BELL
Rabbit's Moon 2007
Mixed media on canvas
160 x 276 cm

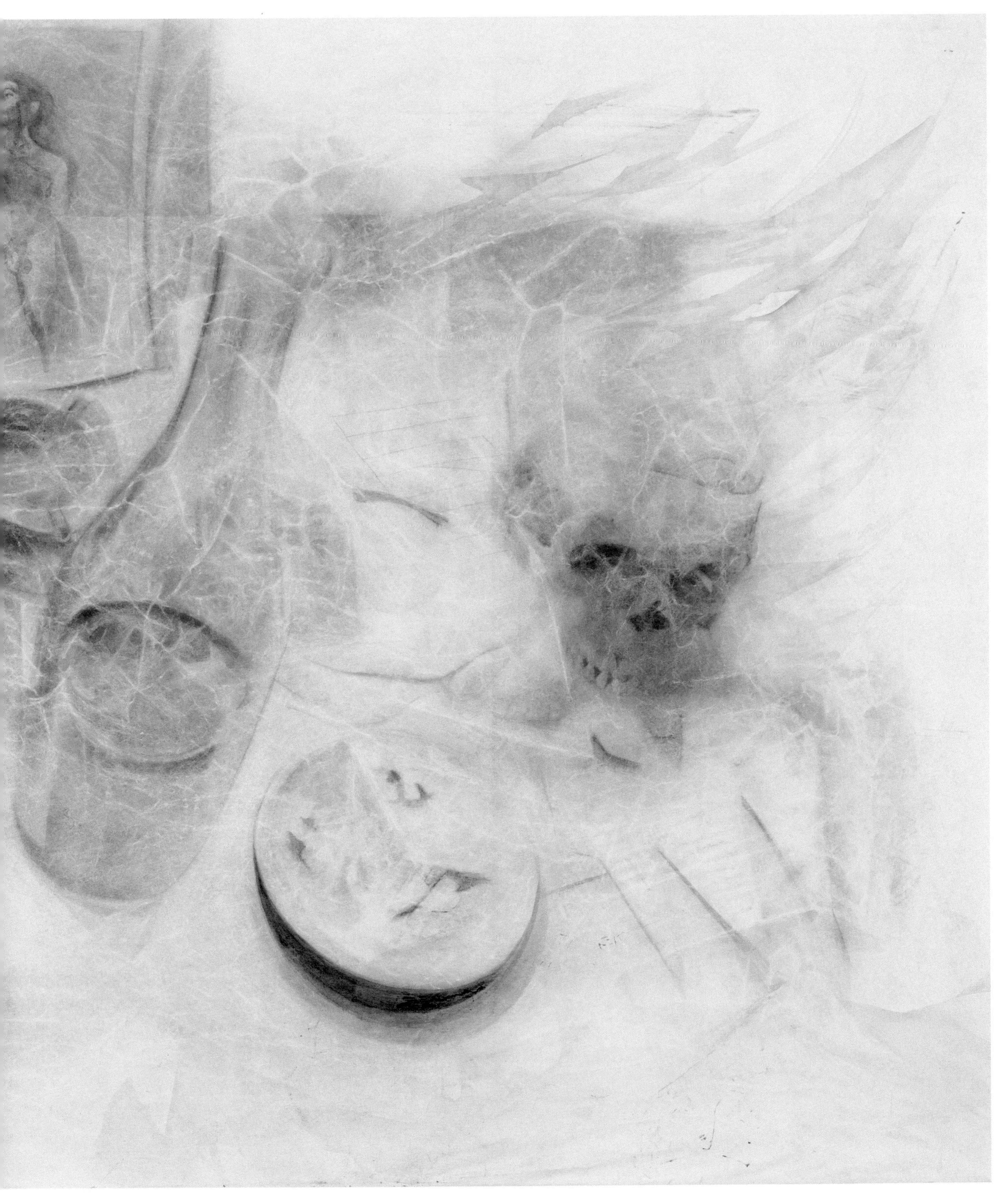

DIRK BELL
Wolf Hamlet Madonna Elmex 2006
Mixed media on canvas
230 x 140 cm

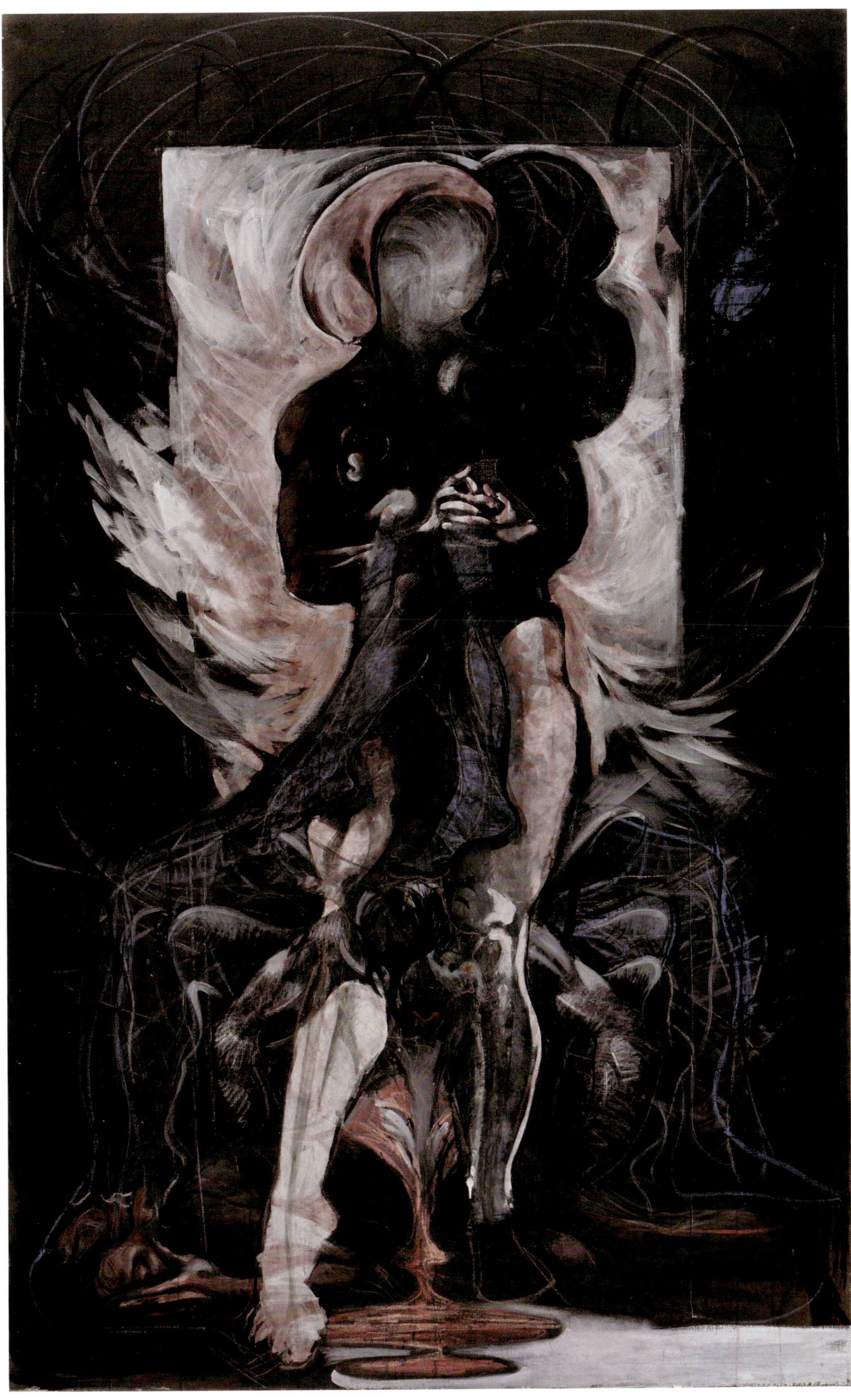

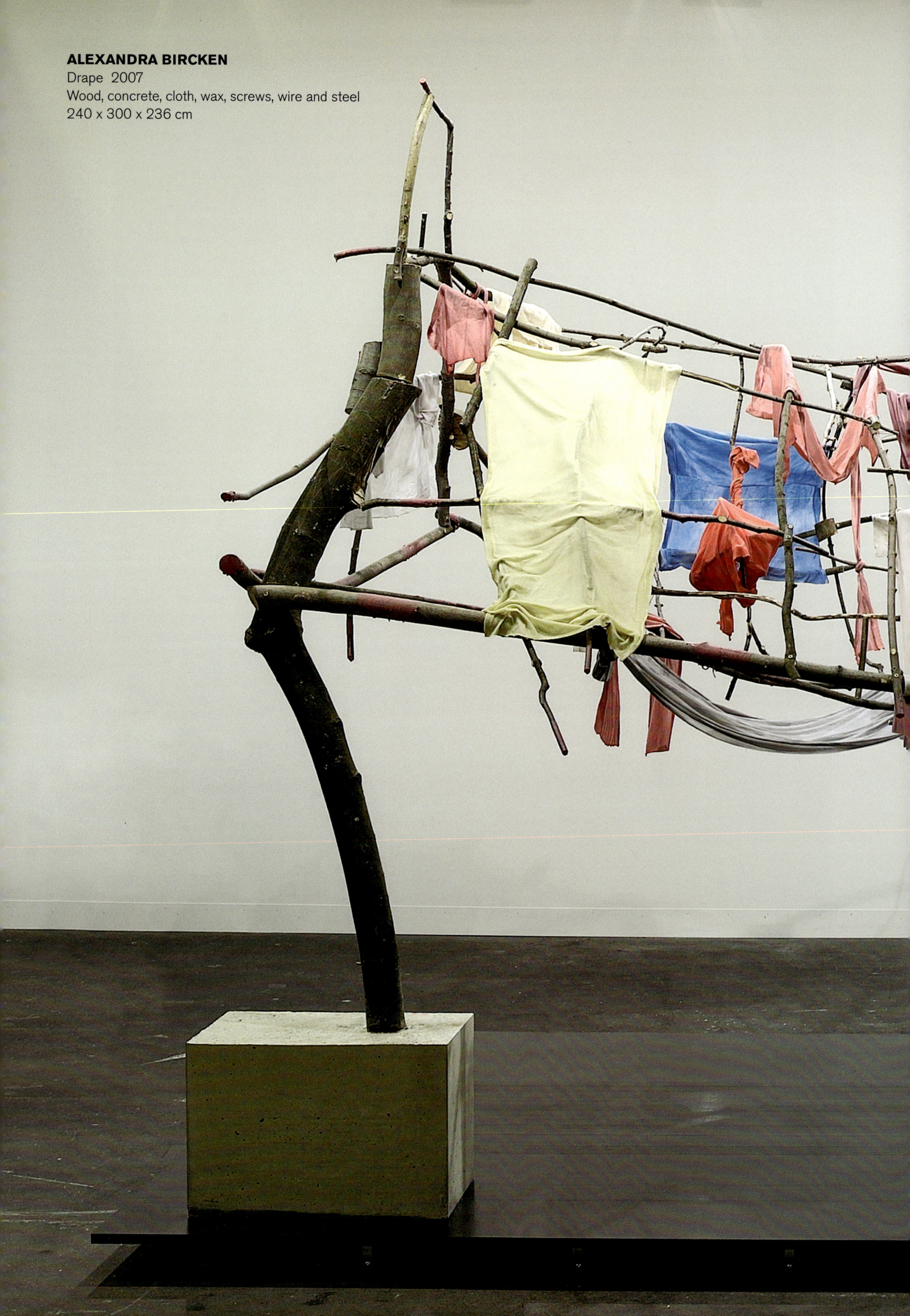

ALEXANDRA BIRCKEN
Drape 2007
Wood, concrete, cloth, wax, screws, wire and steel
240 x 300 x 236 cm

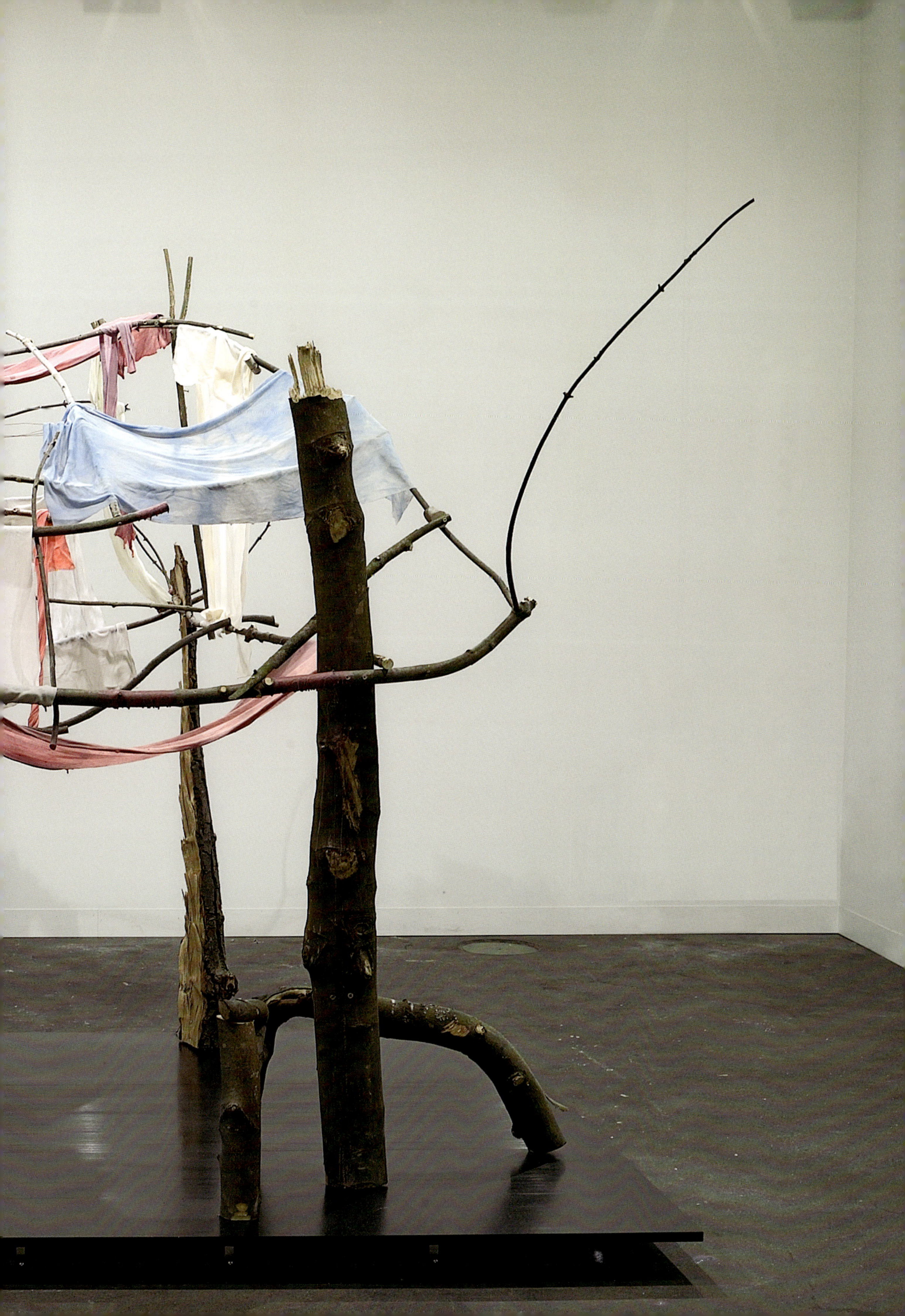

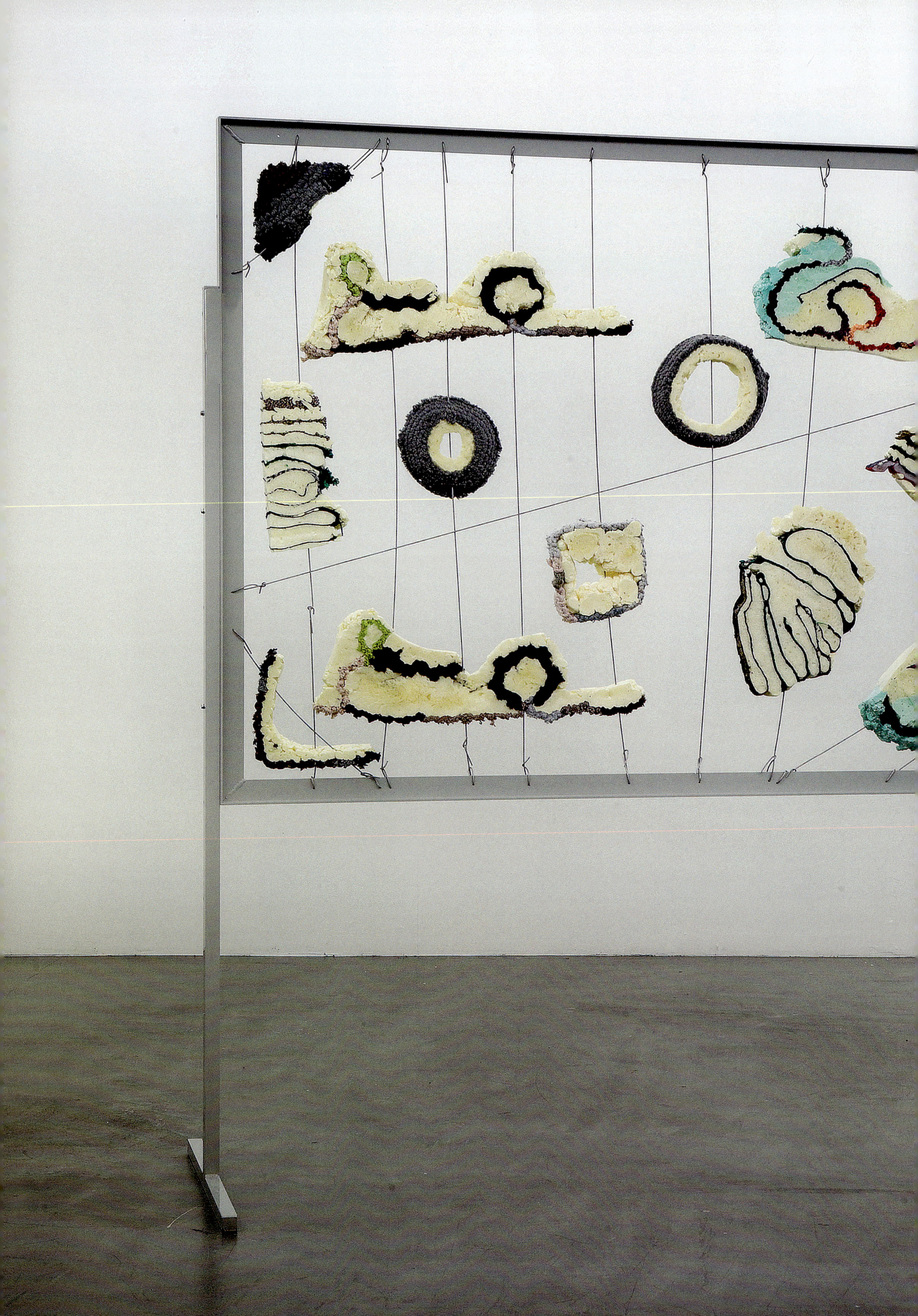

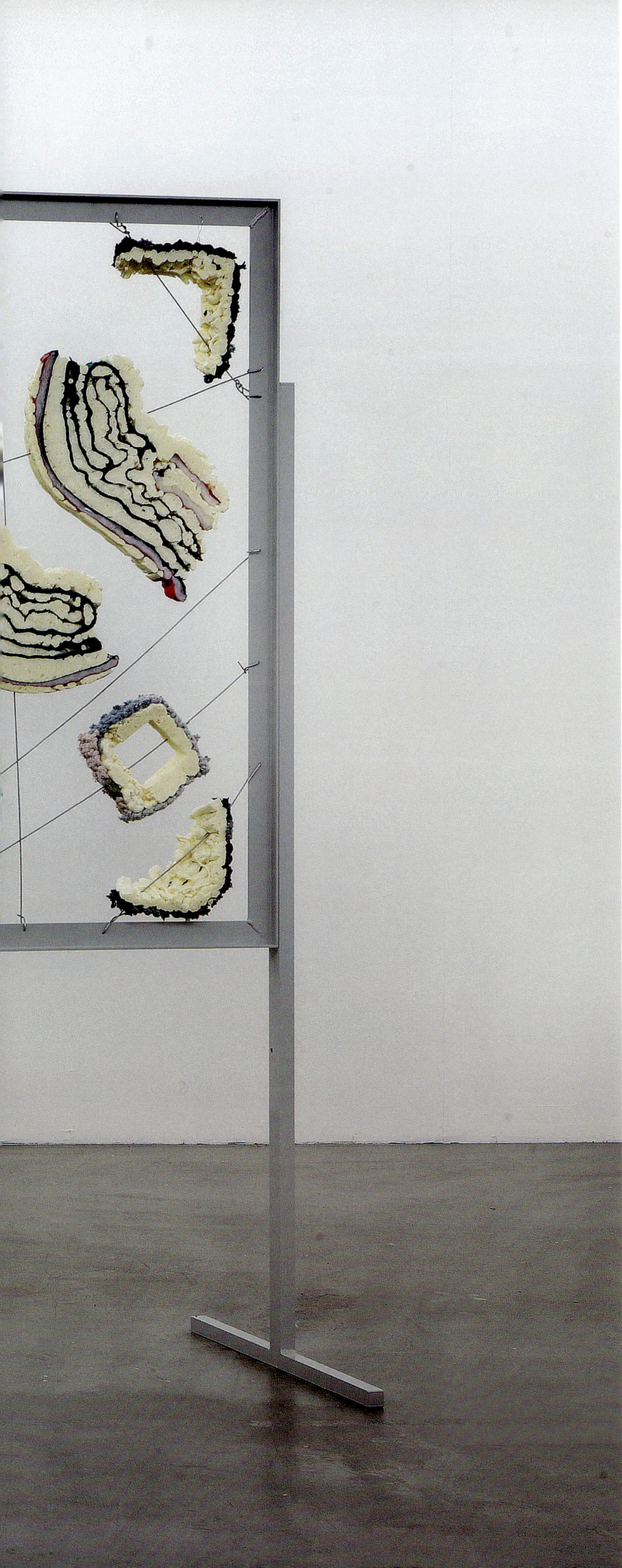

ALEXANDRA BIRCKEN
Unit 1 2008
Coated aluminium, aluminium rods, polyurethane
foam, fabric, wool
Frame: 140 x 220 cm
Base: 80 x 185 cm

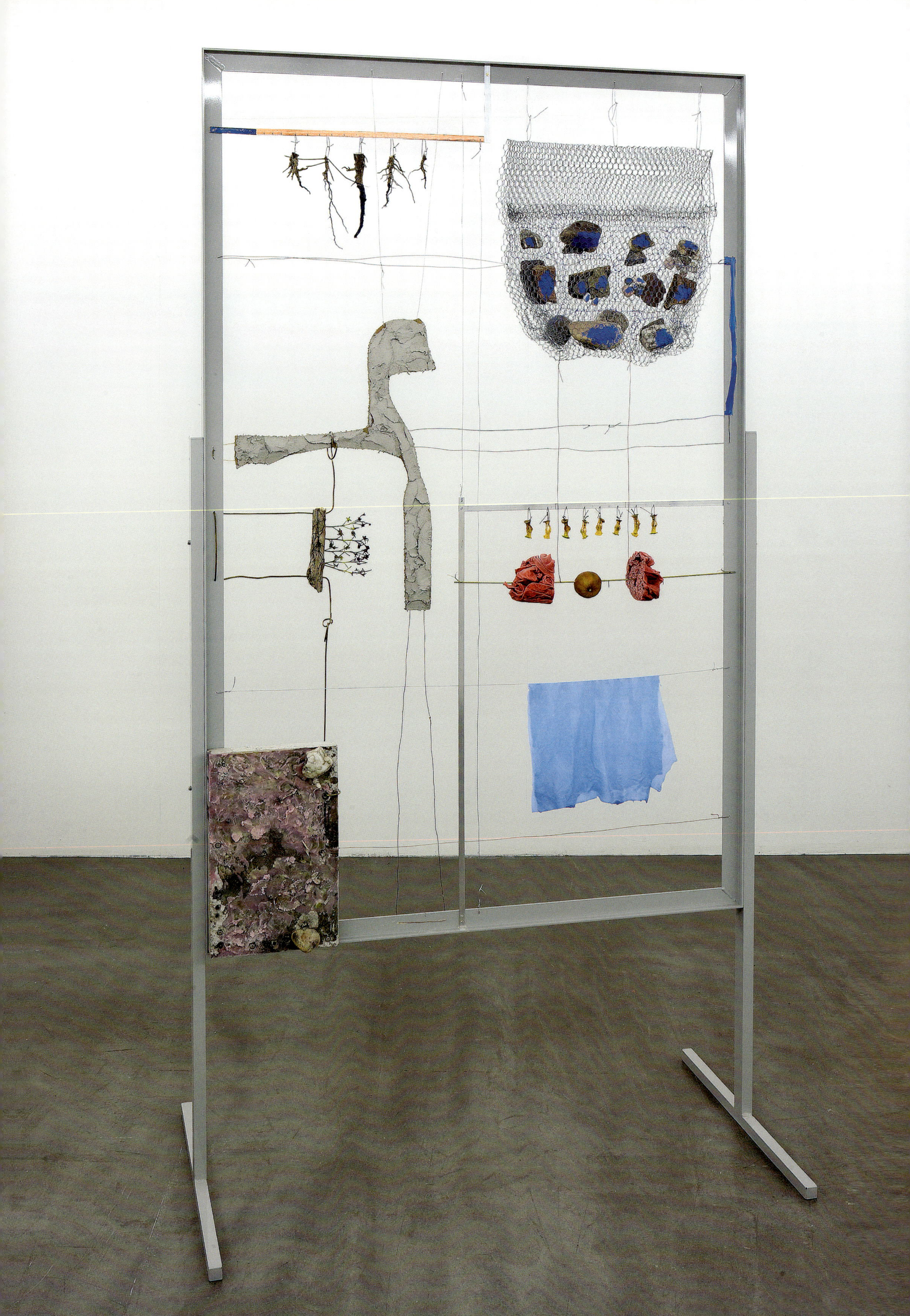

ALEXANDRA BIRCKEN
Unit 3 2008
Coated aluminium, copper, brass, wire, roots, stones, acrylic paint,
spray paint, cardboard, mortar, branches, tomato panicle, steel,
concrete, wax, oilcloth, tangerine, apple cores, screws
Frame: 220 x 140 cm Base: 80 x 185 cm

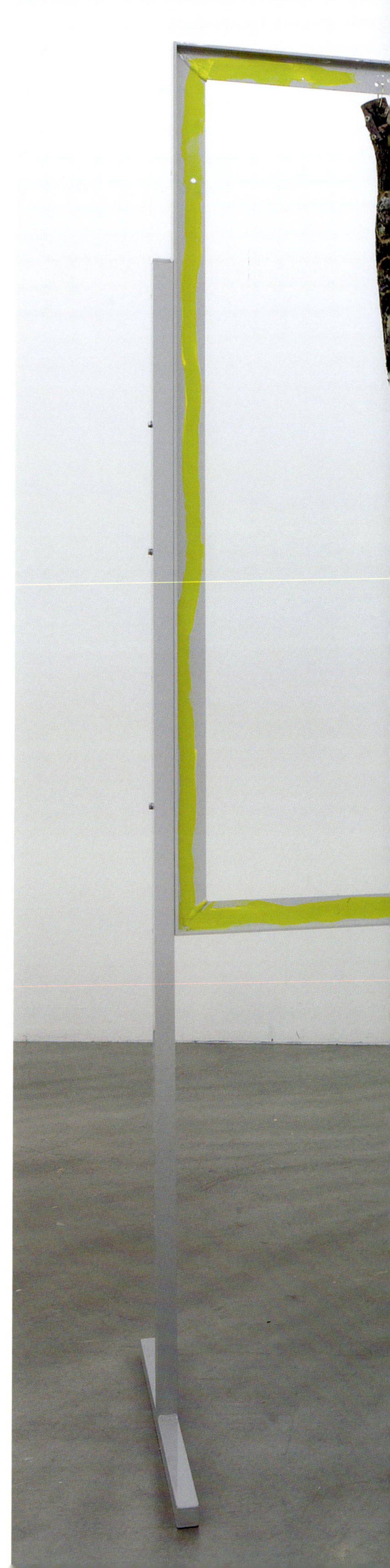

ALEXANDRA BIRCKEN
Unit 4 2008
Coated aluminium, branches, plastic tube, acrylic paint,
stone slices, bread, wire, screws
Frame: 140 x 220 cm Base: 80 x 185 cm

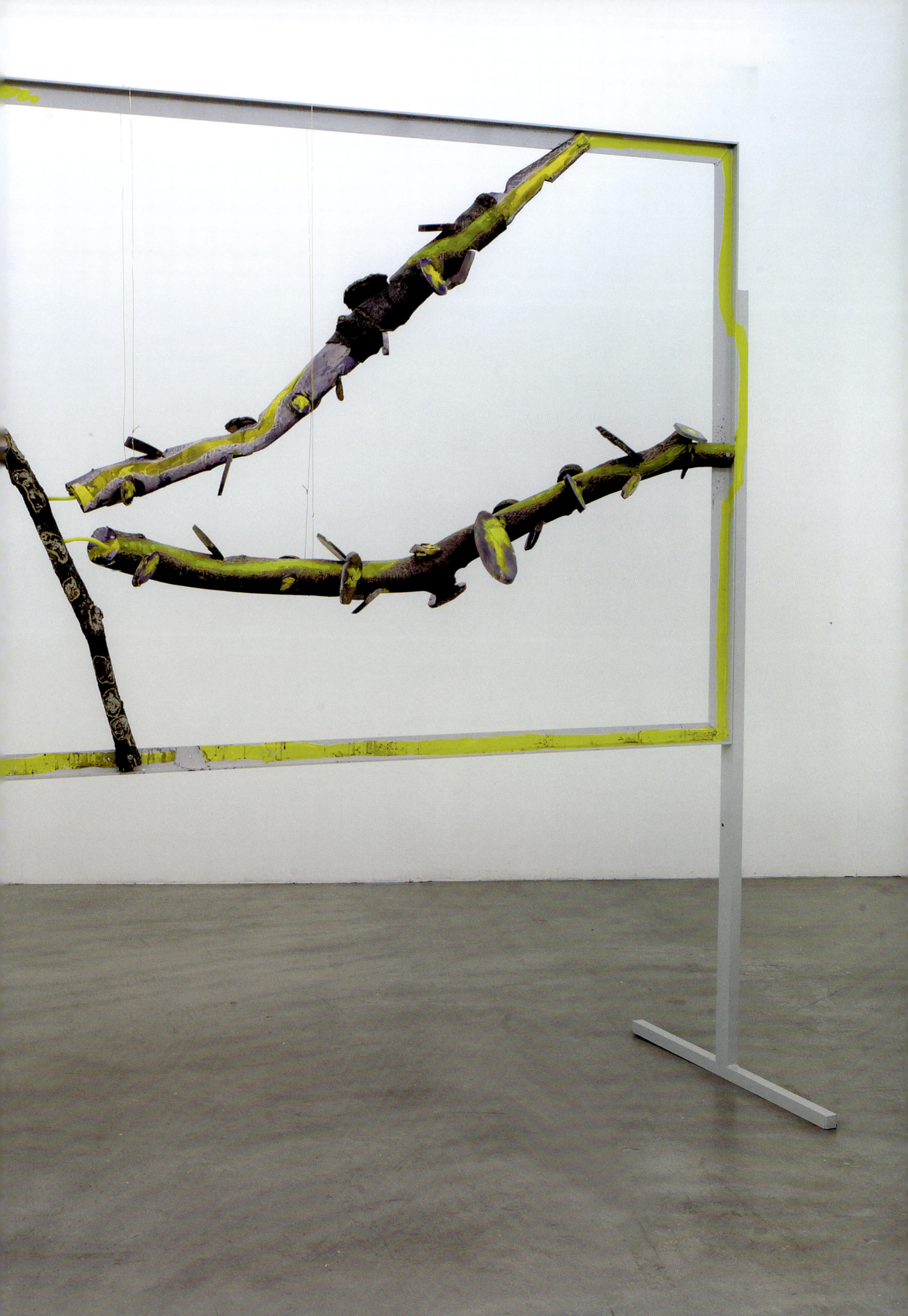

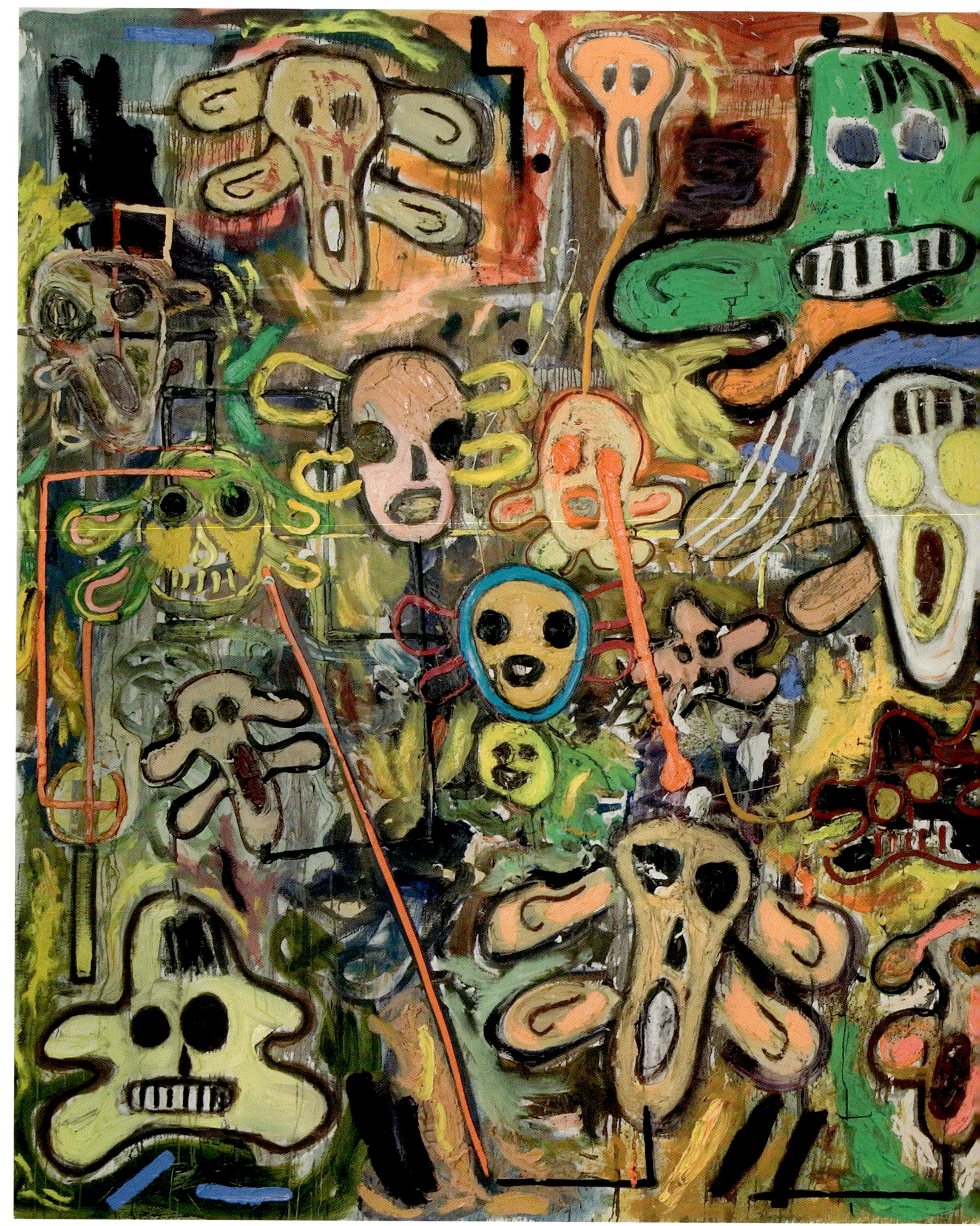

ANDRÉ BUTZER
Ahnenbild 2411 2006
Oil on canvas
280 x 460 cm

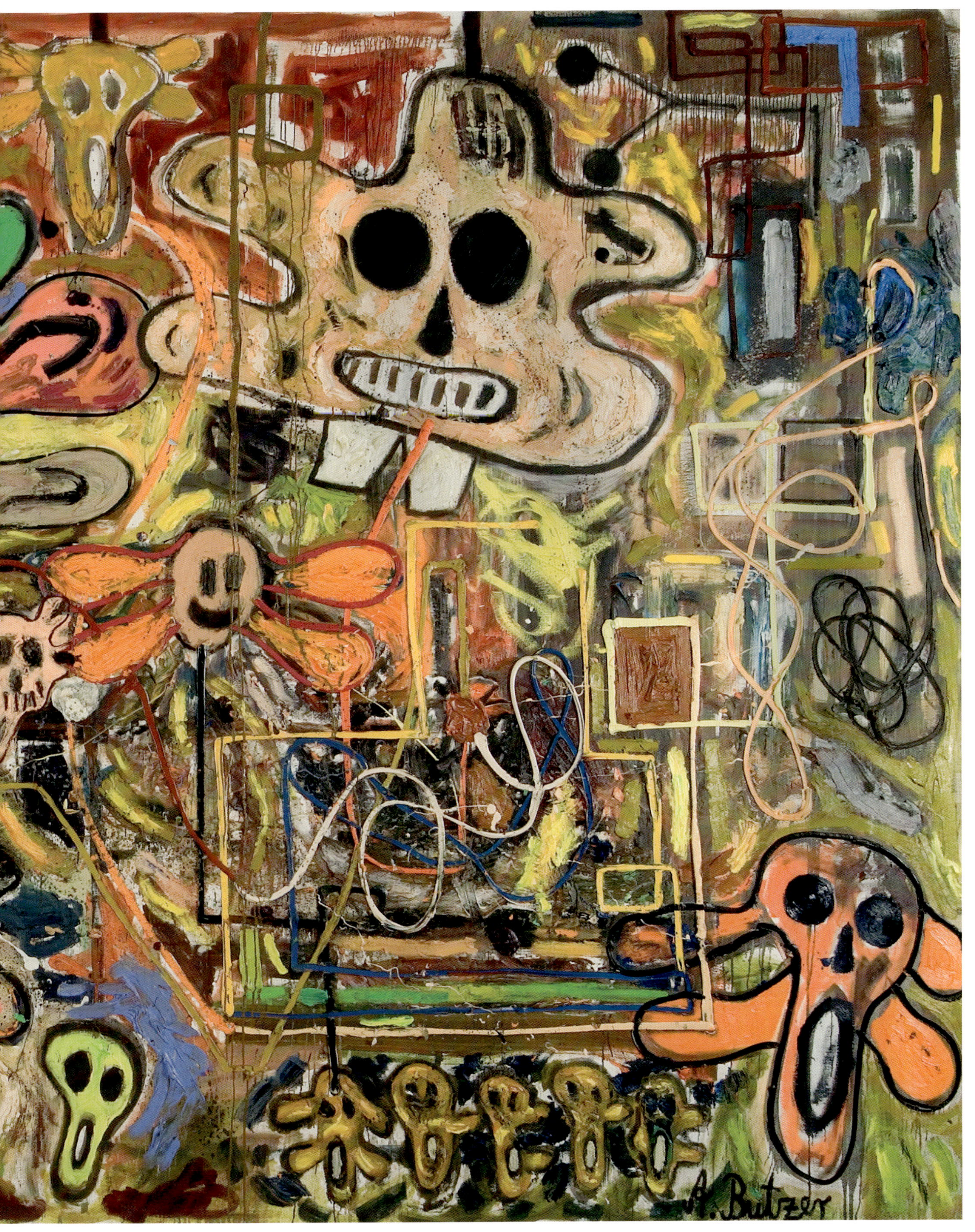

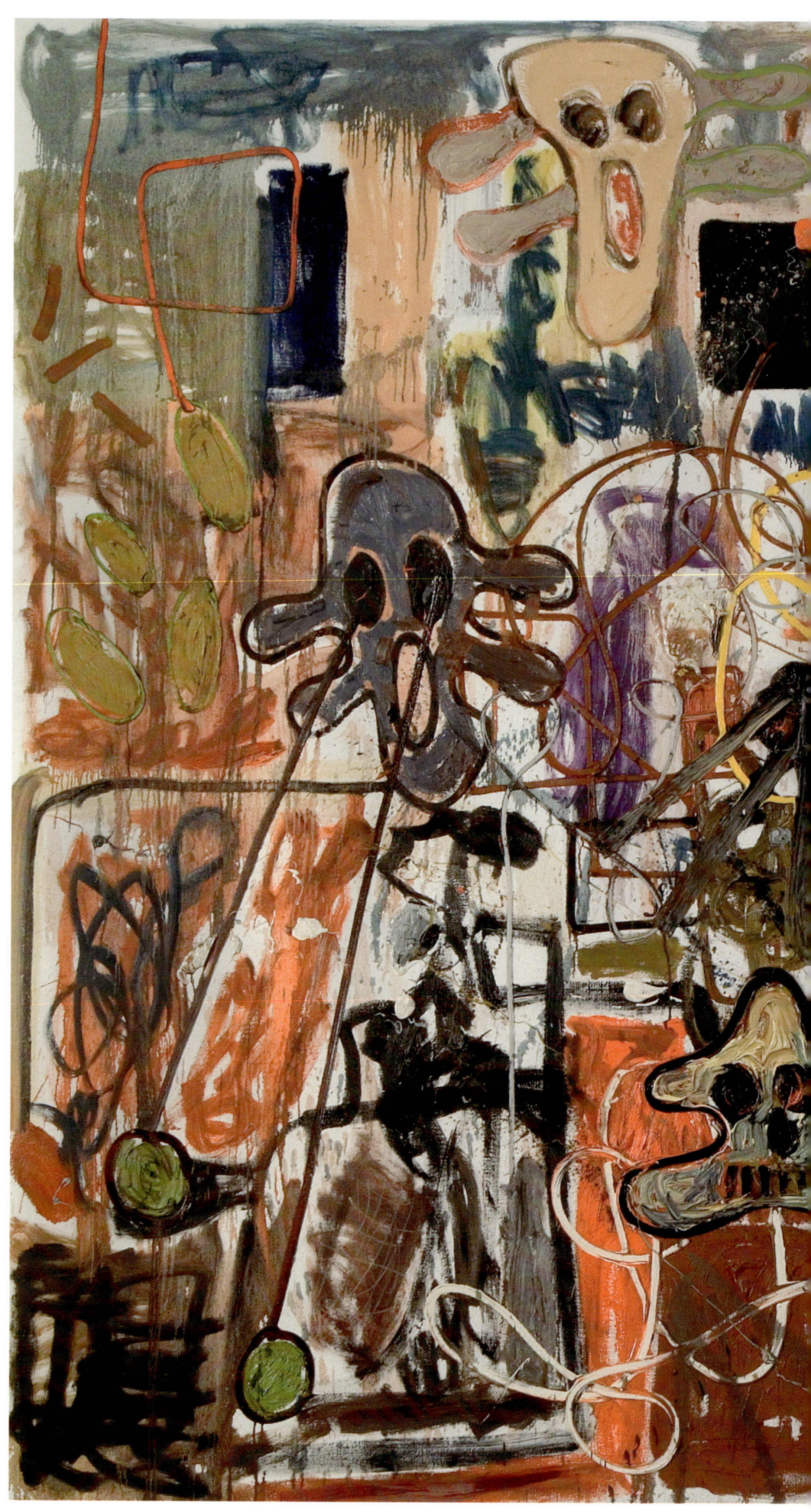

ANDRÉ BUTZER
Untitled 2007
Oil on canvas
260 x 340 cm

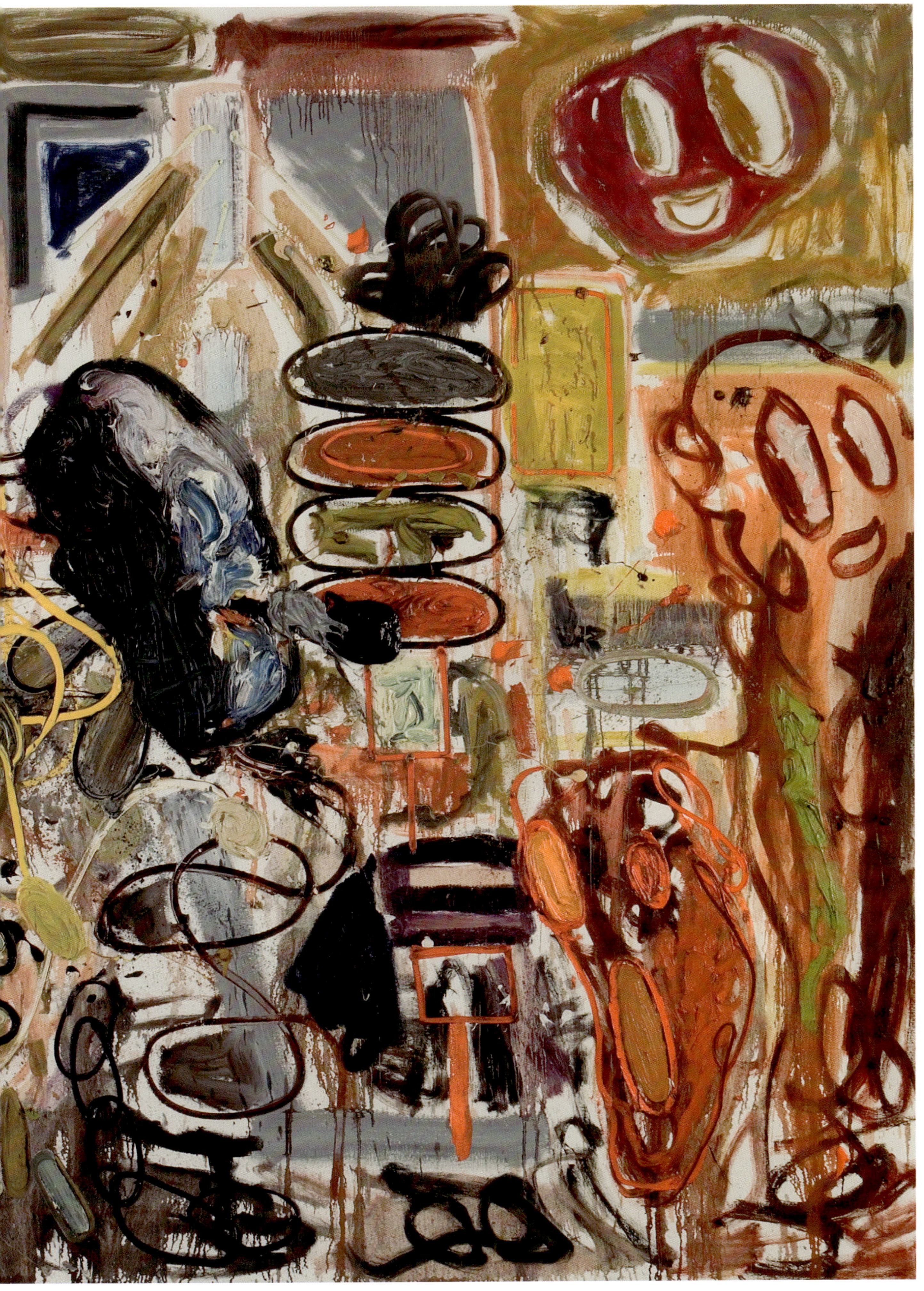

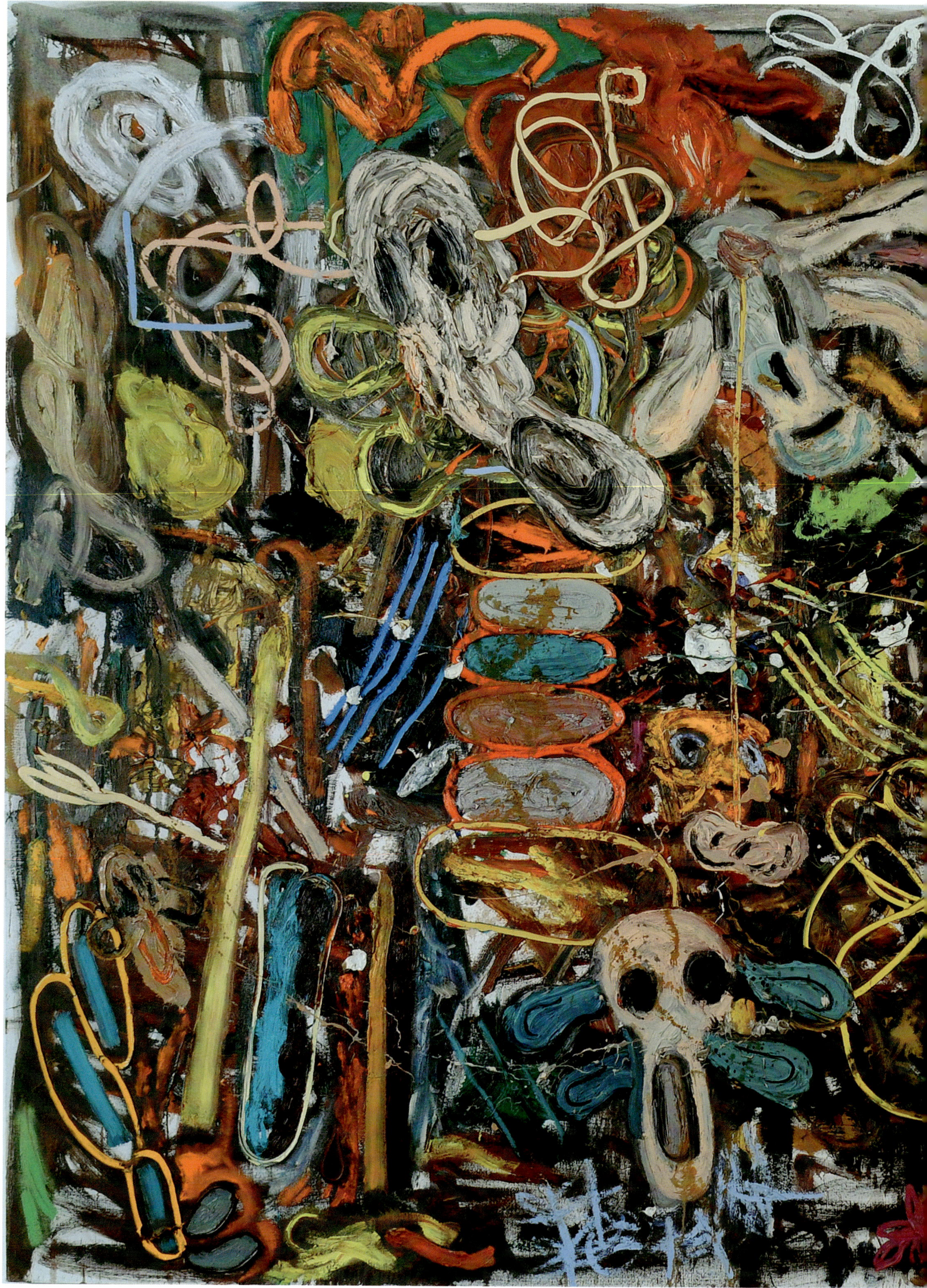

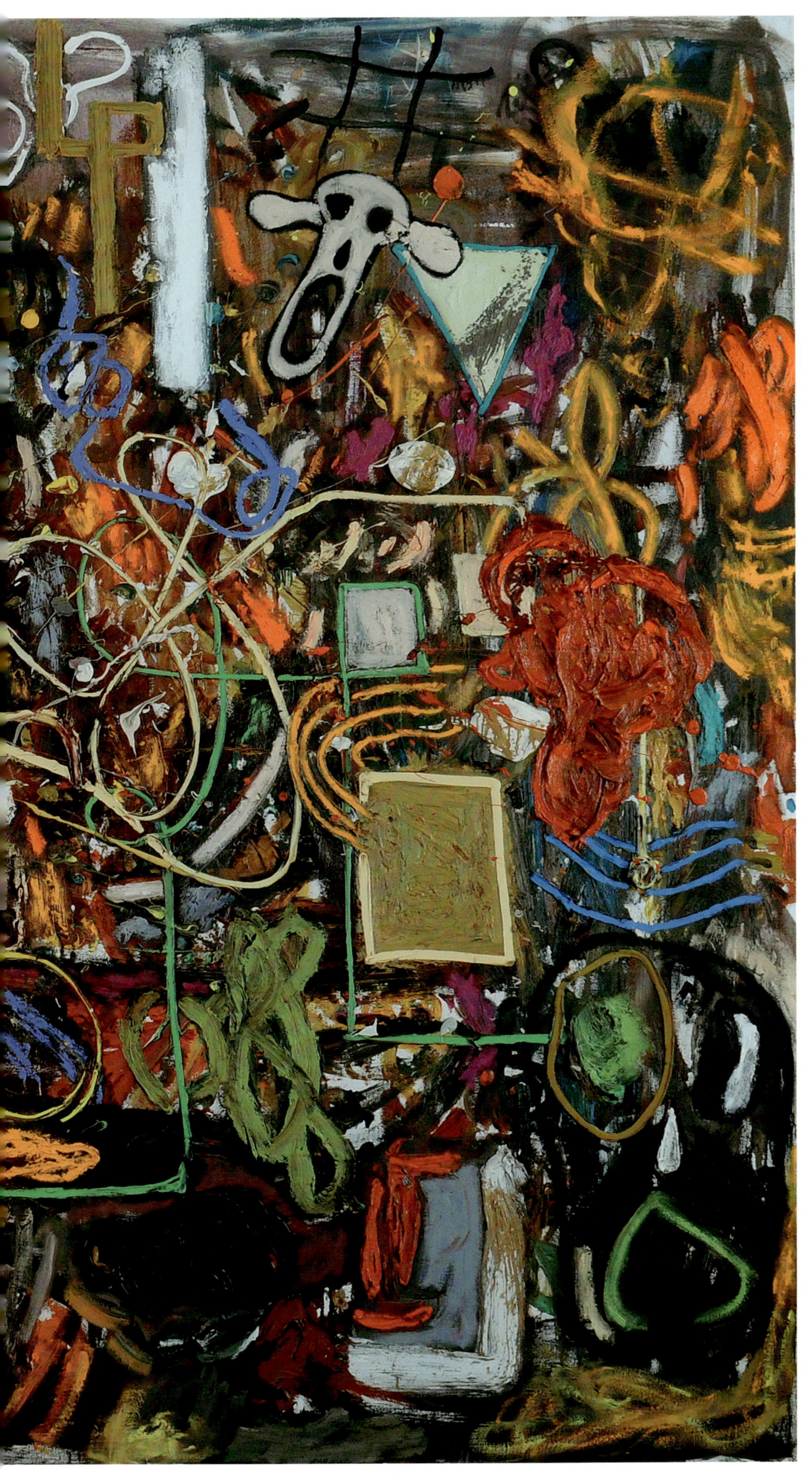

ANDRÉ BUTZER
Untitled 2007
Oil on canvas
260 x 340 cm

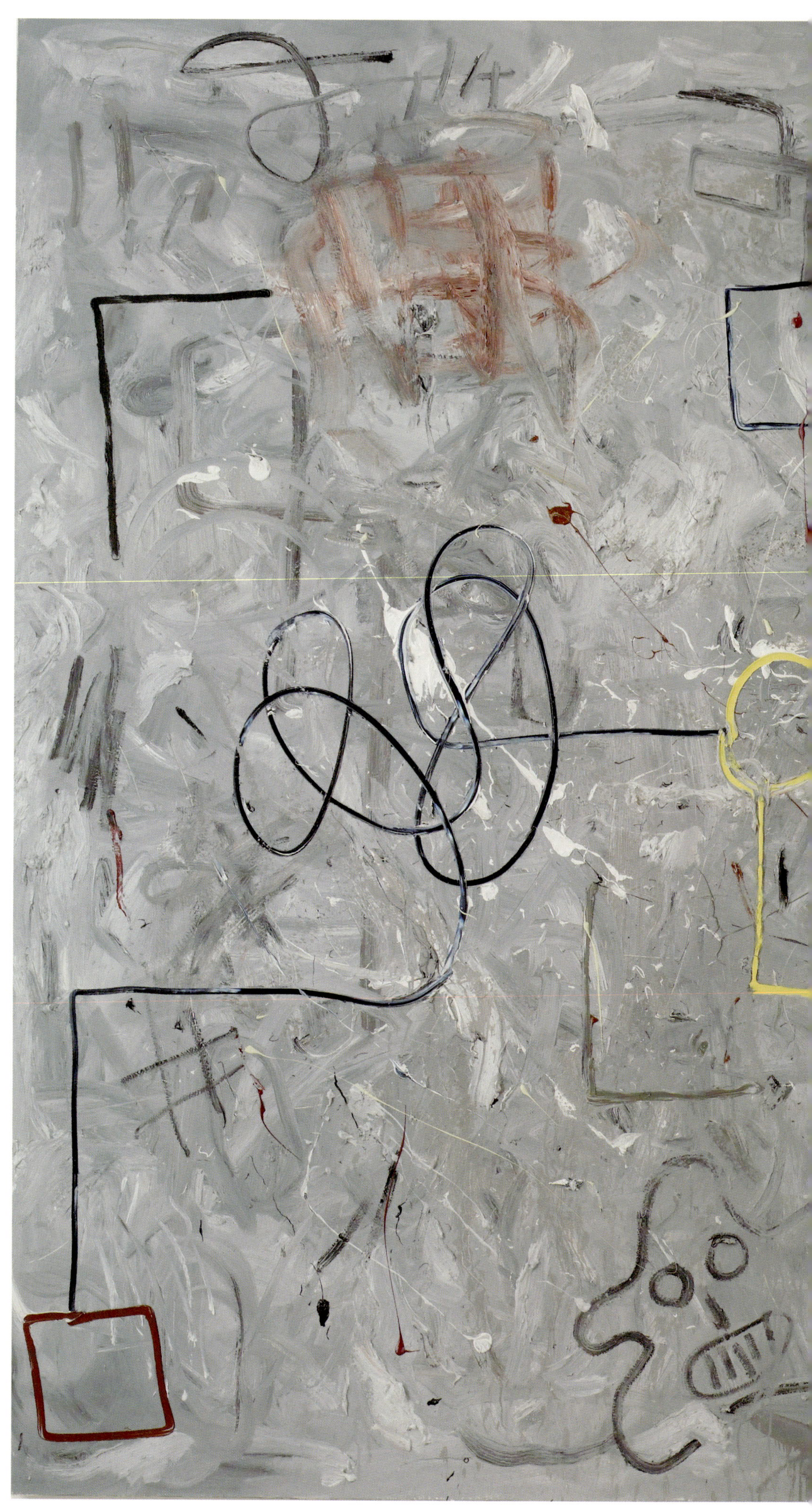

ANDRÉ BUTZER
Untitled 2007
Oil on canvas
260 x 340 cm

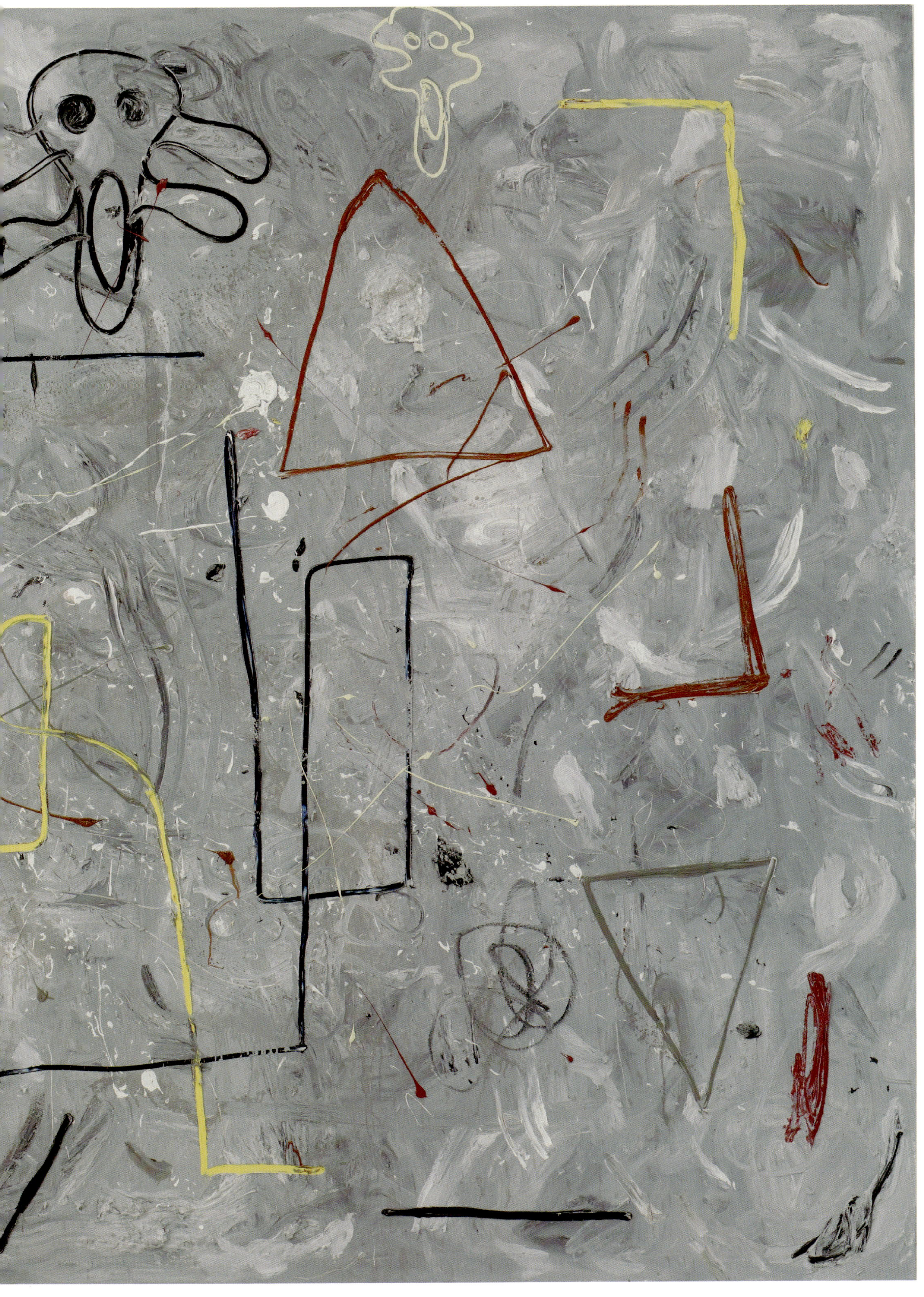

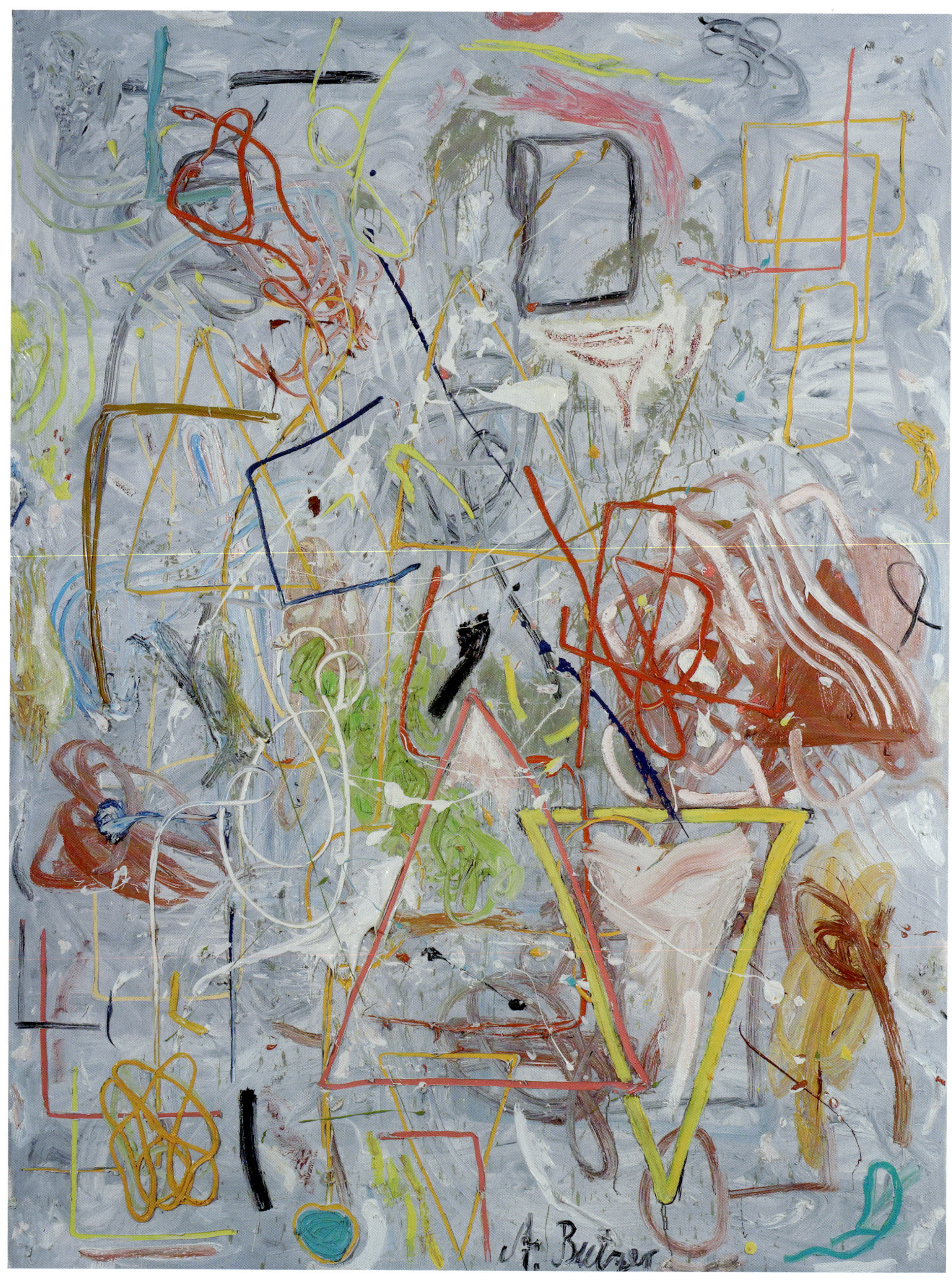

ANDRÉ BUTZER
Untitled 2008
Oil on canvas
340 x 250 cm

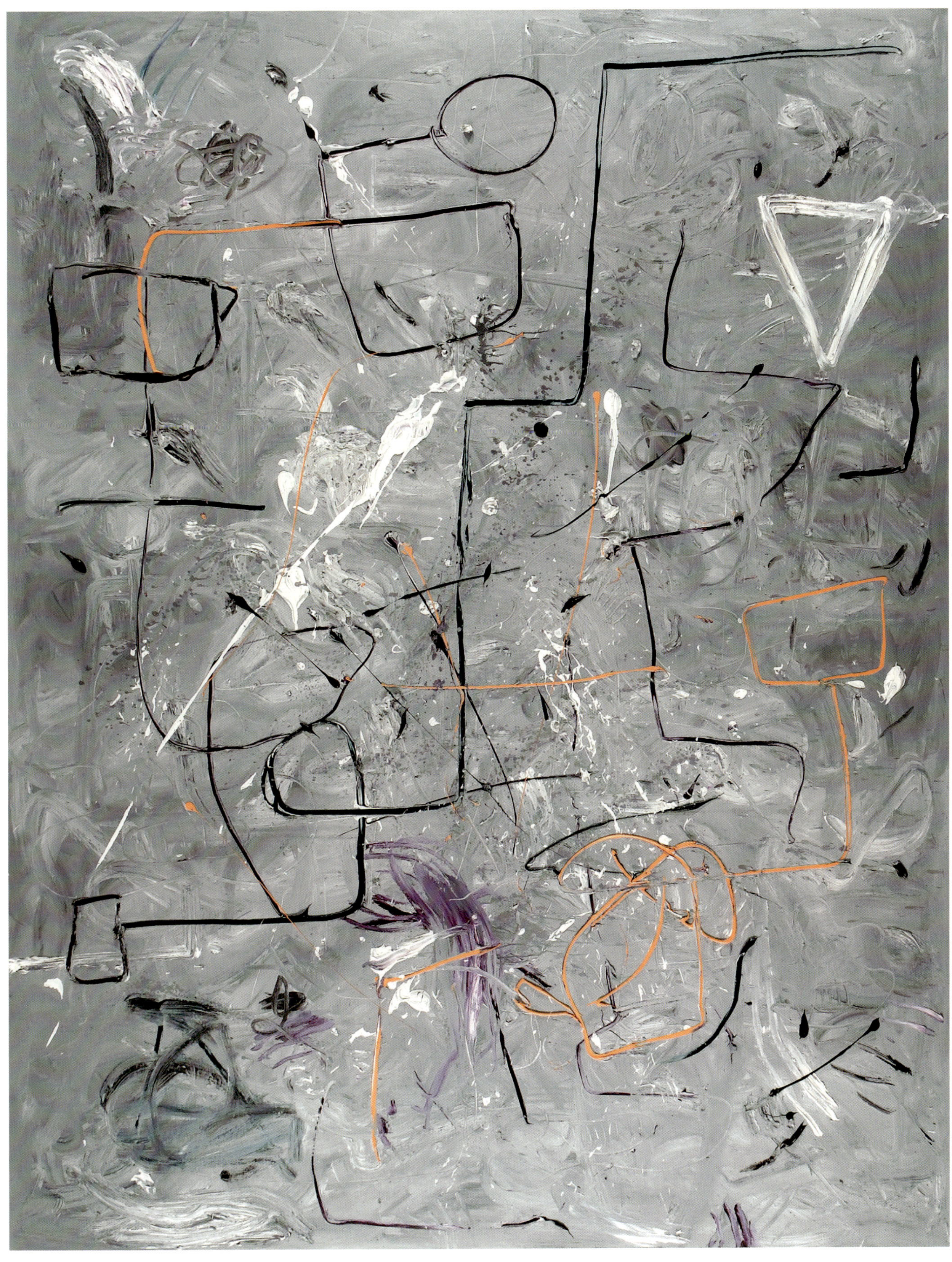

ANDRÉ BUTZER
Untitled 2007
Oil on canvas
340 x 260 cm

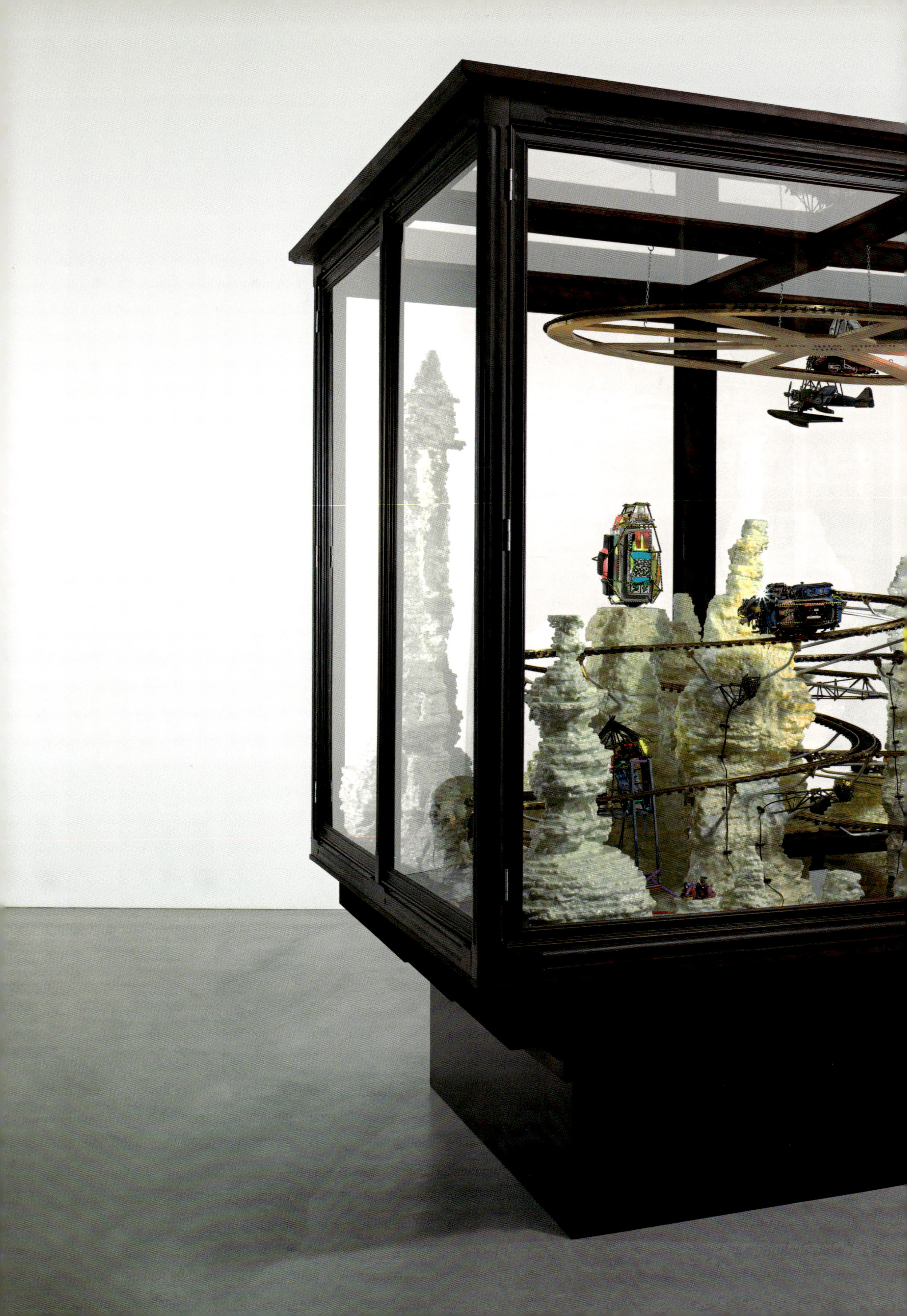

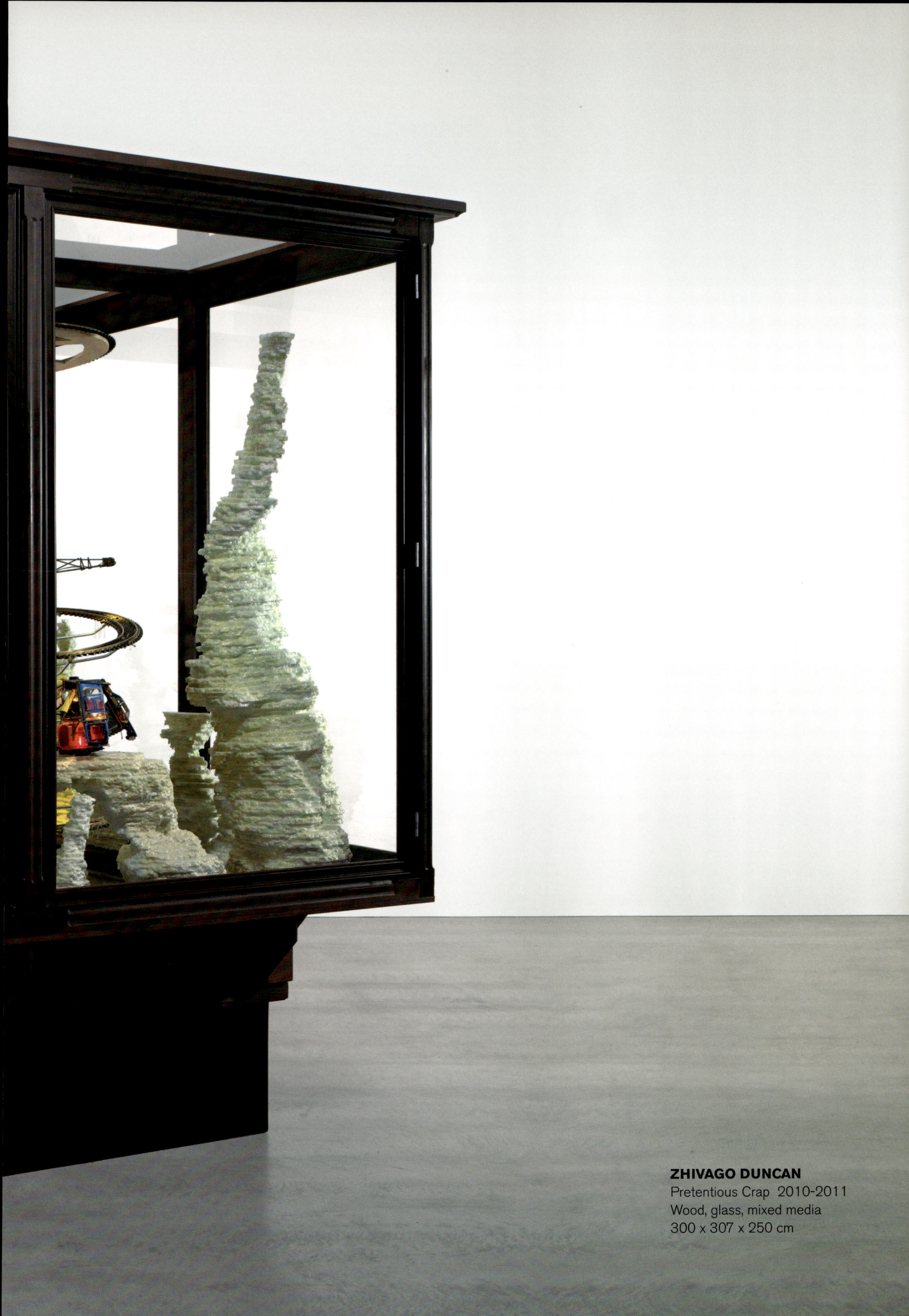

ZHIVAGO DUNCAN
Pretentious Crap 2010-2011
Wood, glass, mixed media
300 x 307 x 250 cm

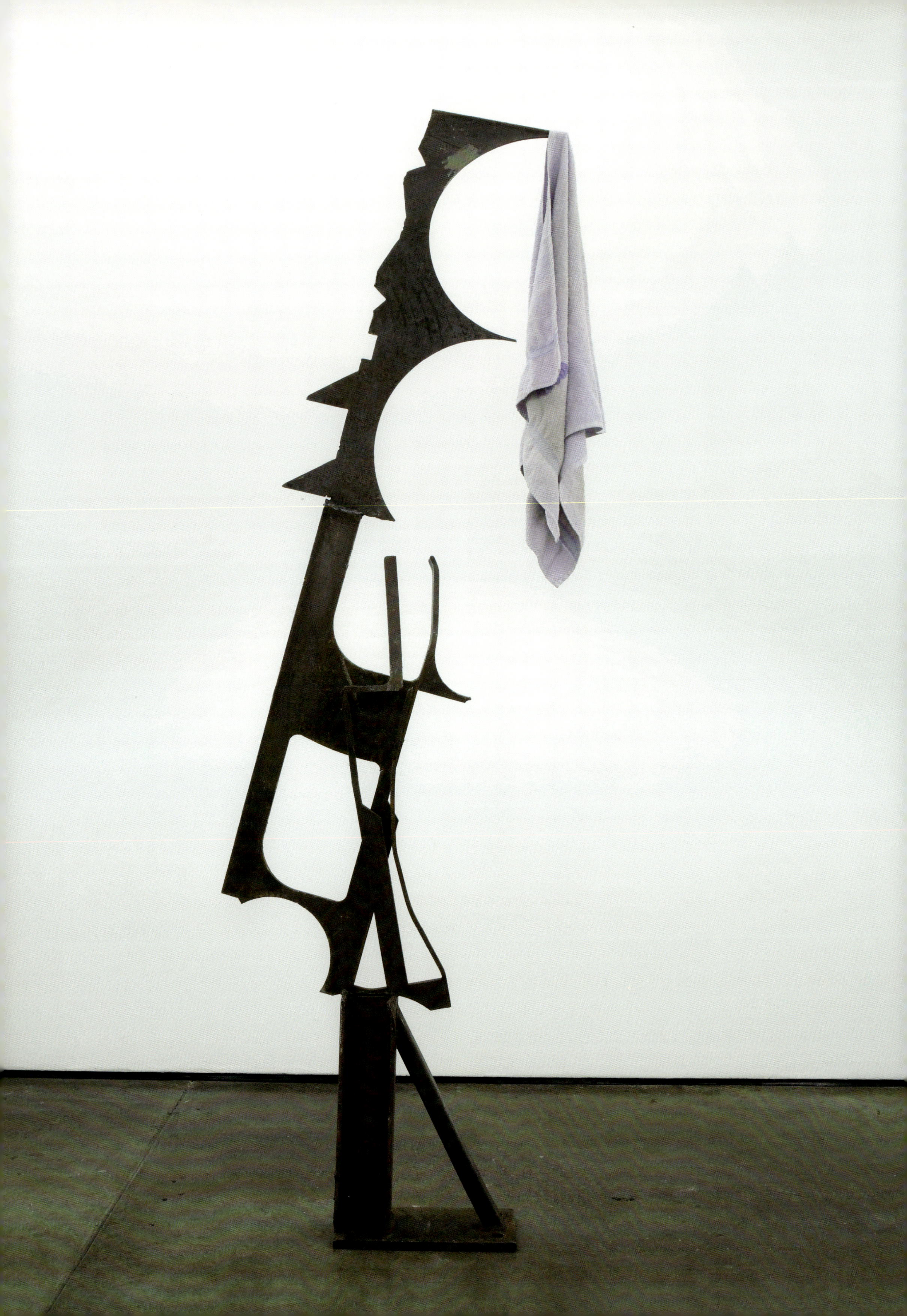

IDA EKBLAD
Tennessee Hills 2010
Welded steel, found object
252 x 72 x 20 cm

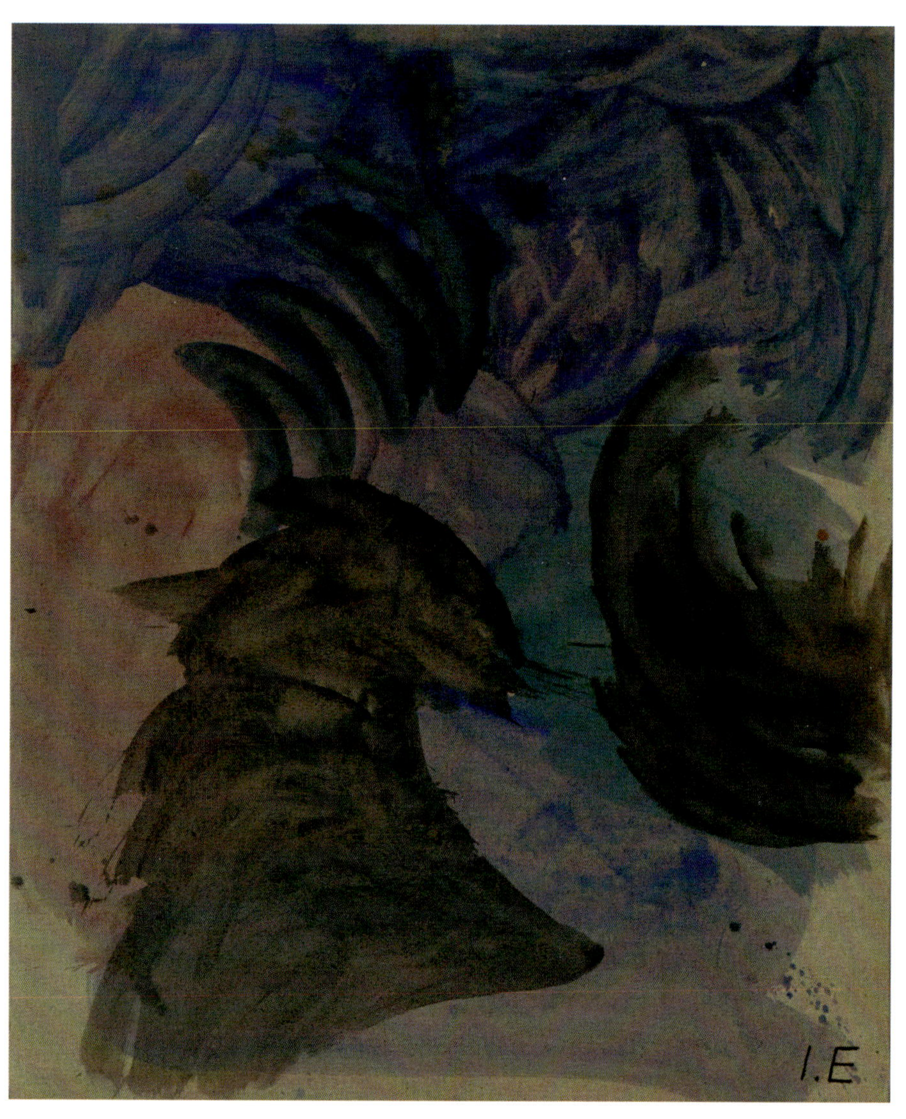

IDA EKBLAD
Missing Pages 2010
Oil on canvas
160 x 130 cm

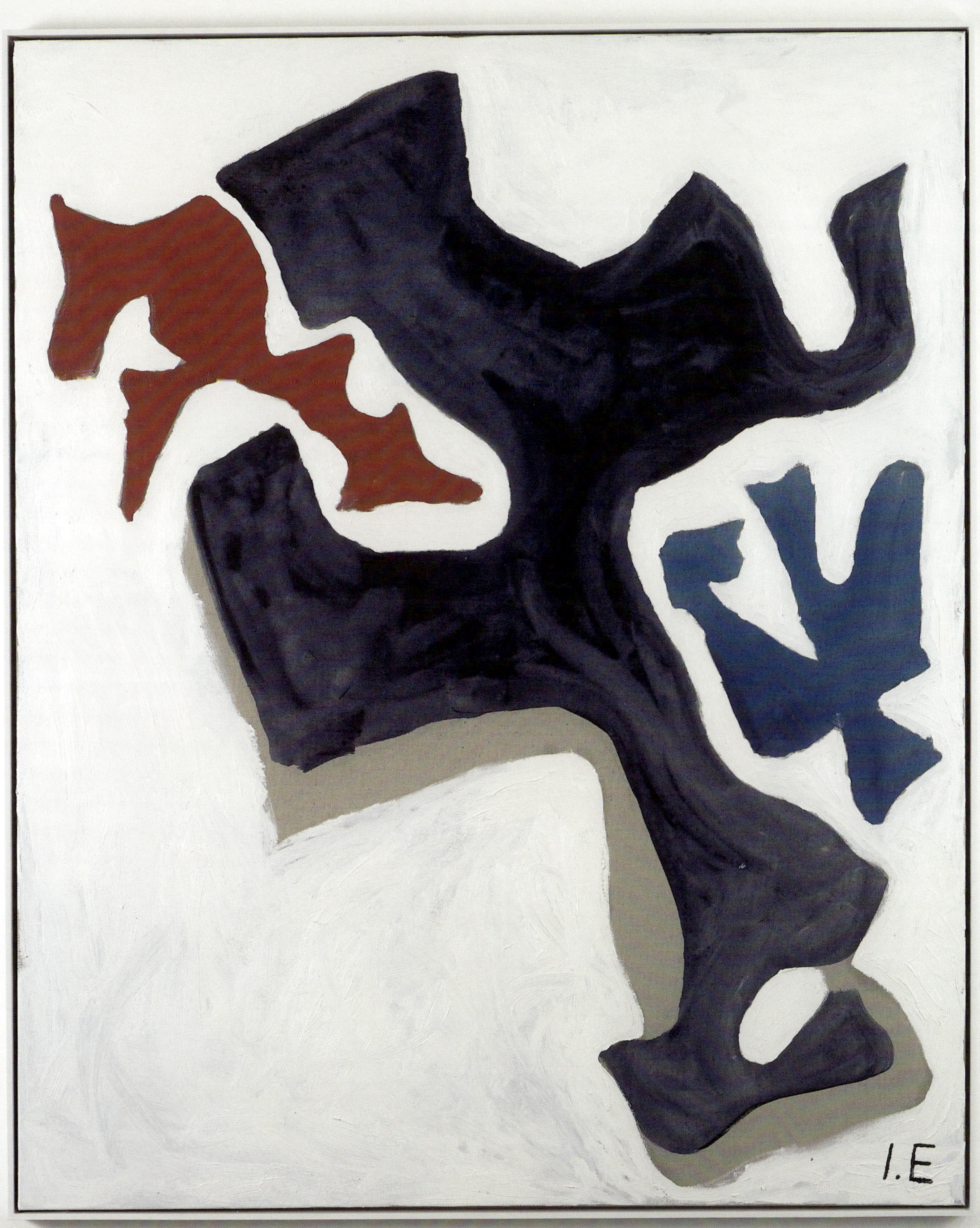

IDA EKBLAD
To Drink A Glass Of Melted Snow 2010
Oil on canvas
203.5 x 163.5 cm

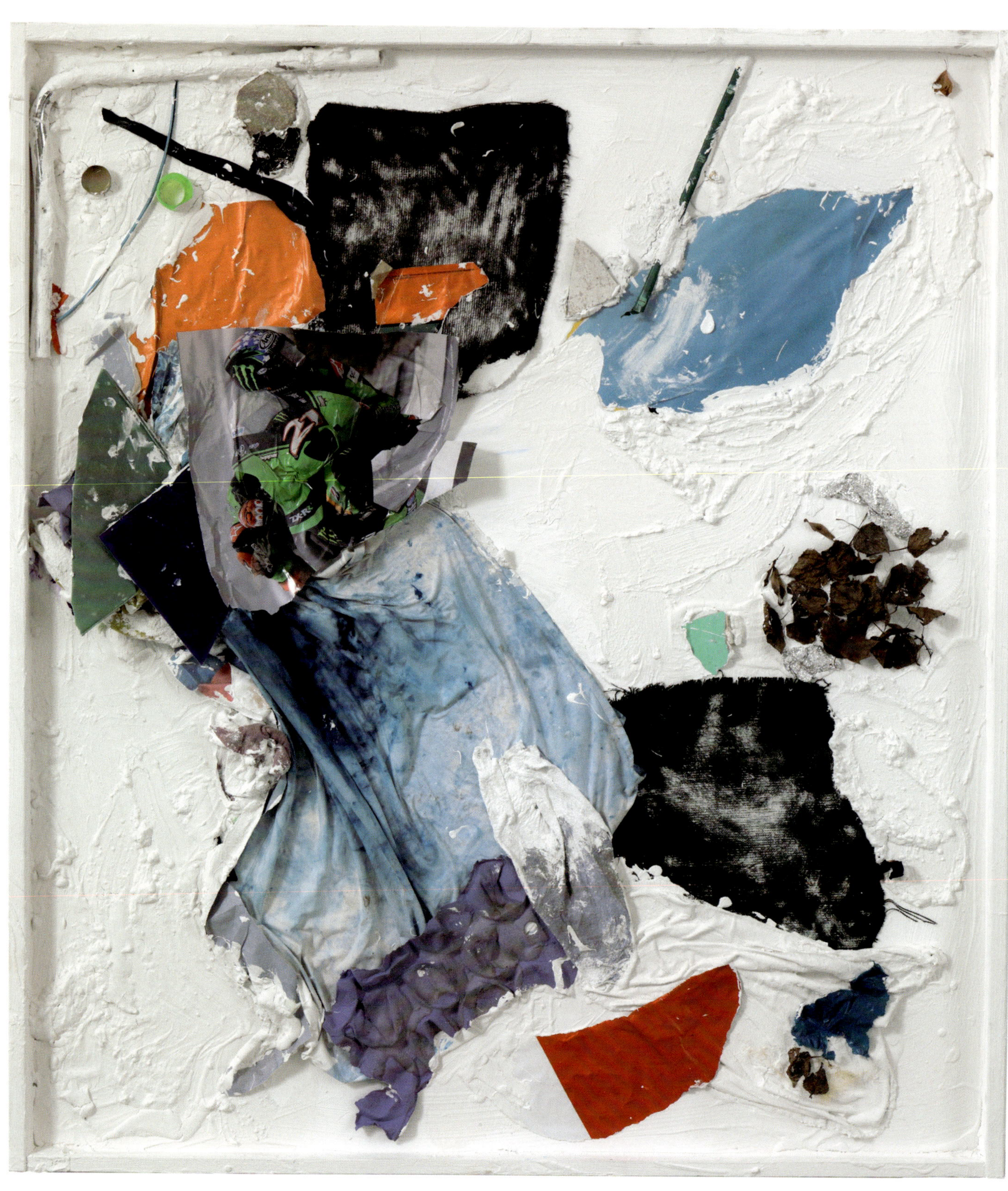

IDA EKBLAD
Dusty Dry On The Tongue Swallowed Some 2010
Mixed materials
150 x 100 cm

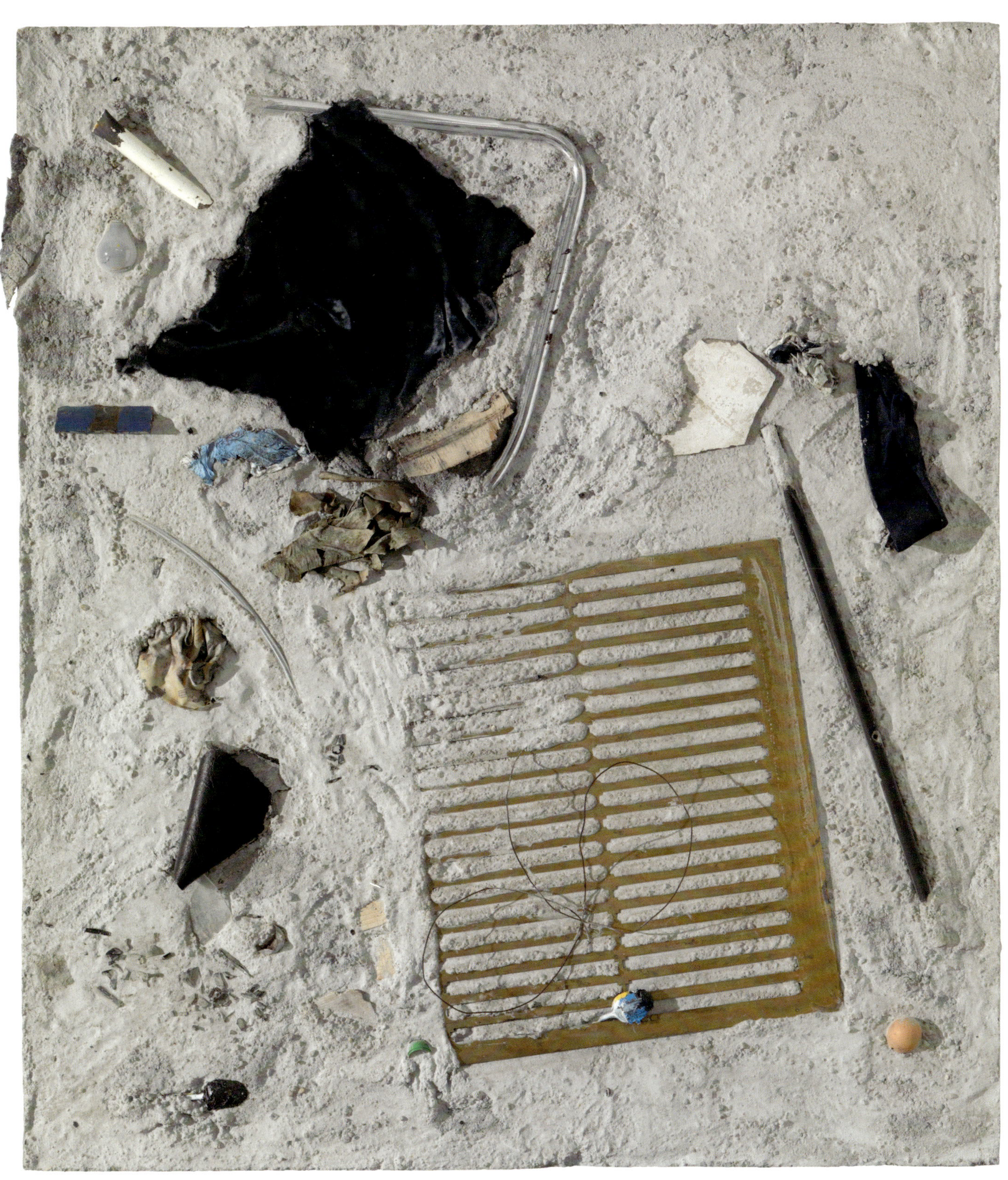

IDA EKBLAD
Night Ocean Return Without And Without Hesitate 2010
Mixed media, concrete
144 x 123 cm

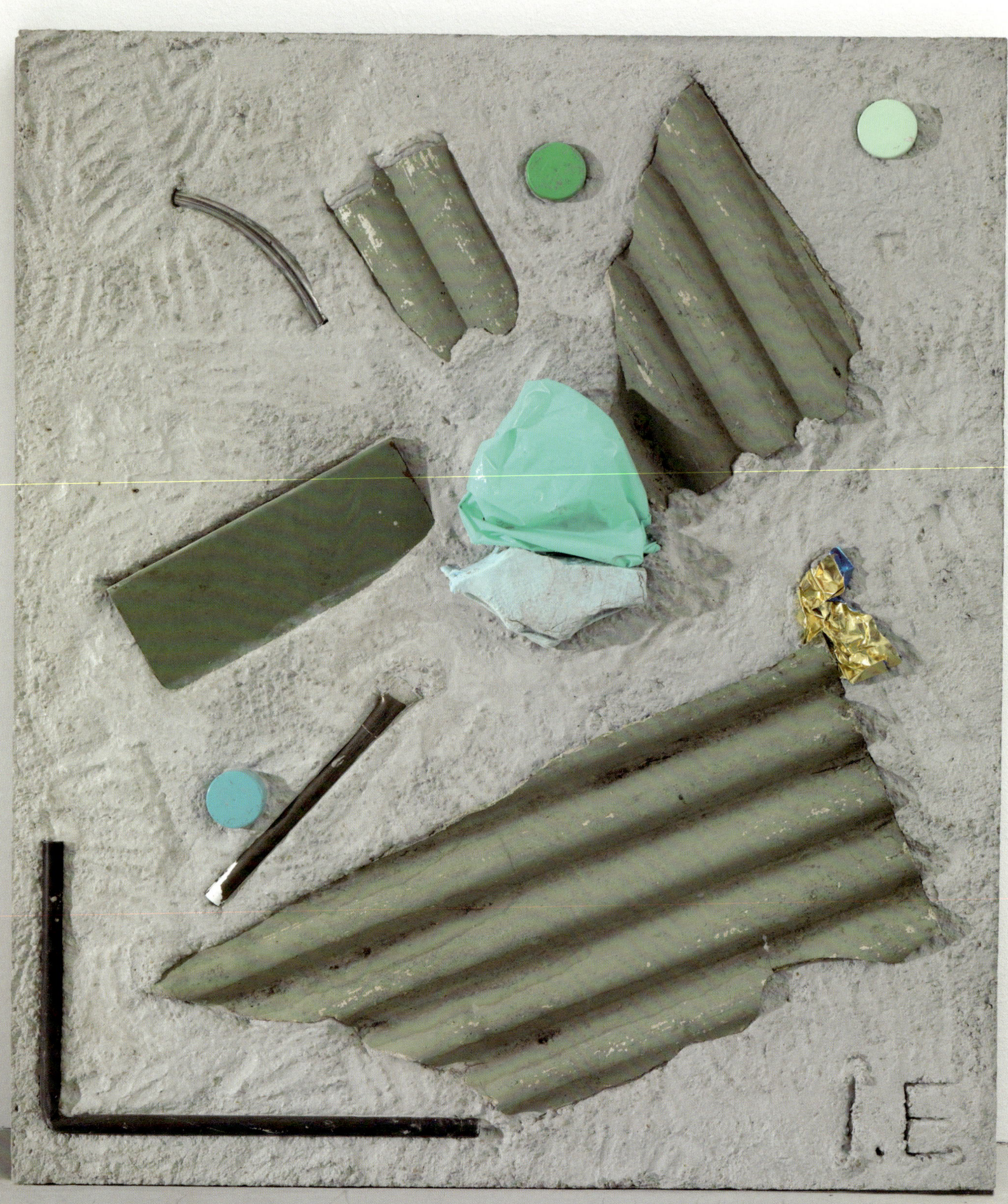

IDA EKBLAD
Banging 2010
Mixed media
110 x 95 cm

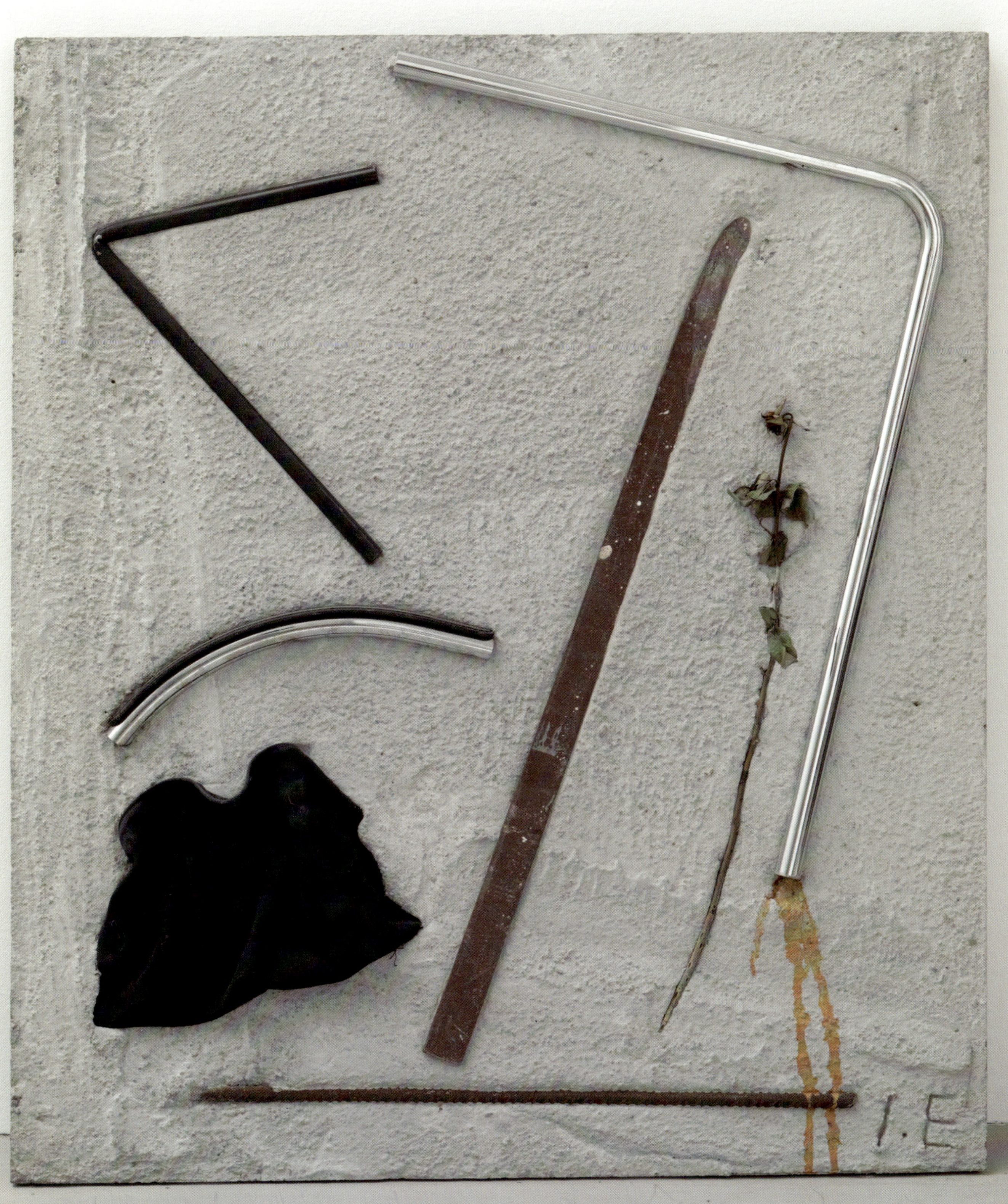

IDA EKBLAD
Dubbed 2010
Concrete, found objects
110 x 90 cm

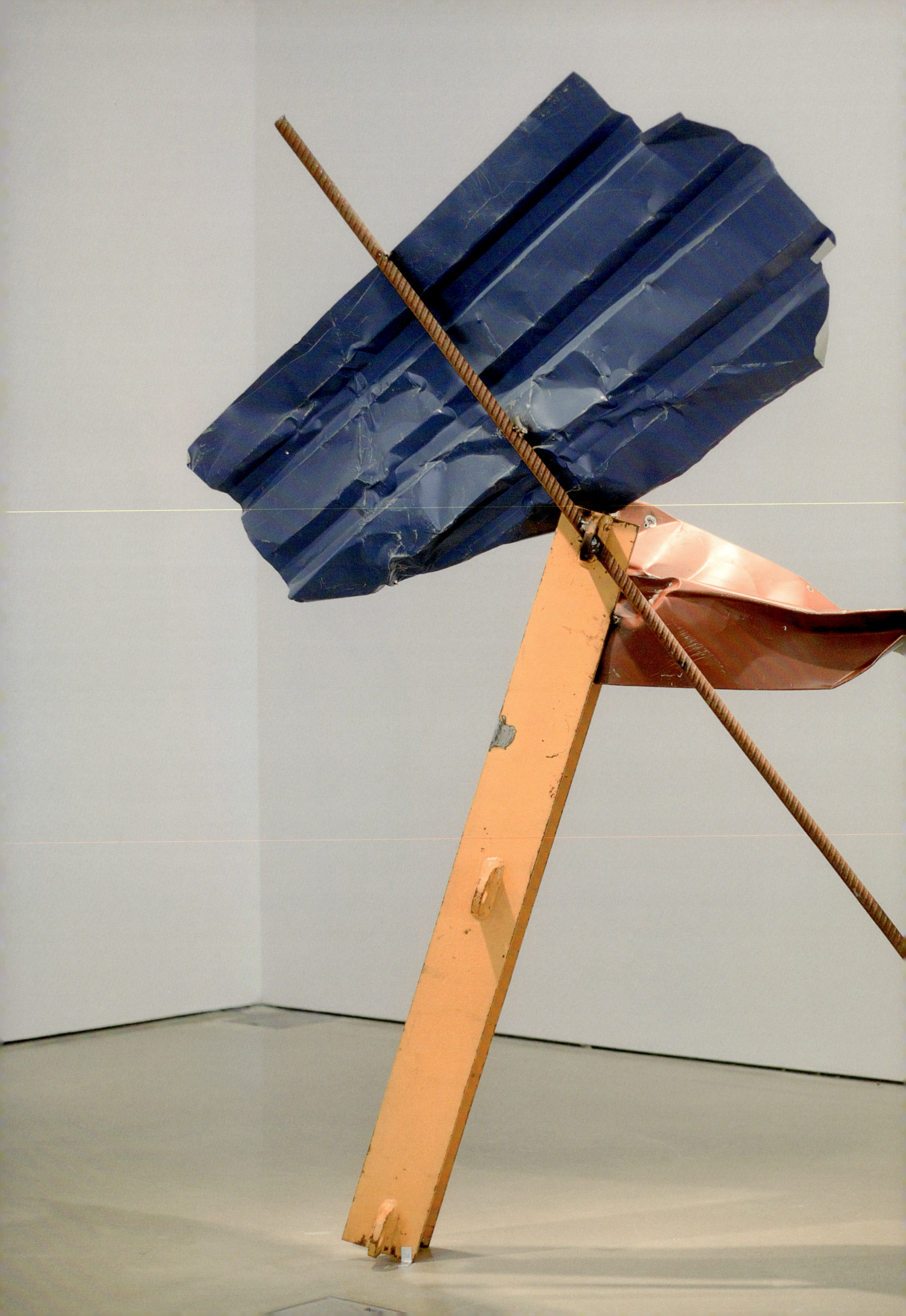

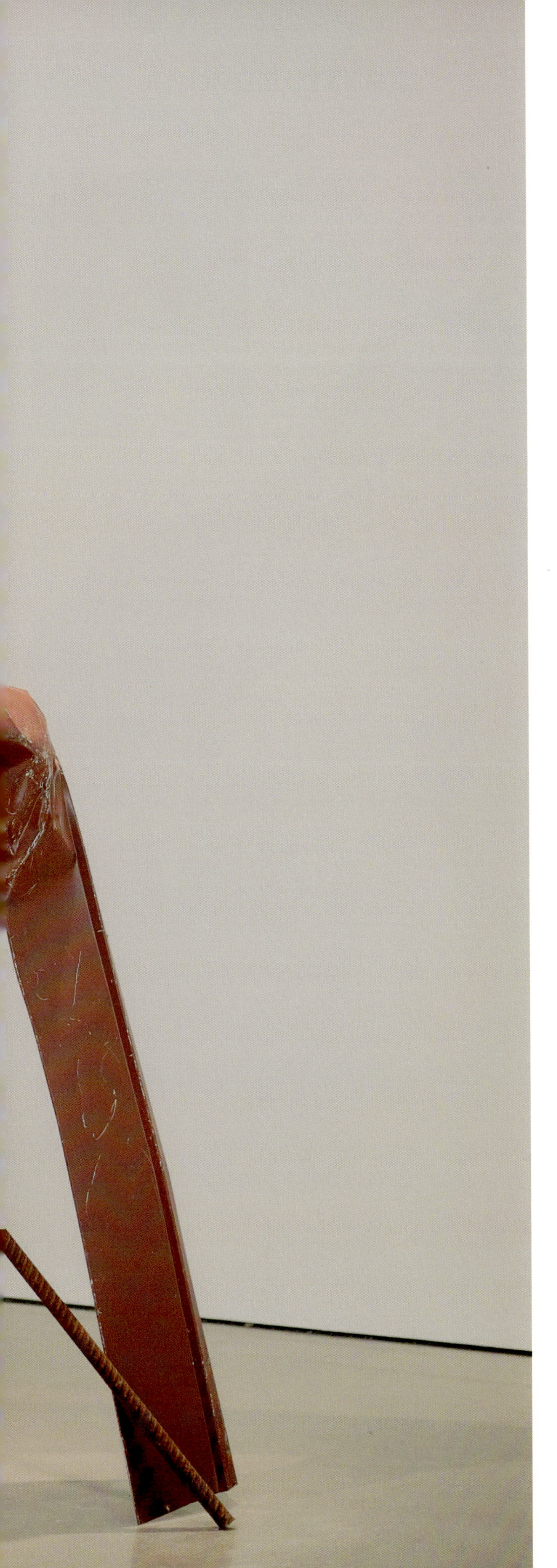

IDA EKBLAD
Organ Invention 2010
Welded steel
190 x 210 x 120 cm

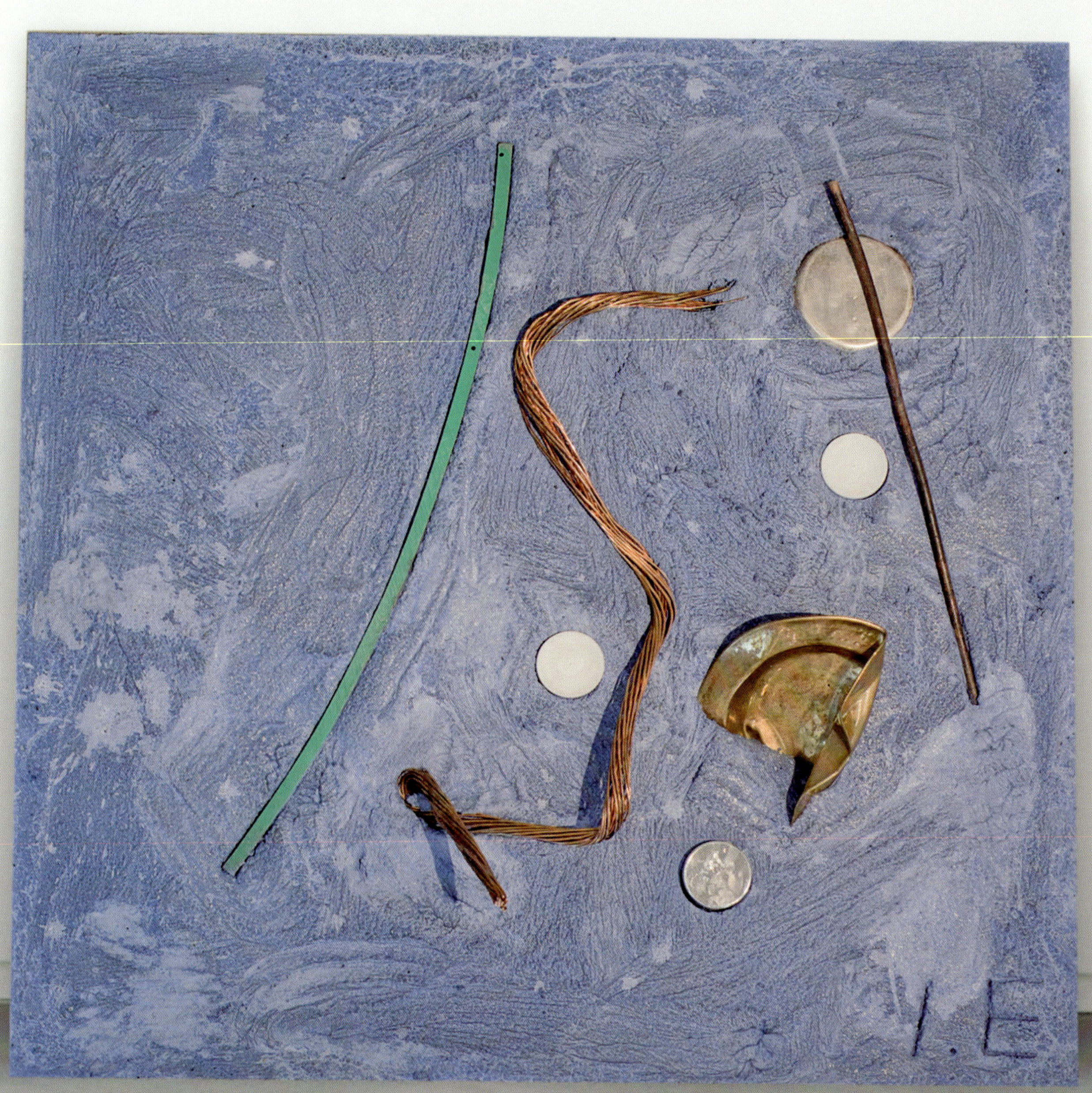

IDA EKBLAD
The L, The LL, The Lapis Lazuli 2010
Cast concrete, pigment, found objects
120 x 120 x 5 cm

opposite:
Loops 2010
Cast concrete, steel
134 x 82 x 62 cm

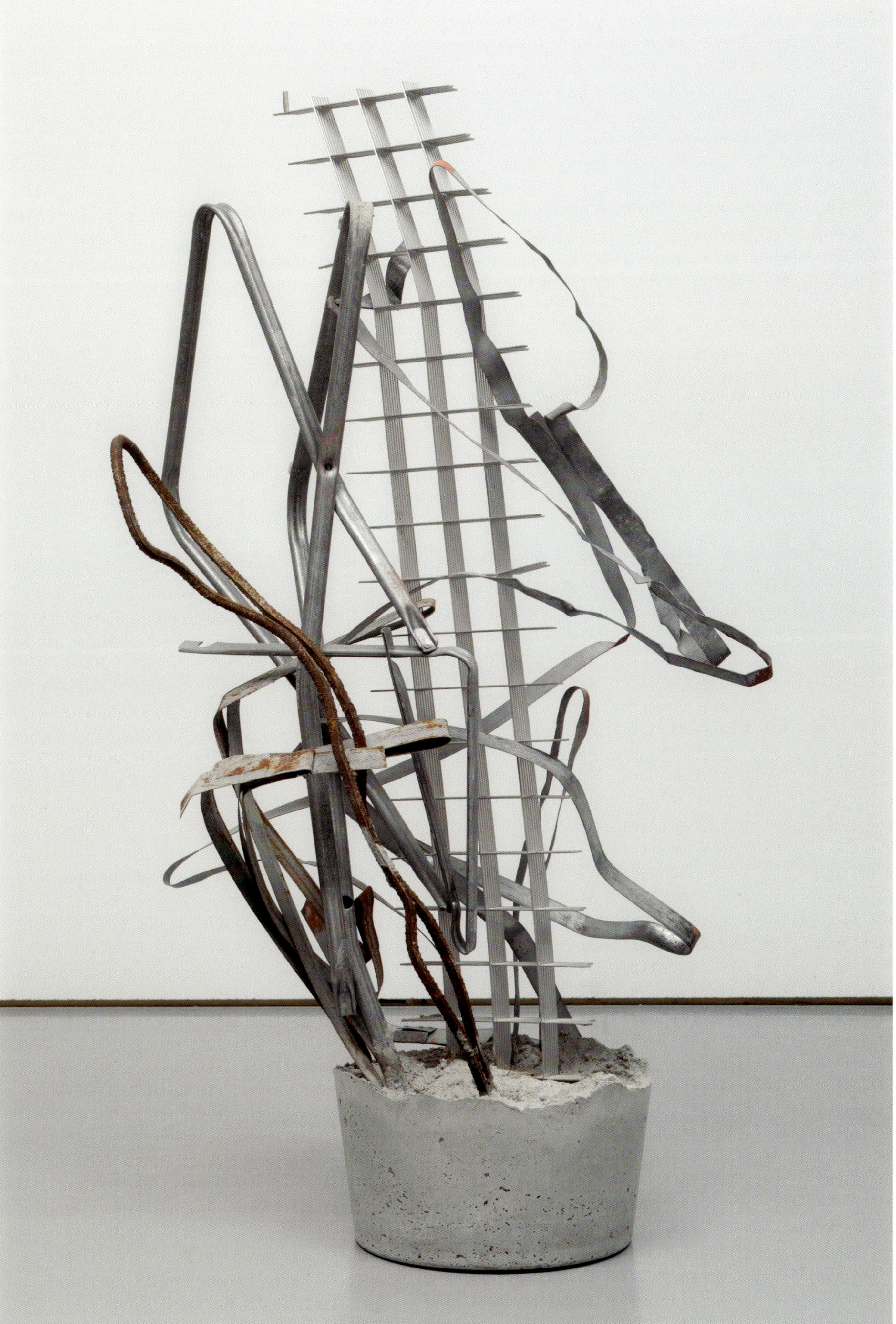

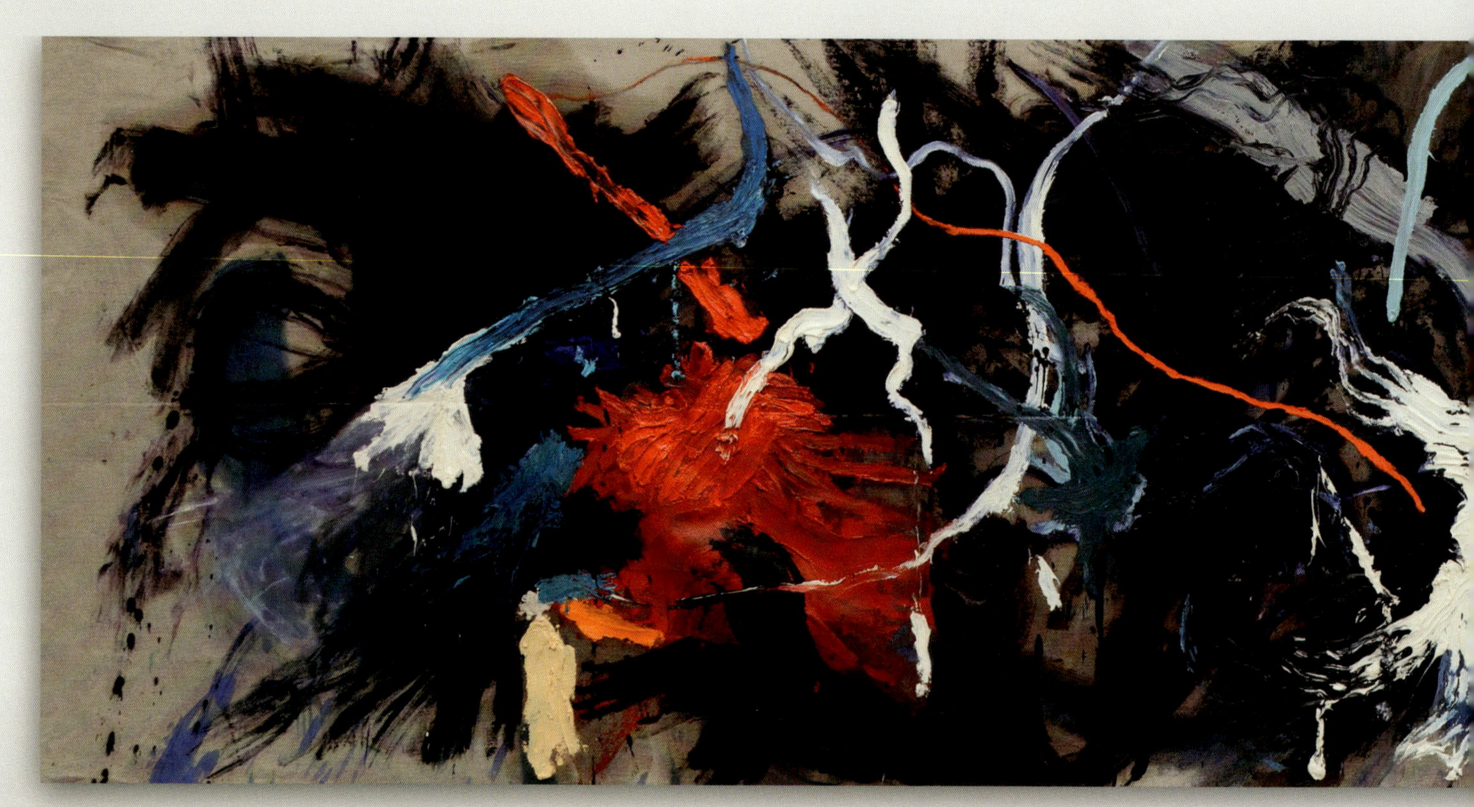

IDA EKBLAD
Stalk Gills And Caps Of Goodbye 2009
Oil on canvas
140 x 560 cm

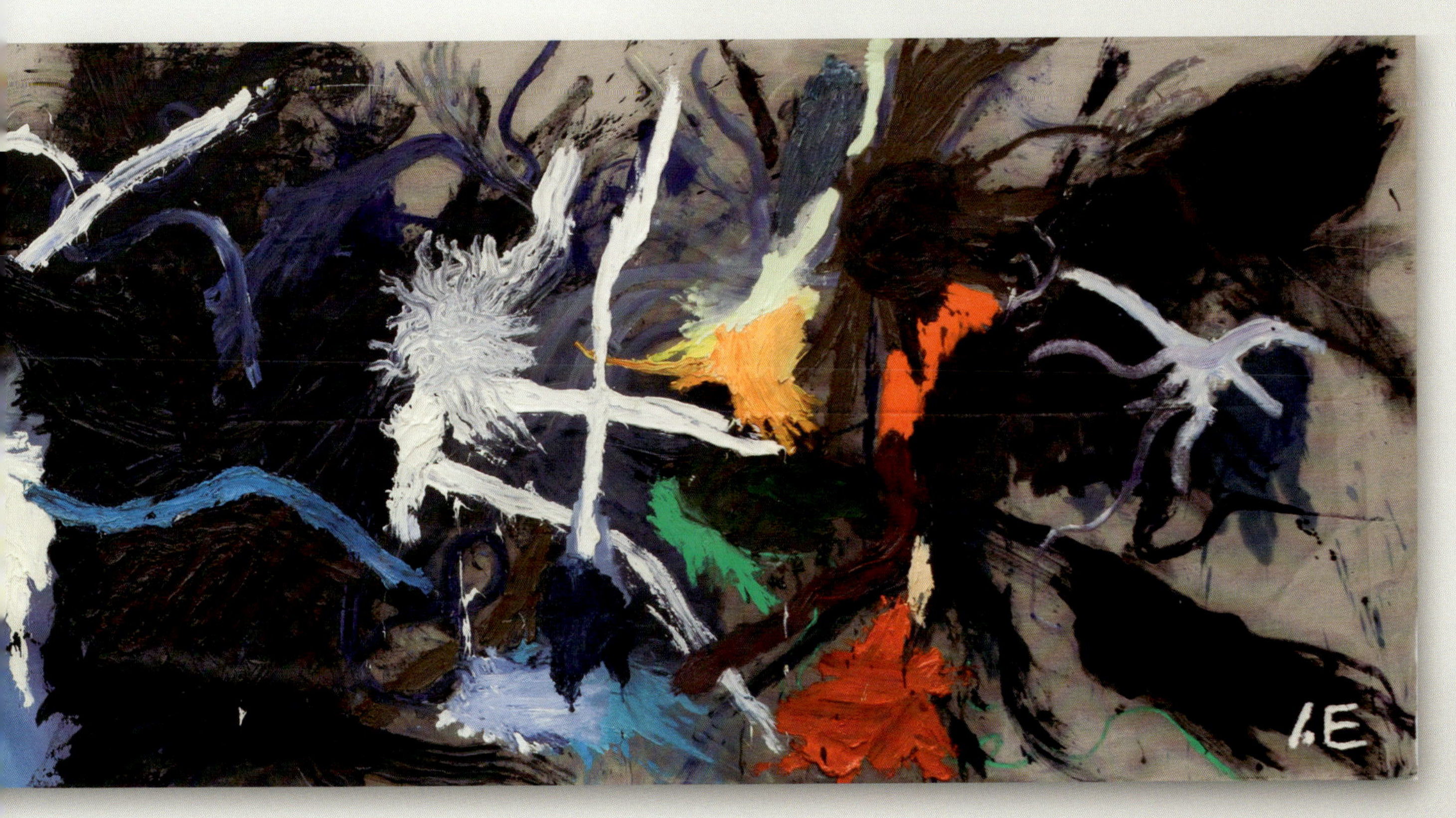

IDA EKBLAD
Figurine With Horns   2010
Cast concrete, found objects
265 x 100 x 60 cm

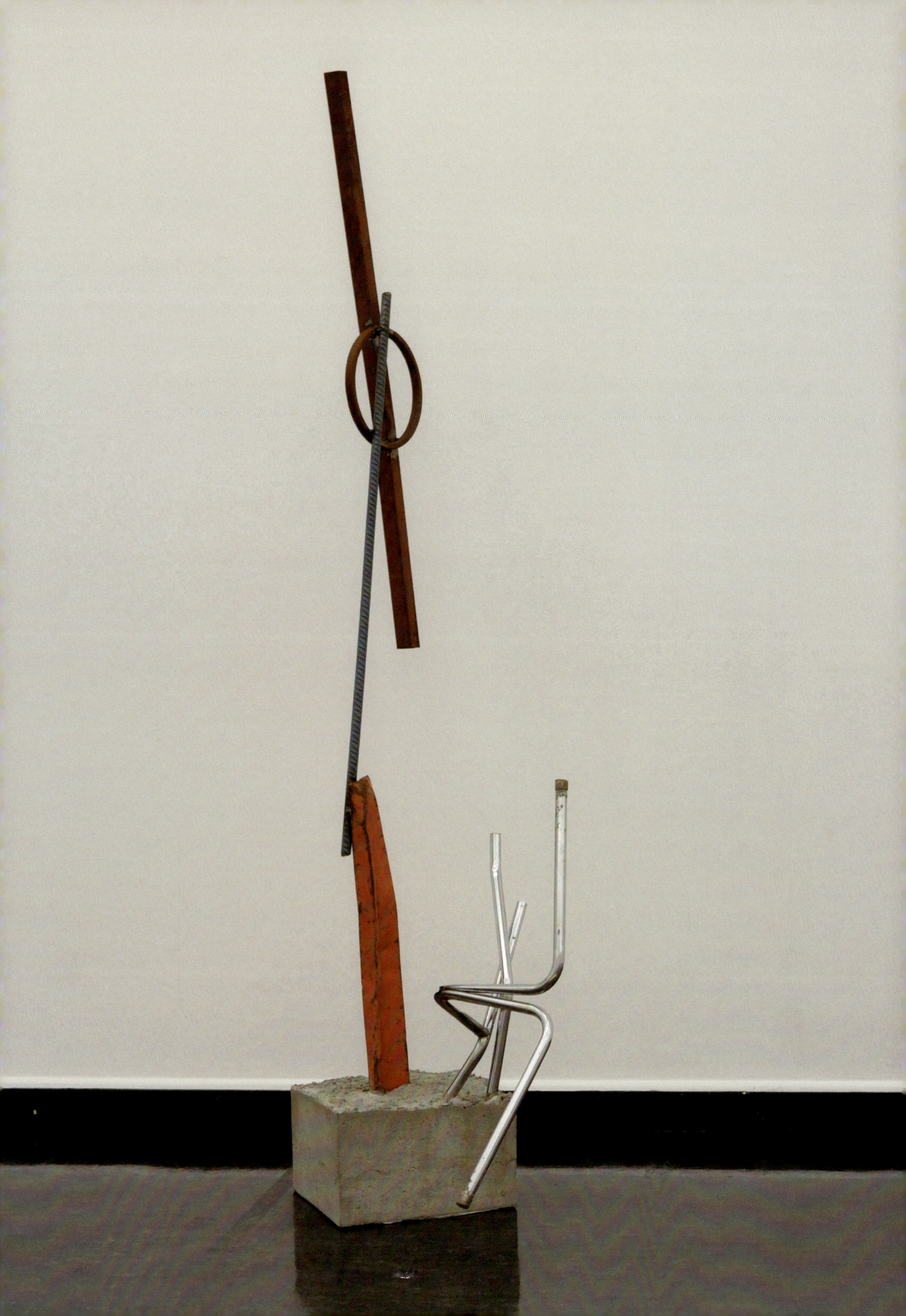

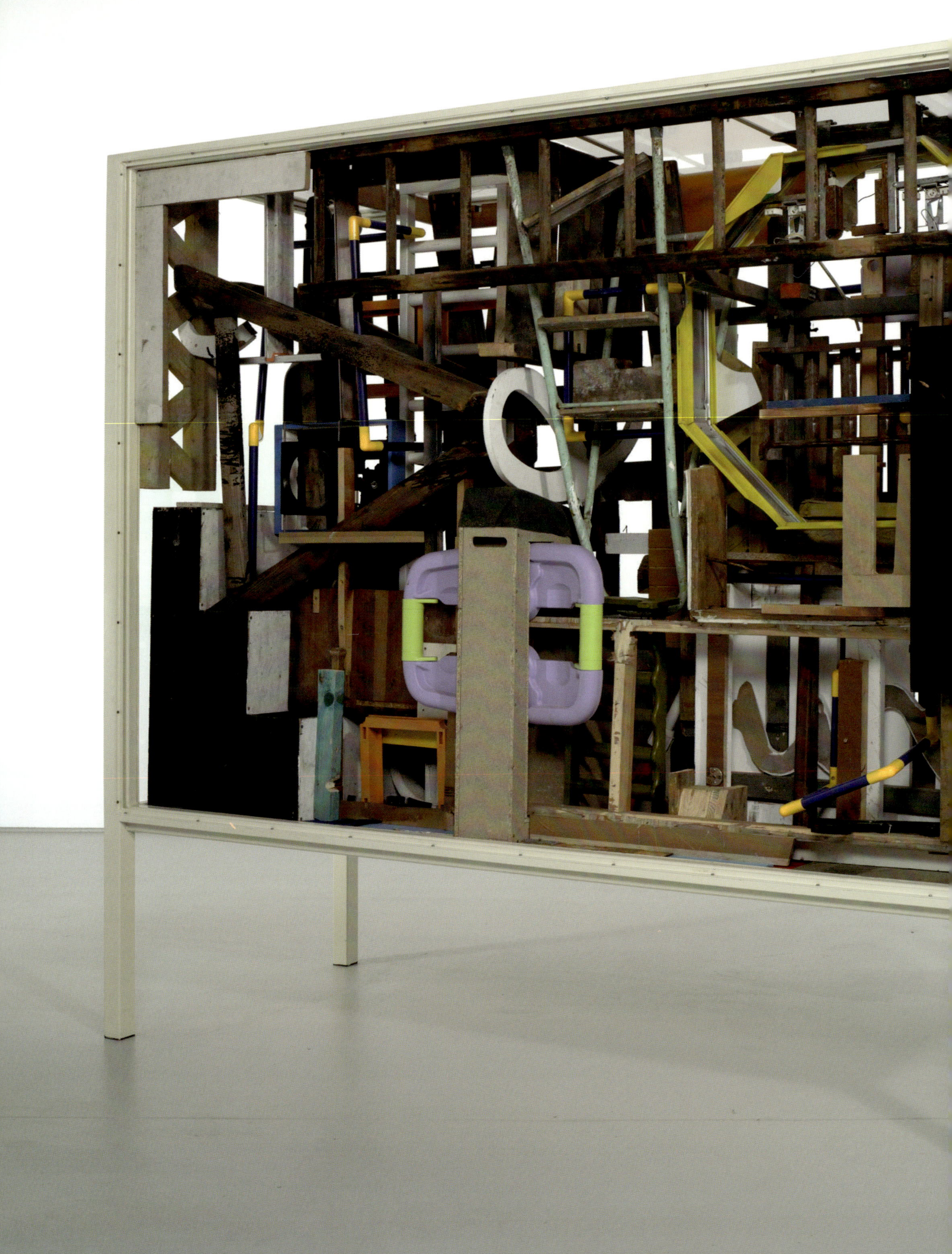

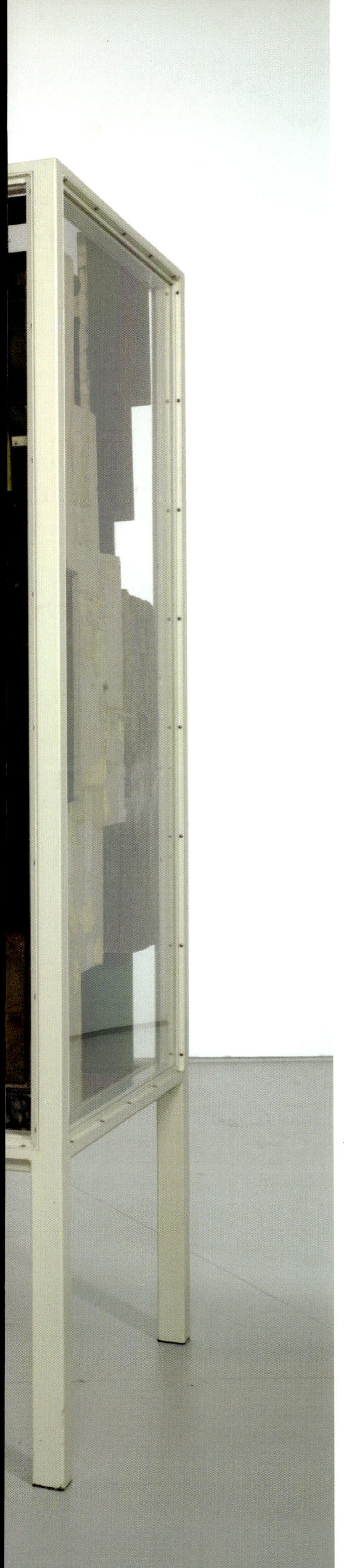

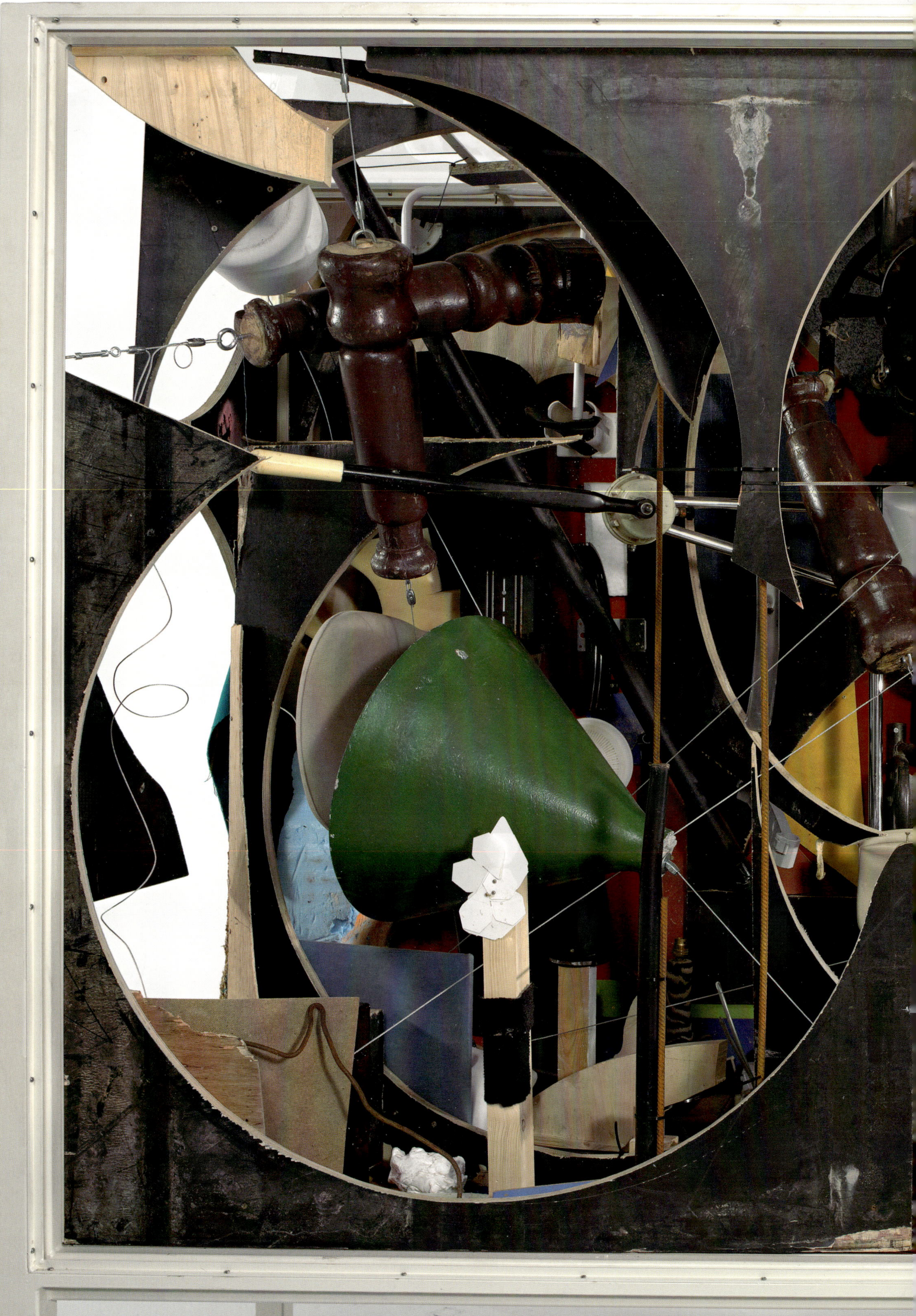

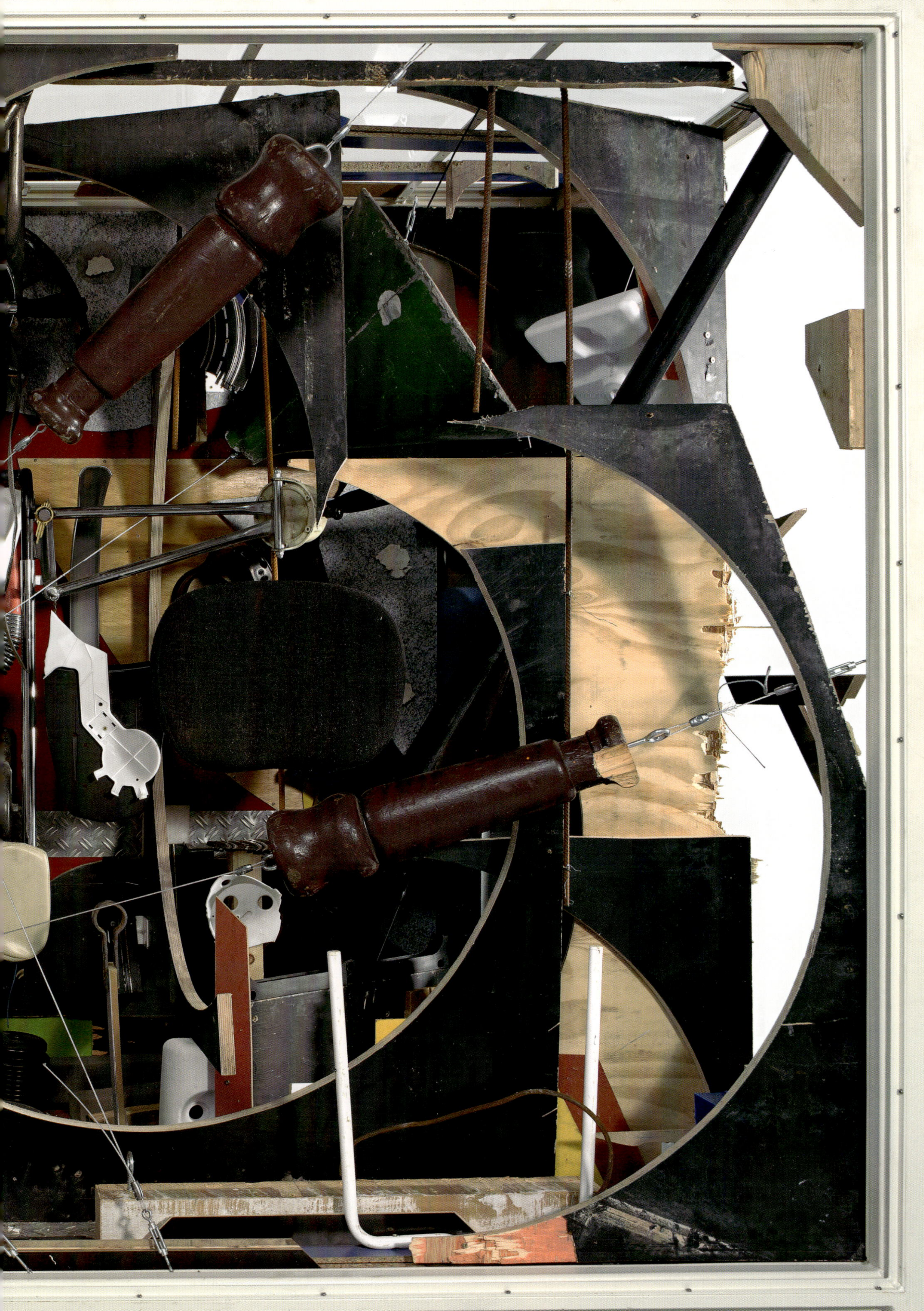

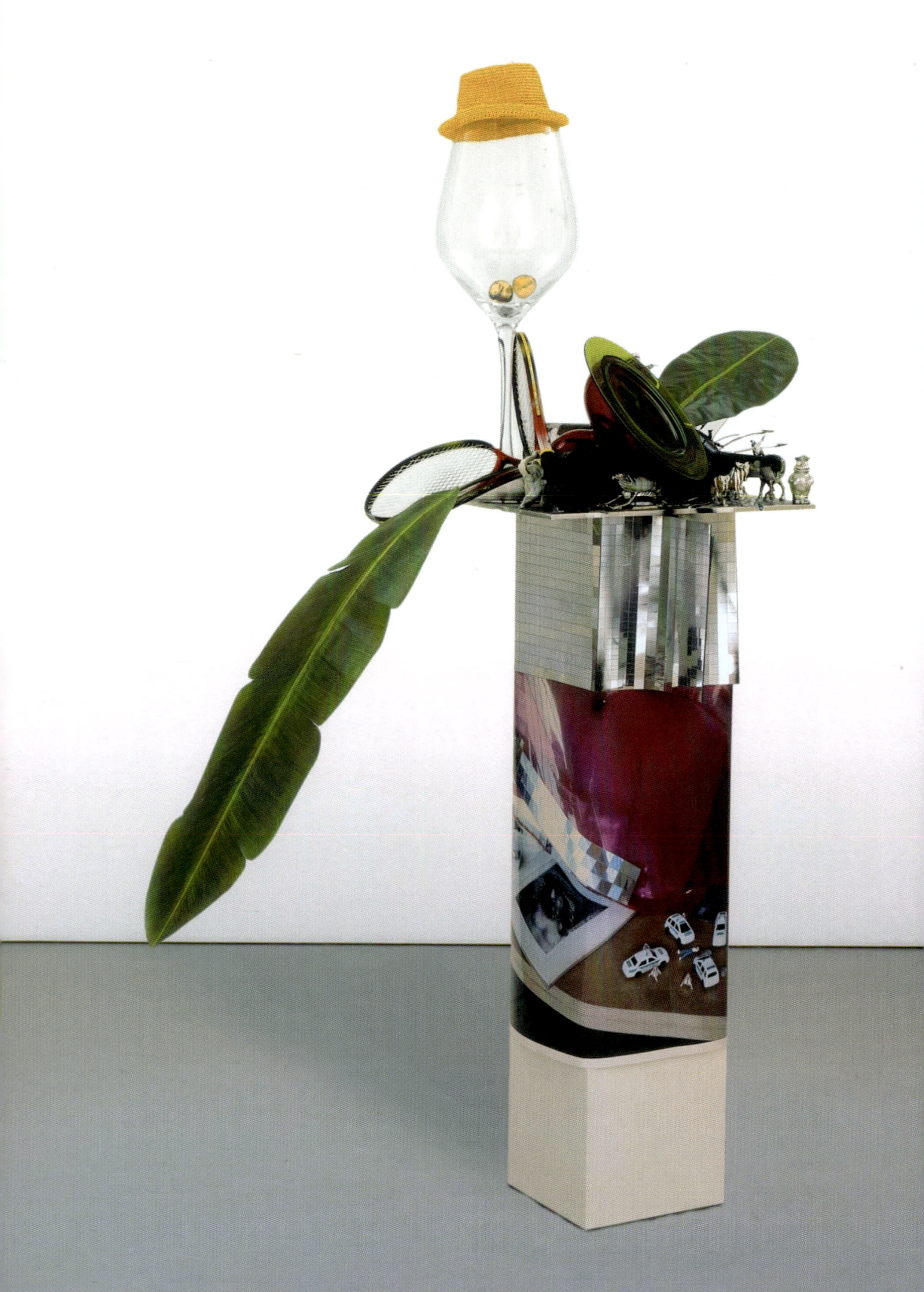

ISA GENZKEN
Urlaub 2004
Glass, lacquer, plastics, metal, wood, photograph
227 x 165 x 55 cm

ISA GENZKEN
Bouquet 2004
Plastic, wood, lacquer, mirror foil, glass
260 x 115 x 130 cm

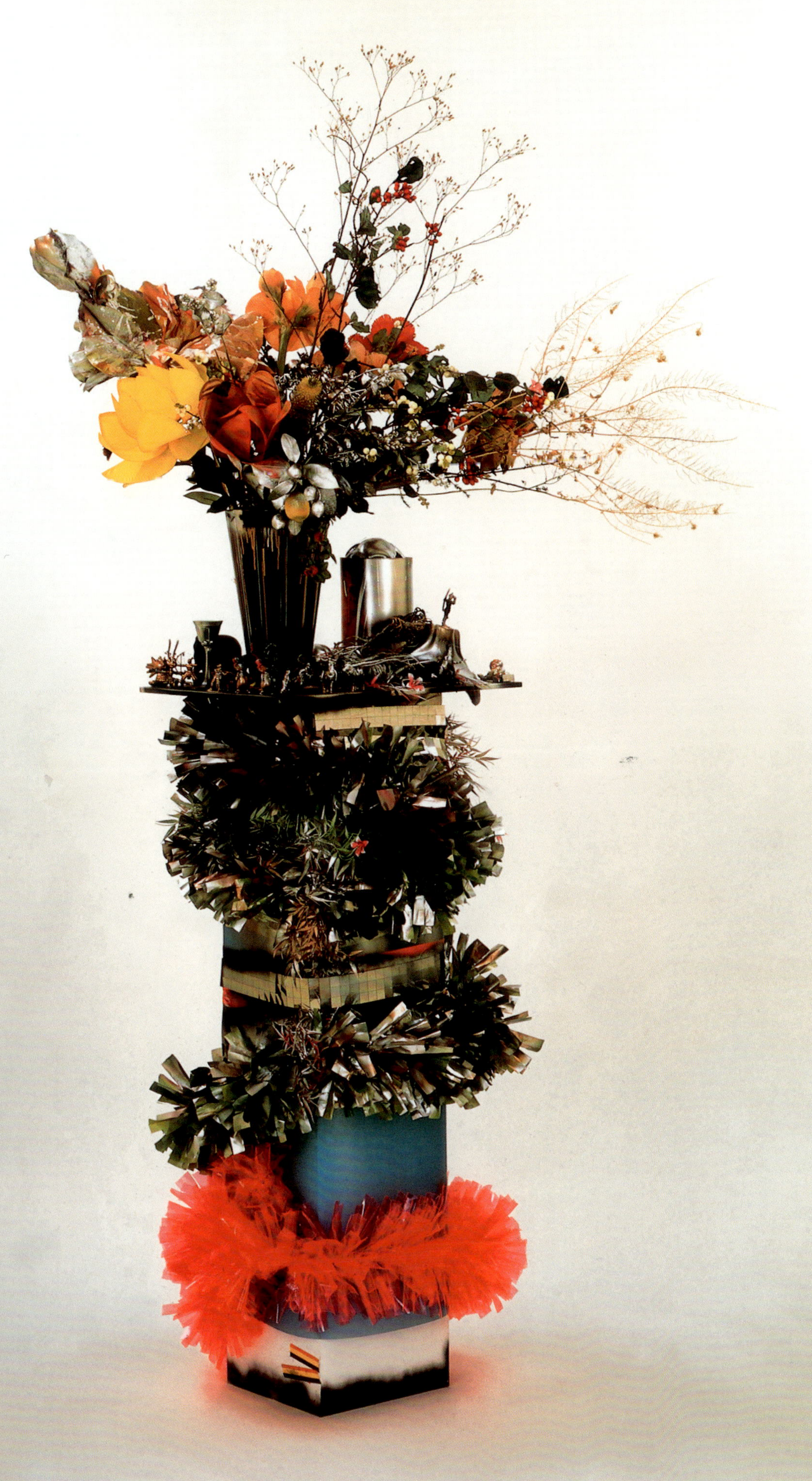

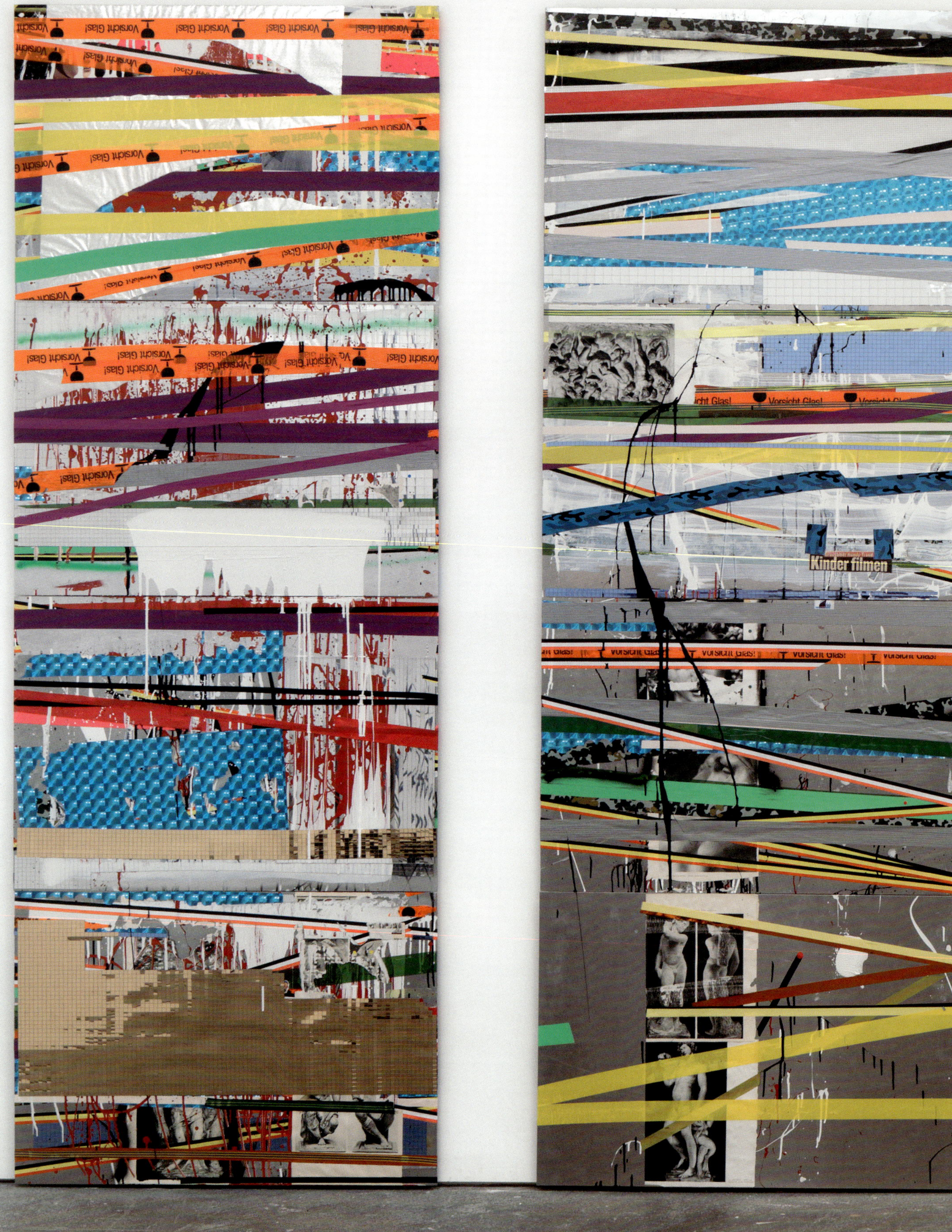

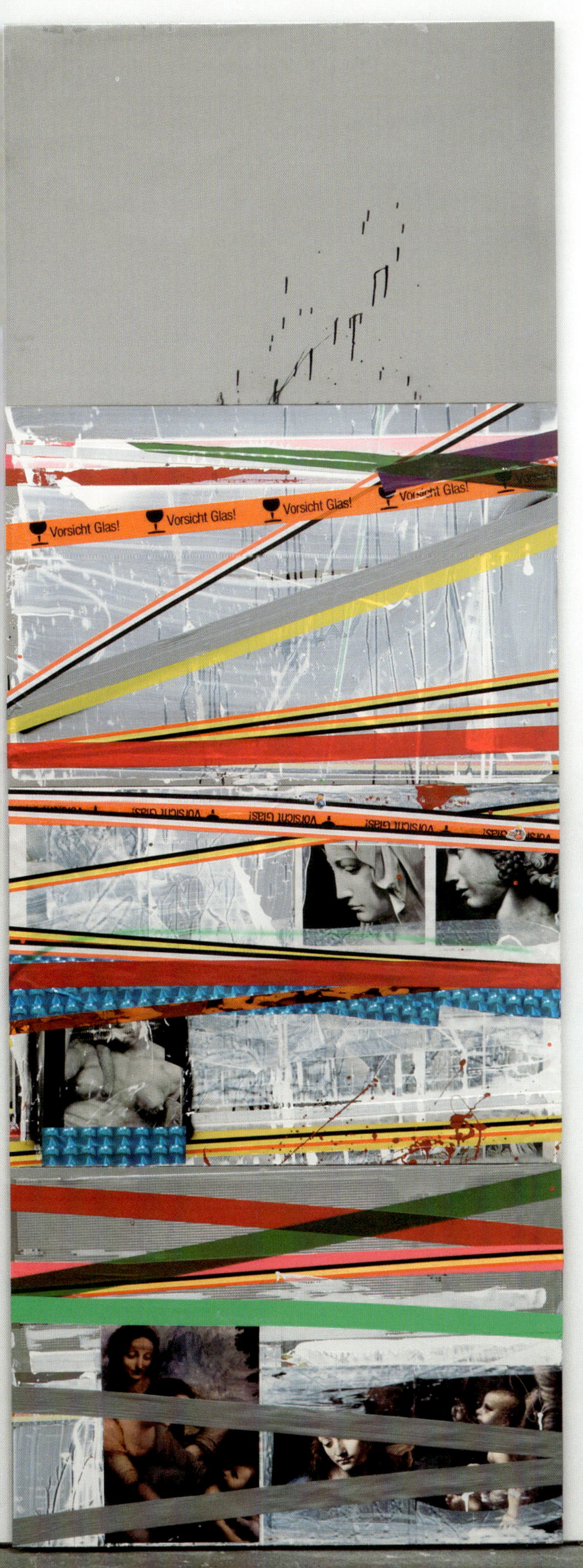
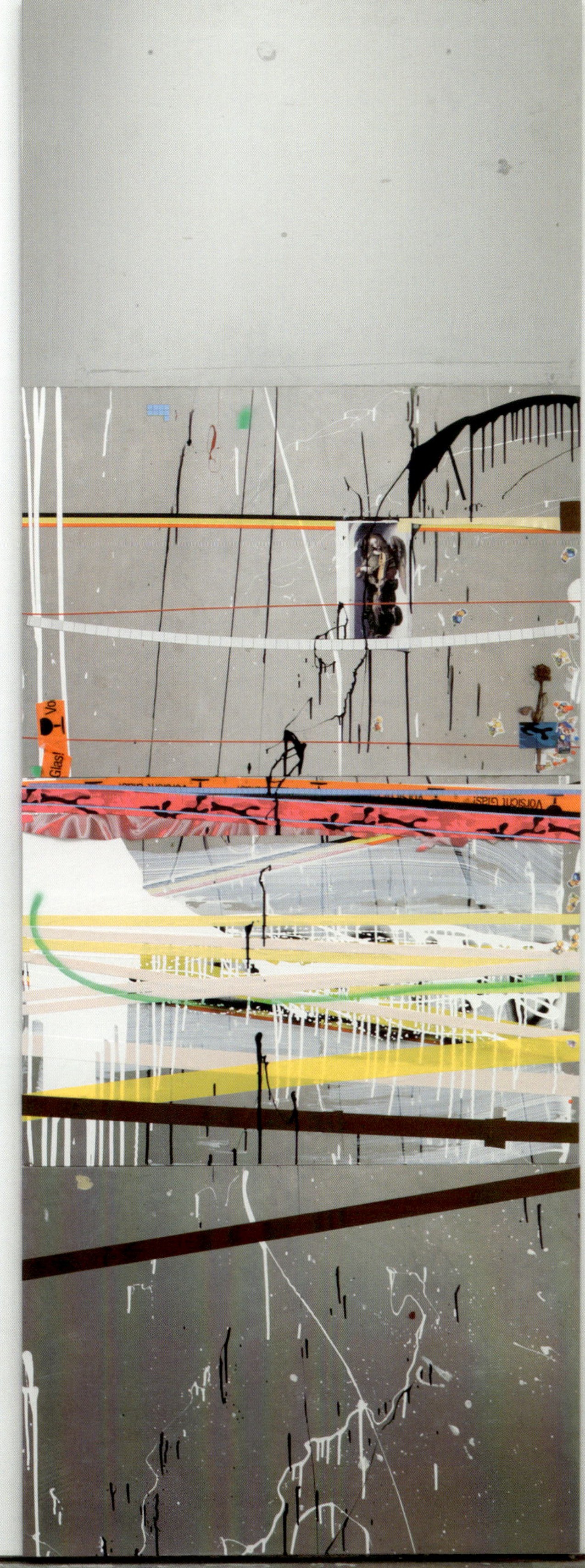

ISA GENZKEN
Kinder Filmen I 2005
Mirror, metal, adhesive tape, magazine and book pages,
stamps acrylic, lacquer, spray paint.
280 x 100 cm each panel

ISA GENZKEN
Untitled 2006
Wheelchair, hologram foil, belts, fabric, colour print, mirror foil,
two ceramic bowls, clips, lacquer
88.9 x 63.5 x 105.4 cm

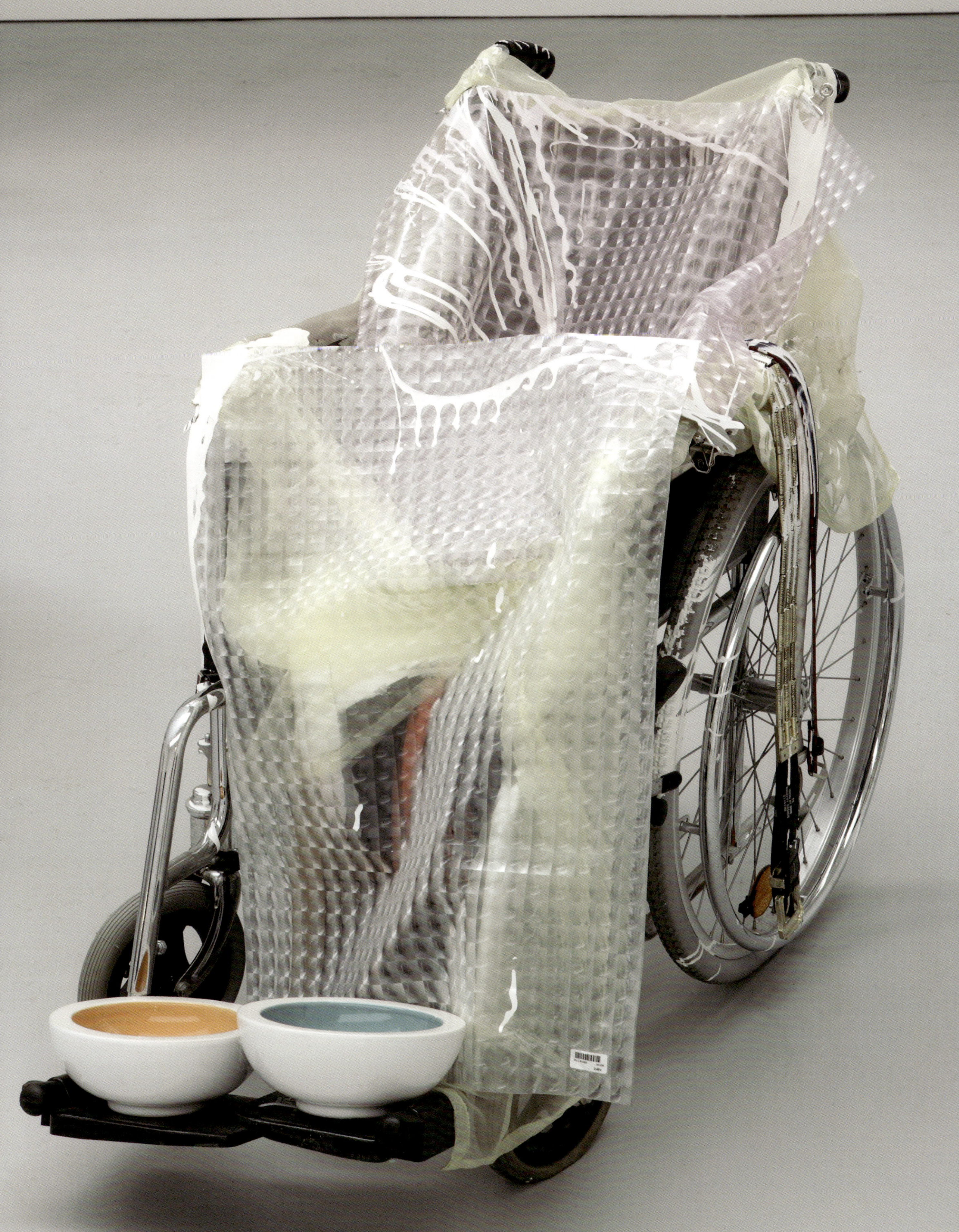

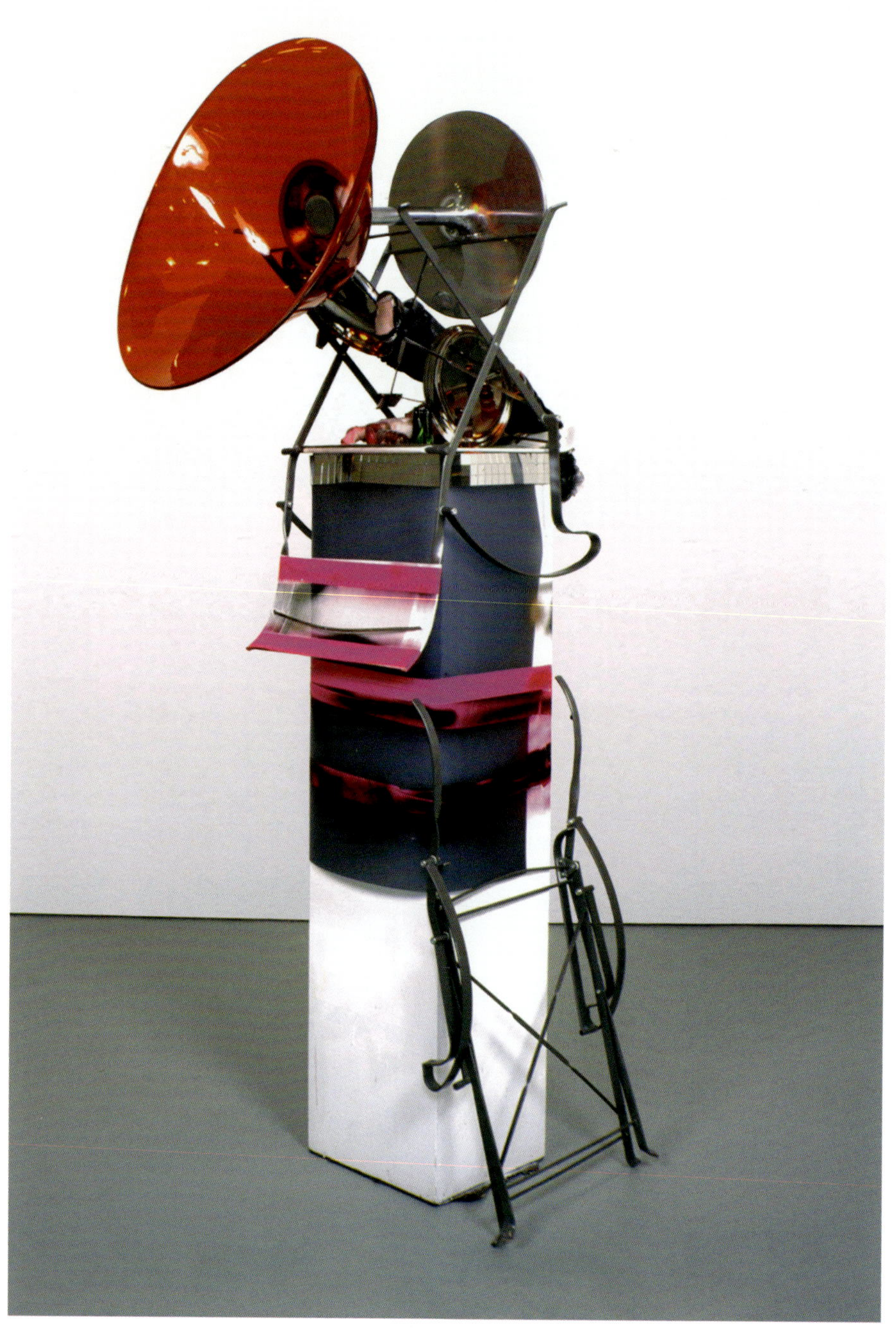

ISA GENZKEN

above:
Geschwister 2004
Plastic, lacquer, mirror foil, glass, metal, wood, fabric
220 x 60 x 100 cm

right:
Mutter Mit Kind 2004
Plastic, fabric, mirror foil, wood, metal, lacquer
194 x 60 x 100 cm

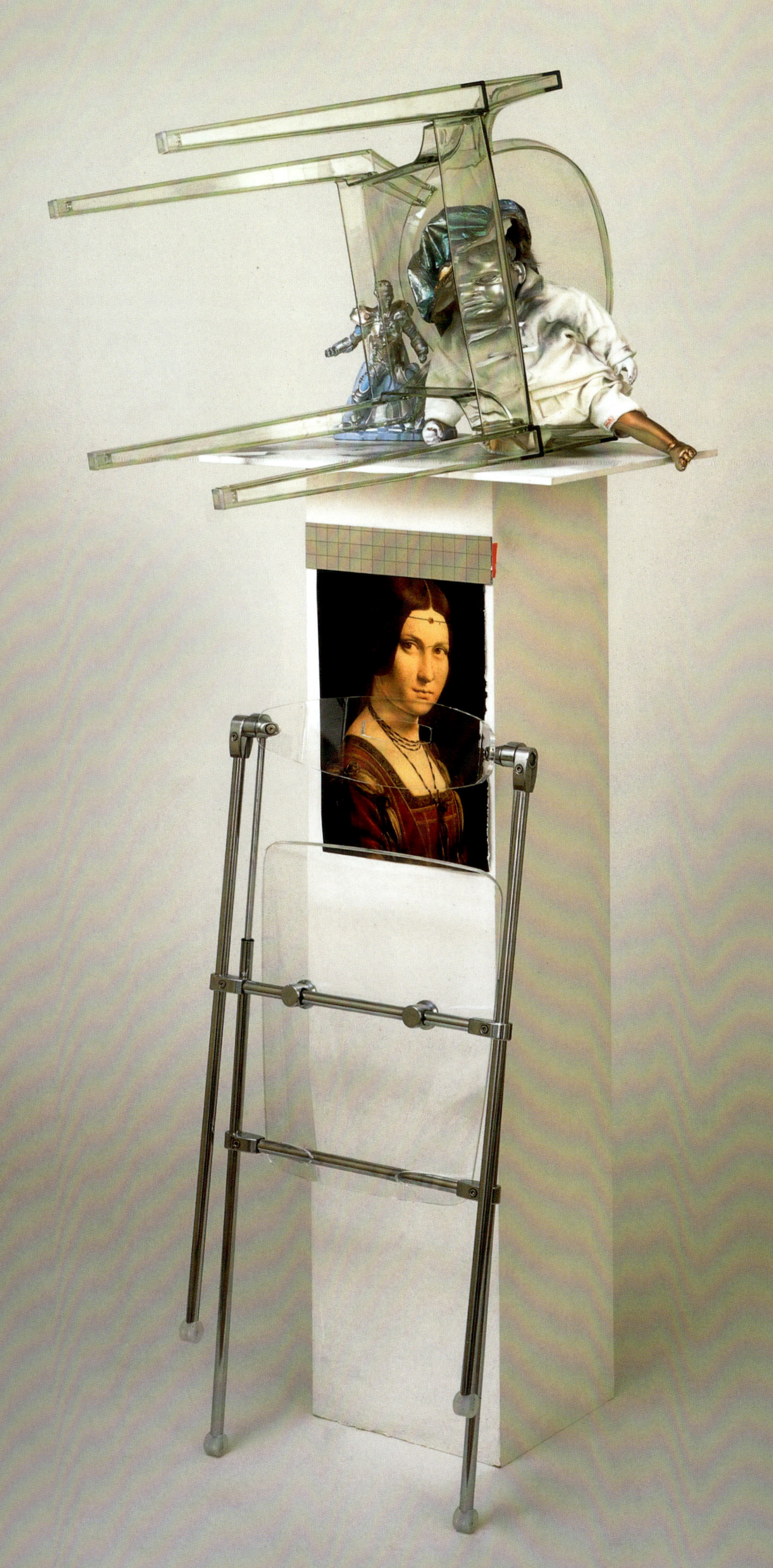

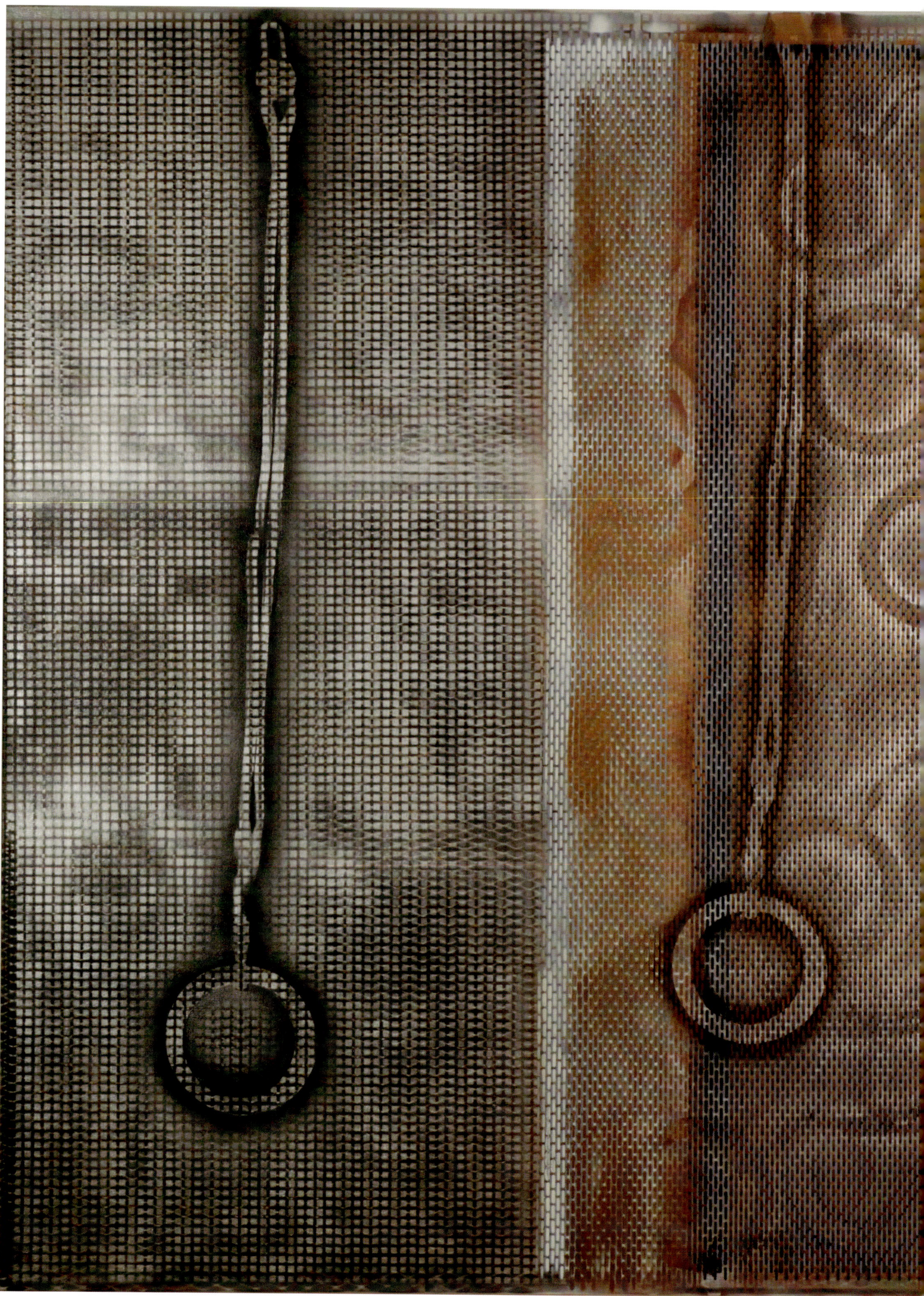

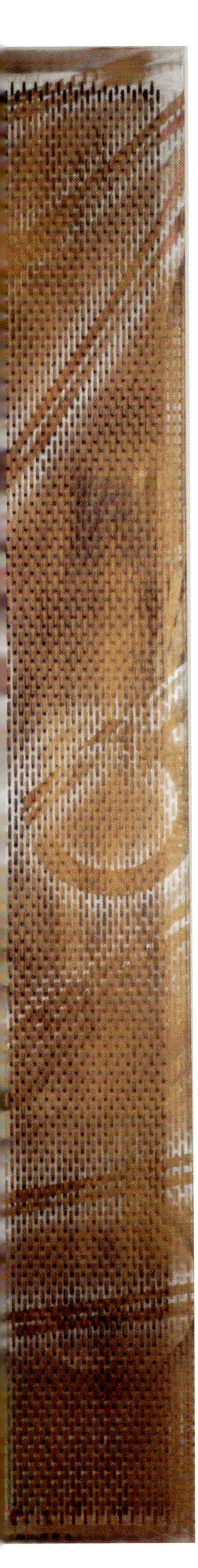

ISA GENZKEN
MLR 1992
Lacquer on canvas
206 x 185 cm

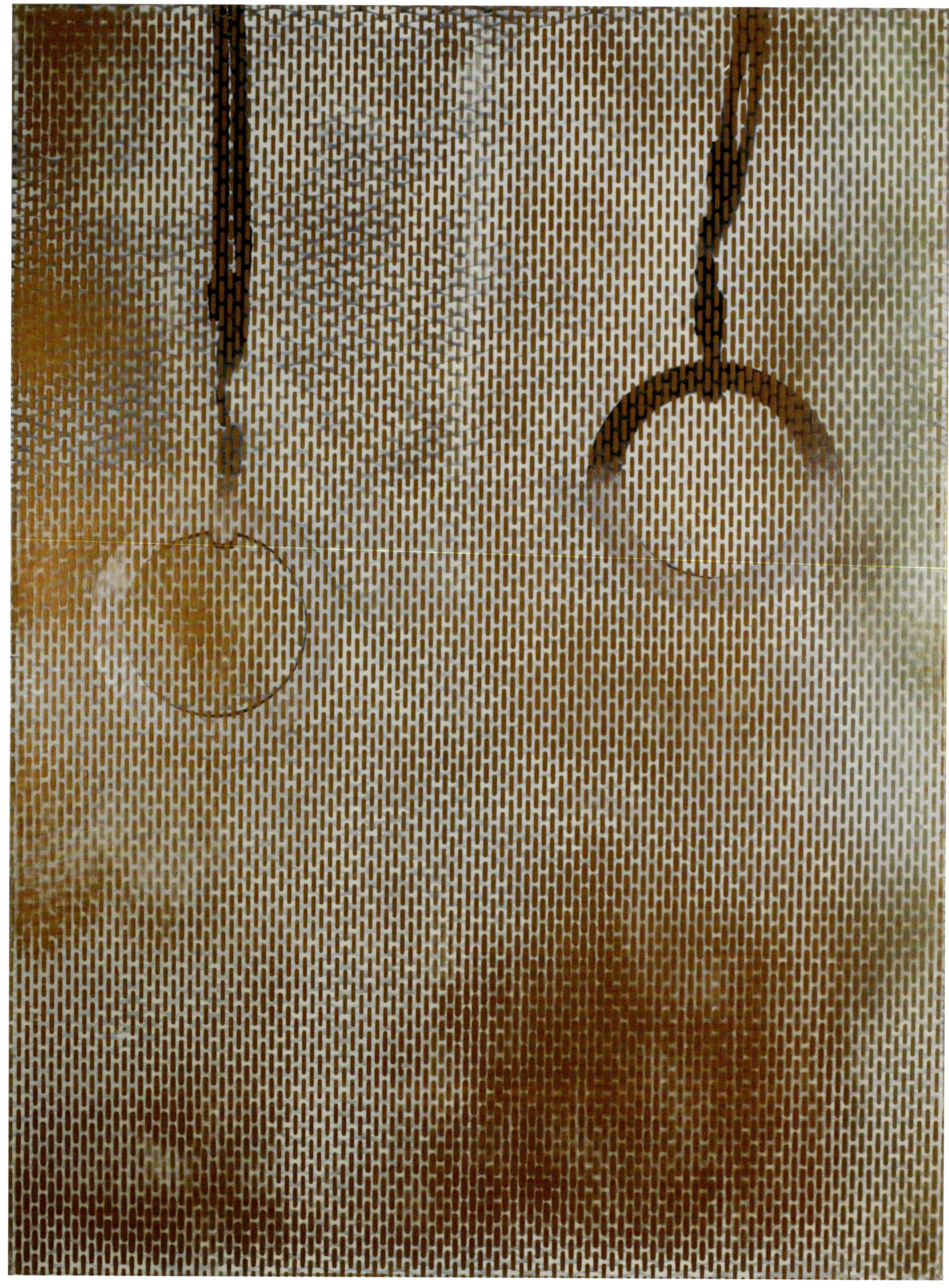

ISA GENZKEN
MLR 1992
Lacquer on canvas
126 x 91.5 cm

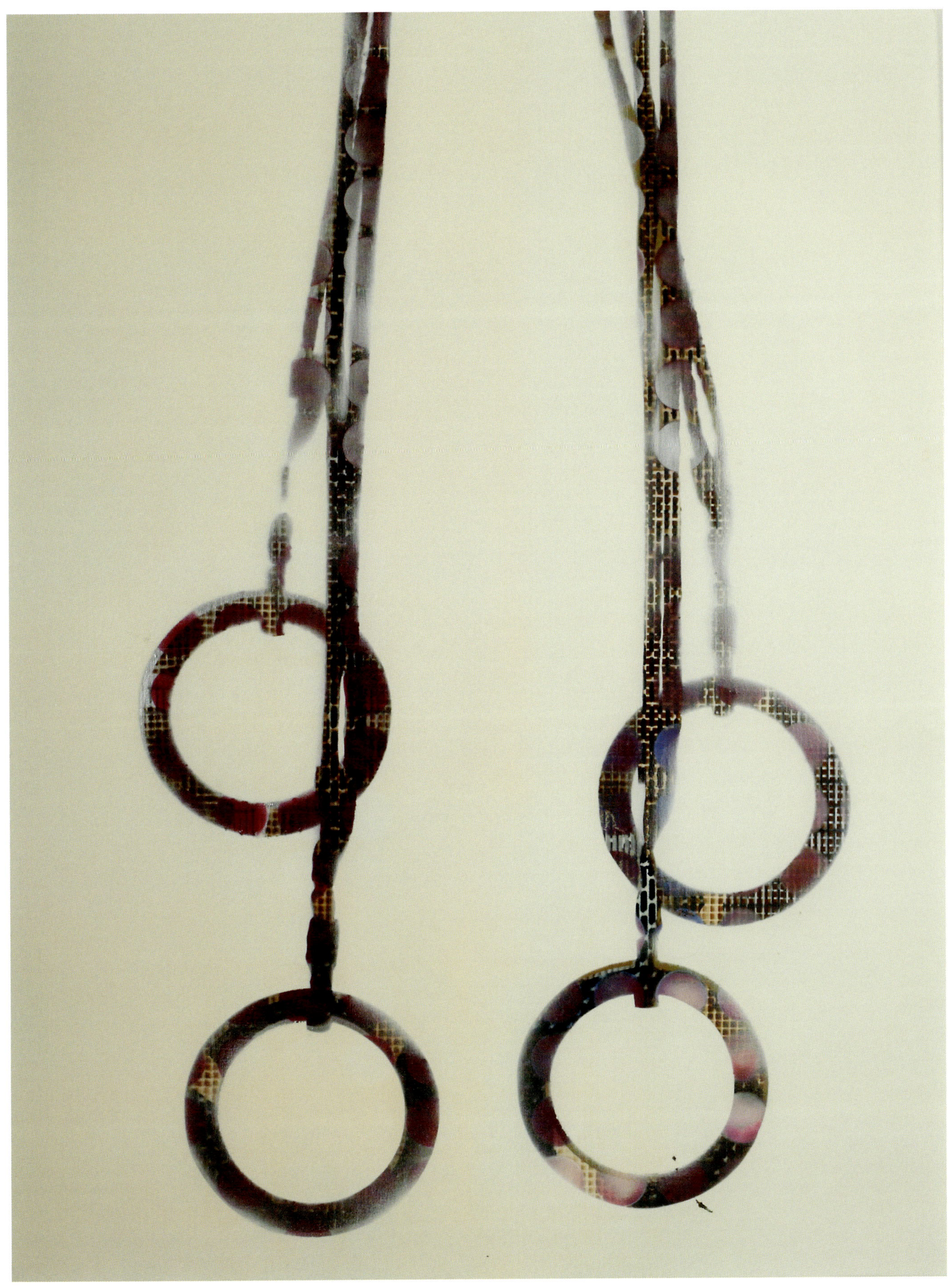

ISA GENZKEN
MRL 1992
Lacquer on MDF
120 x 80 cm

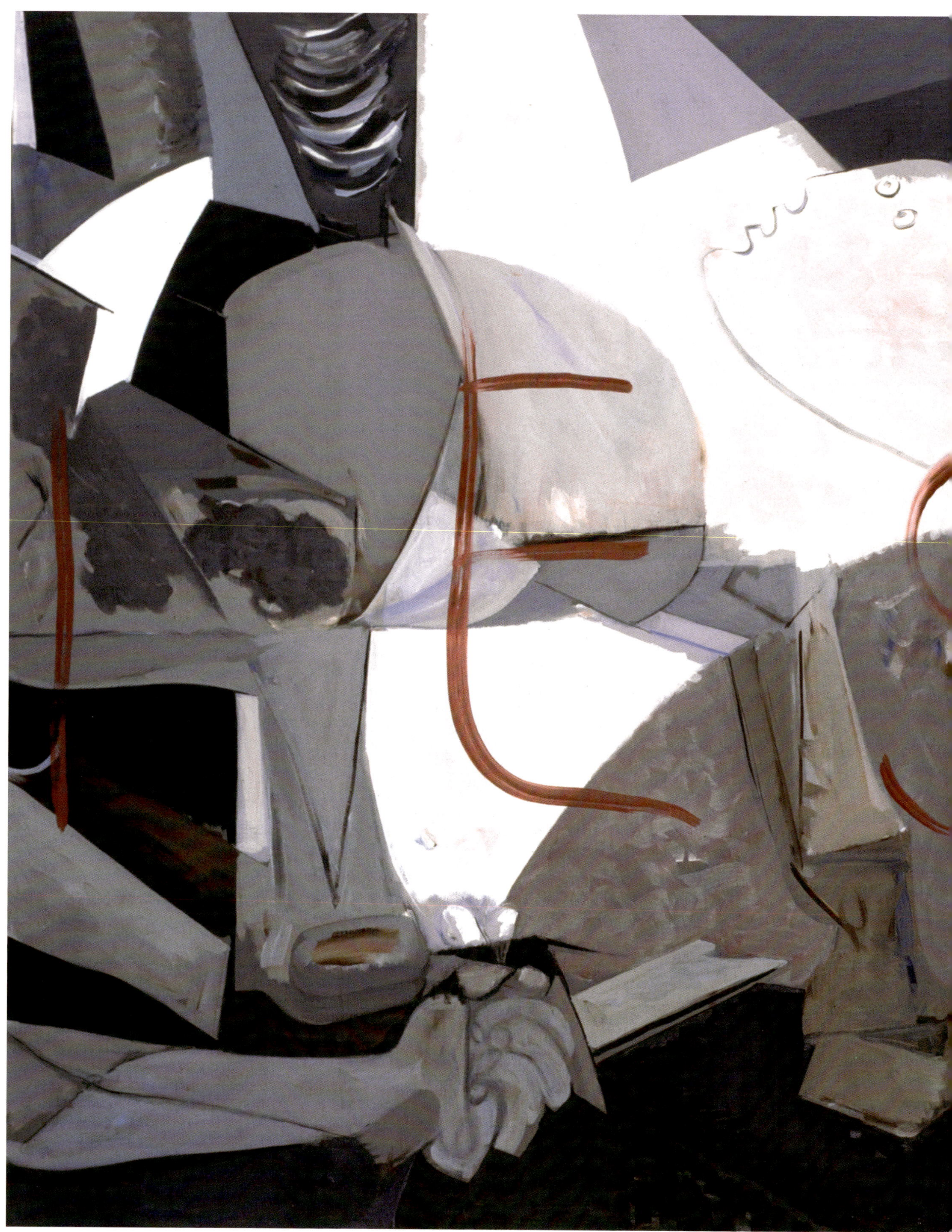

FELIX GMELIN
Kill Lies All After Pablo Picasso (1937) and Tony Shafrazi (1974) 1996
Oil on canvas
195 x 295 cm

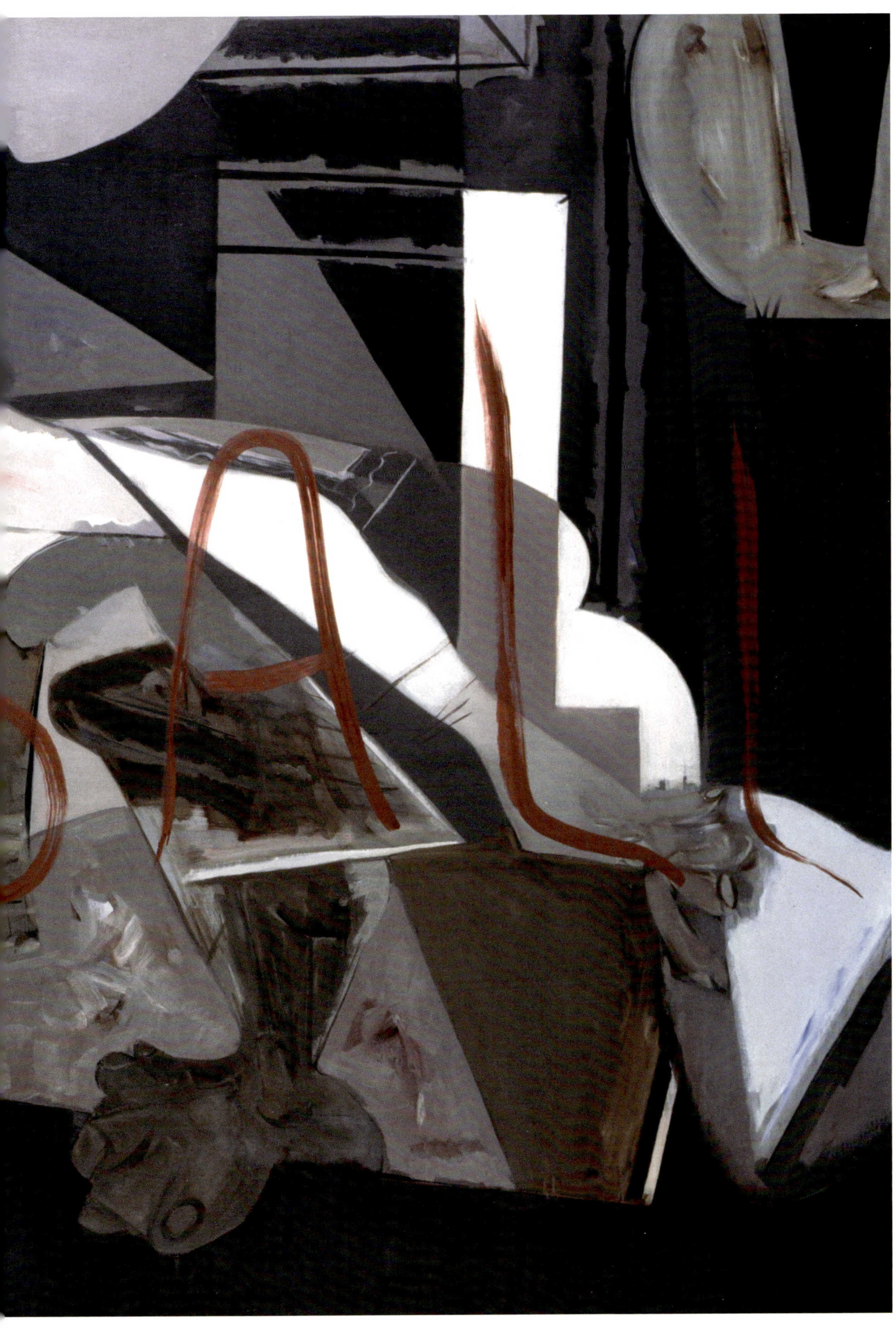

JEPPE HEIN
Mirror Wall 2010
Mirror foil, wooden frame substructure,
vibration system
200 x 356 cm

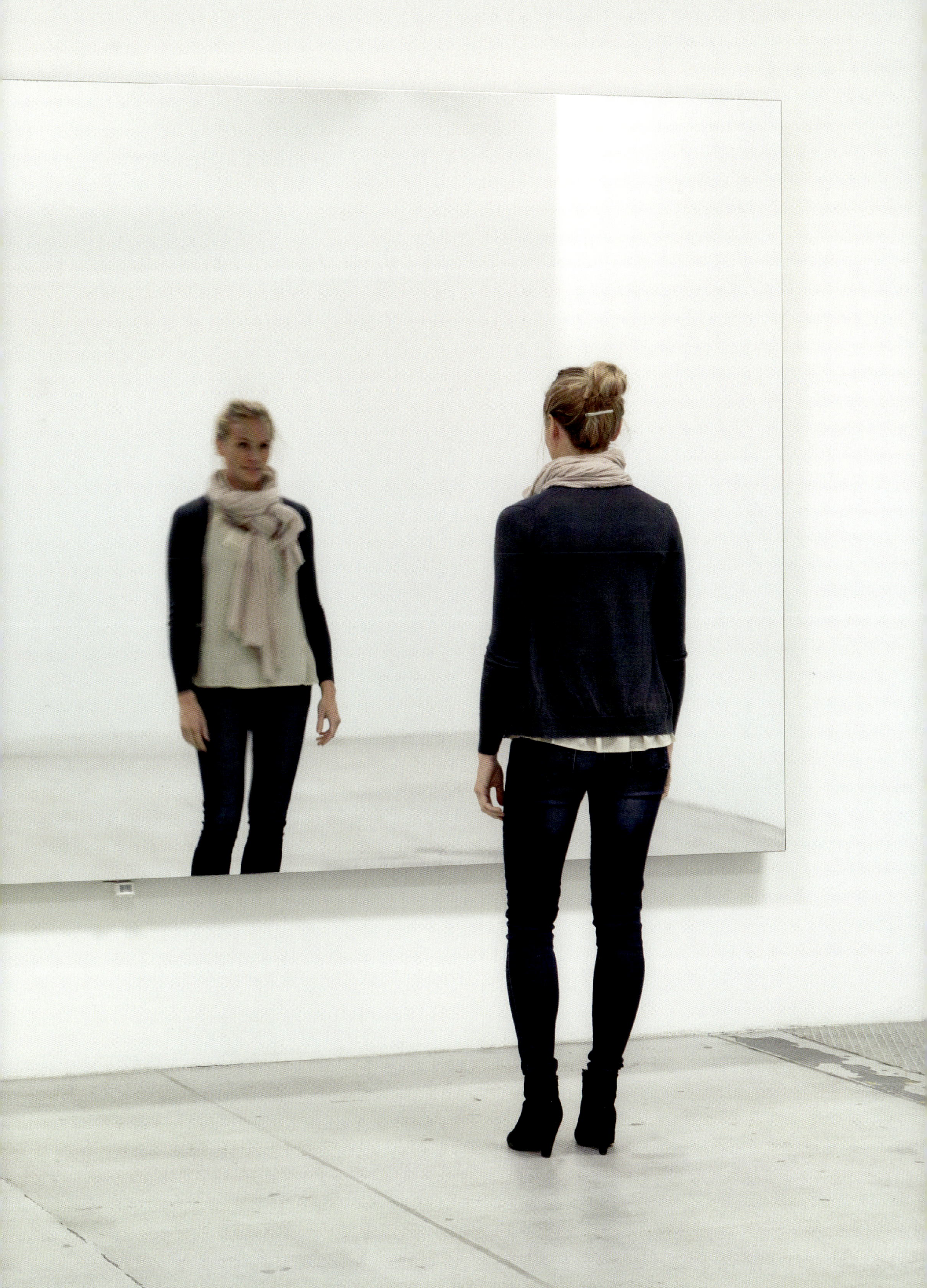

JEPPE HEIN
Shaking Cube 2004
Aluminium and motor
50 x 50 x 50 cm

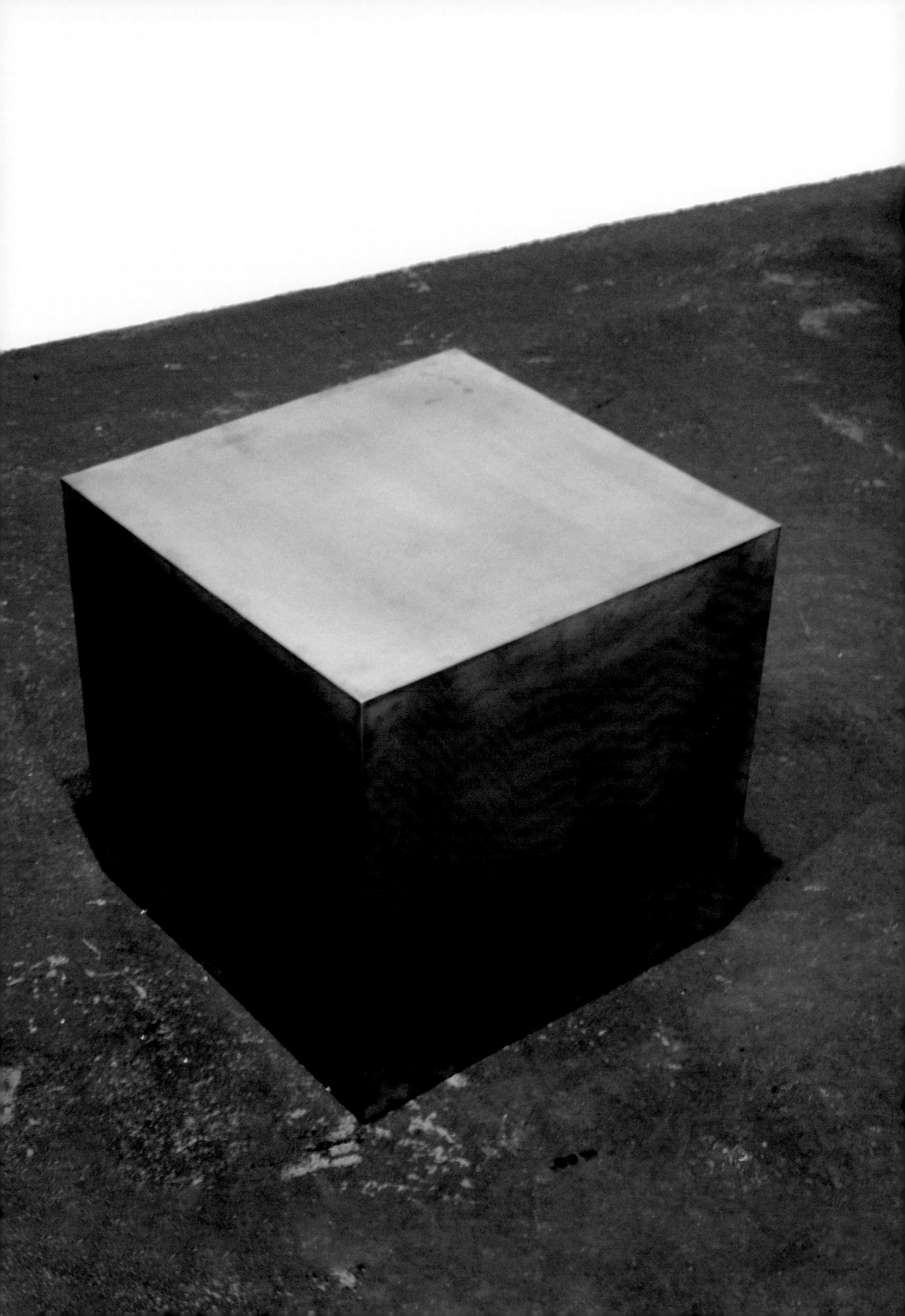

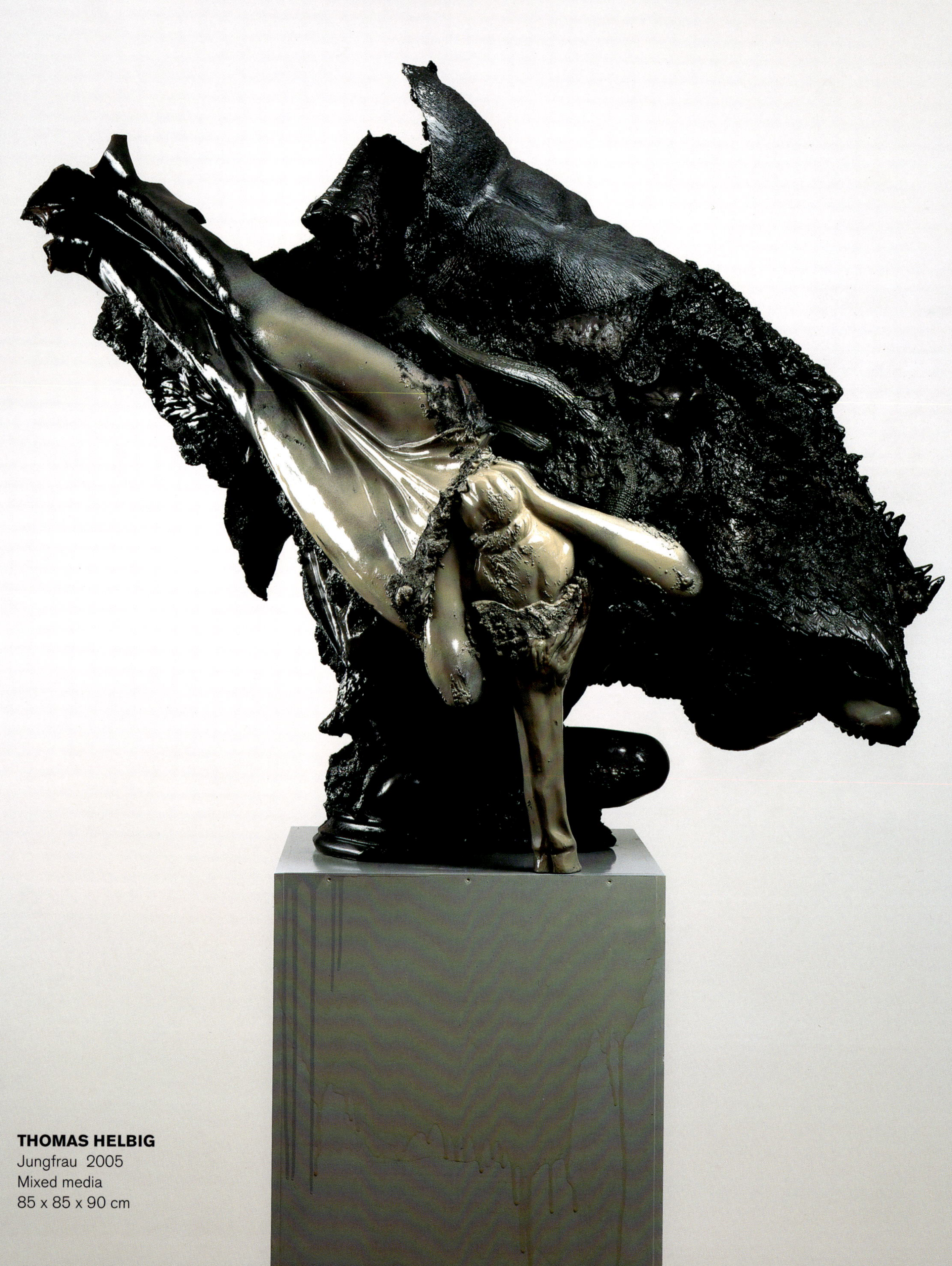

THOMAS HELBIG
Jungfrau 2005
Mixed media
85 x 85 x 90 cm

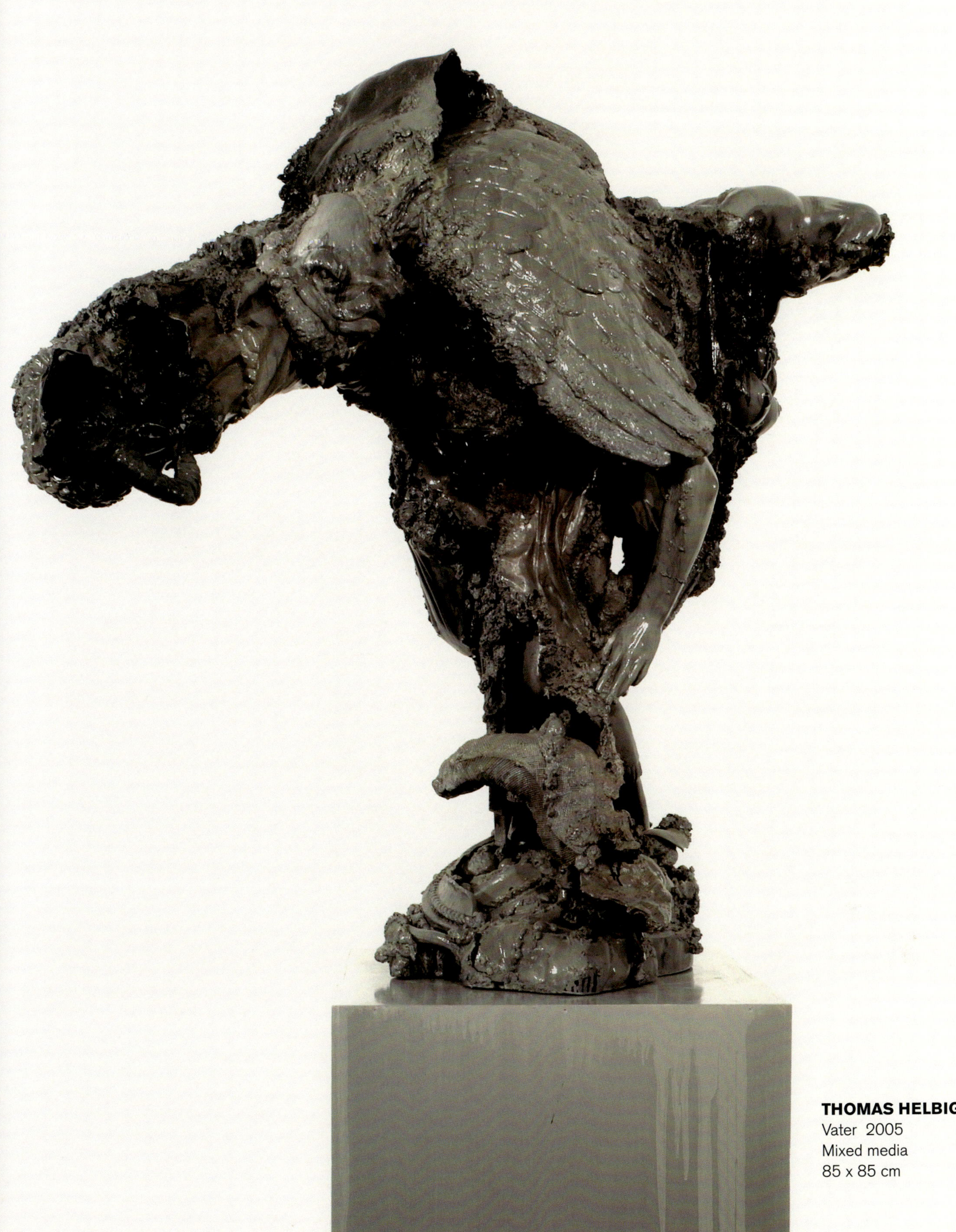

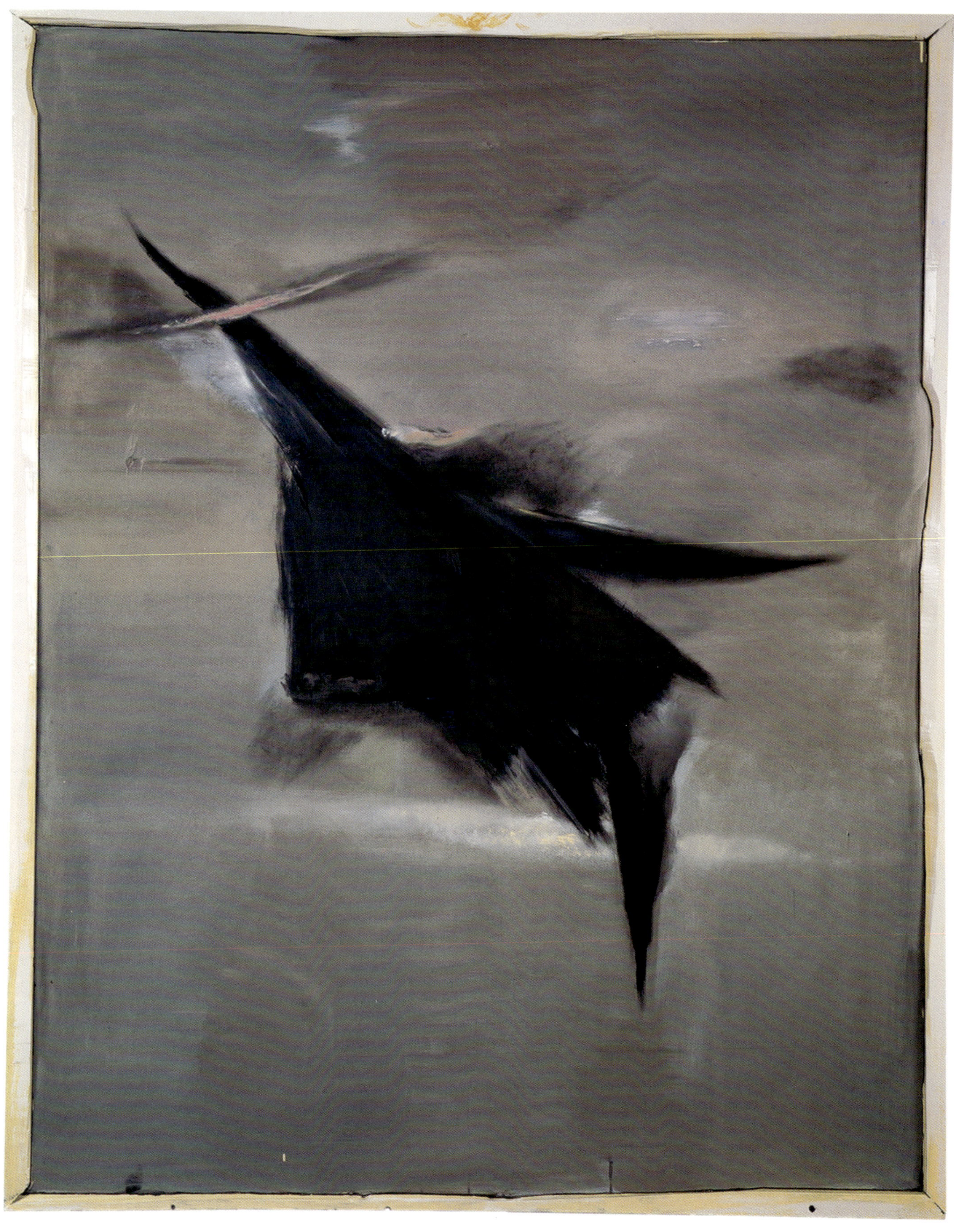

THOMAS HELBIG
Maschine 2005
Oil on canvas
250 x 185 cm

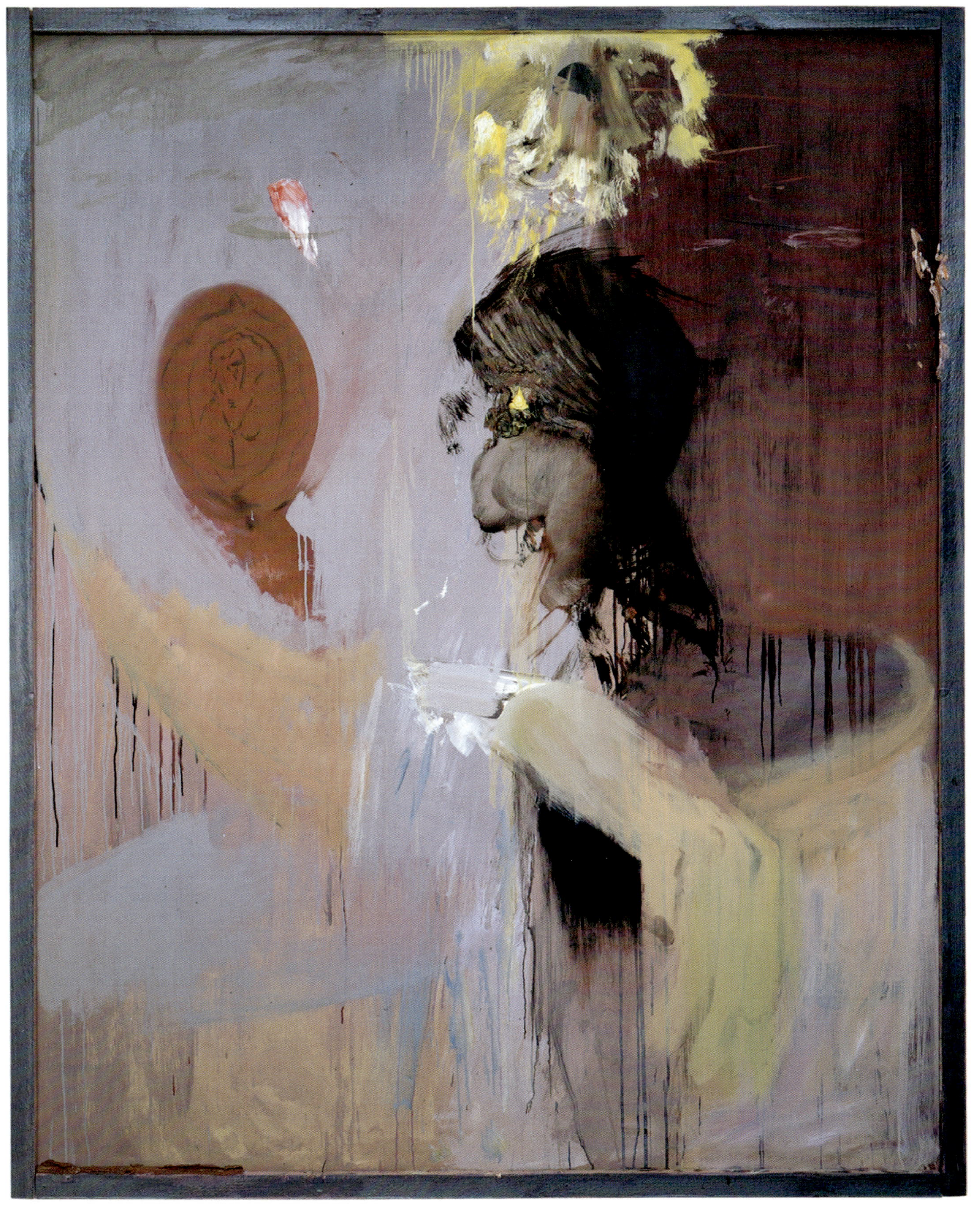

THOMAS HELBIG
Wilde Mit Spiegel 2004
Oil on wood
200 x 160 cm

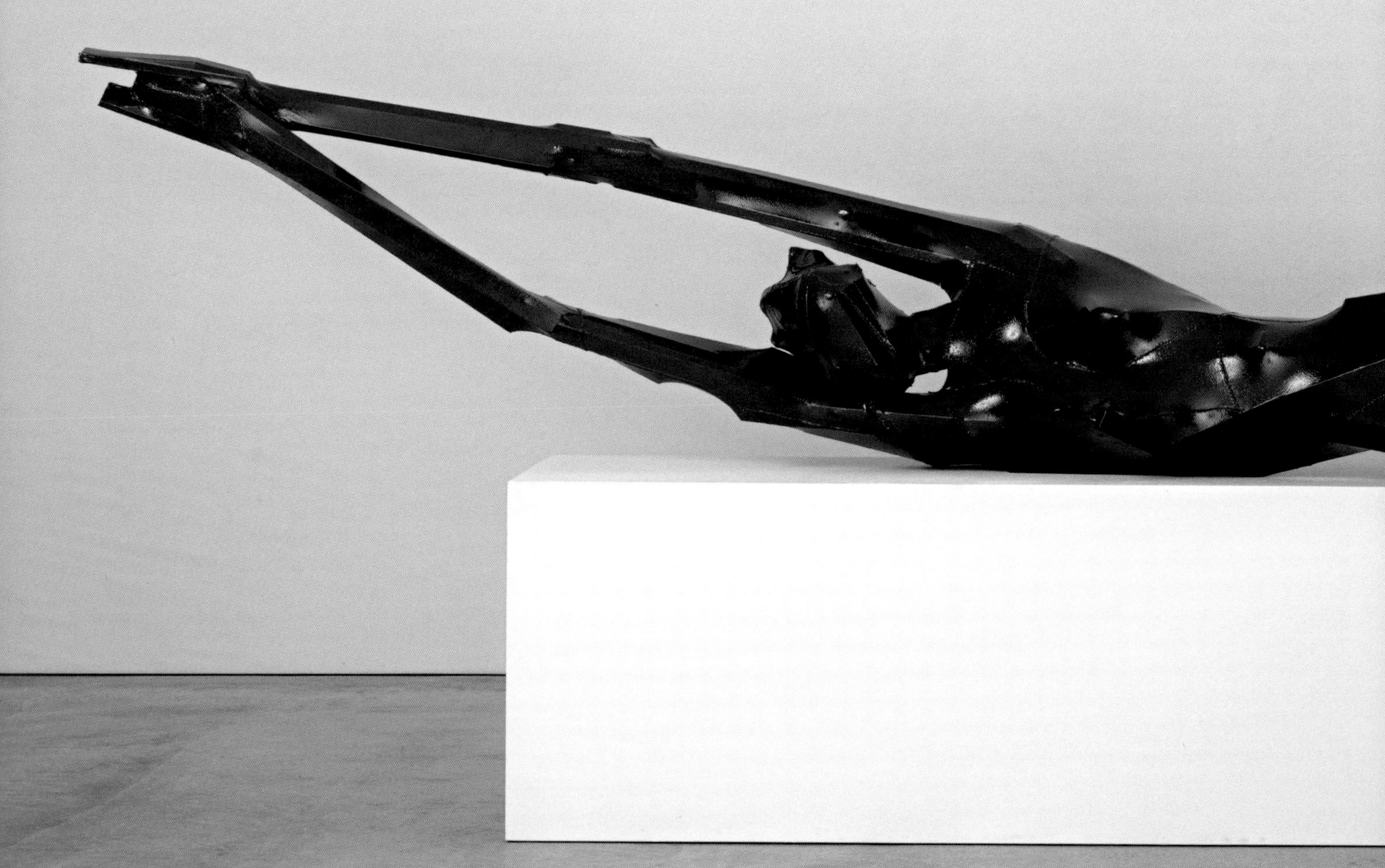

GEORG HEROLD
Untitled 2010
Batten, canvas, lacquer, thread and screws
115 x 510 x 65 cm

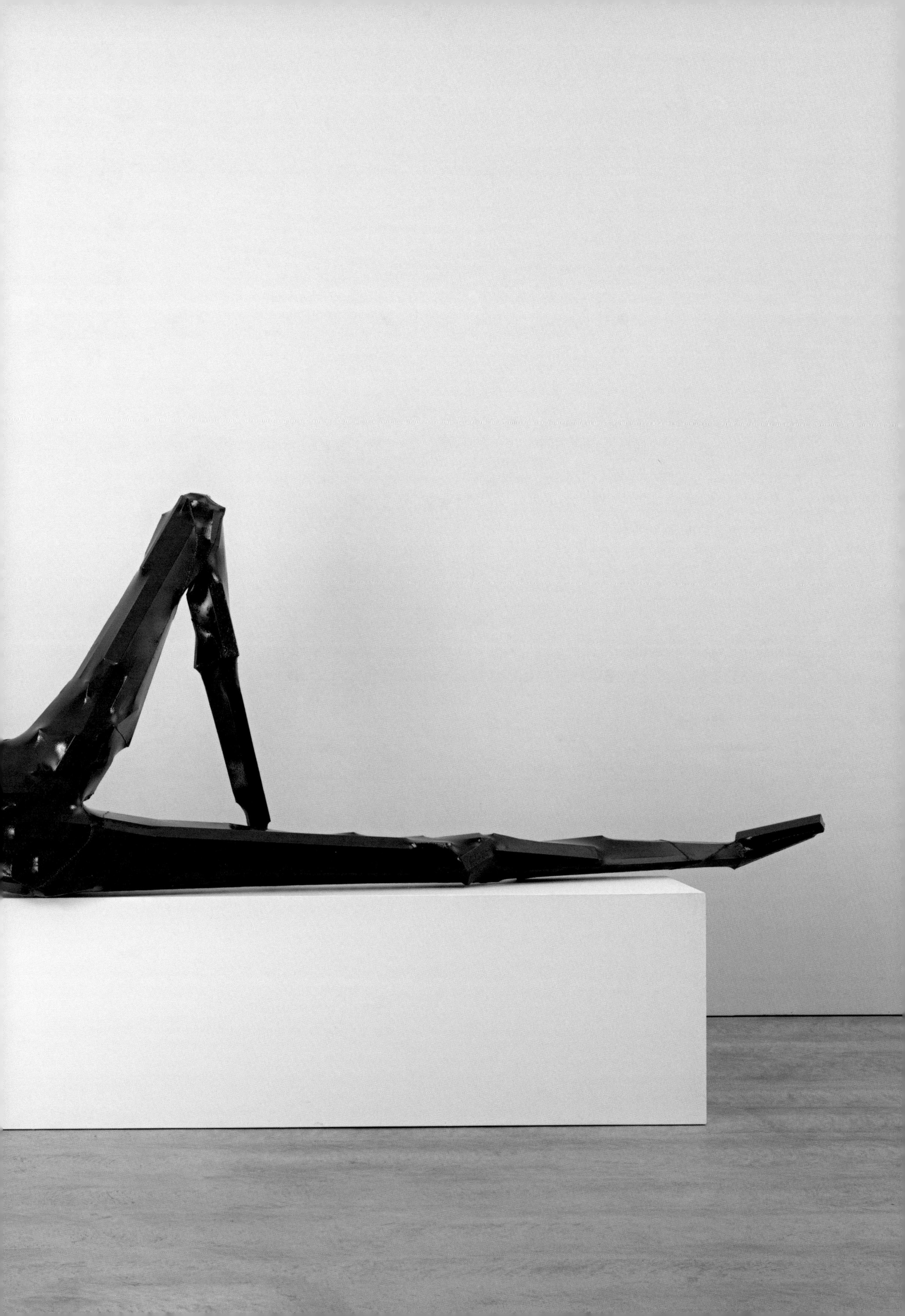

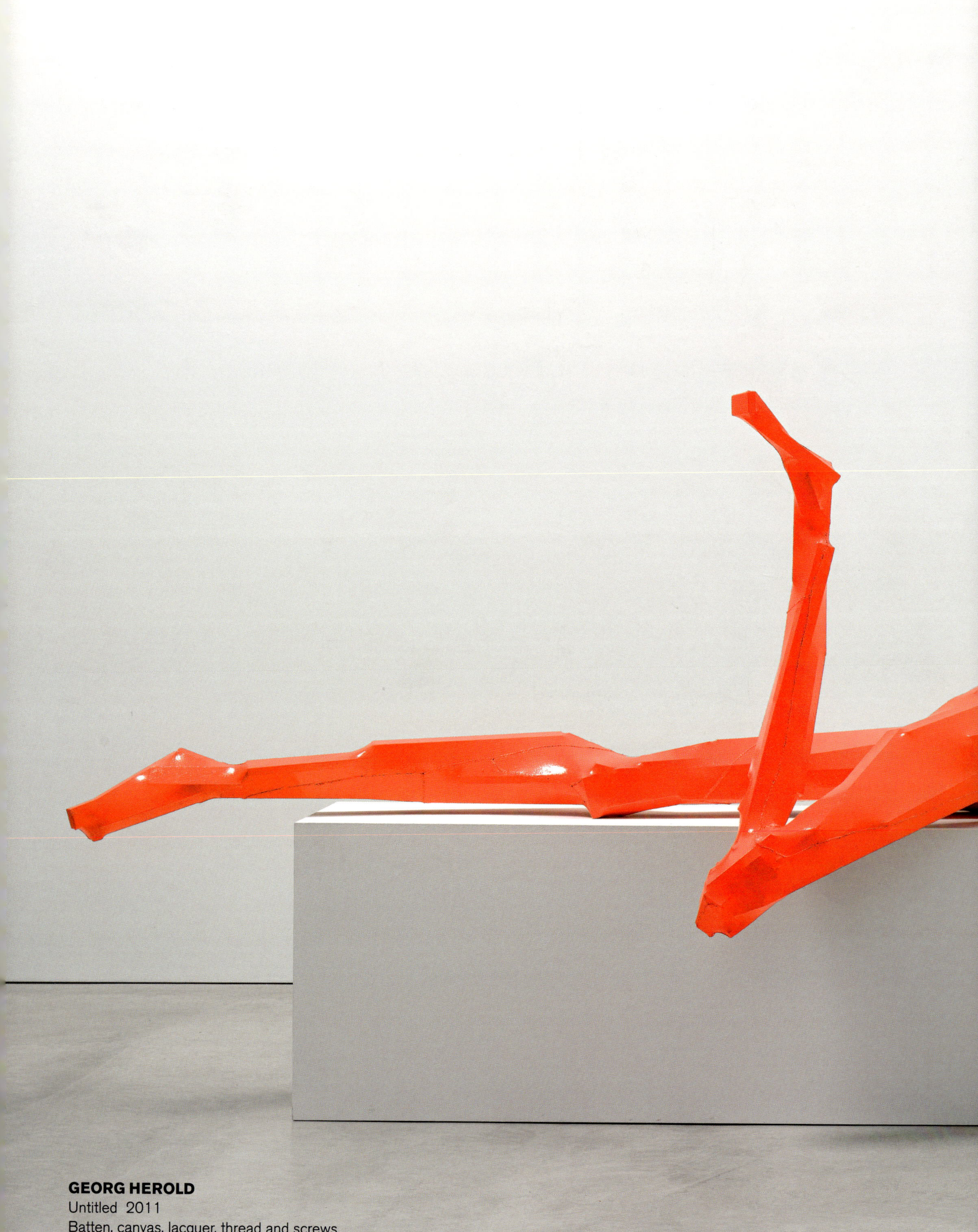

GEORG HEROLD
Untitled 2011
Batten, canvas, lacquer, thread and screws
120 x 420 x 165 cm

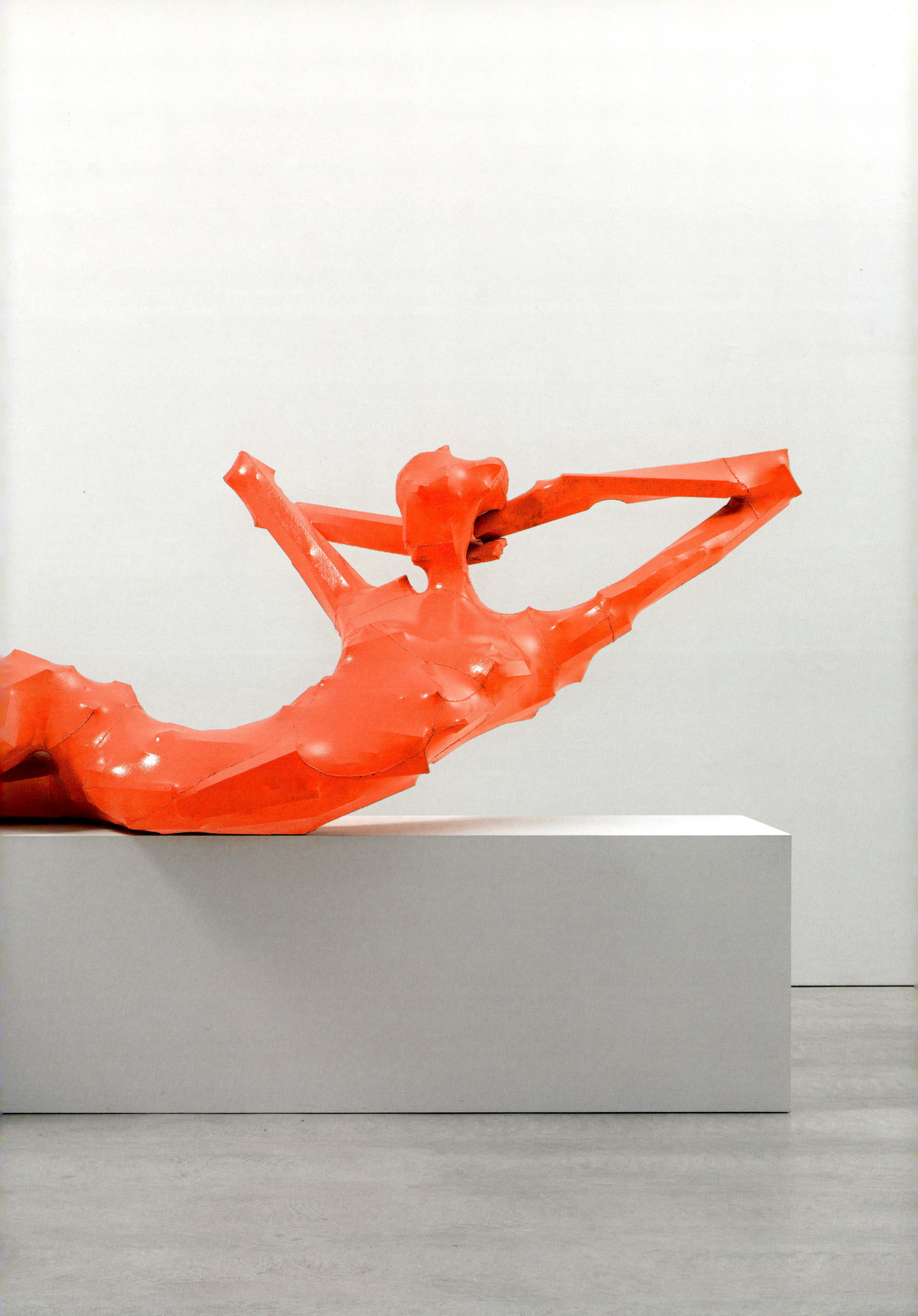

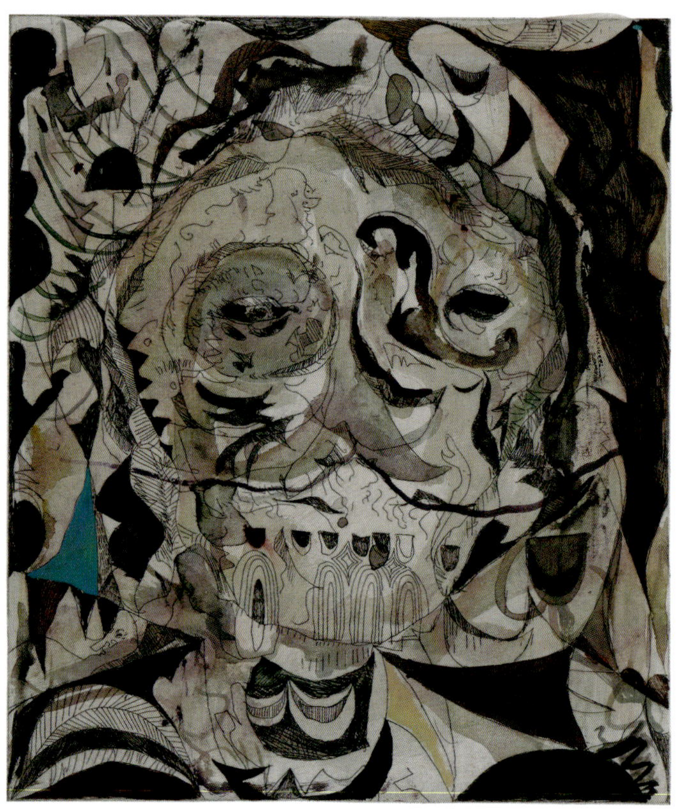

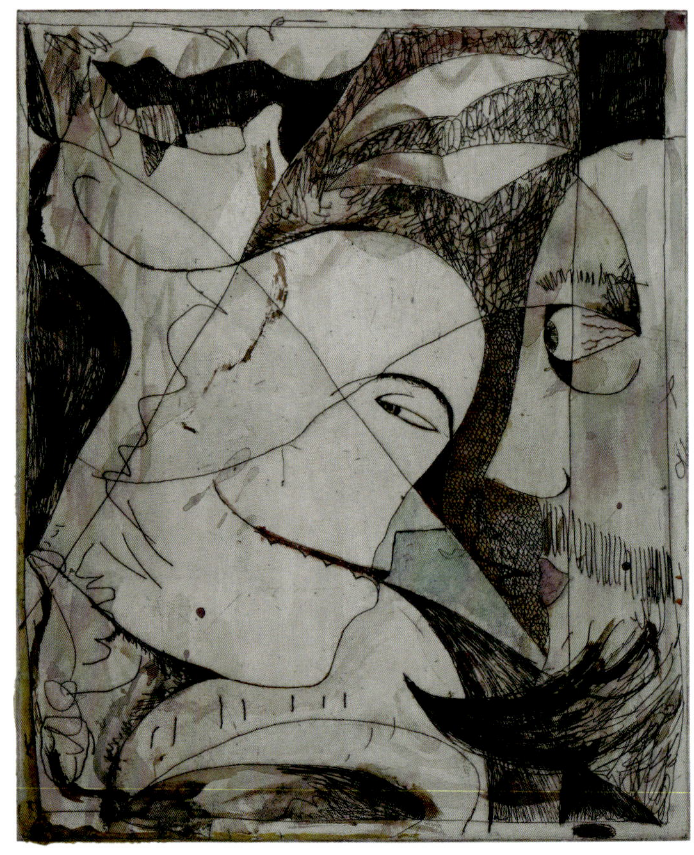

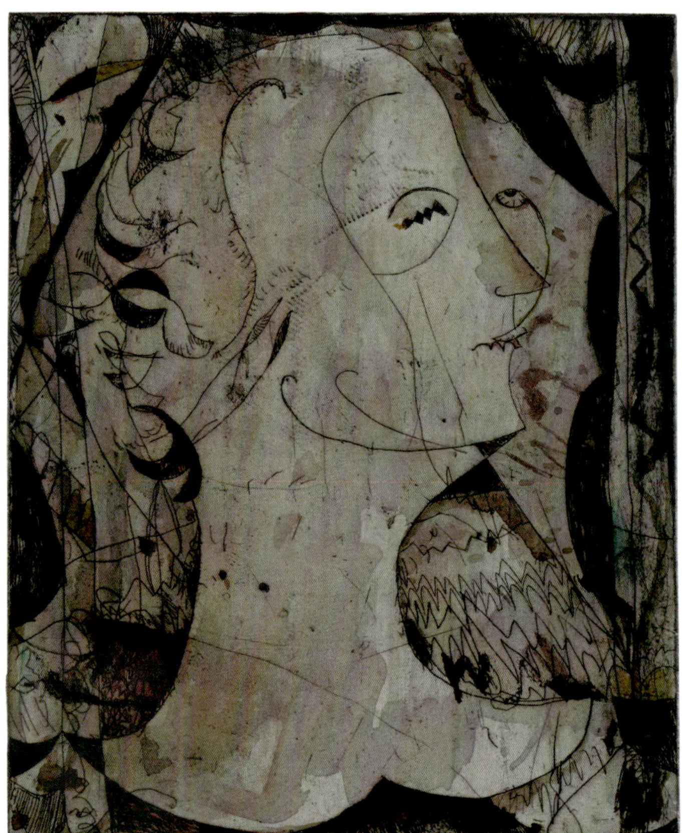

VOLKER HUELLER

above:
My Portrait In The Year 2080 2007
Etching, watercolour
Image: 29 x 25 cm

above right:
Puppetmaster 2009
Etching with watercolour and shellac
30 x 24 cm

above right:
Wohin-Sehen 2009
Etching with watercolour and shellac
30 x 24 cm

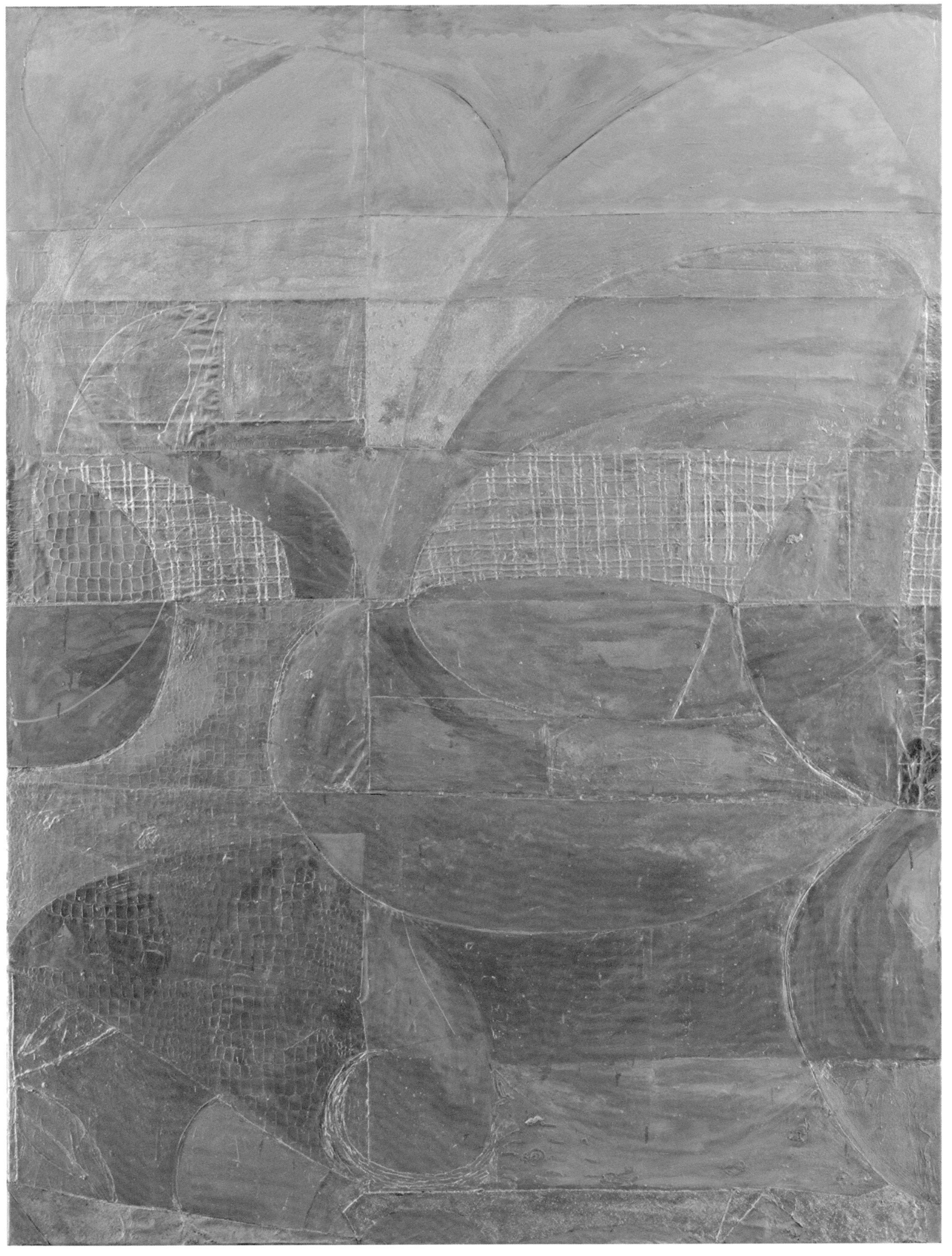

VOLKER HUELLER
Sie Sind Unter Uns XII 2009
Mixed media on canvas
250 x 200 cm

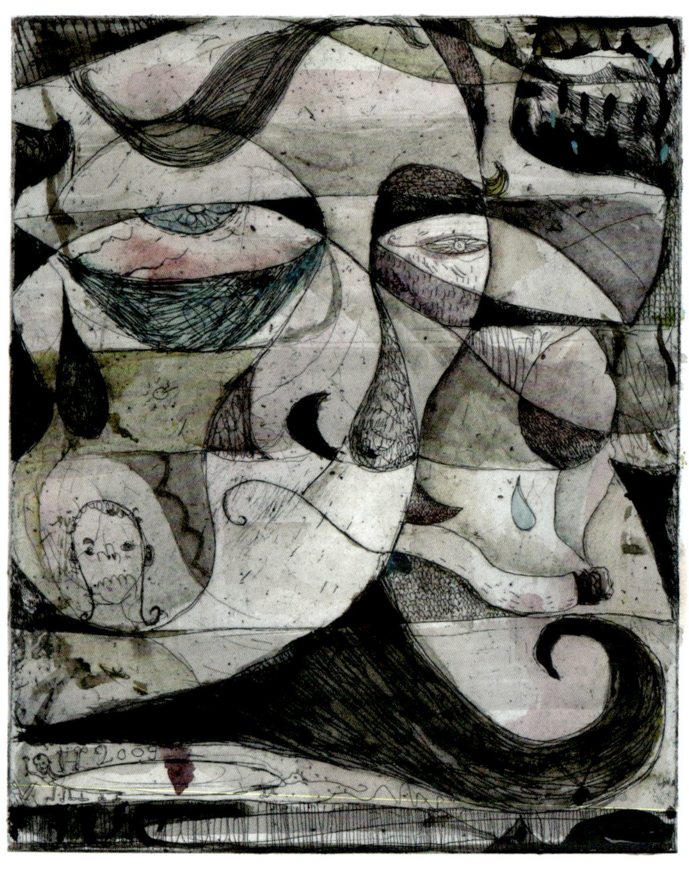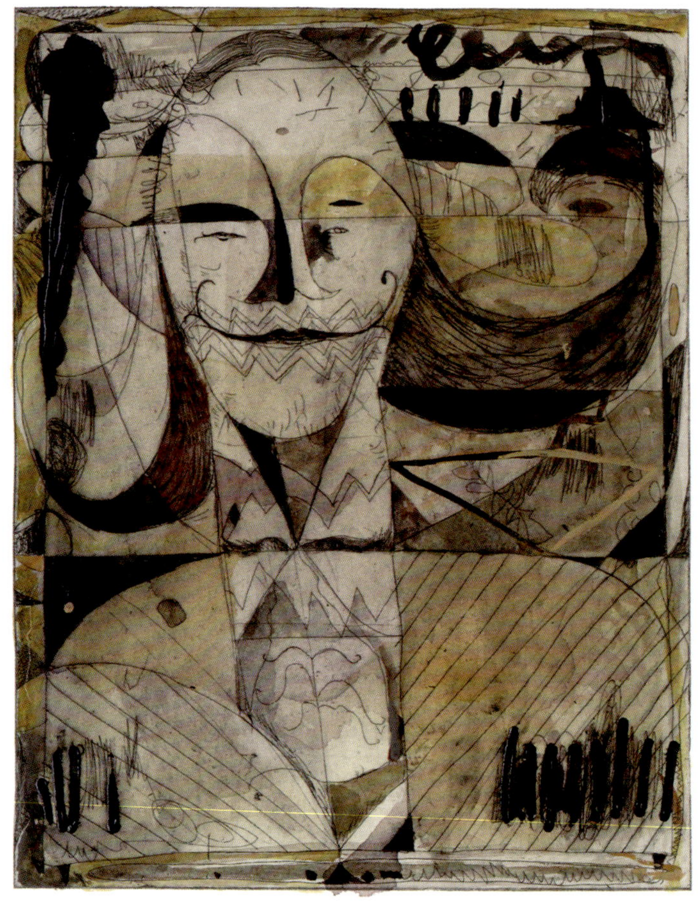

VOLKER HUELLER

above:
Rauch Im Aug 2009
Watercolour, shellac
25 x 20 cm

above top:
Untitled (Haupt) 2009
Etching, watercolour, shellac, red wine
40 x 30 cm

above right:
Elegy 2009
Etching, watercolour, shellac, red wine
40 x 30 cm

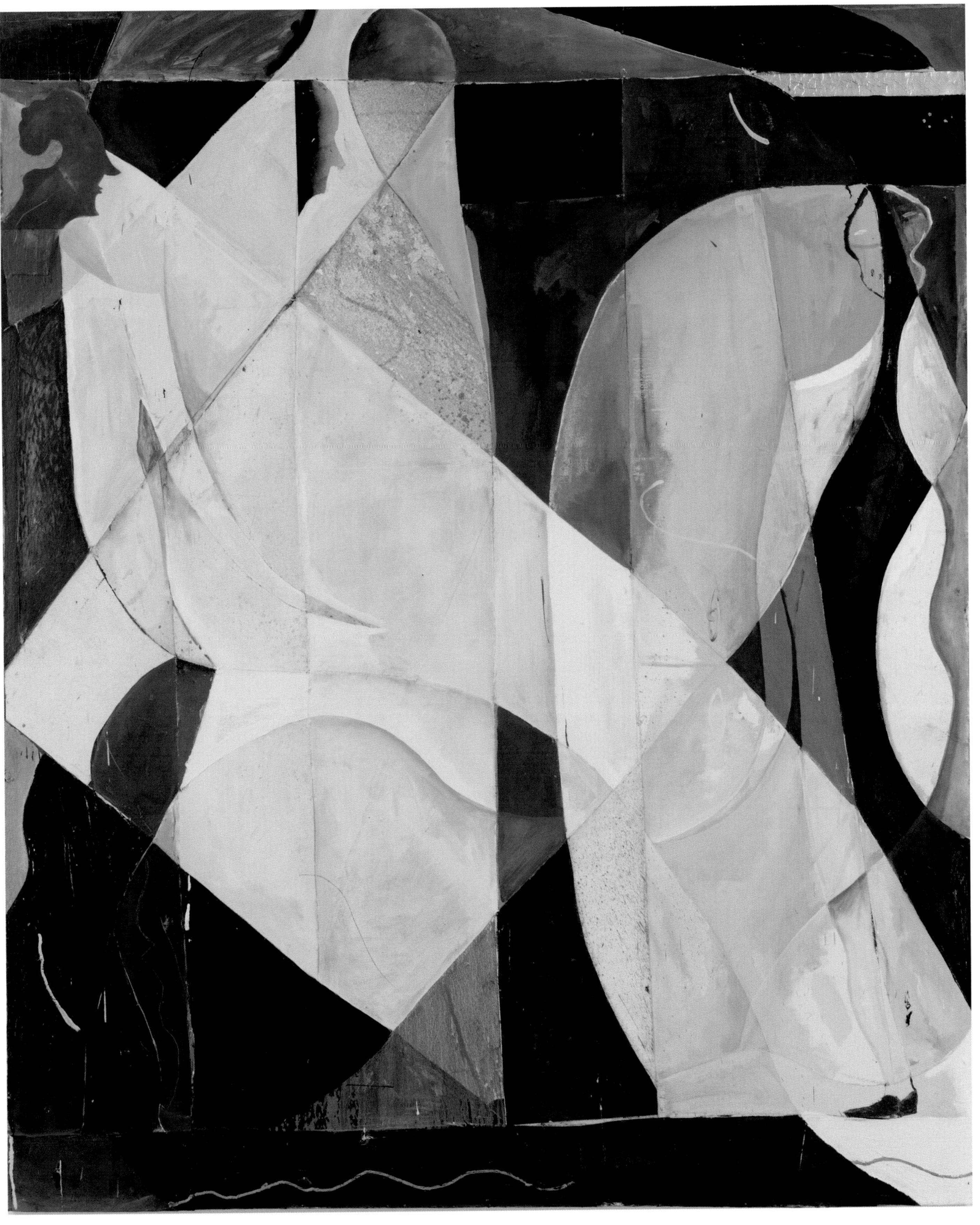

VOLKER HUELLER
Drei Halunken Und Ein Halleluja 2009
Mixed media on canvas
240 x 180 cm

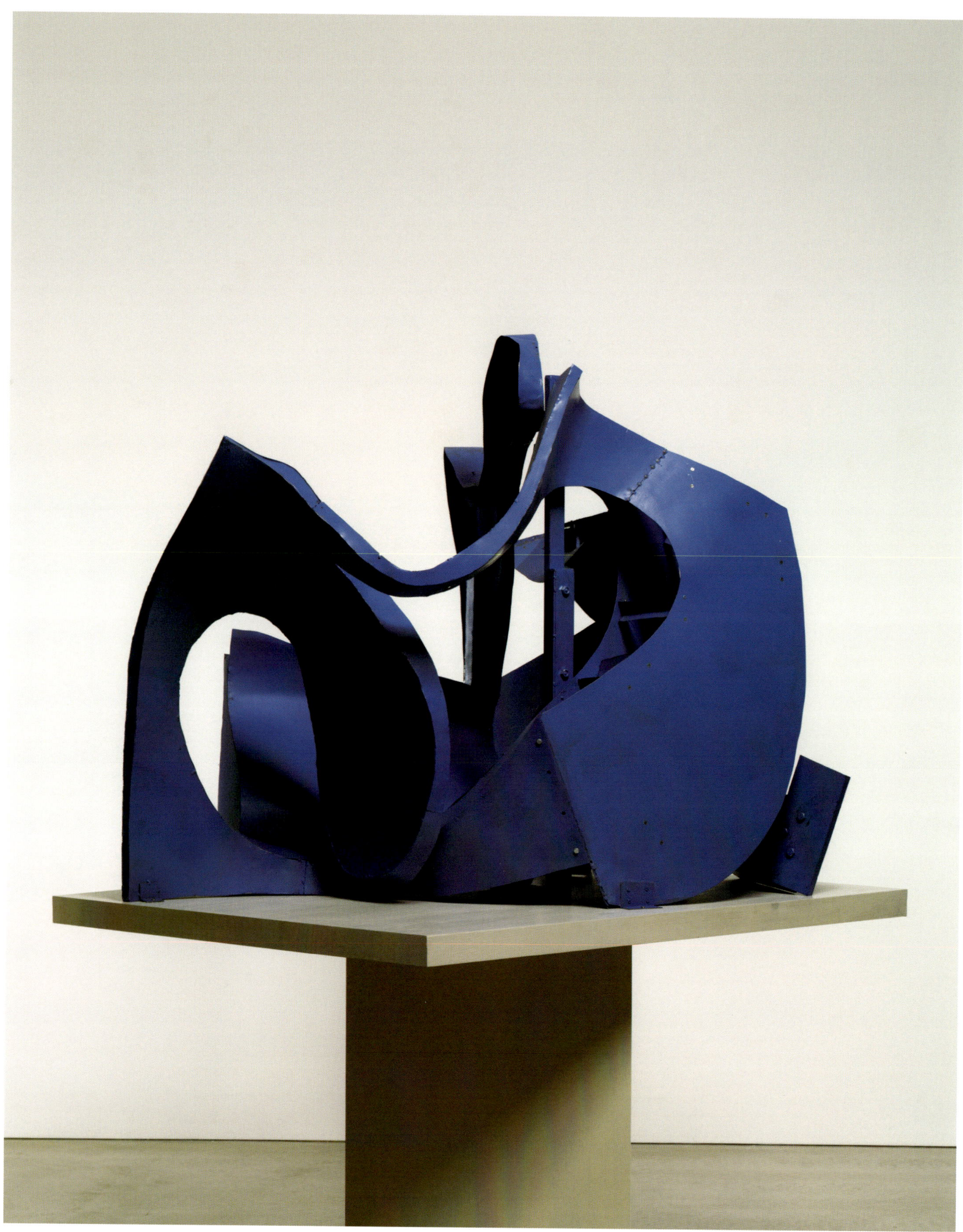

THOMAS KIESEWETTER
Matisse Blau 2010
Sheet metal, steel, lacquer
117.5 x 156 x 133 cm

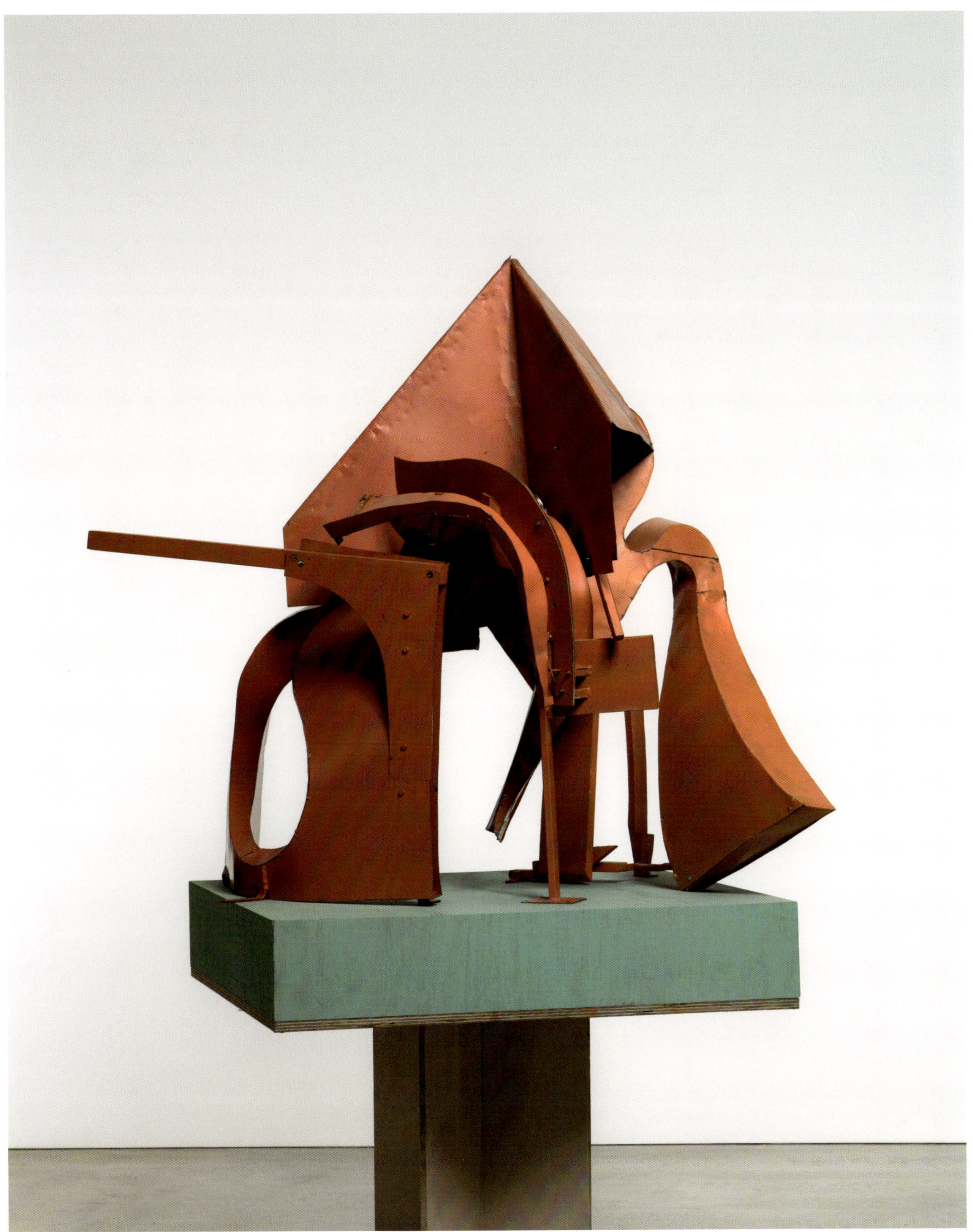

THOMAS KIESEWETTER
Barriere 2010
Sheet metal, steel, spray paint
135 x 149 x 89 cm

THOMAS KIESEWETTER
Untitled 2004
Sheet metal, paint
215 x 142 x 160 cm

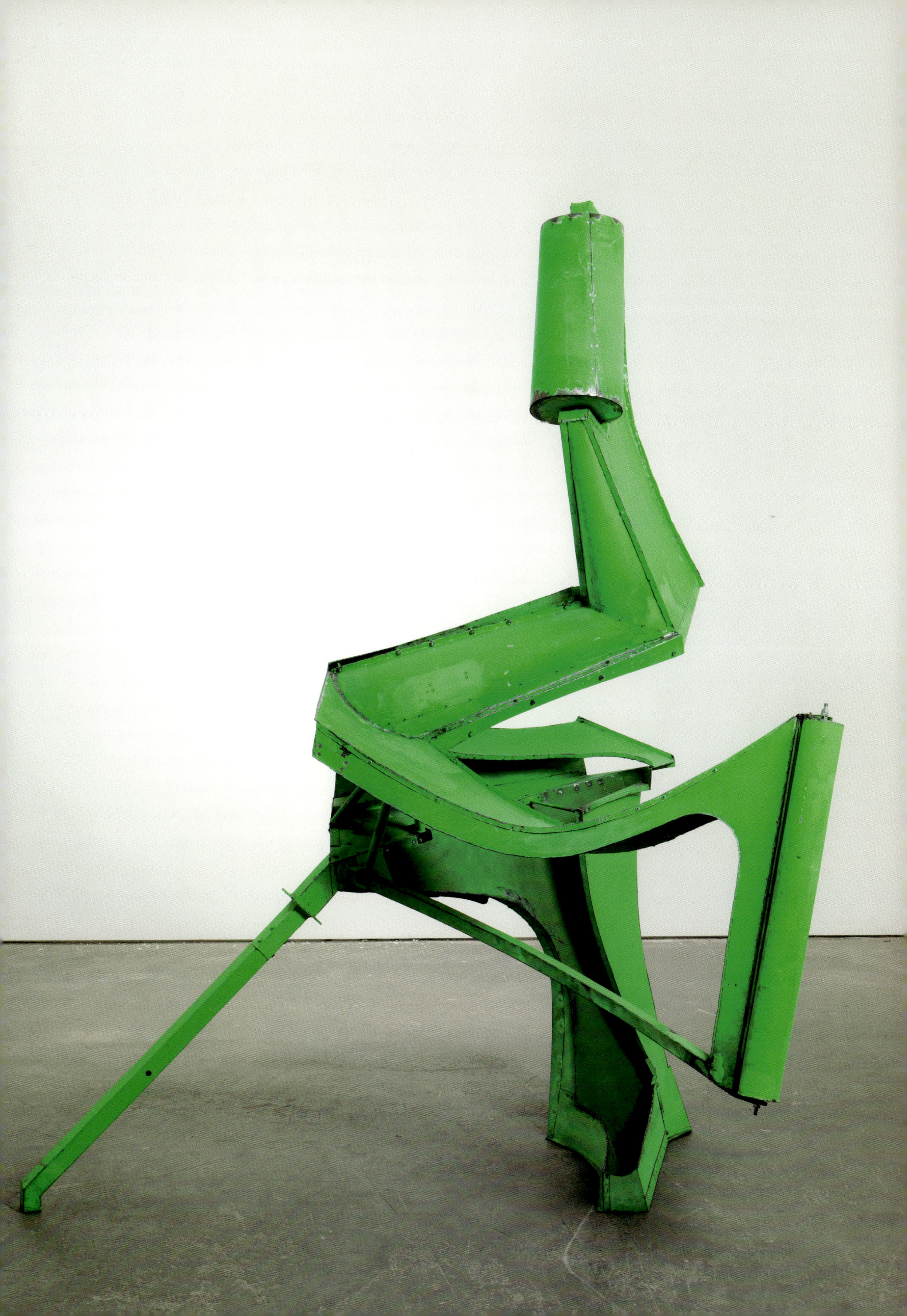

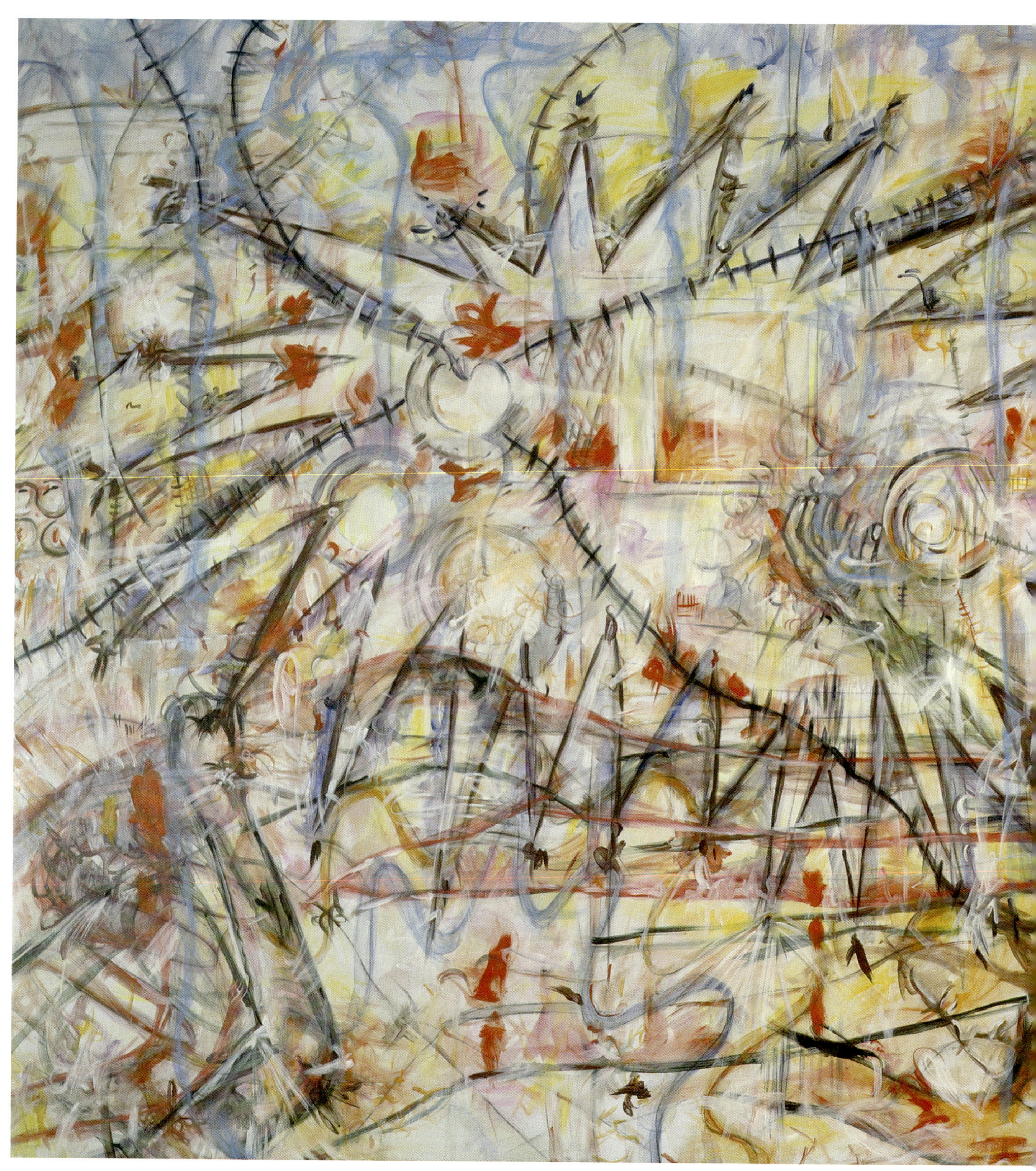

JUTTA KOETHER
Frontage (Well, Show Me Nothing) 1994
Oil on canvas
188 x 290 cm

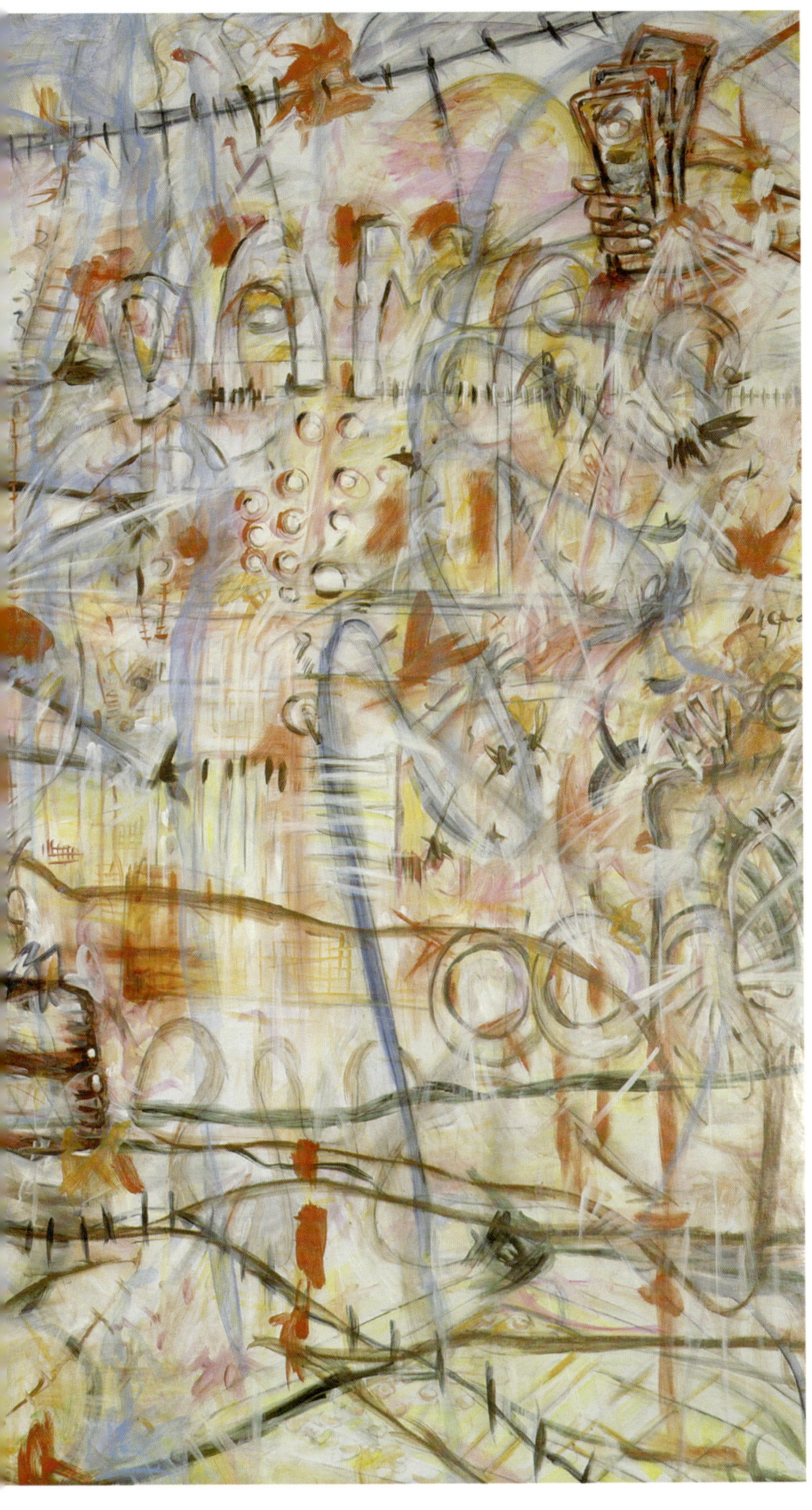

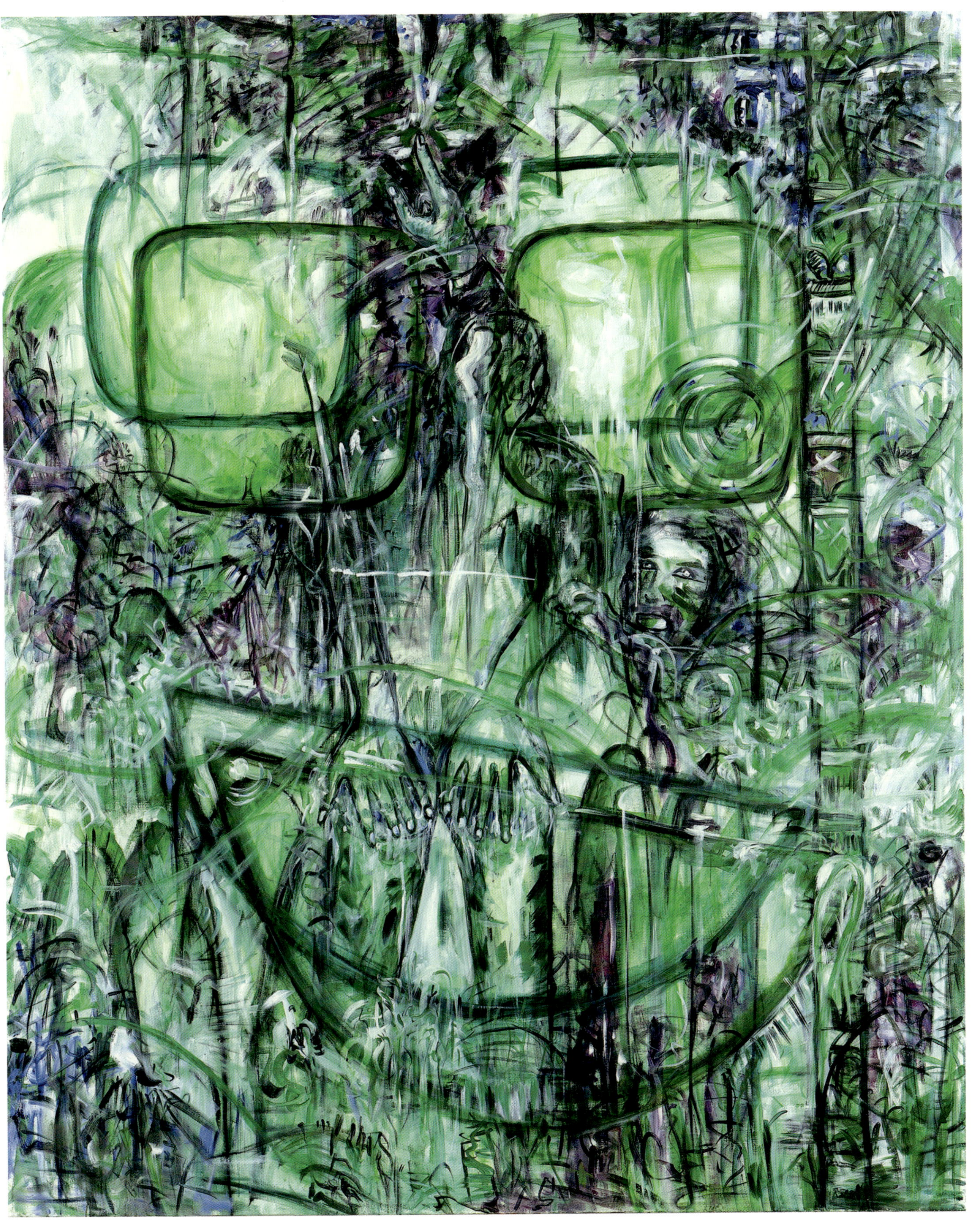

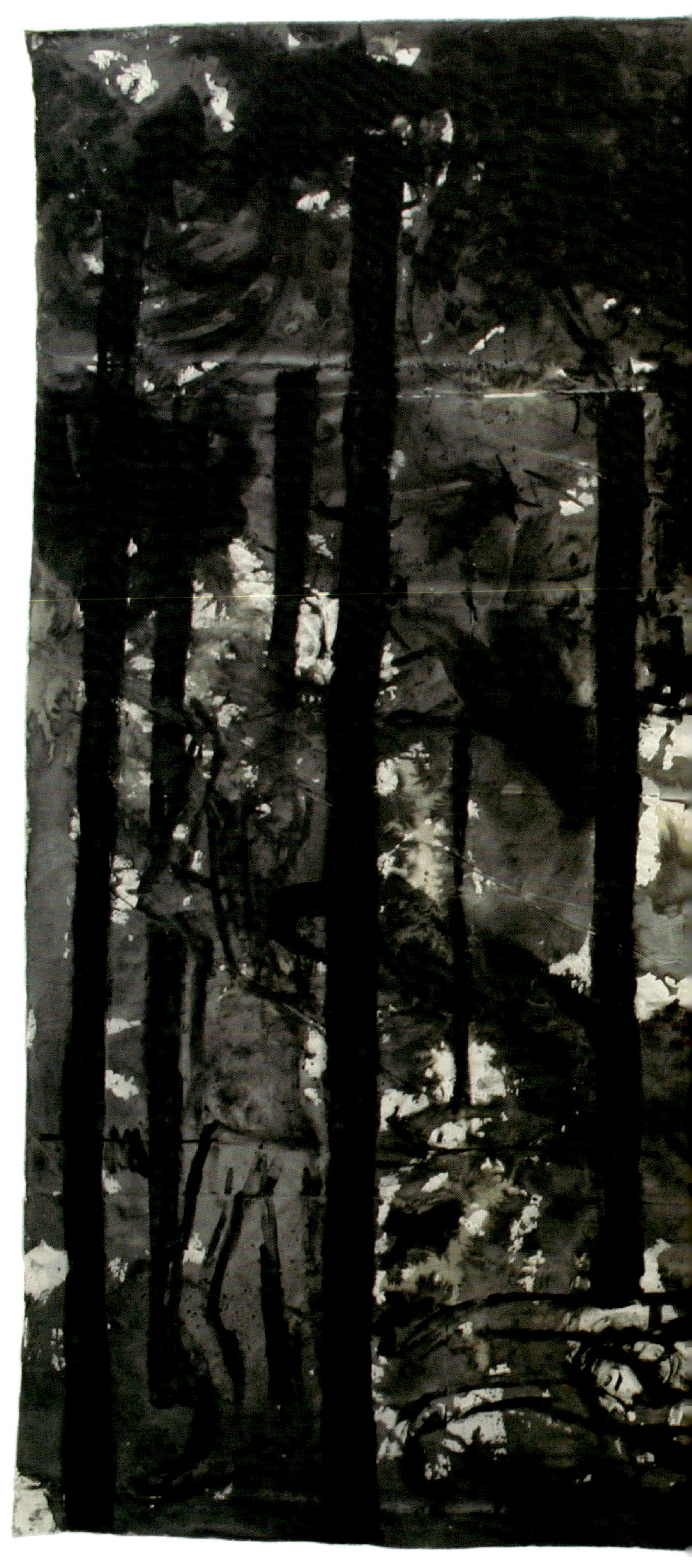

JUTTA KOETHER
Leibhaftige Malerei 2007
Acrylic on linen
400 x 484 cm

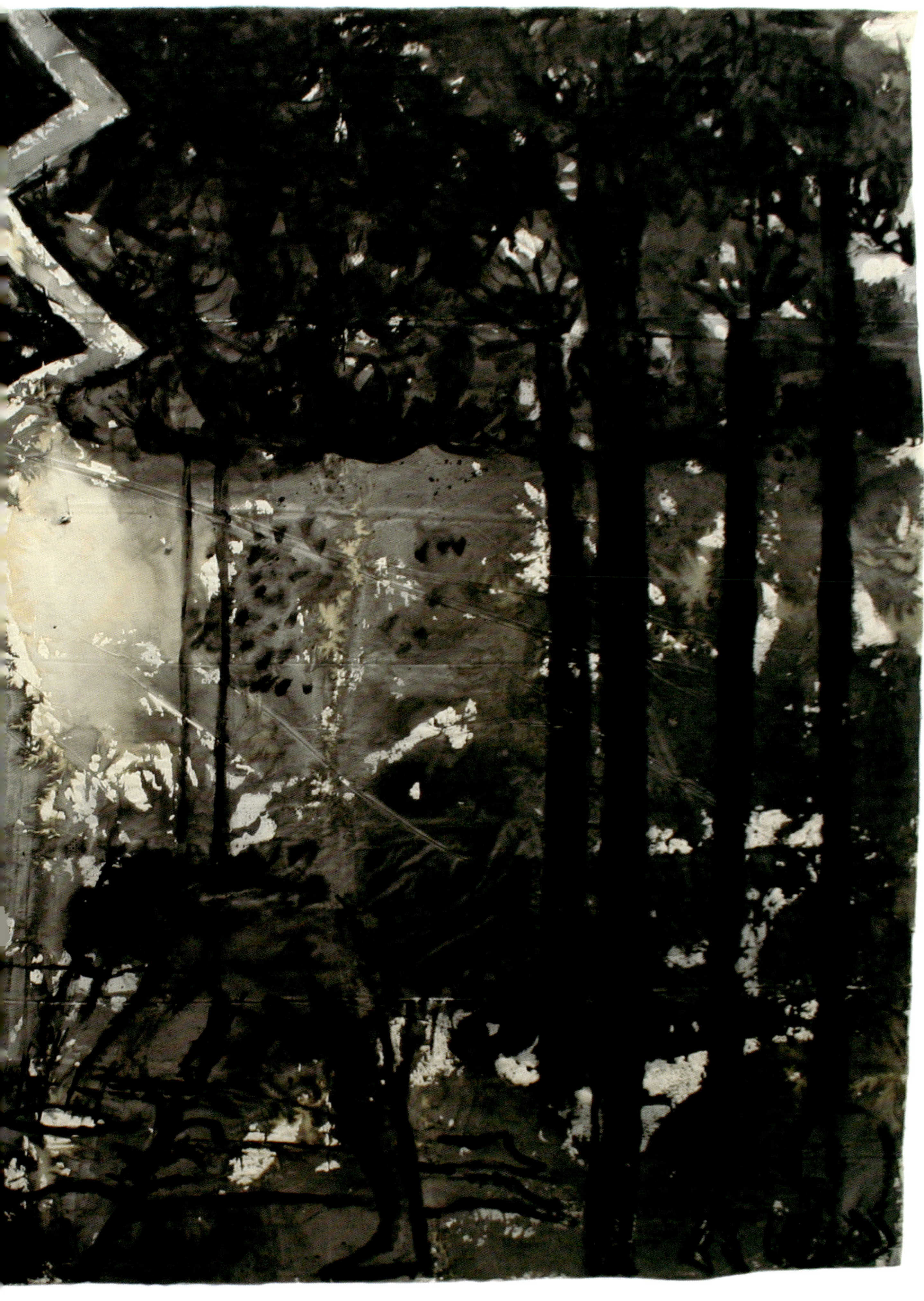

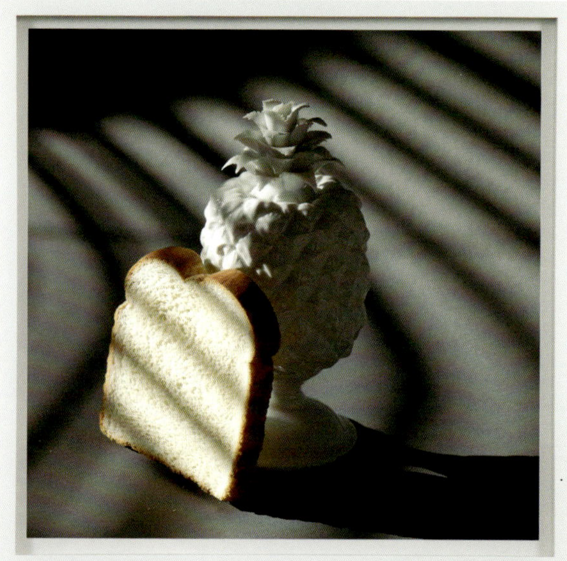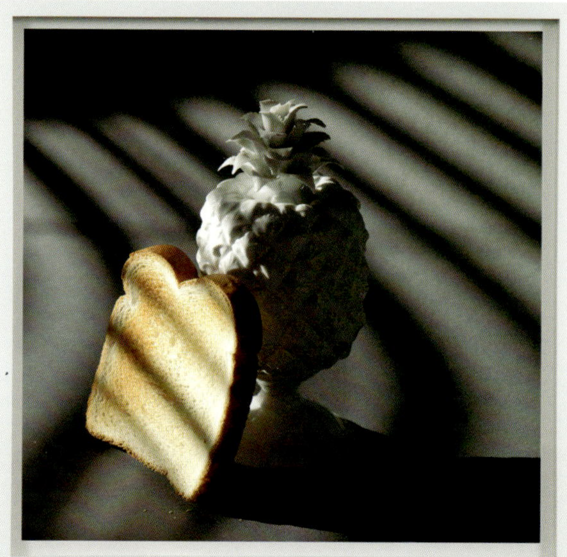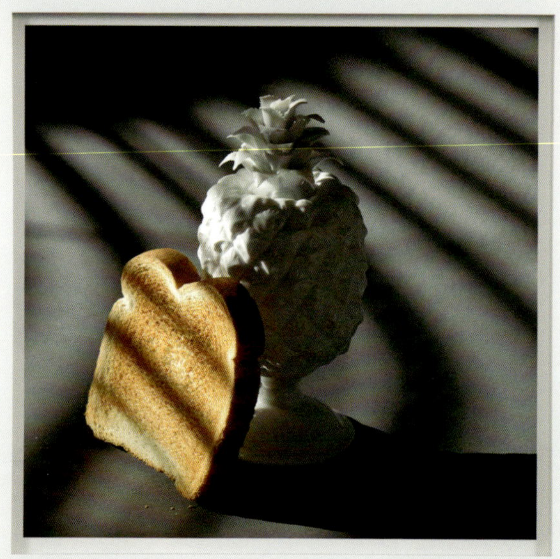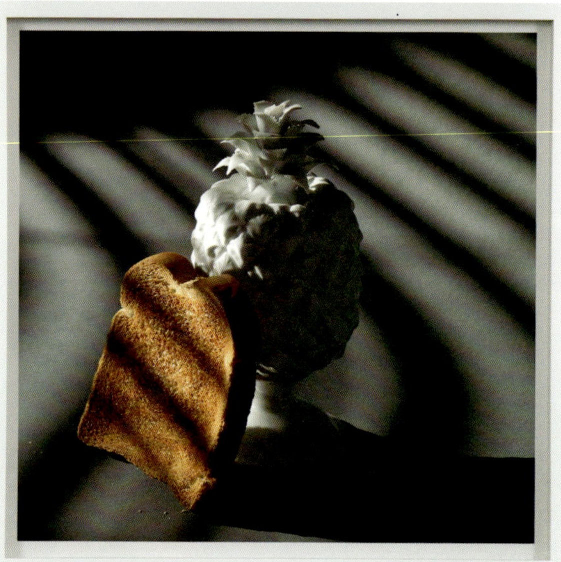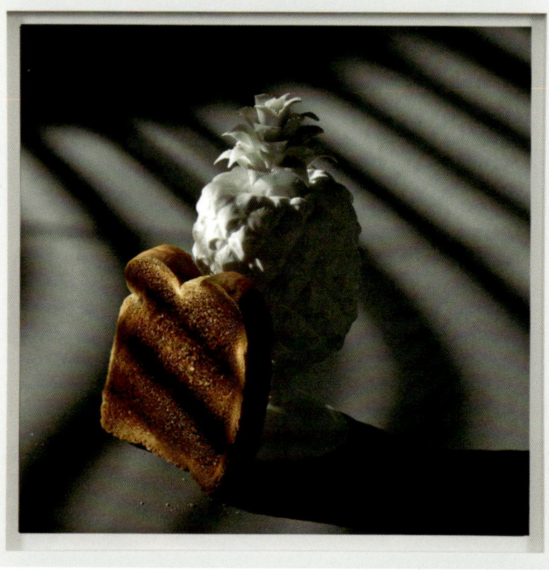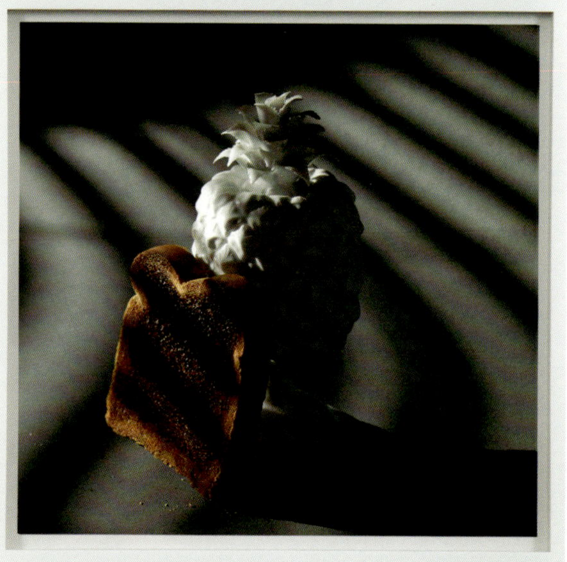

FRIEDRICH KUNATH
First Life Takes Time Then Time Takes Life 2010
Seven c-prints
Overall size 41.6 x 414 cm

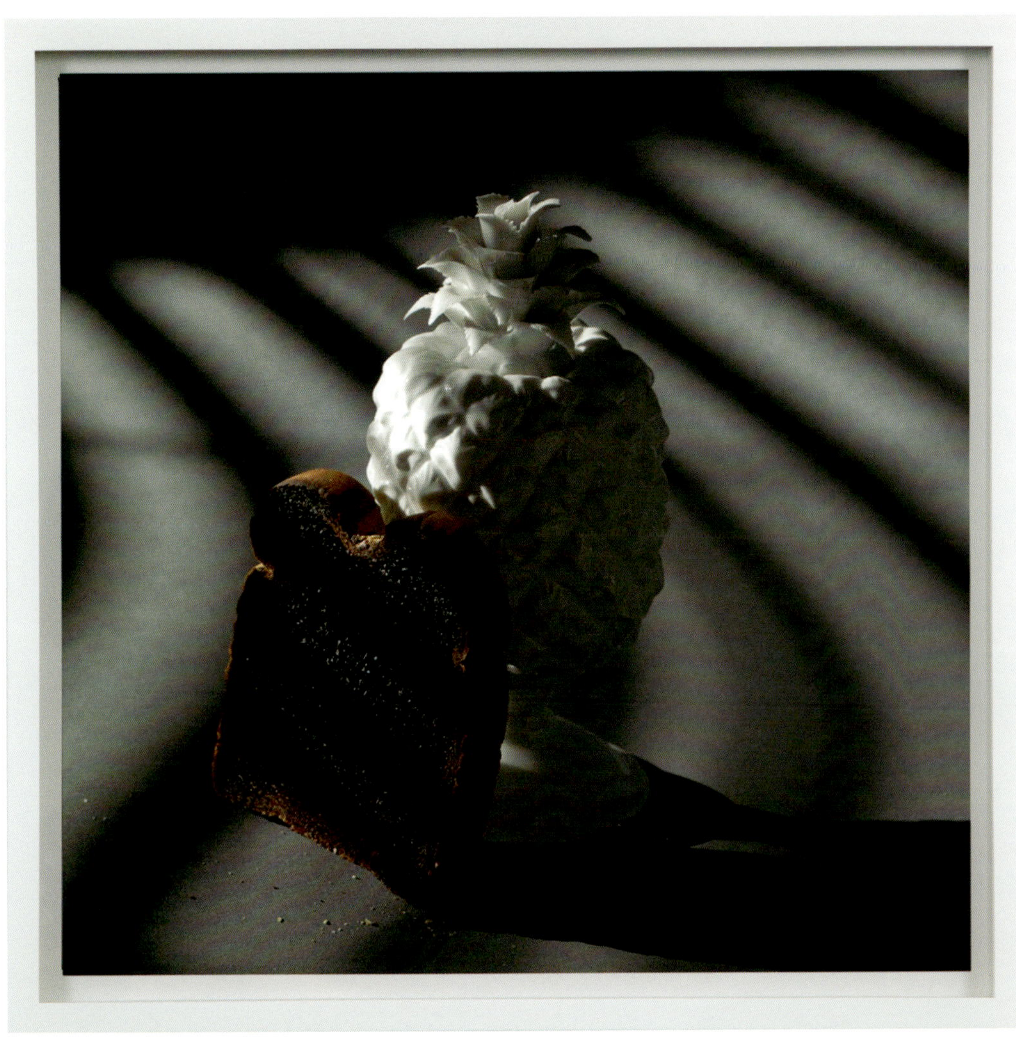

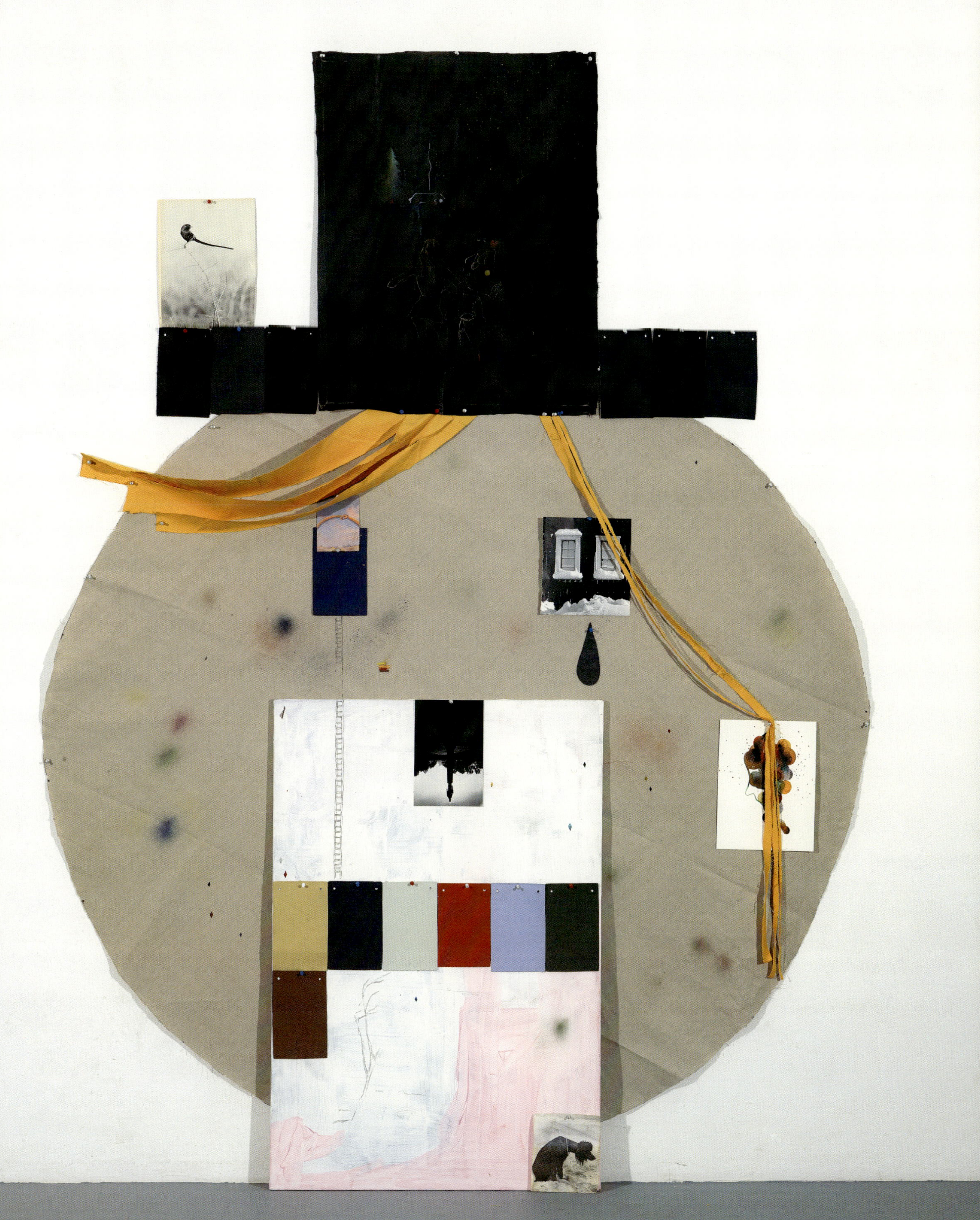

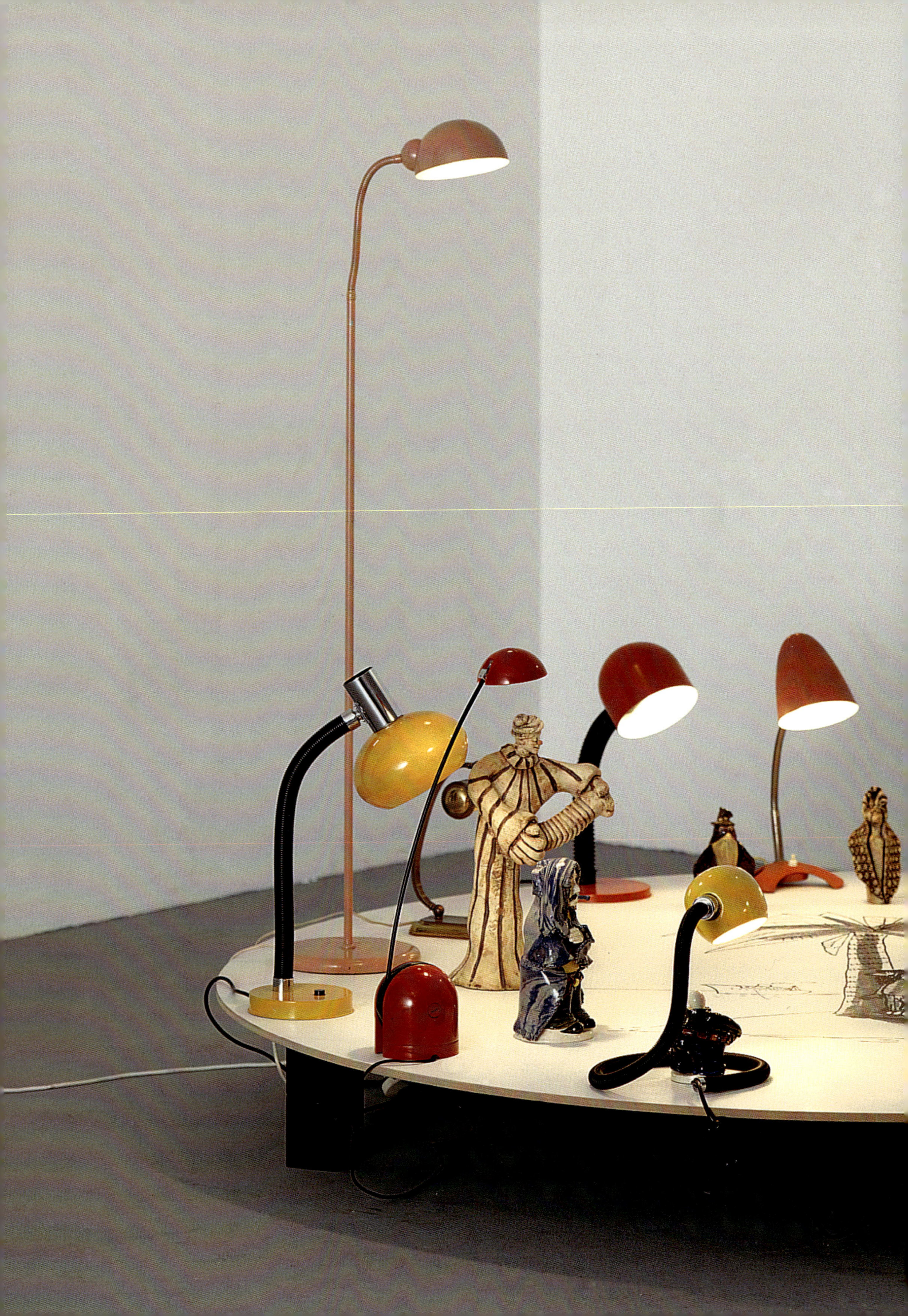

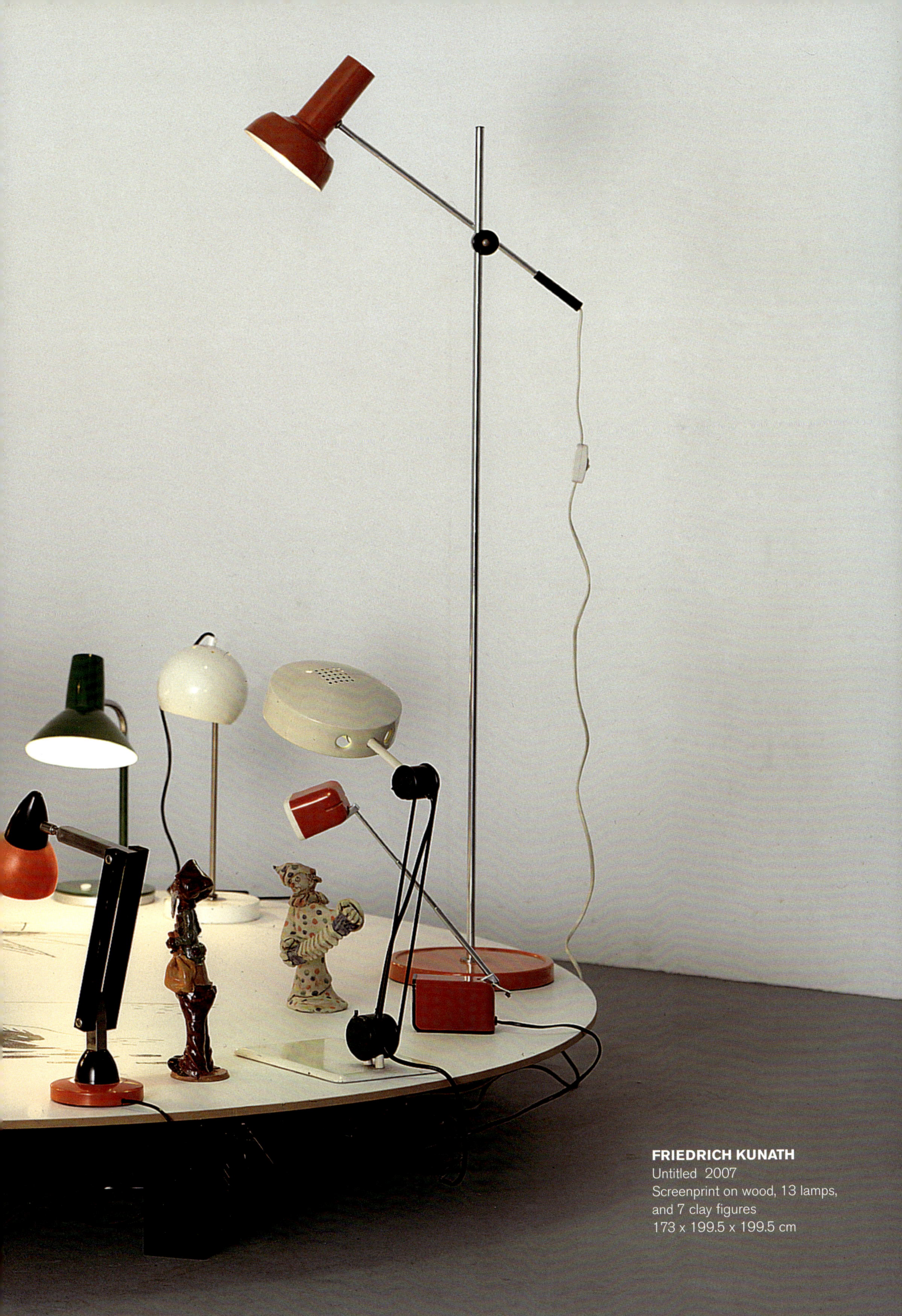

FRIEDRICH KUNATH
Untitled 2007
Screenprint on wood, 13 lamps,
and 7 clay figures
173 x 199.5 x 199.5 cm

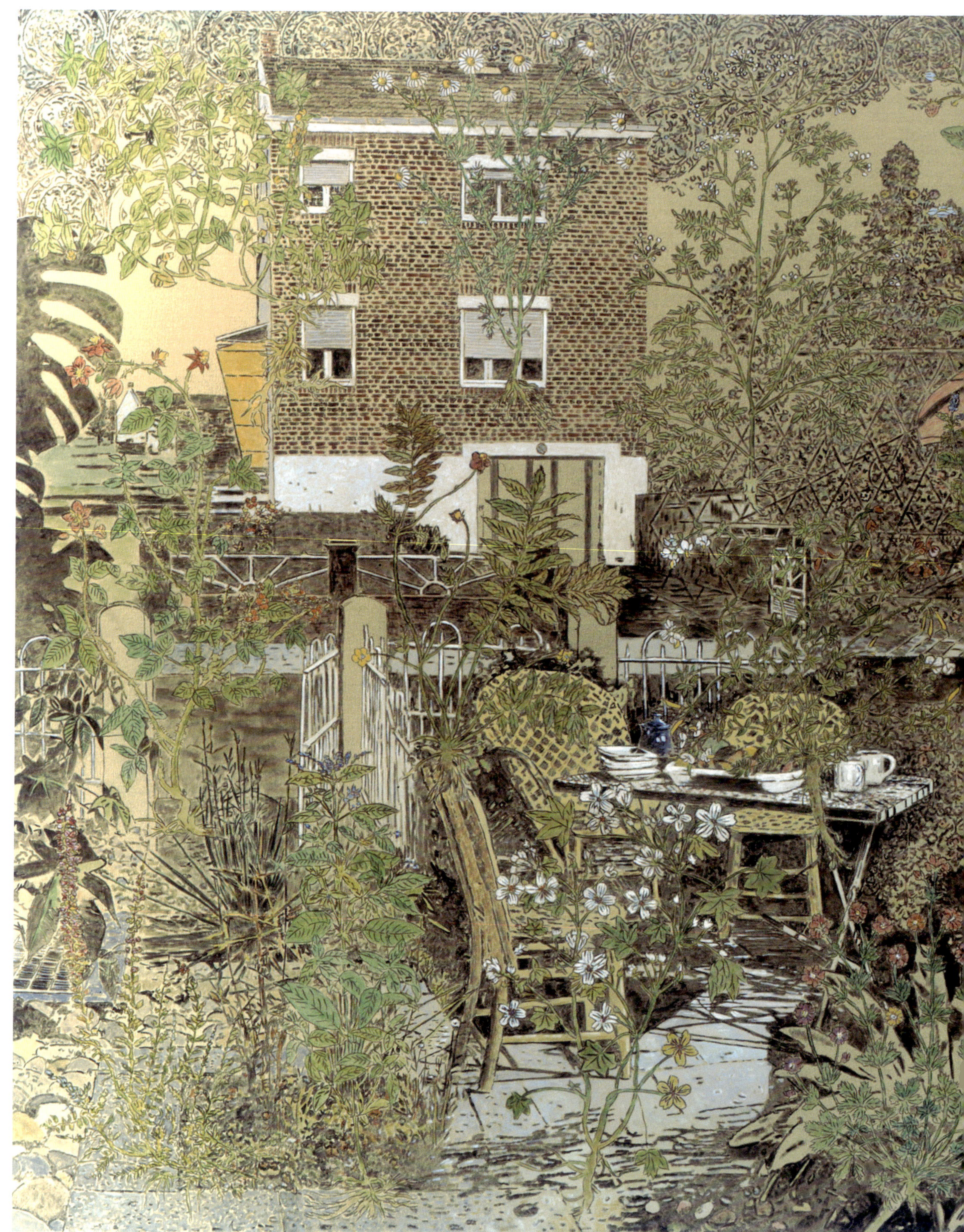

STEFAN KÜRTEN
The Handsome Family 2004
Oil on canvas
190 x 270 cm

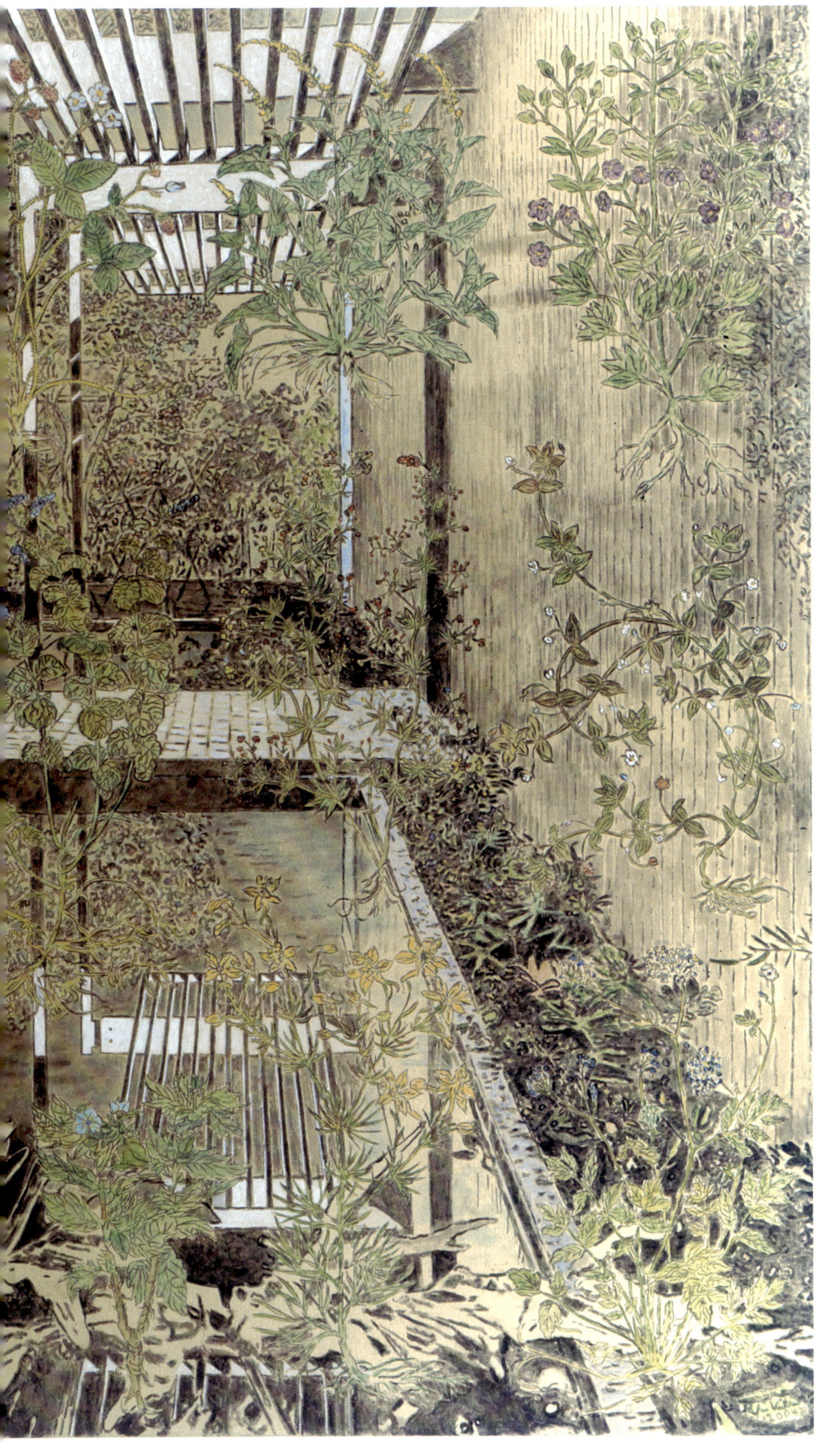

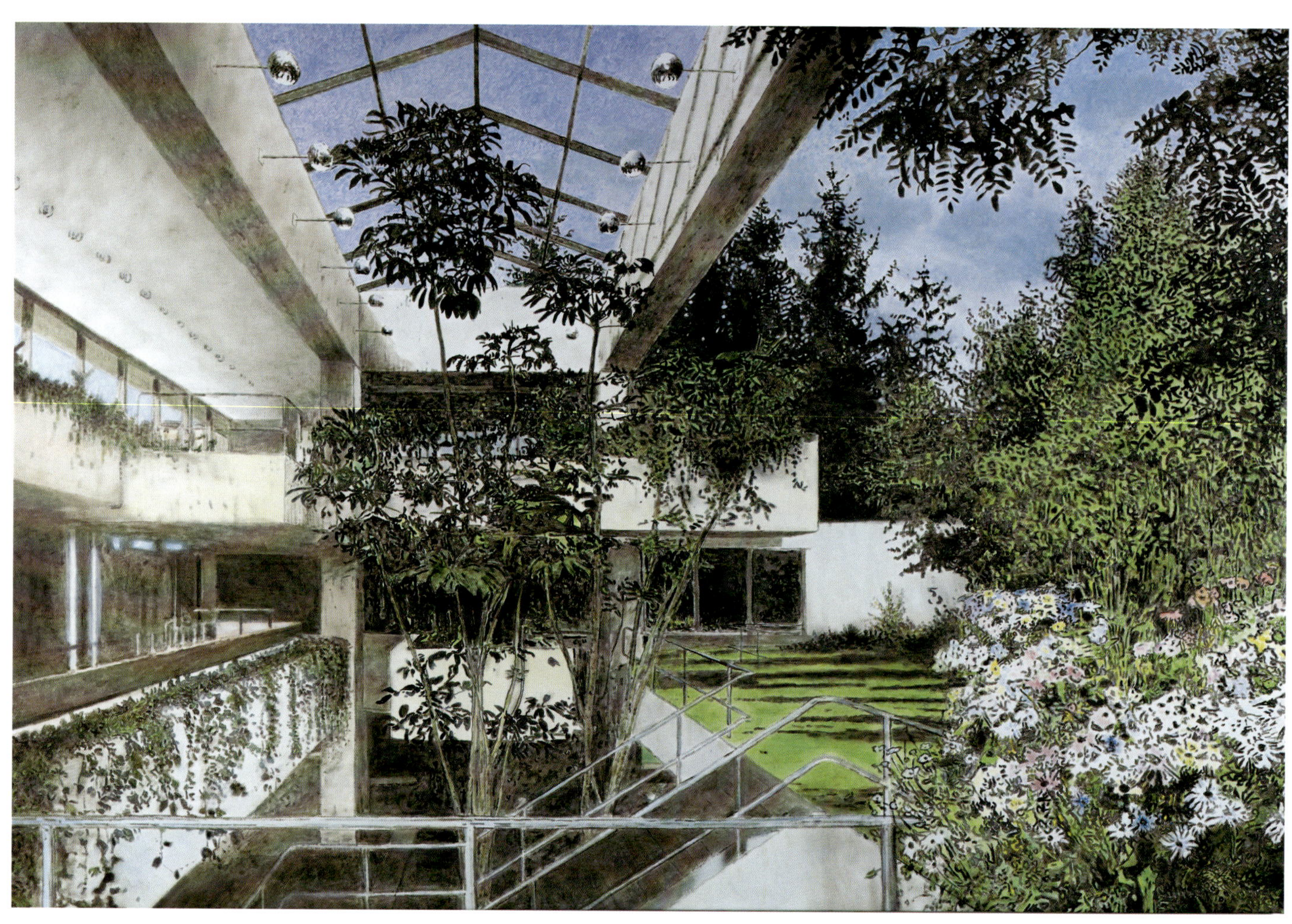

STEFAN KÜRTEN
Silence 2001
Oil on canvas
188 x 267 cm

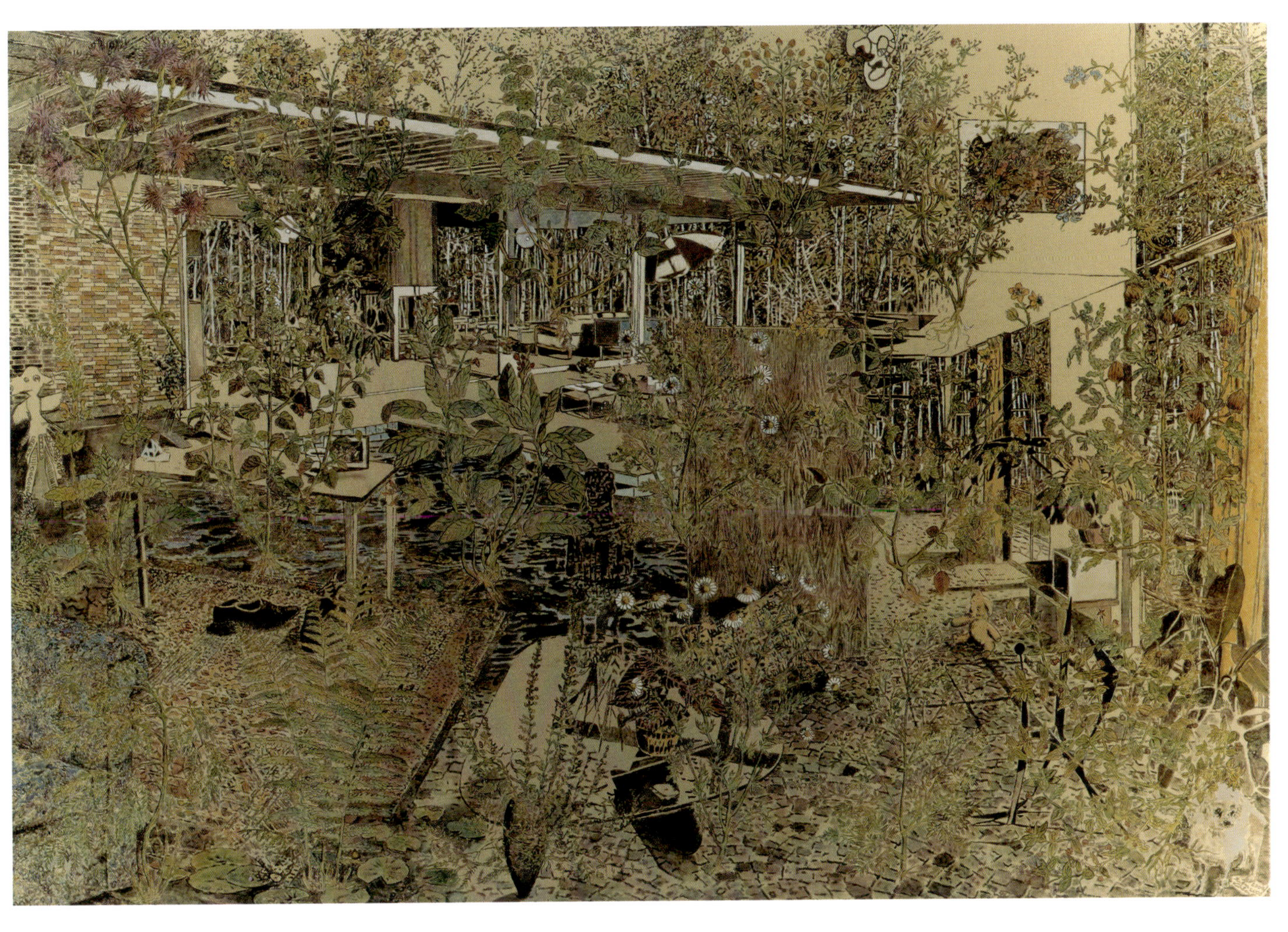

STEFAN KÜRTEN
Heartbeat 2004-5
Oil on canvas
190 x 270 cm

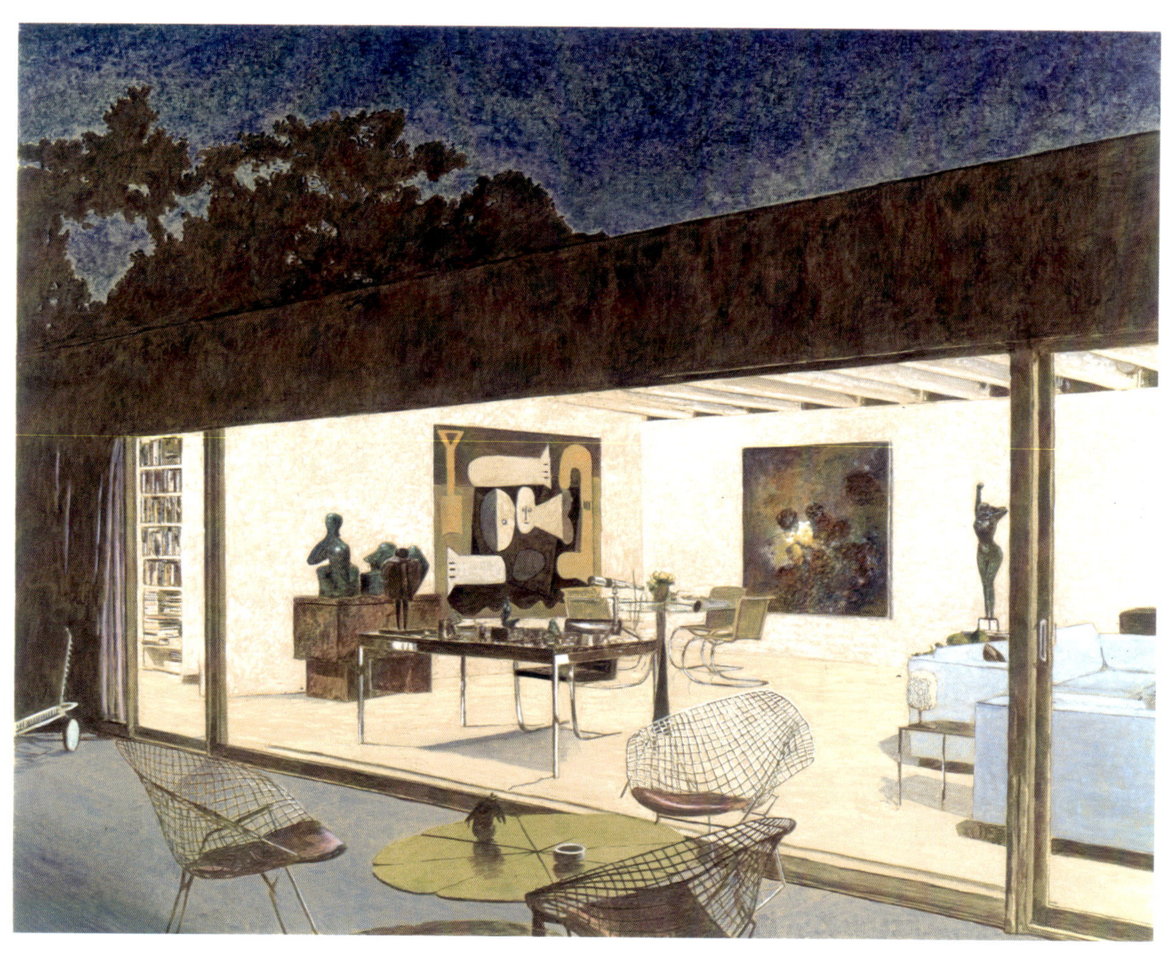

STEFAN KÜRTEN
Ultramarine II 2004
Oil on canvas
120 x 150 cm

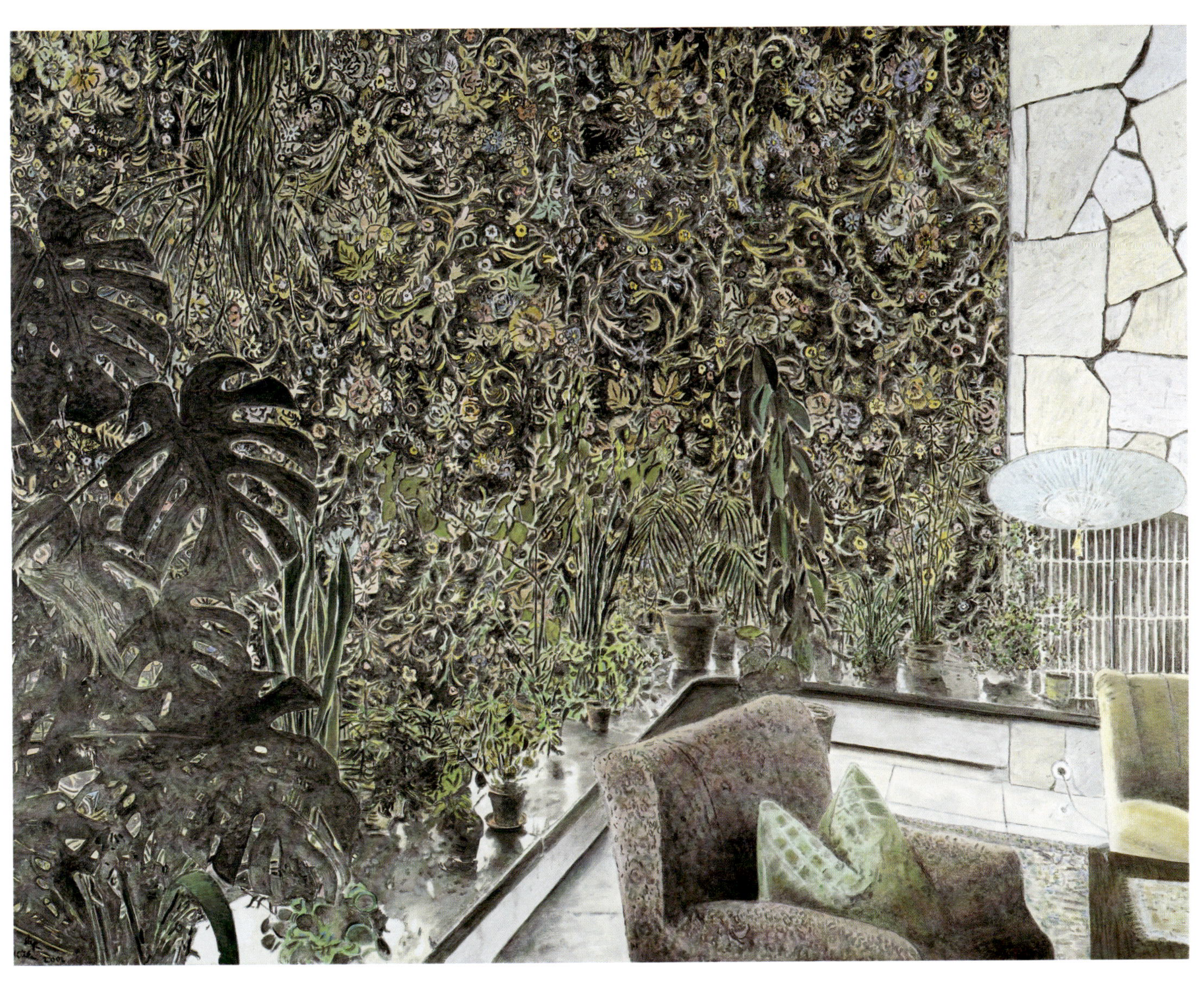

STEFAN KÜRTEN
Long Time Now 2002
Oil on canvas
145 x 190 cm

JOSEPHINE MECKSEPER
Blow Up (Michelli) 2006
Mixed media in display vitrine
208.3 x 243.8 x 68.6 cm

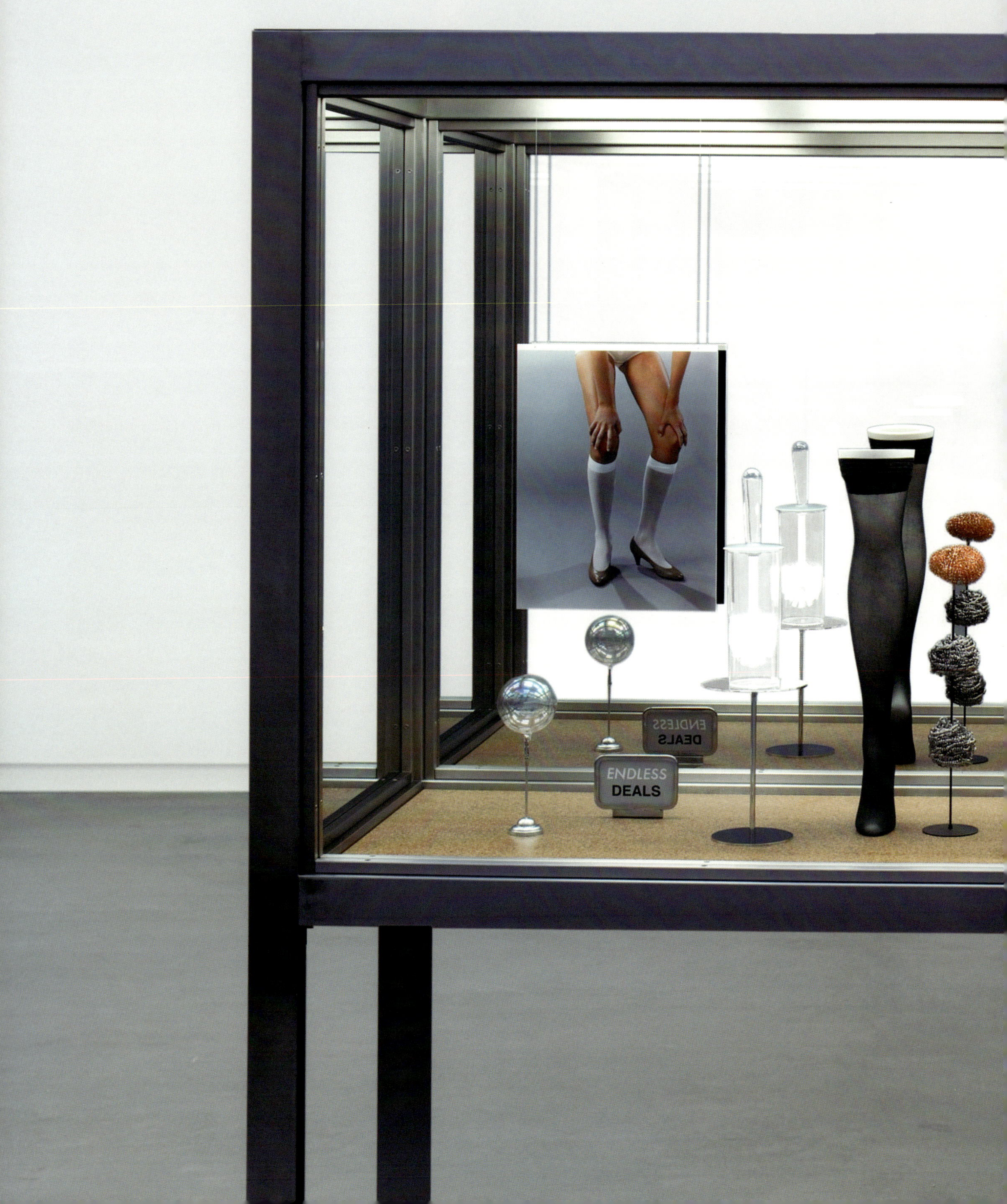

ENDLESS
DEALS

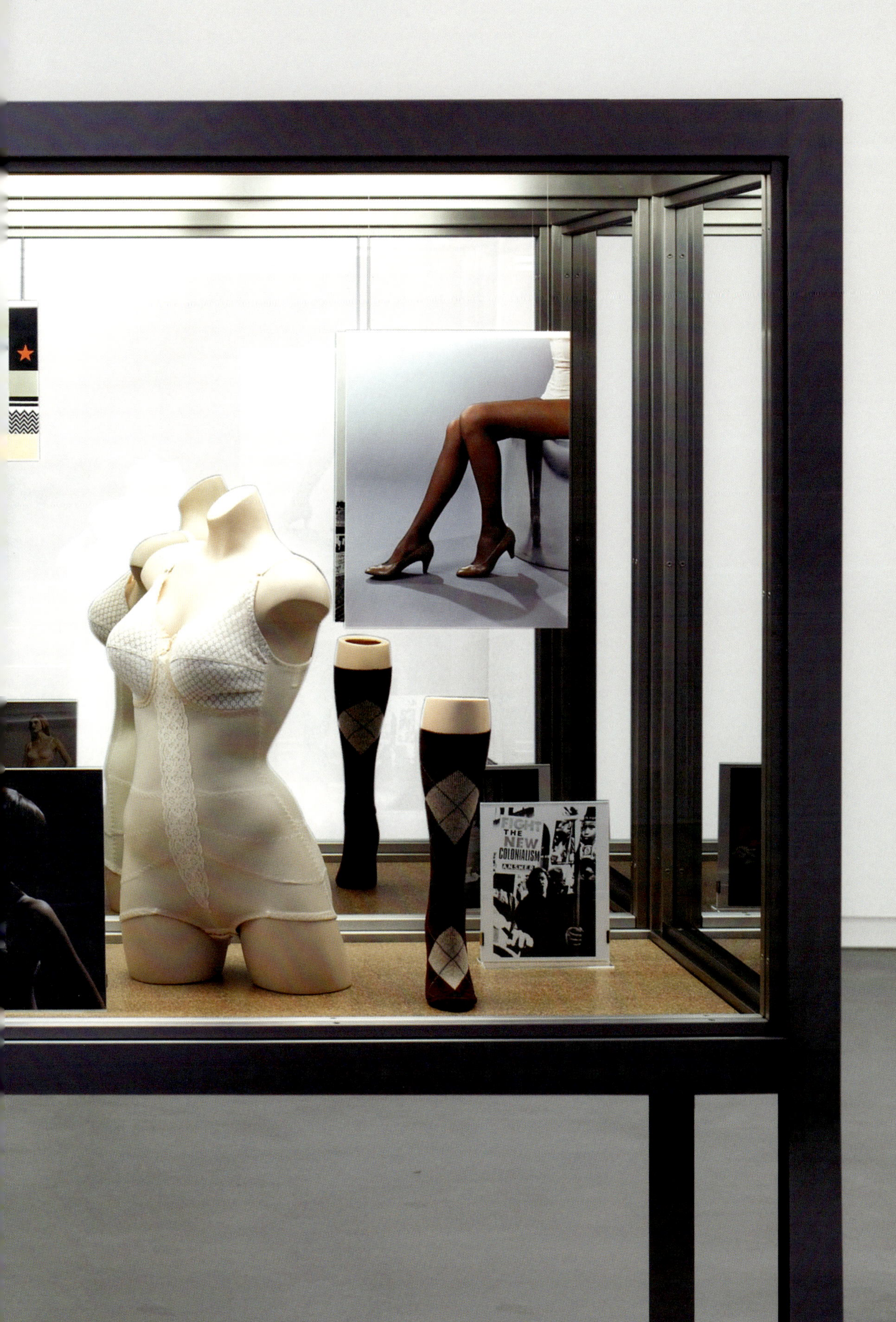
FIGHT
THE
NEW
COLONIALISM

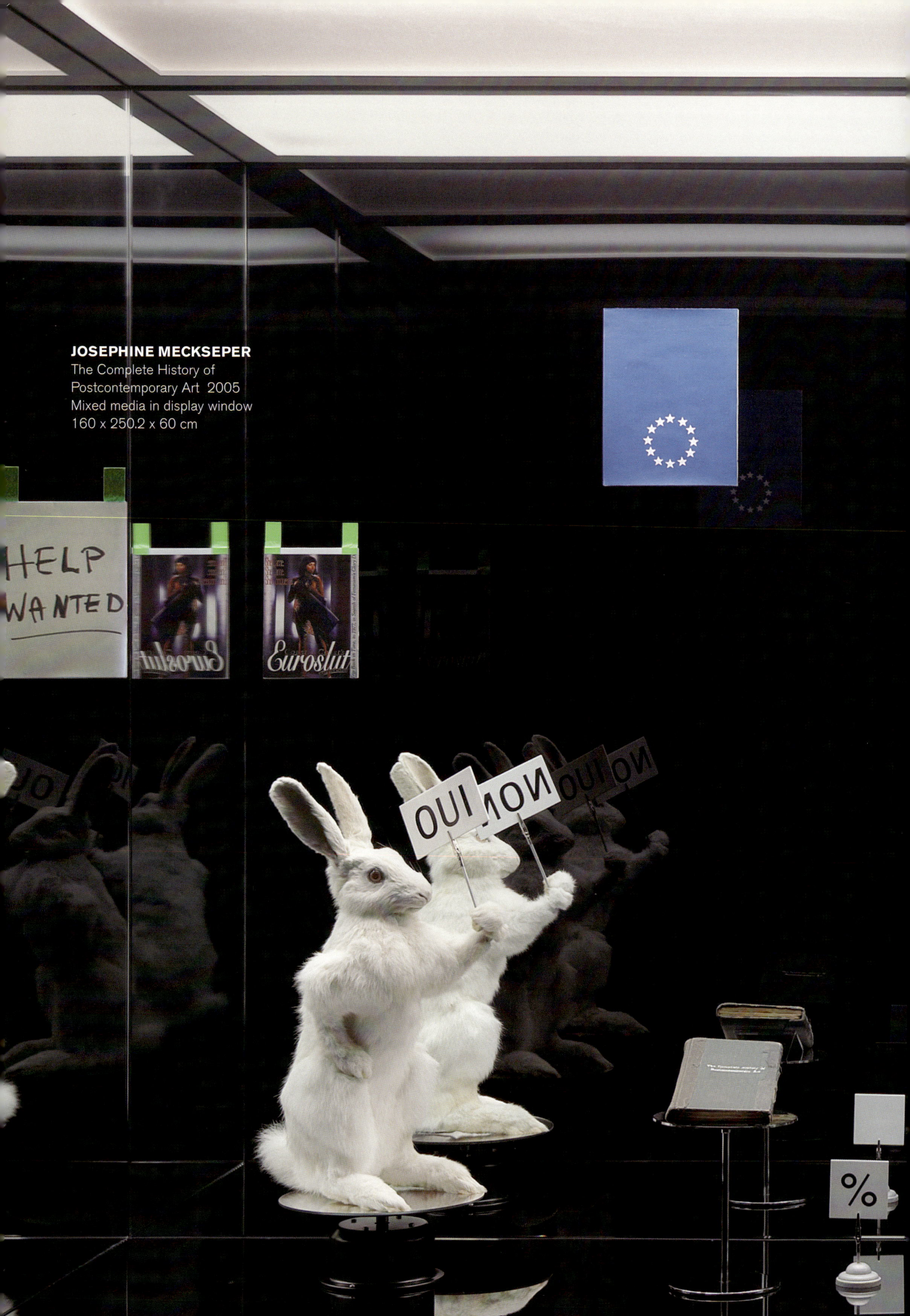

JOSEPHINE MECKSEPER
The Complete History of
Postcontemporary Art 2005
Mixed media in display window
160 x 250.2 x 60 cm

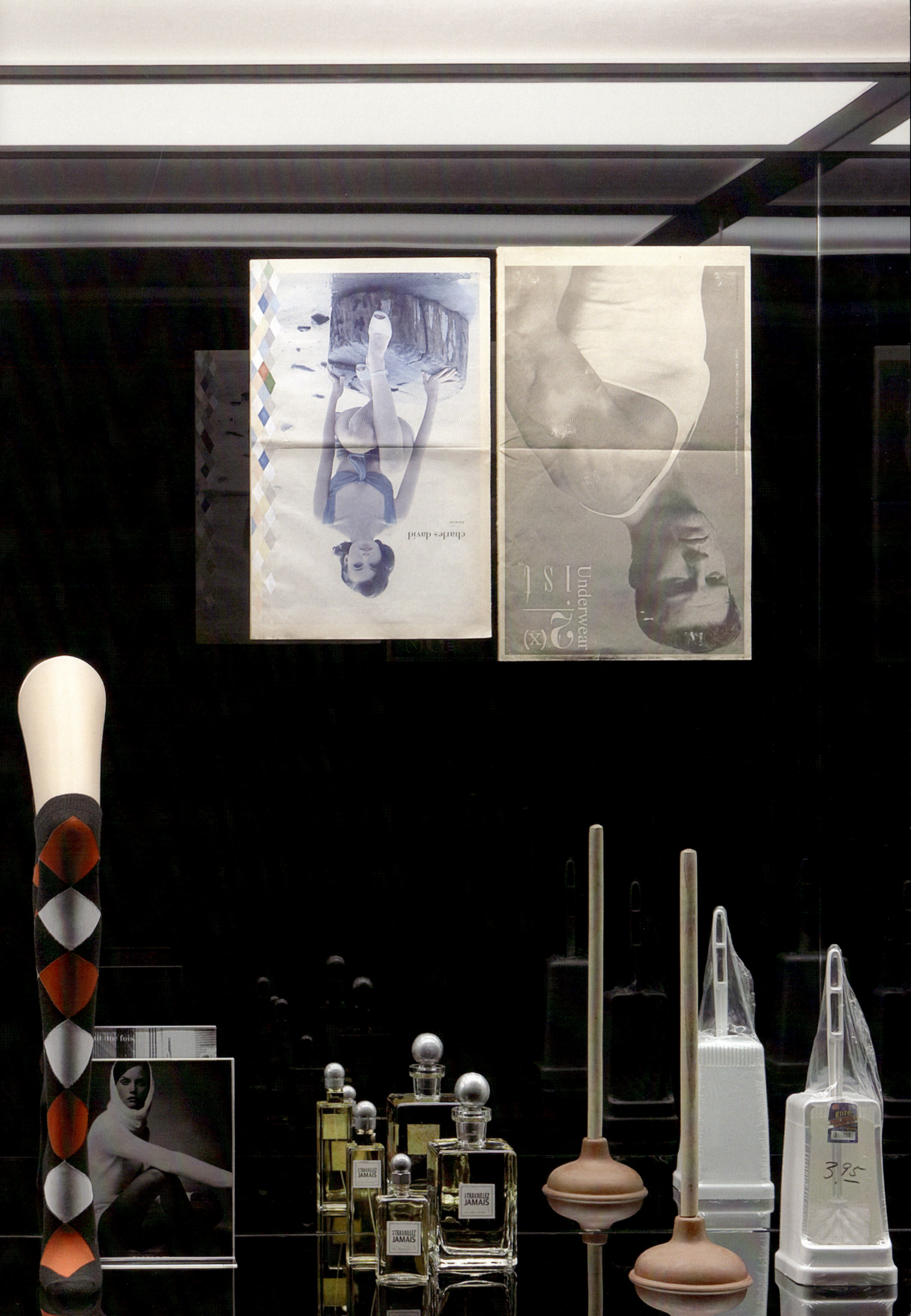

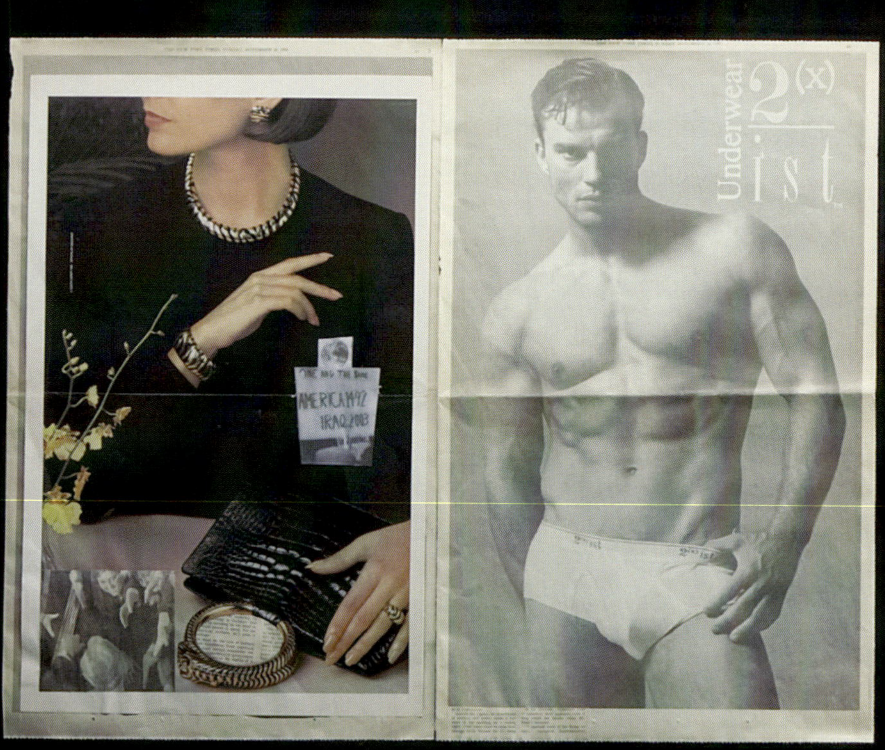

JOSEPHINE MECKSEPER
Tout Va Bien 2005
Mixed media in display window
160 x 250.2 x 60 cm

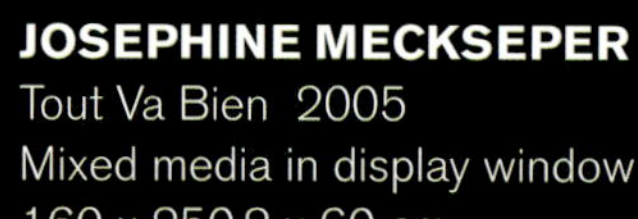
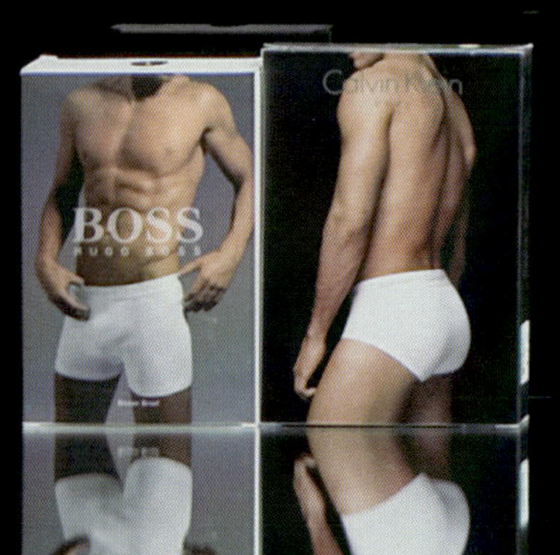
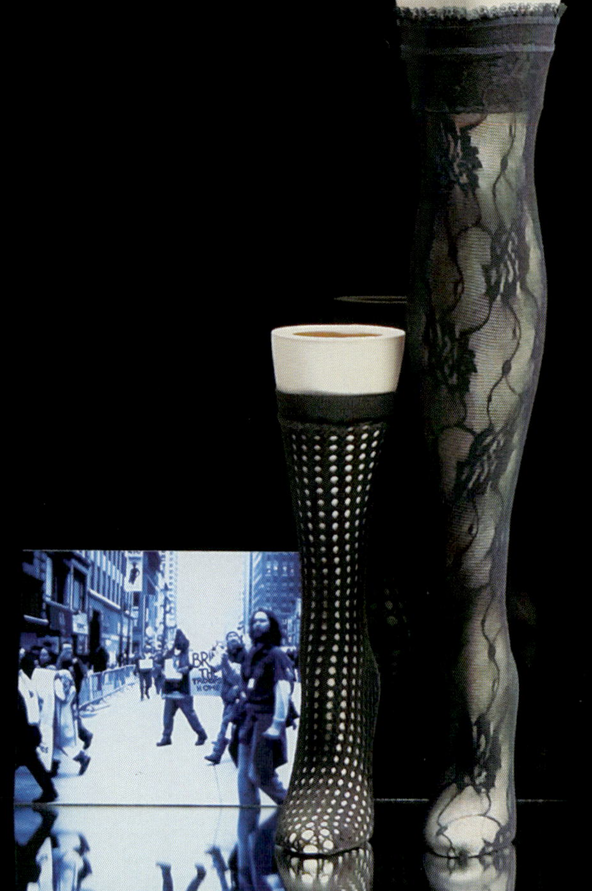
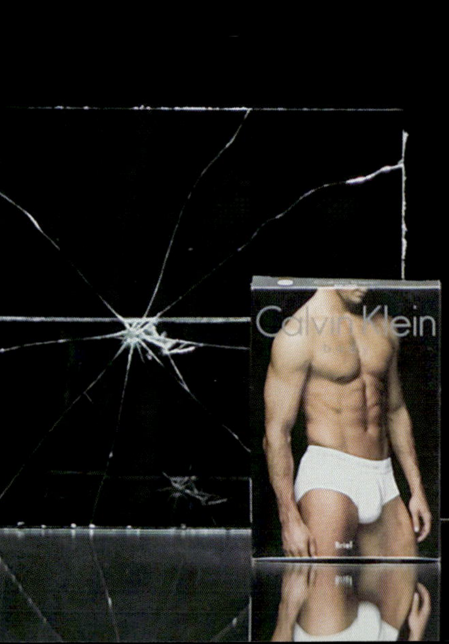

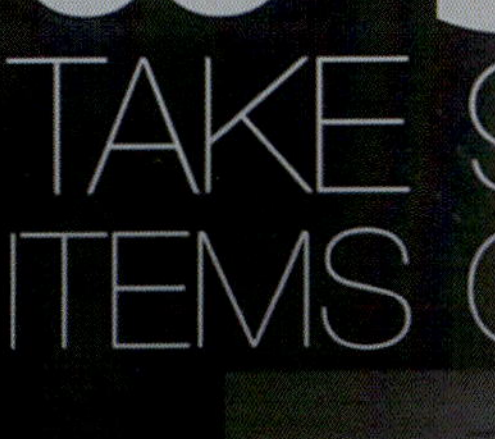
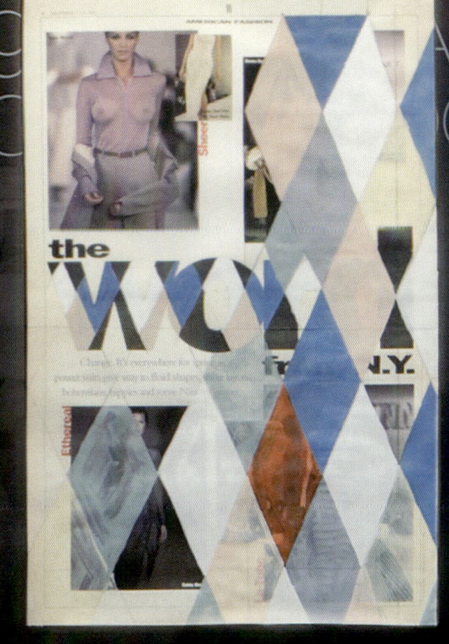
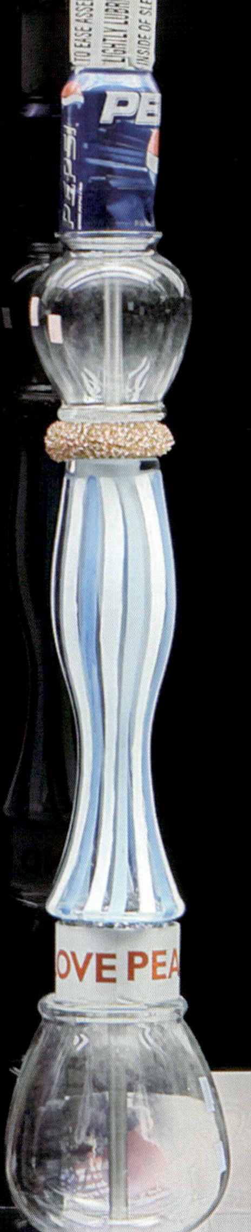
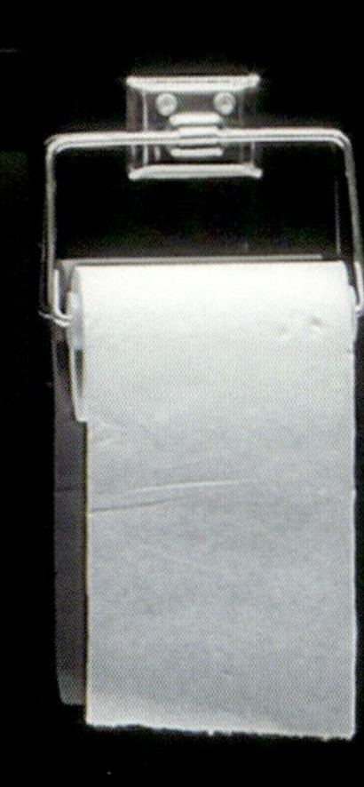
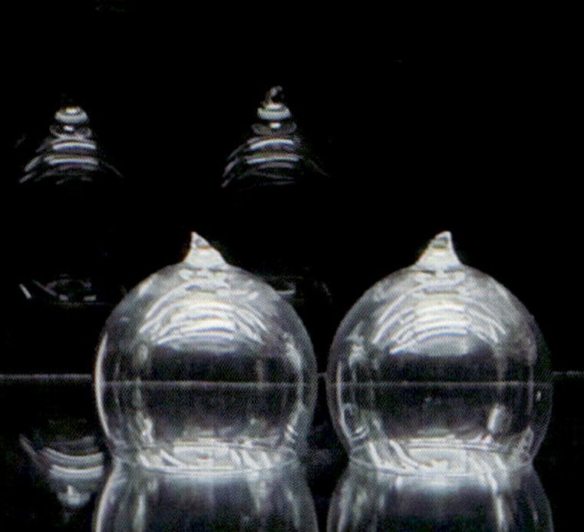
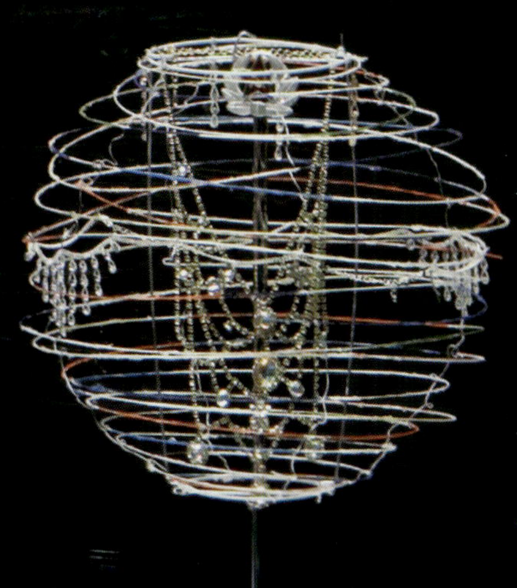
∞ STRIKE
TAKE 99 % OFF ALL
ITEMS ON THIS FLOOR
∞ STRIKE
TAKE 9
ITEMS O

JOSEPHINE MECKSEPER
Untitled (End Democracy) 2005
Inkjet print, Plexiglas, plastic mannequin torso,
metal stand, mirror on wood
144 x 122 x 122 cm

right:
Pyromaniac 2 2003
C-print
101 x 76 cm

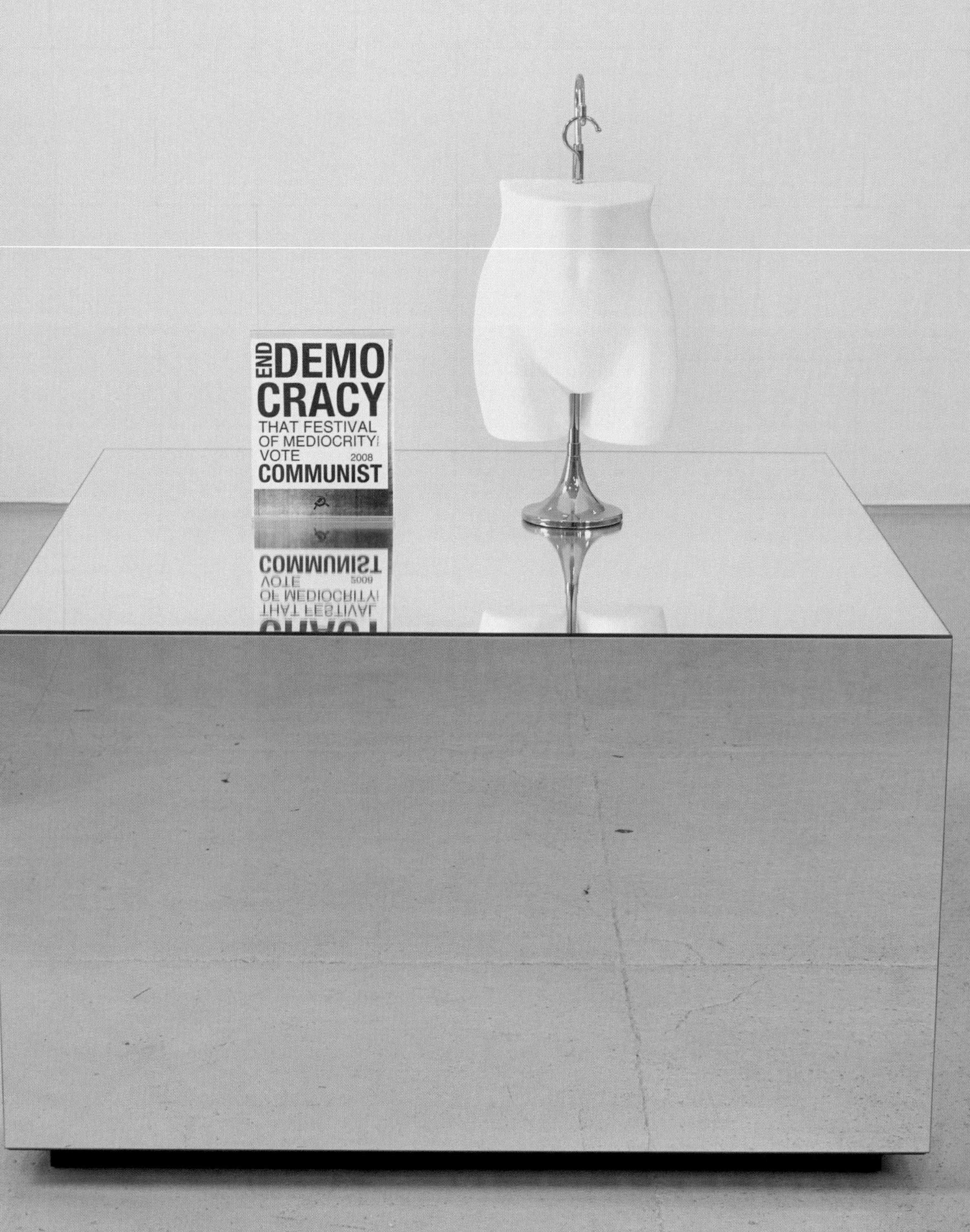

END DEMO
CRACY
THAT FESTIVAL
OF MEDIOCRITY
VOTE 2008
COMMUNIST

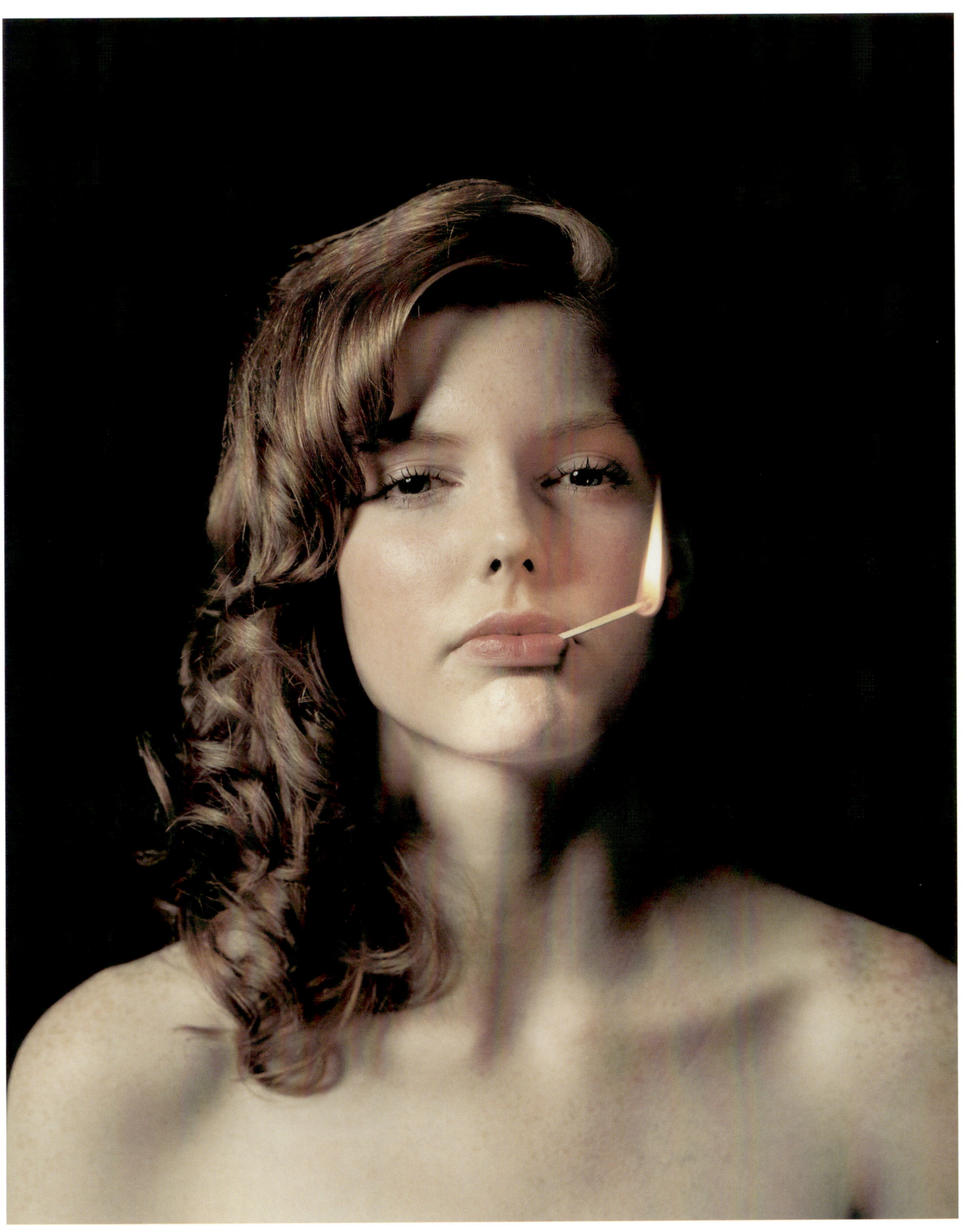

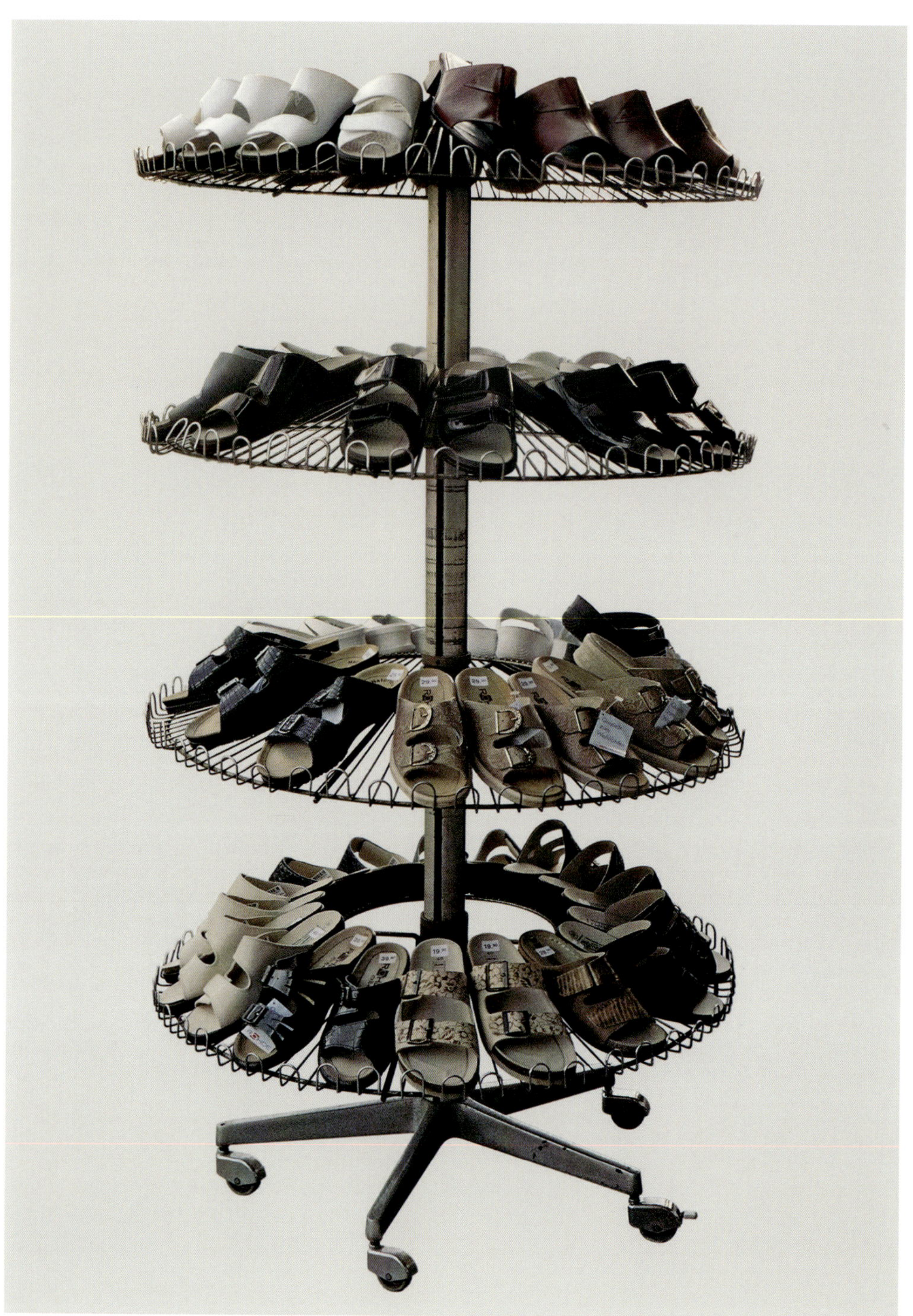

JOSEPHINE MECKSEPER

above:
Ubi Pedes Ibi. Patria. (Where The Feet Are, There Is The Fatherland) 2006
Shoes, display carousel
153 x 83 cm

right:
Untitled 2005
Mannequin, fabric, found jewellery, inkjet print on fabric, acrylic and fabric on canvas
Mannequin: 144.8 x 66 x 43.8 cm Painting: 61 x 61 cm Collage: 41 x 41 cm

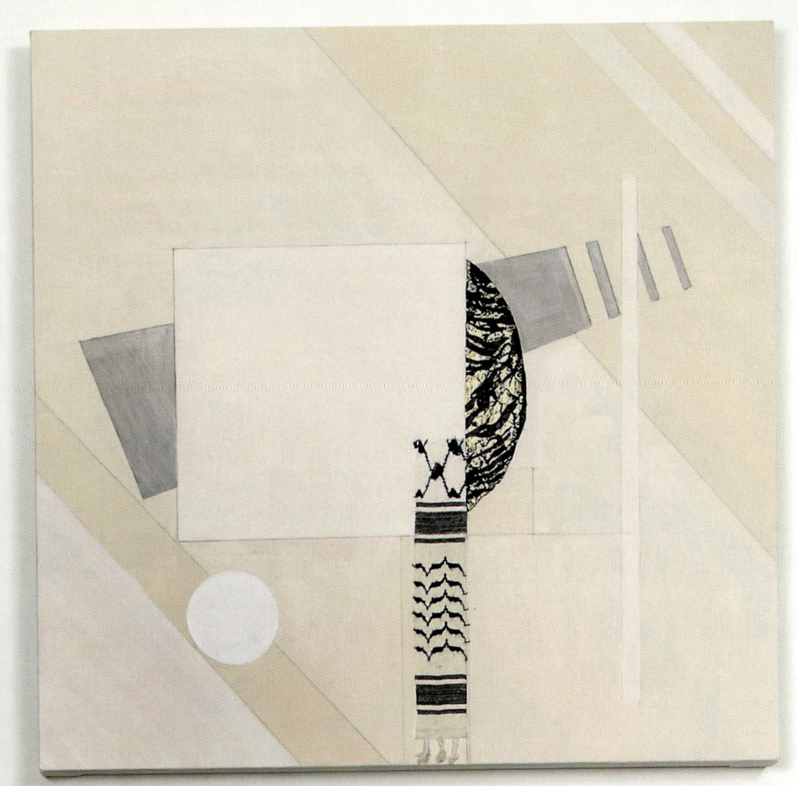

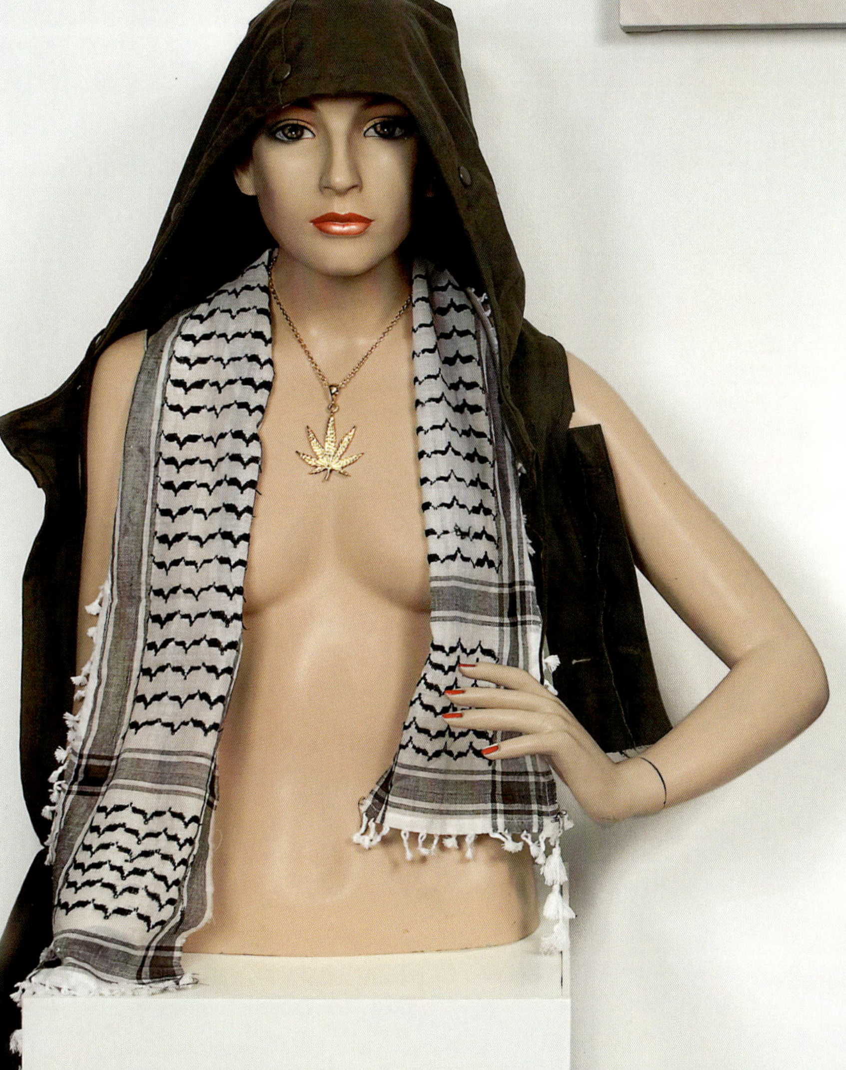

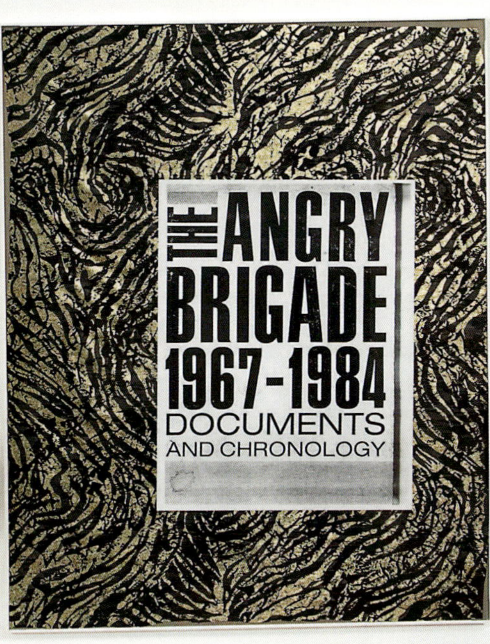

THE ANGRY
BRIGADE
1967-1984
DOCUMENTS
AND CHRONOLOGY

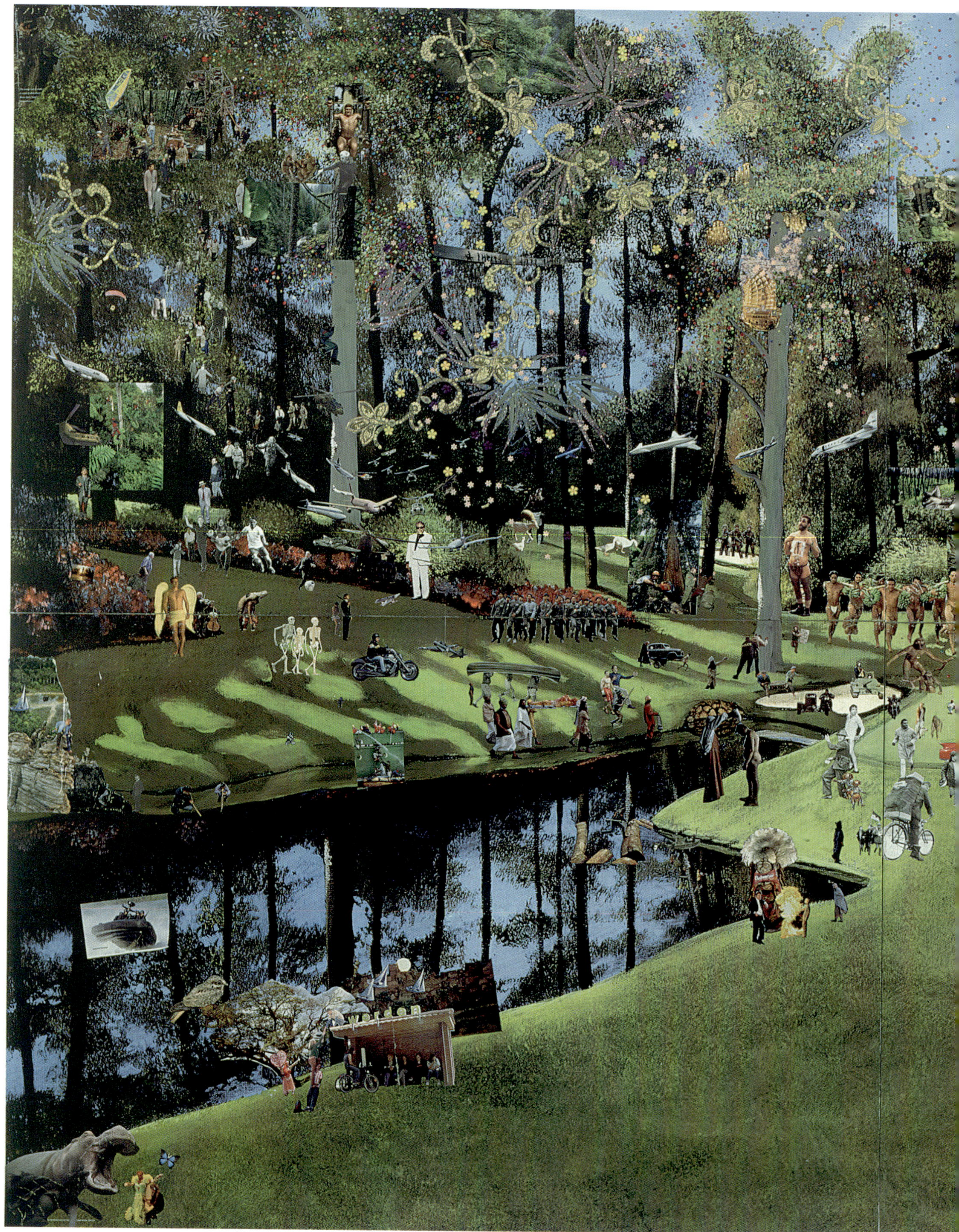

KIRSTINE ROEPSTORFF
You Are Being Lied To 2002
Paper, glitter, pearls, sequins and paint collage on wallpaper, mounted on aluminium
274 x 388 cm

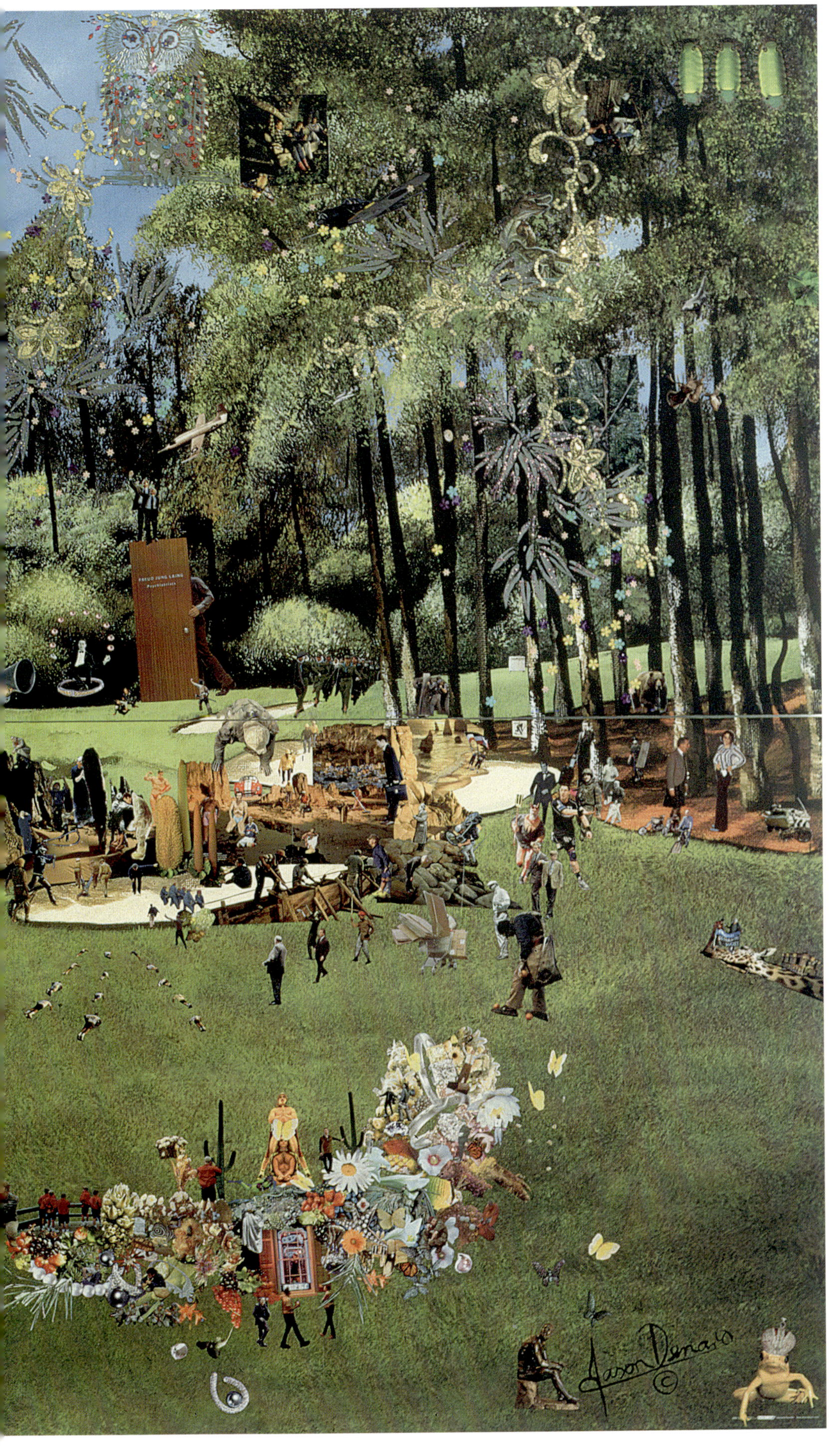

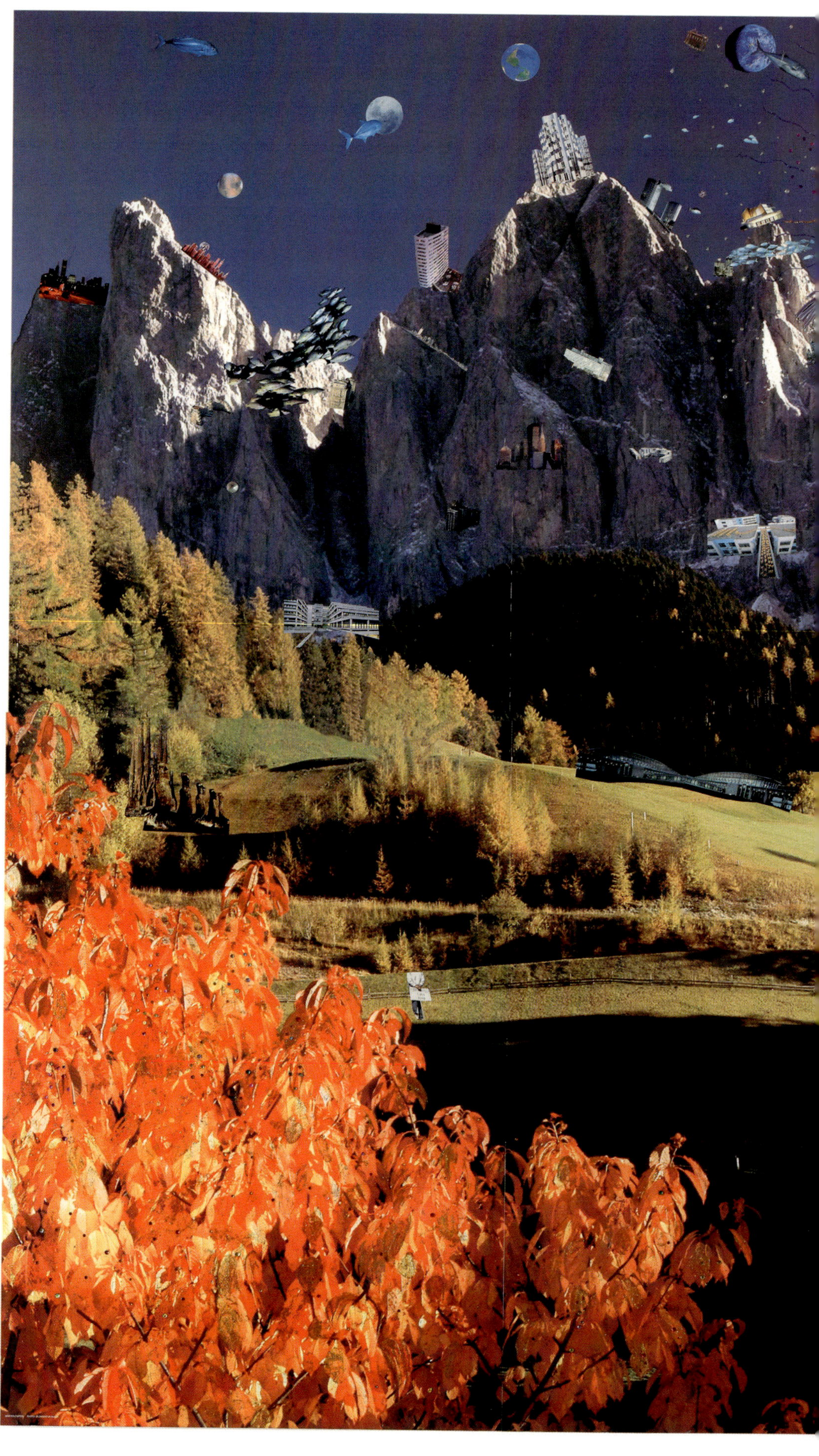

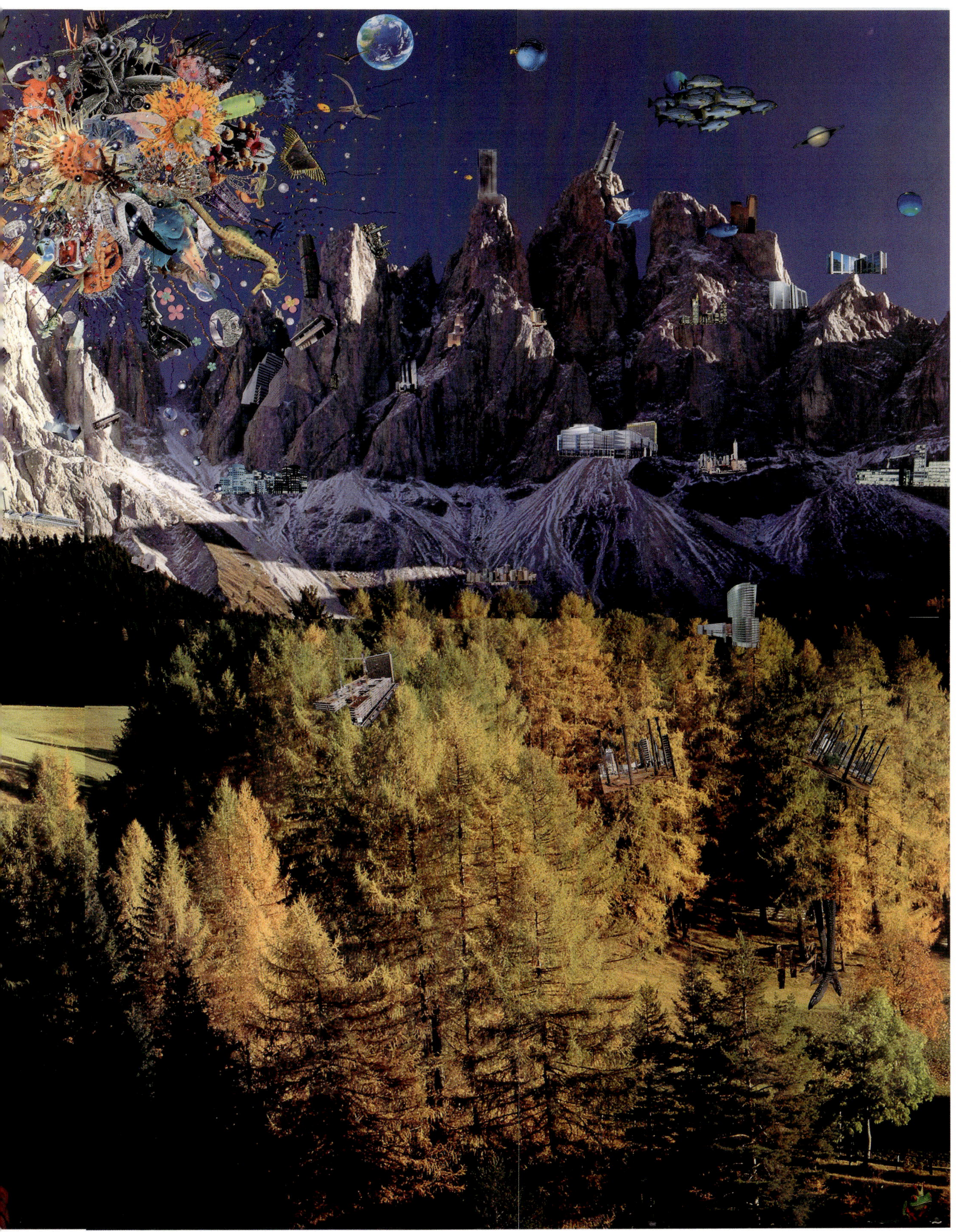

KIRSTINE ROEPSTORFF
Hidden Truth 2002
Paper, glitter, pearls, sequins and paint collage on wallpaper, mounted on aluminium
274 x 388 cm

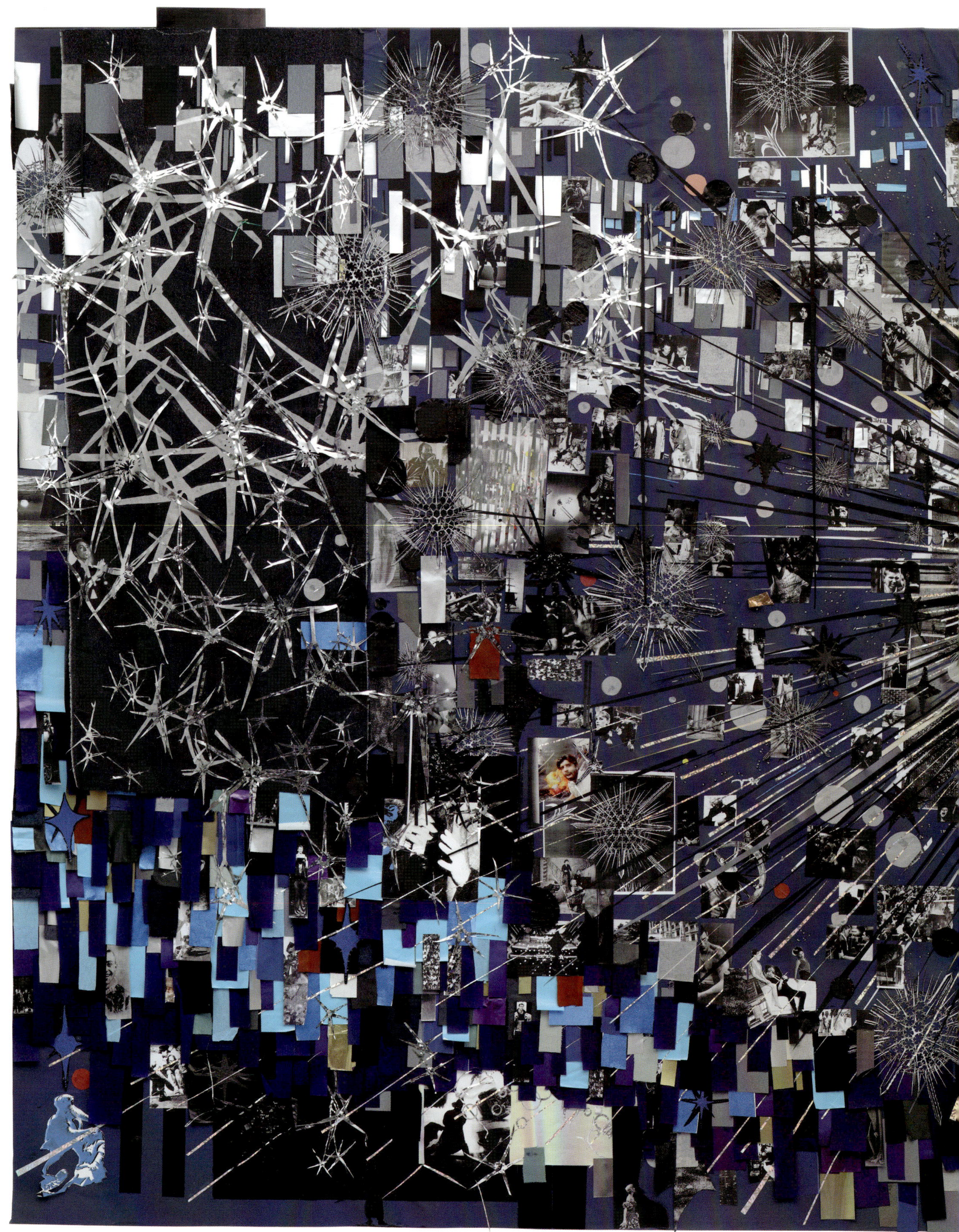

KIRSTINE ROEPSTORFF
All Possible Experiences (From the series "The Inner Sound that Kills the Outer") 2006
Mixed media collage
273 x 444 cm

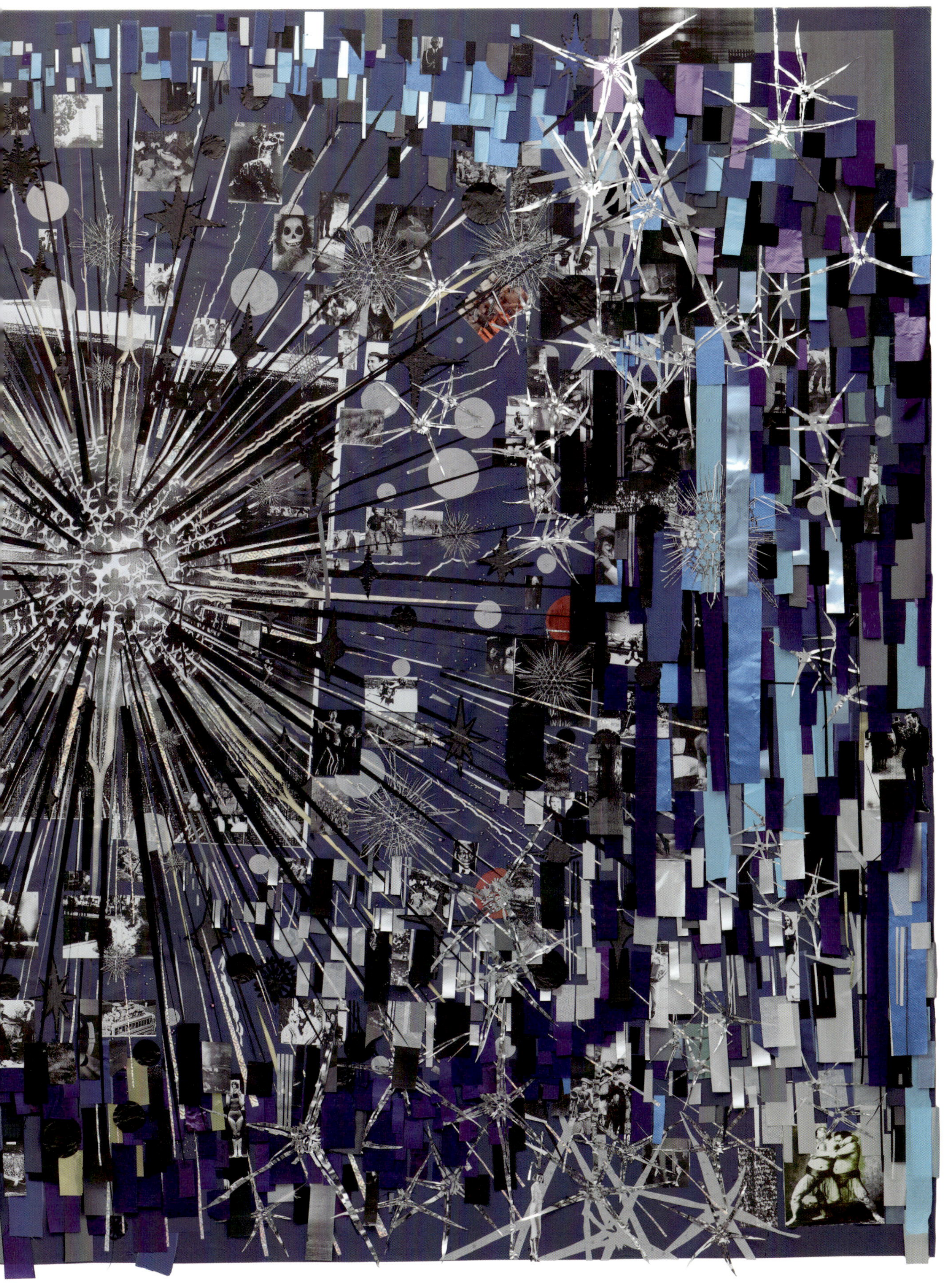

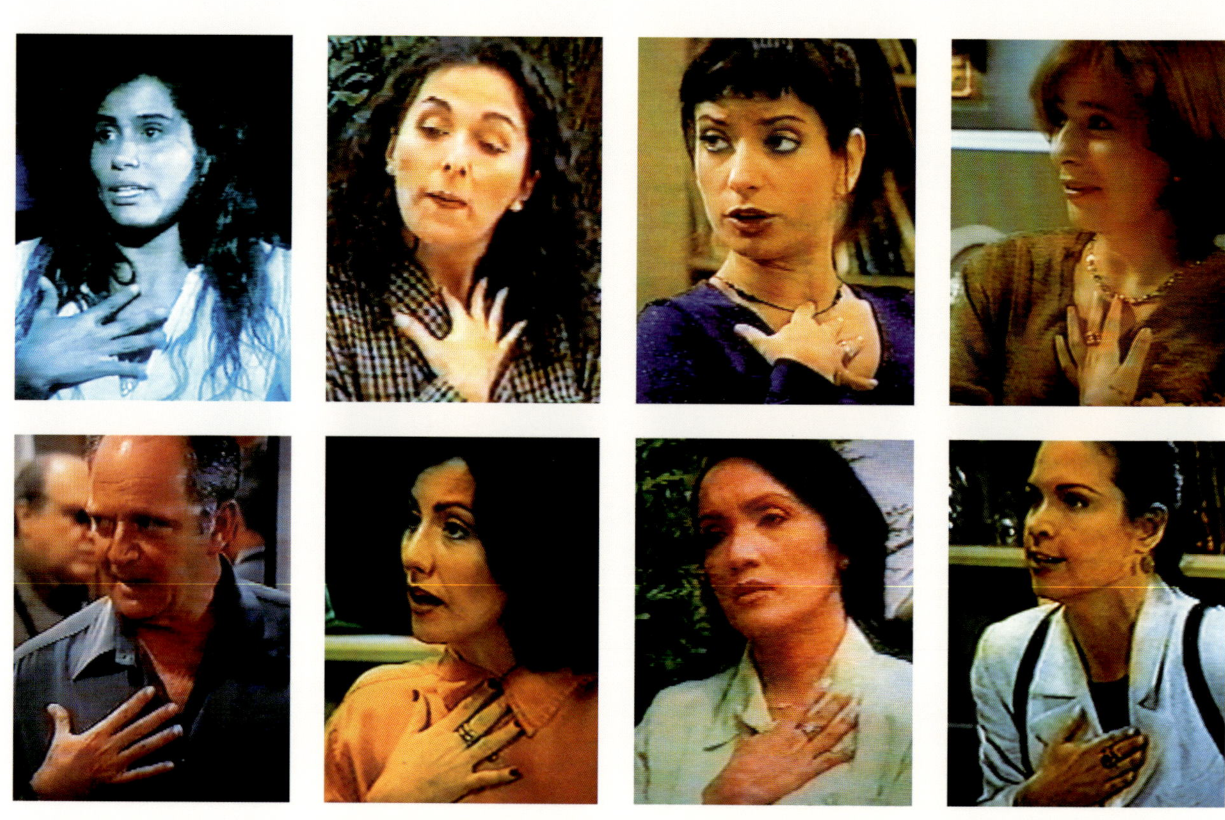

JULIAN ROSEFELDT
Soap Sample IX (*above*), VI (*opposite*) 2000-2004
Lambda print
Each 130 x 130 cm

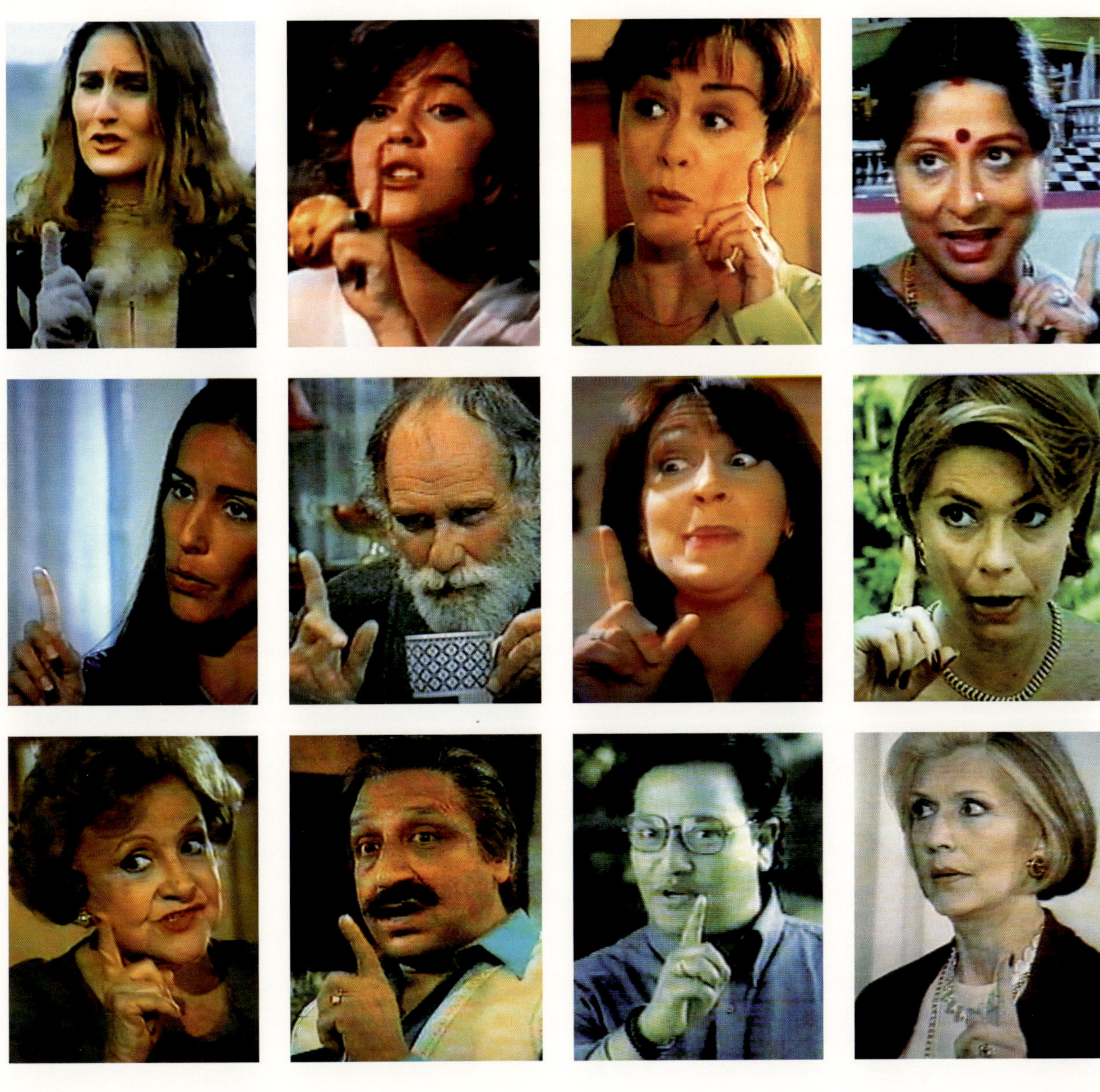

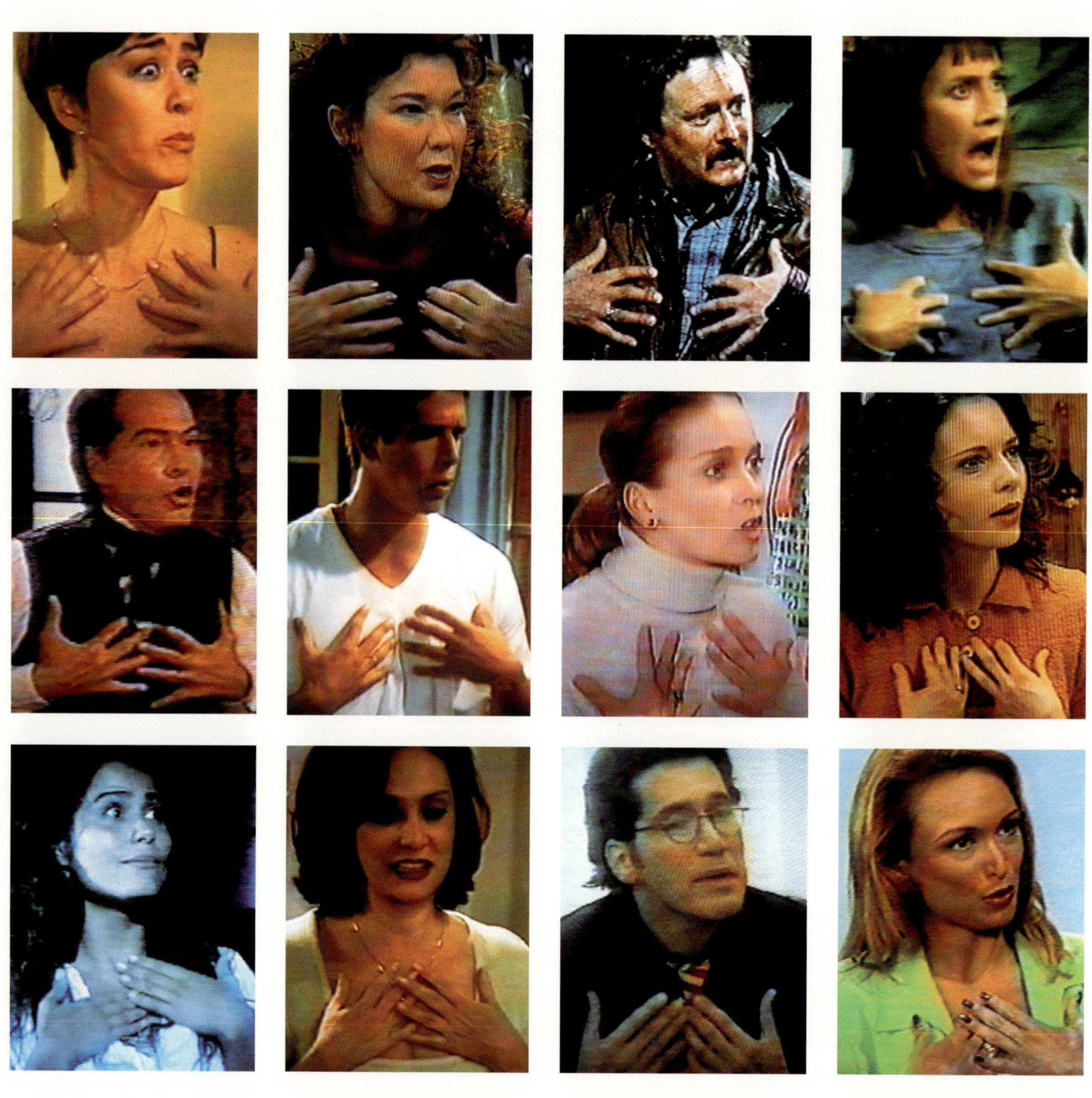

JULIAN ROSEFELDT
Soap Sample V (above), VIII (opposite) 2000-2004
Lambda print
Each 130 x 130 cm

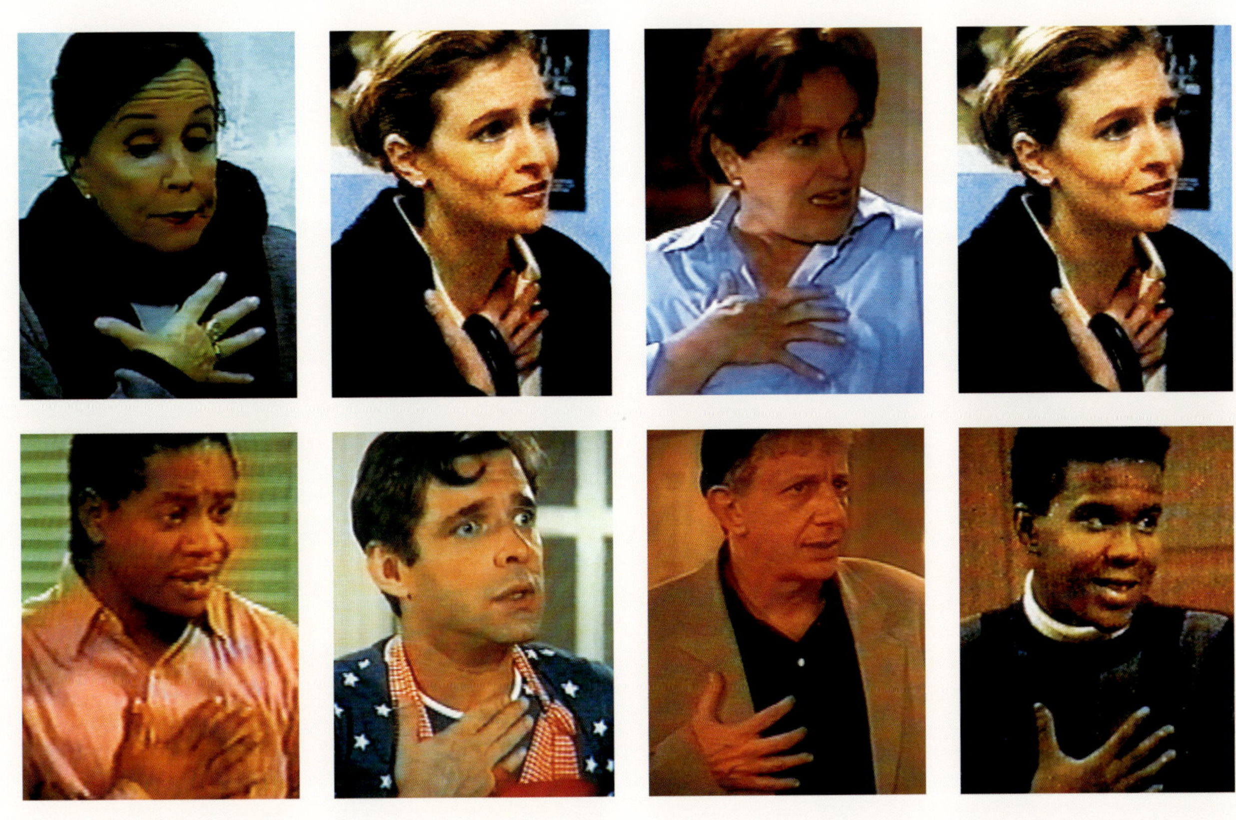

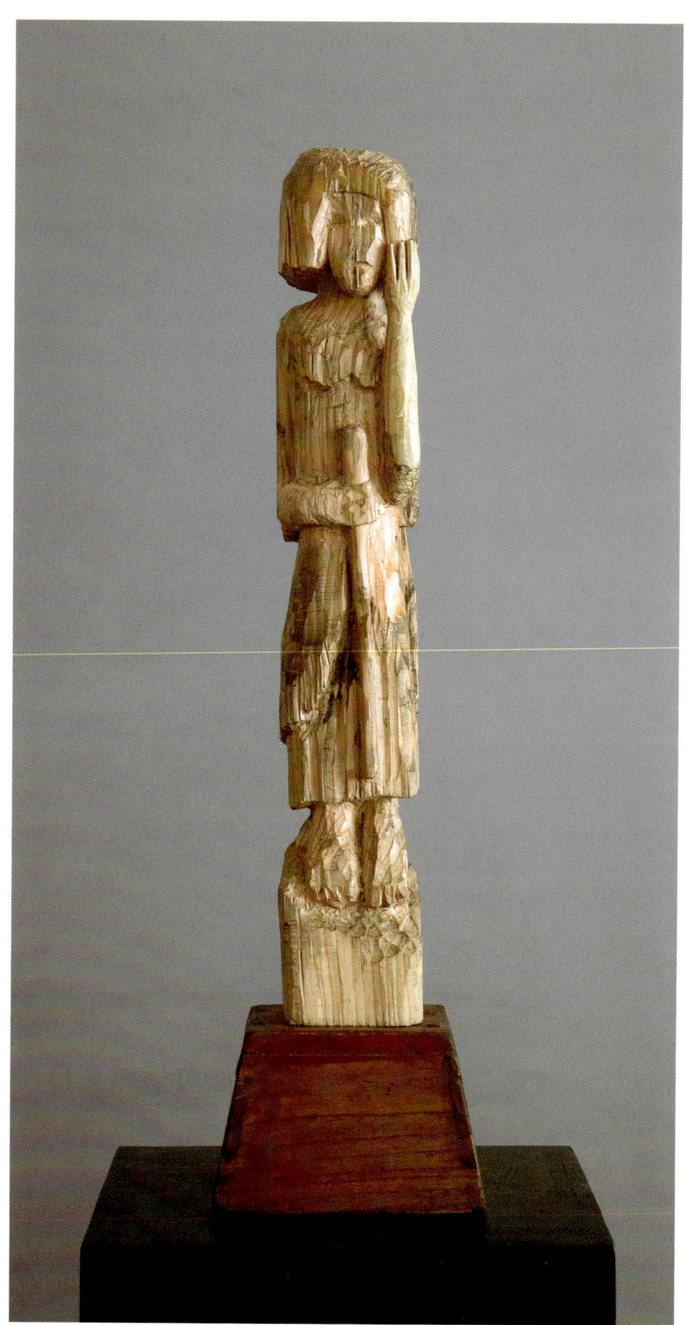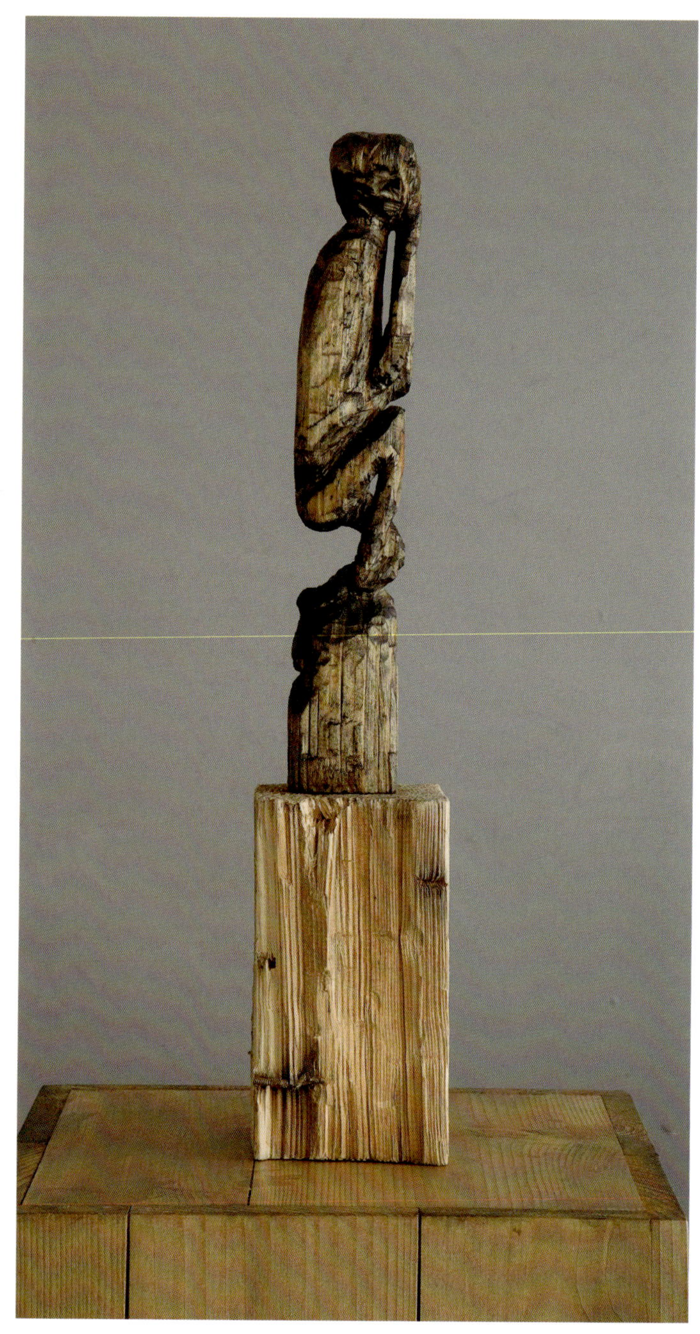

MARKUS SELG

above:
Anima 2010
Wood
100 x 30 x 30 cm

above right:
Abgrund (Abyss) 2010
Wood
110 x 26 cm

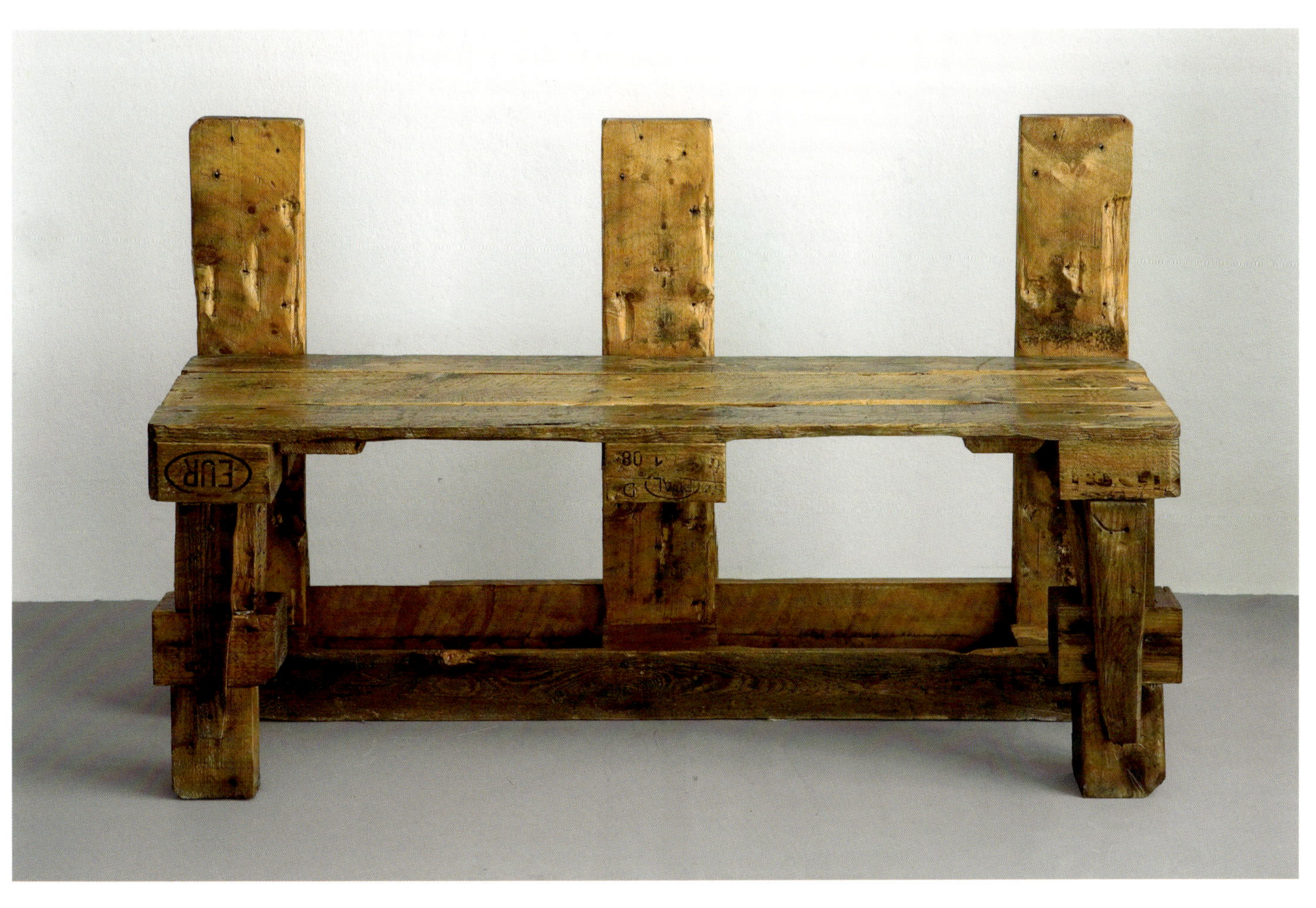

MARKUS SELG
Bench (Tiger) 2010
Collaboration with Astrid Sourkova
Wood
80 x 120 x 38 cm

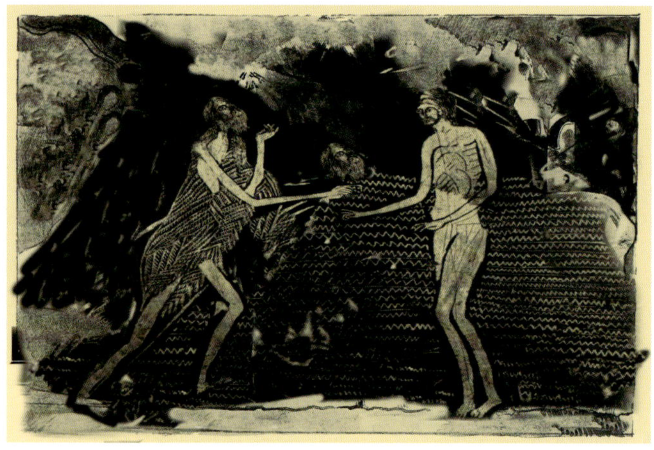

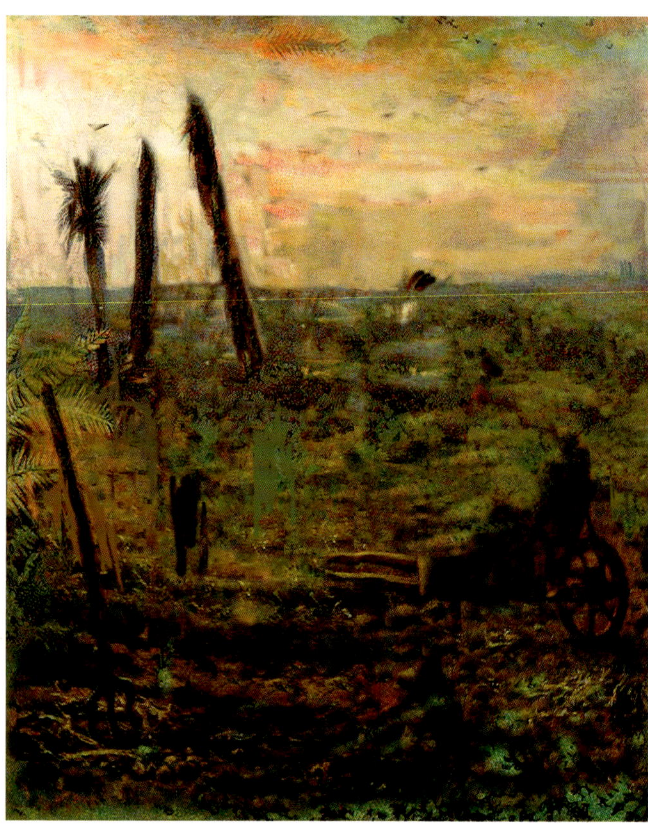

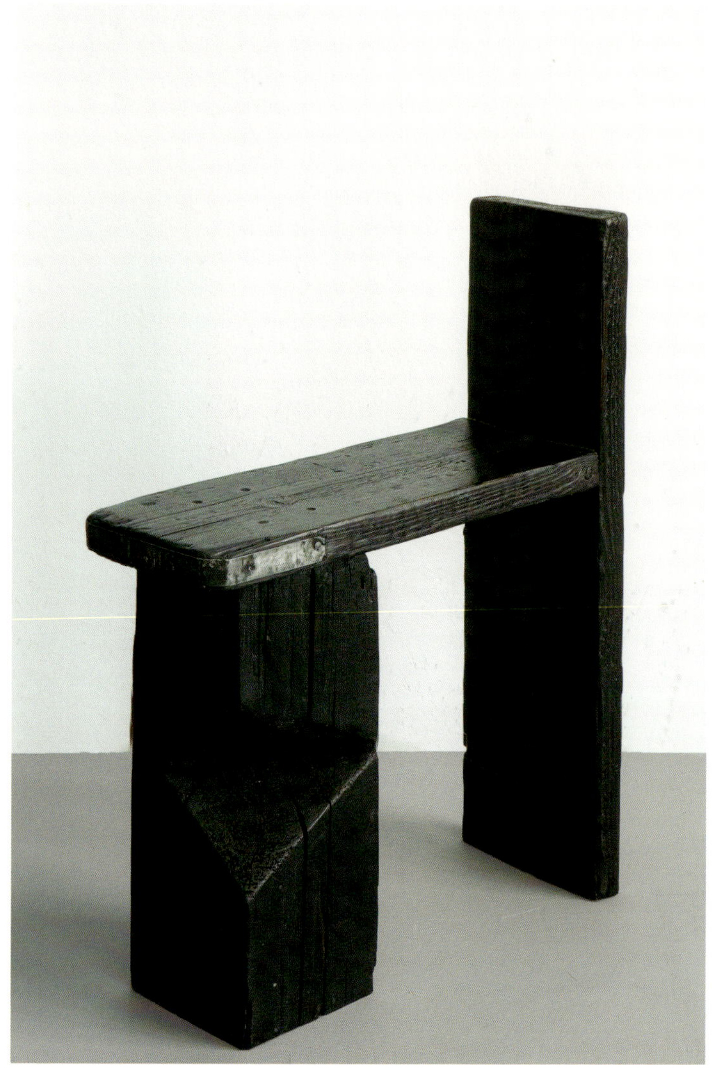

MARKUS SELG
above top:
Vorahnung (Premonition) 2010
Piezo print on paper
37 x 49.5 cm

above:
Angelus 2010
Piezo print on paper
49.5 x 39.5 cm

above right:
Chair (Hanush) 2010
Collaboration with Astrid Sourkova
Wood
88 x 64 x 24 cm

opposite:
Mild Und Leise Wie Er Lächelt (Mild And Quiet As He Smiles) 2008
Metal, wood, straw, plaster and shellac
150 x 38 x 34 cm

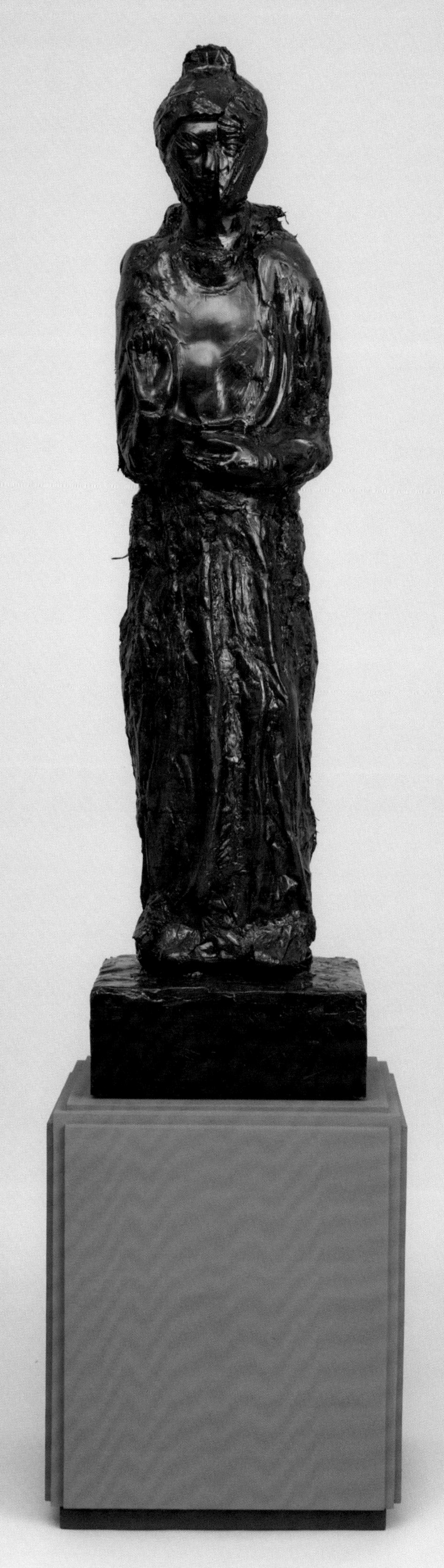

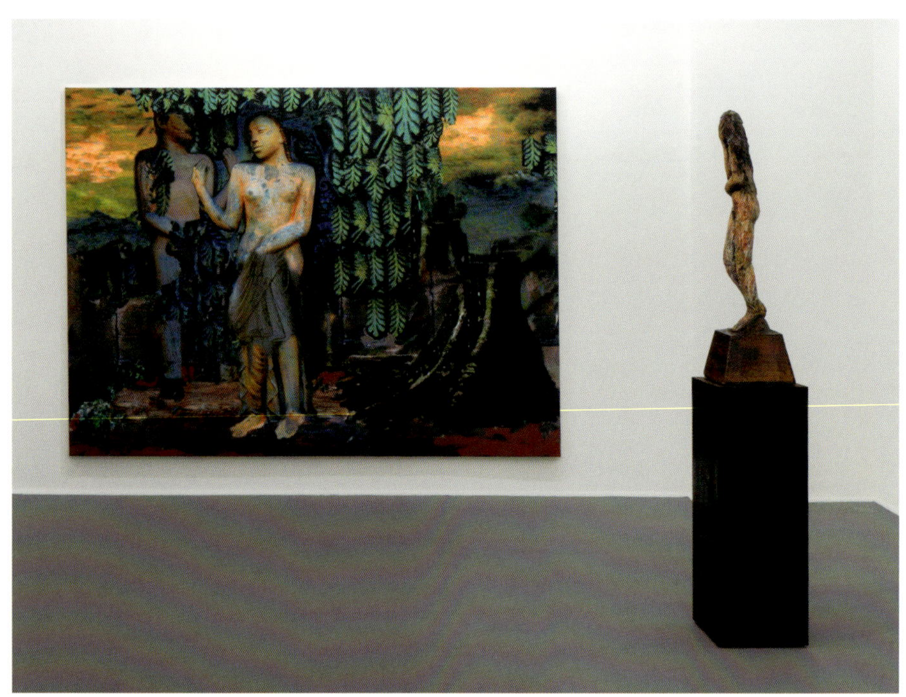

MARKUS SELG

opposite:
Eva 2010
Plaster, wood, jute, metal
95 x 26 x 26 cm / 88 x 33 x 33 cm (pedestal)

above:
Installation shot

overleaf:
Searching For Ruwenzori 2010
Sublimation print on fabric
195 x 260 cm

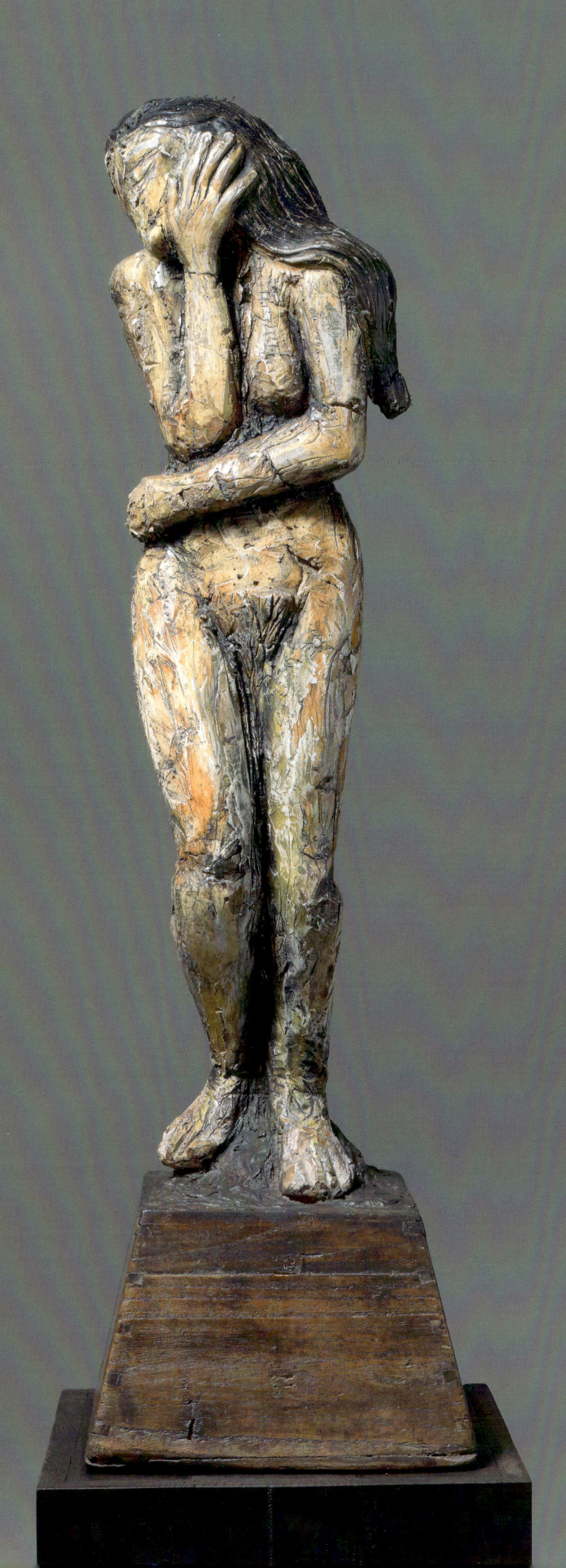

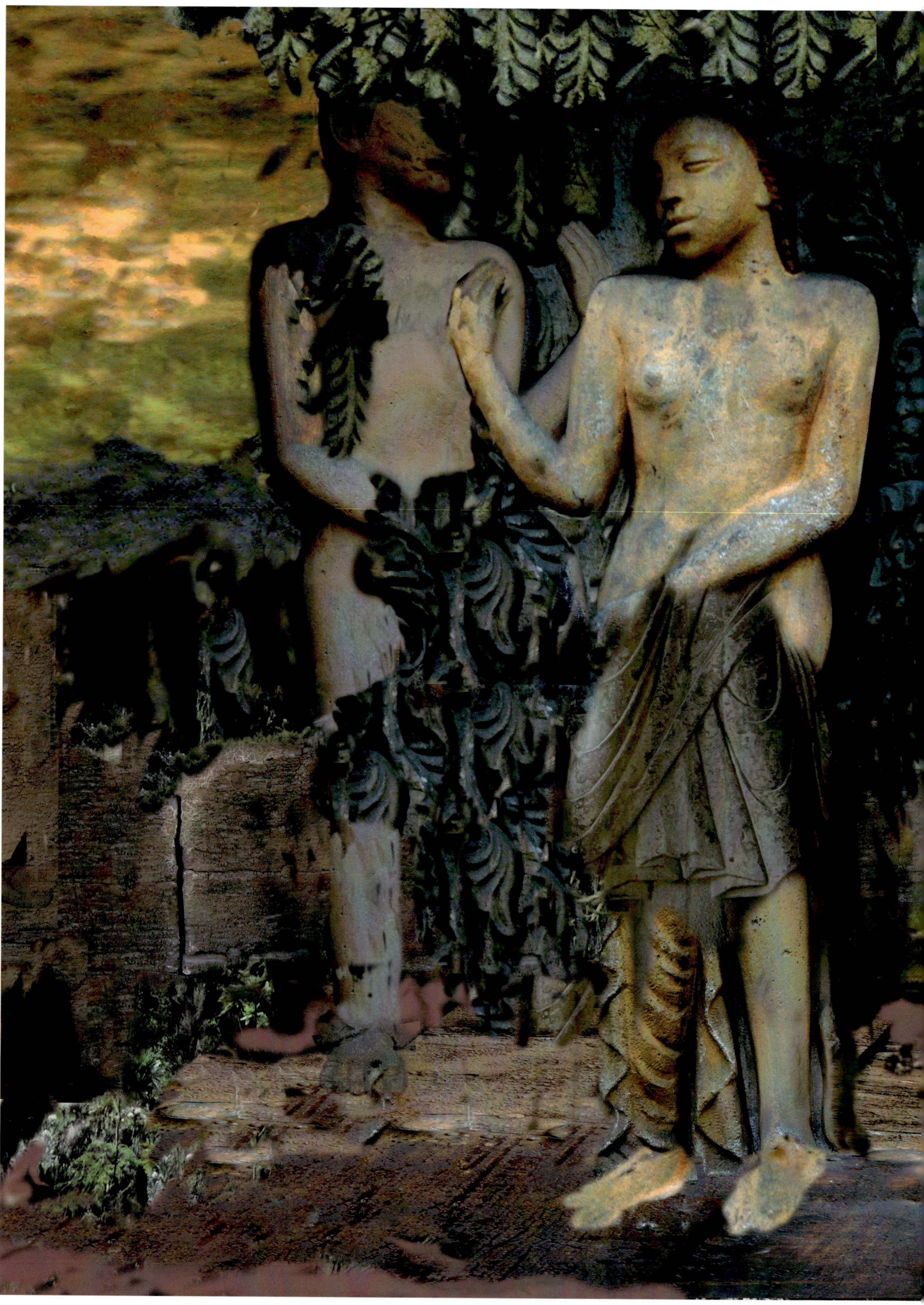

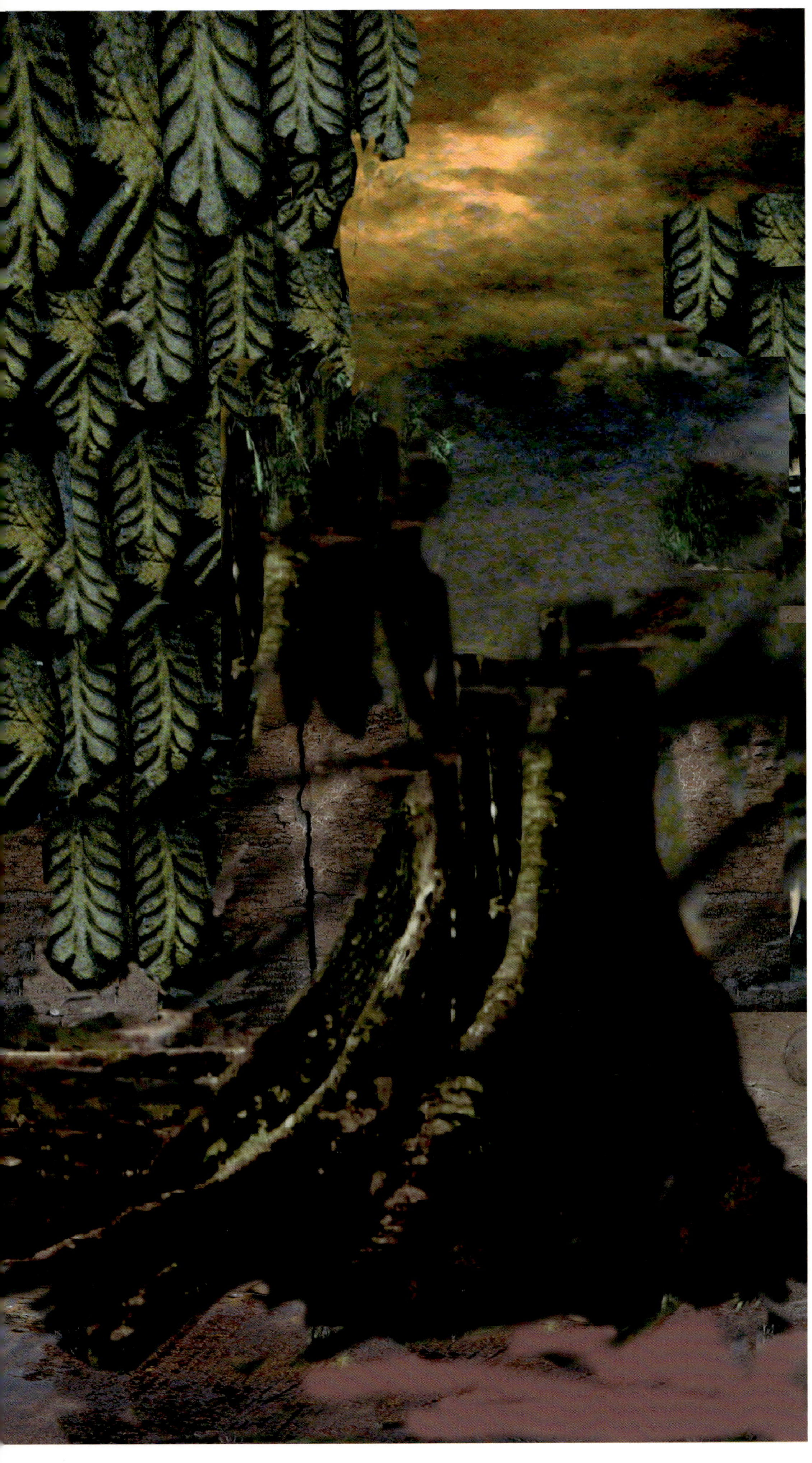

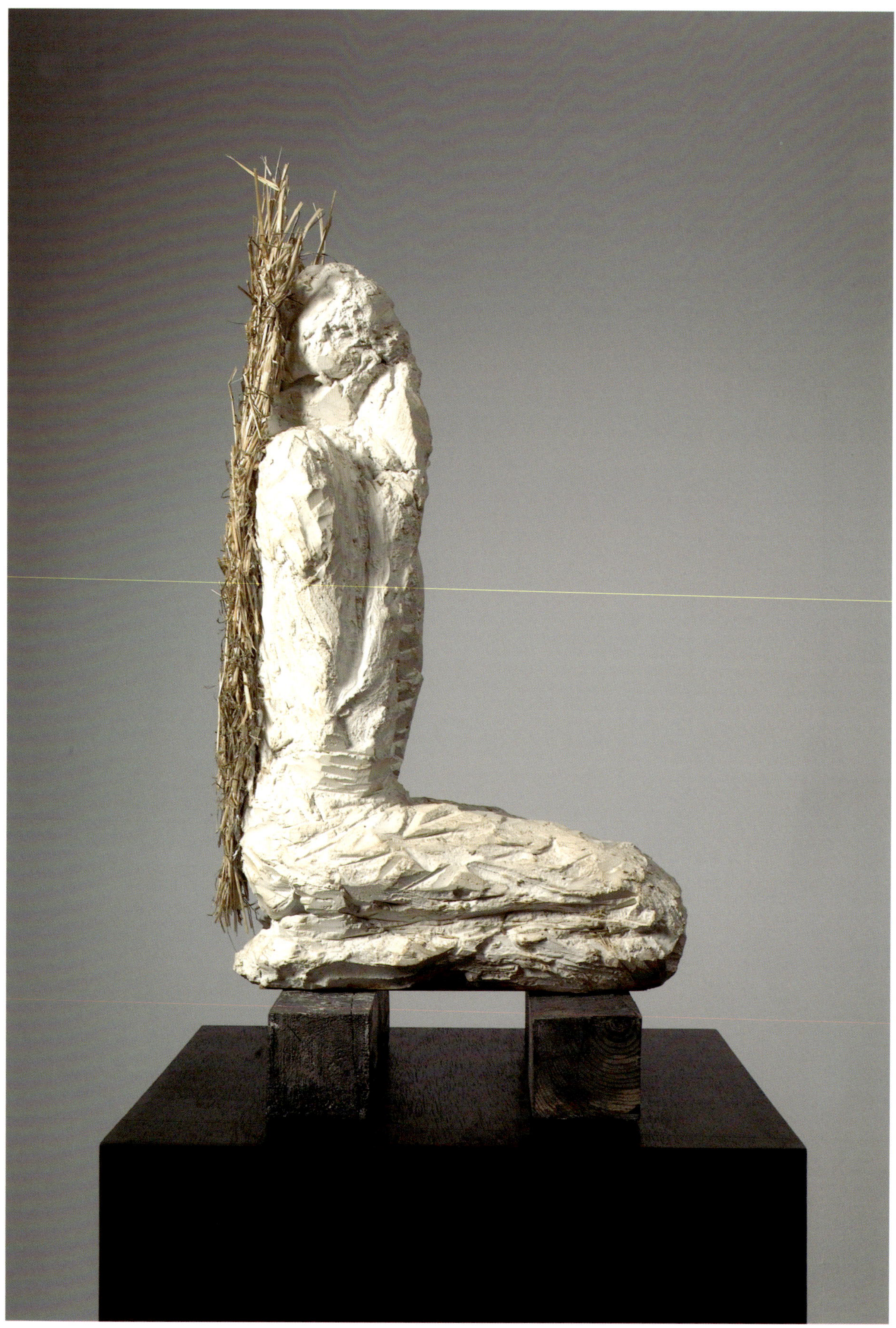

MARKUS SELG
above and opposite:
Betender 2009
Plaster, straw, jute, metal, wood
Artwork: 86 x 20 x 47 cm
Pedestal: 85 x 60 x 60 cm

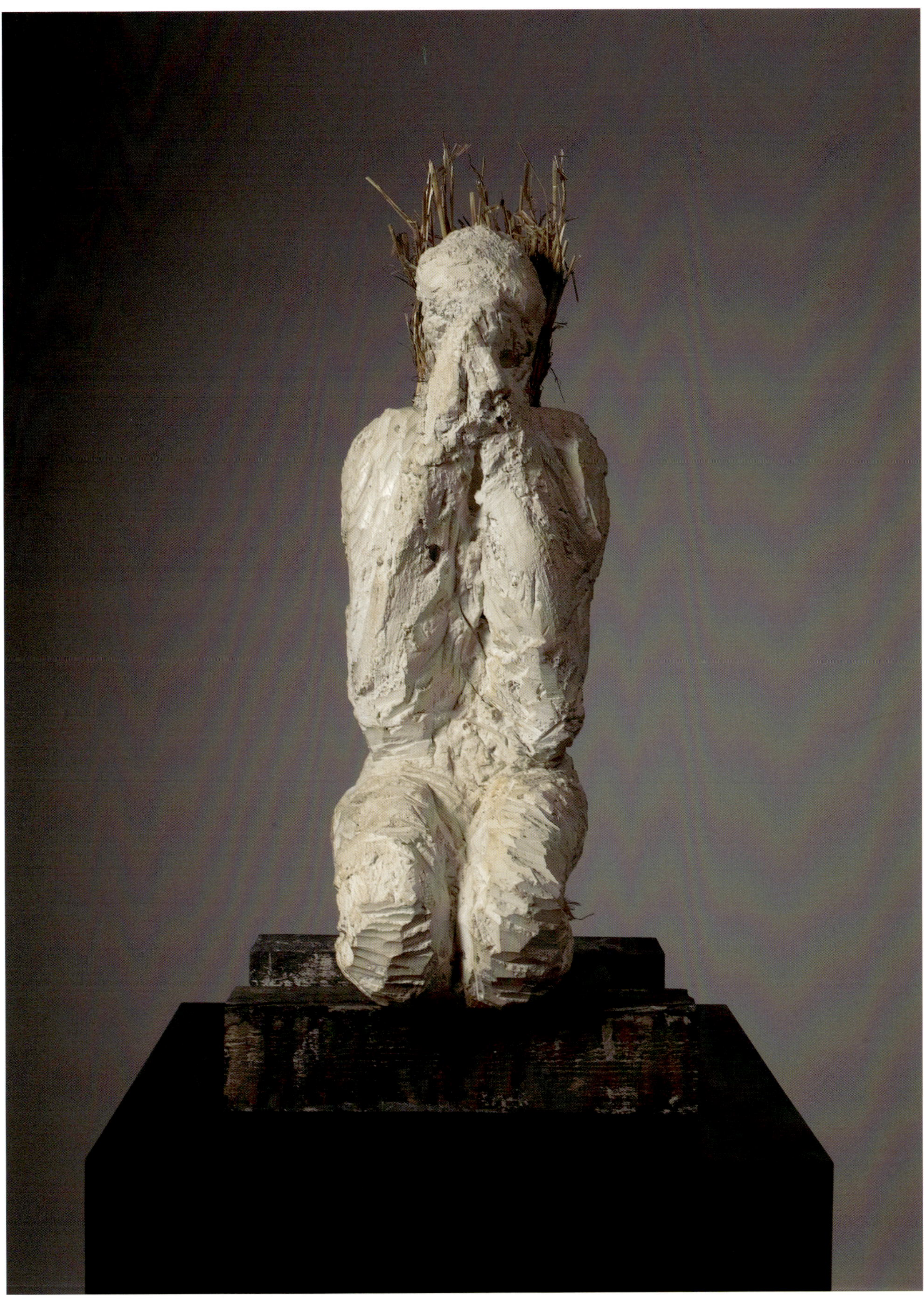

MARKUS SELG
Trauernde 2008
Plaster, straw, jute, metal, shellac
Artwork: 125 x 30 x 30 cm
Pedestal: 62 x 36 x 36 cm

overleaf:
Traum Der Sarazenin 2007
Sublimation print on fabric
240 x 350 cm

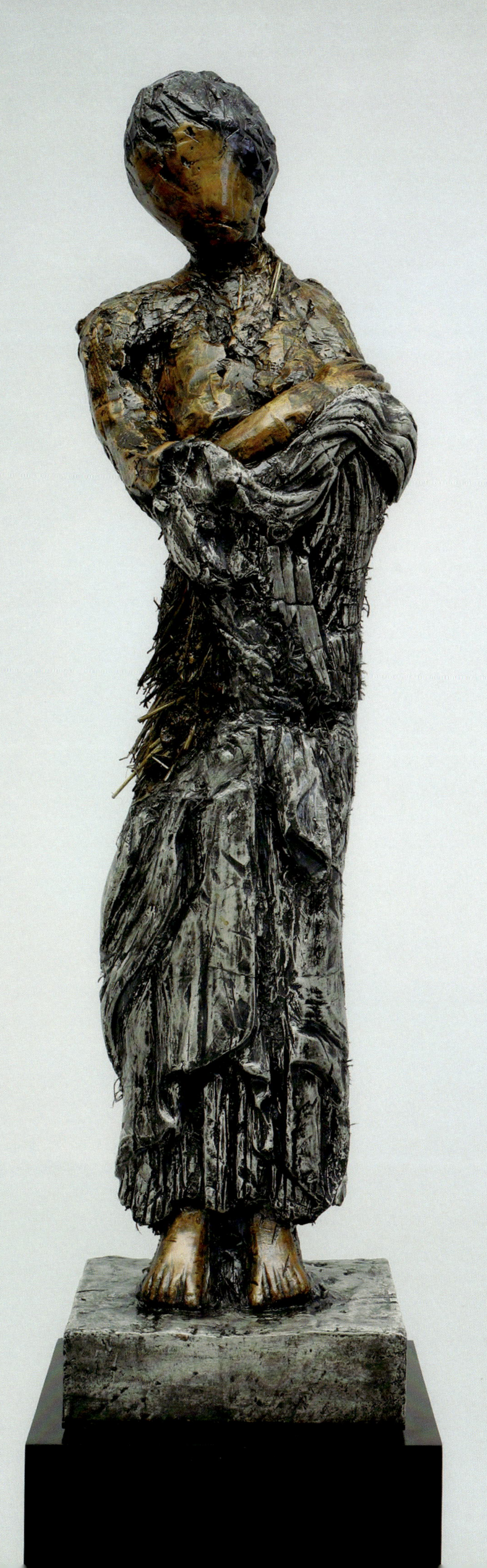

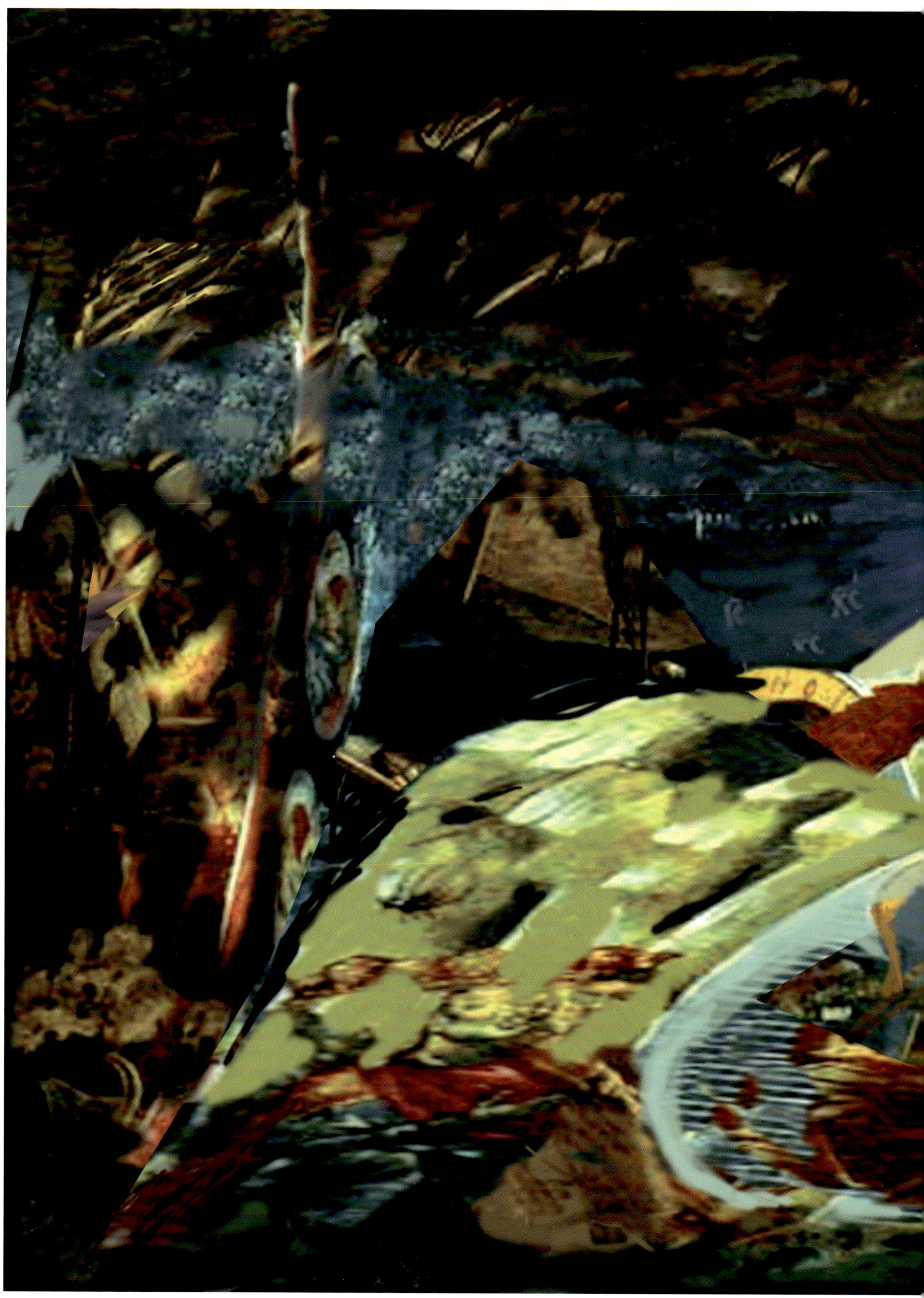

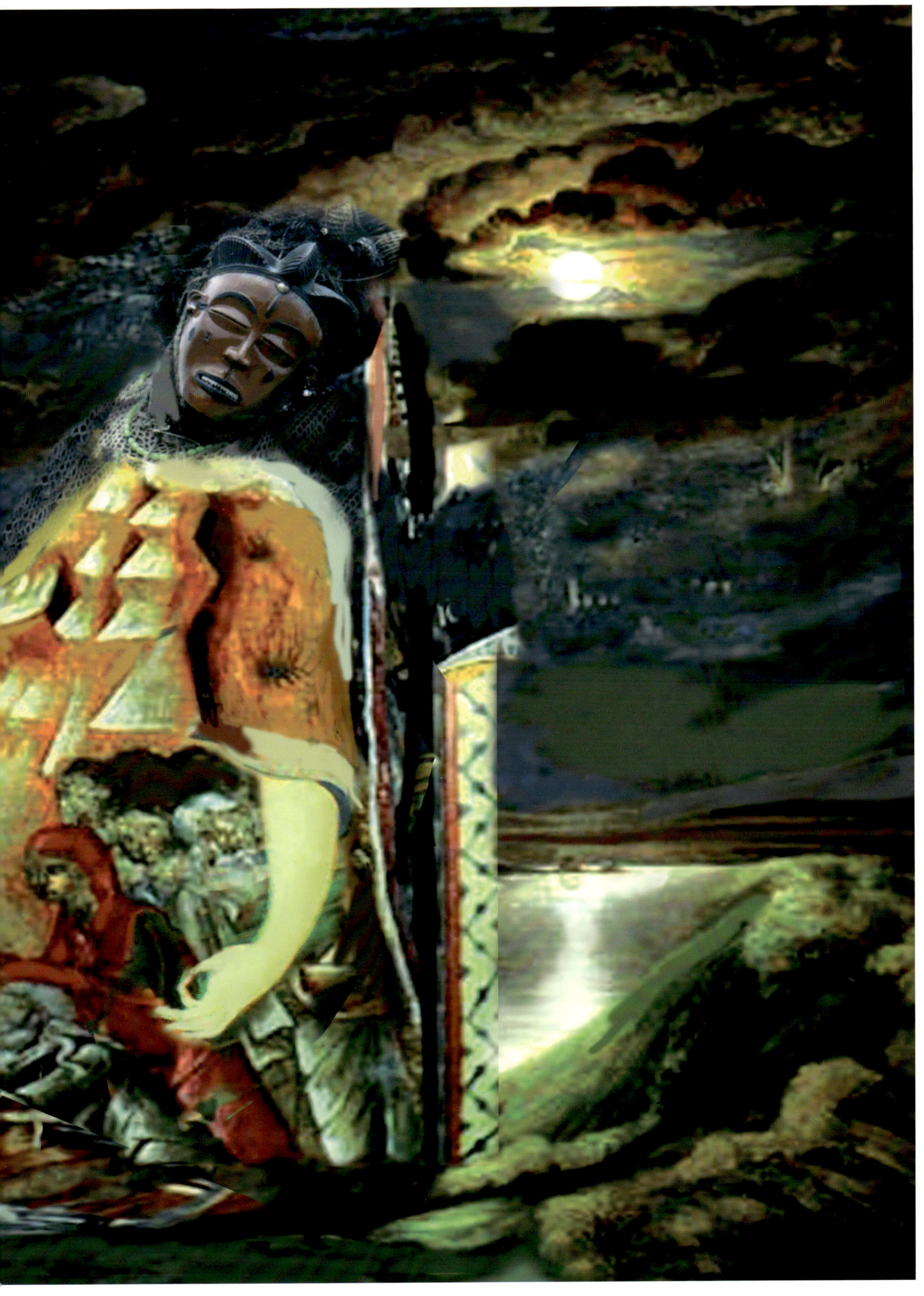

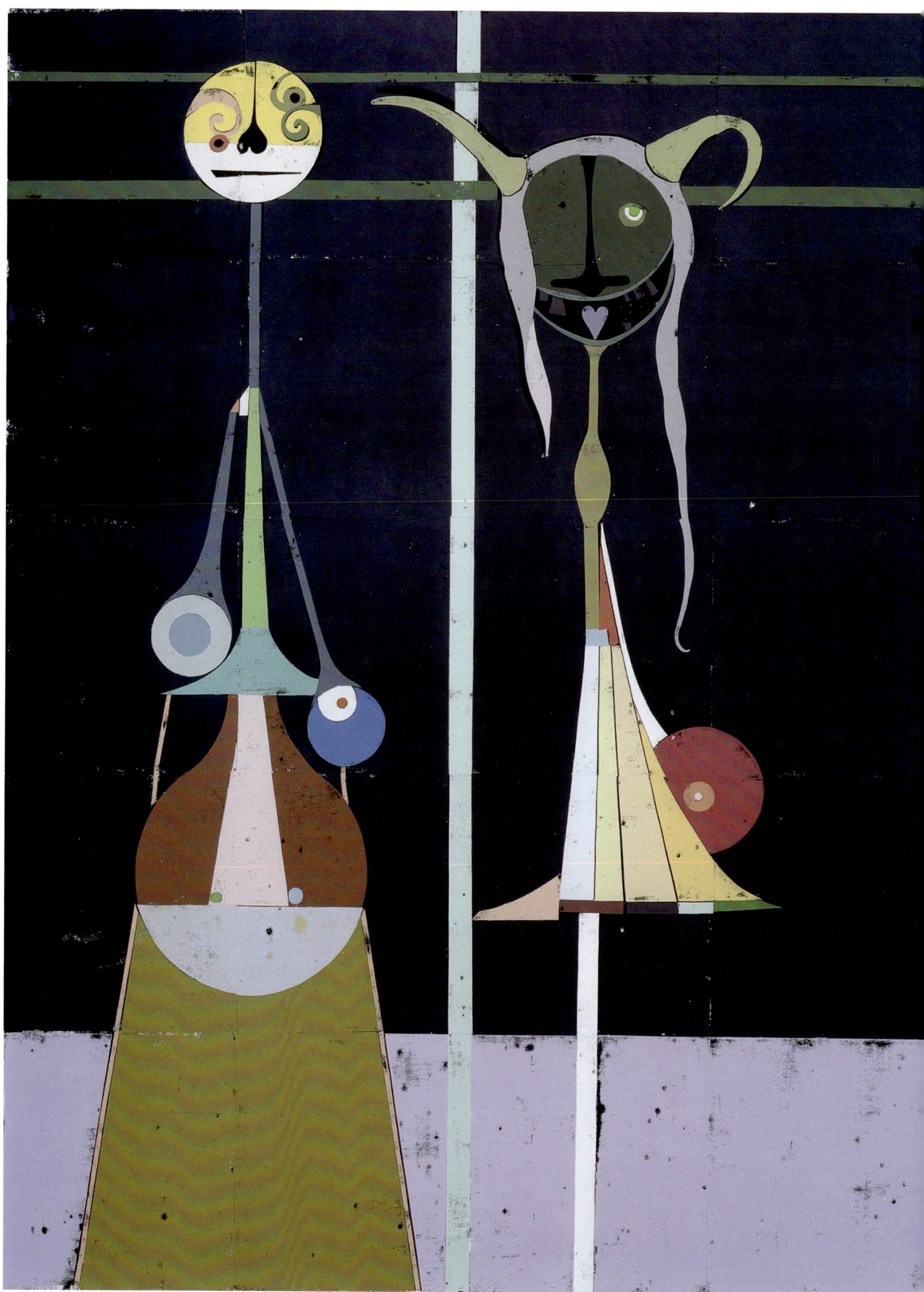

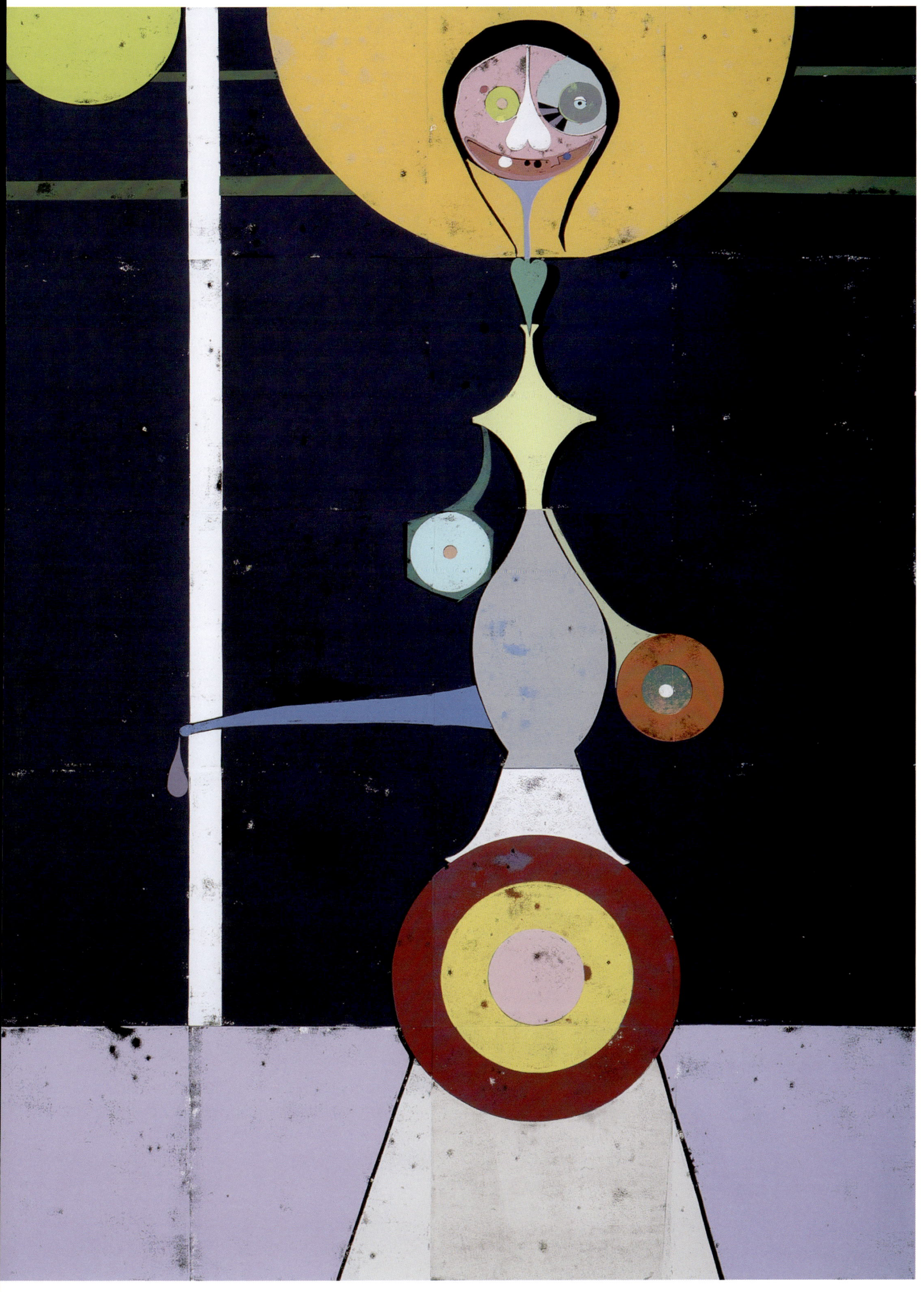

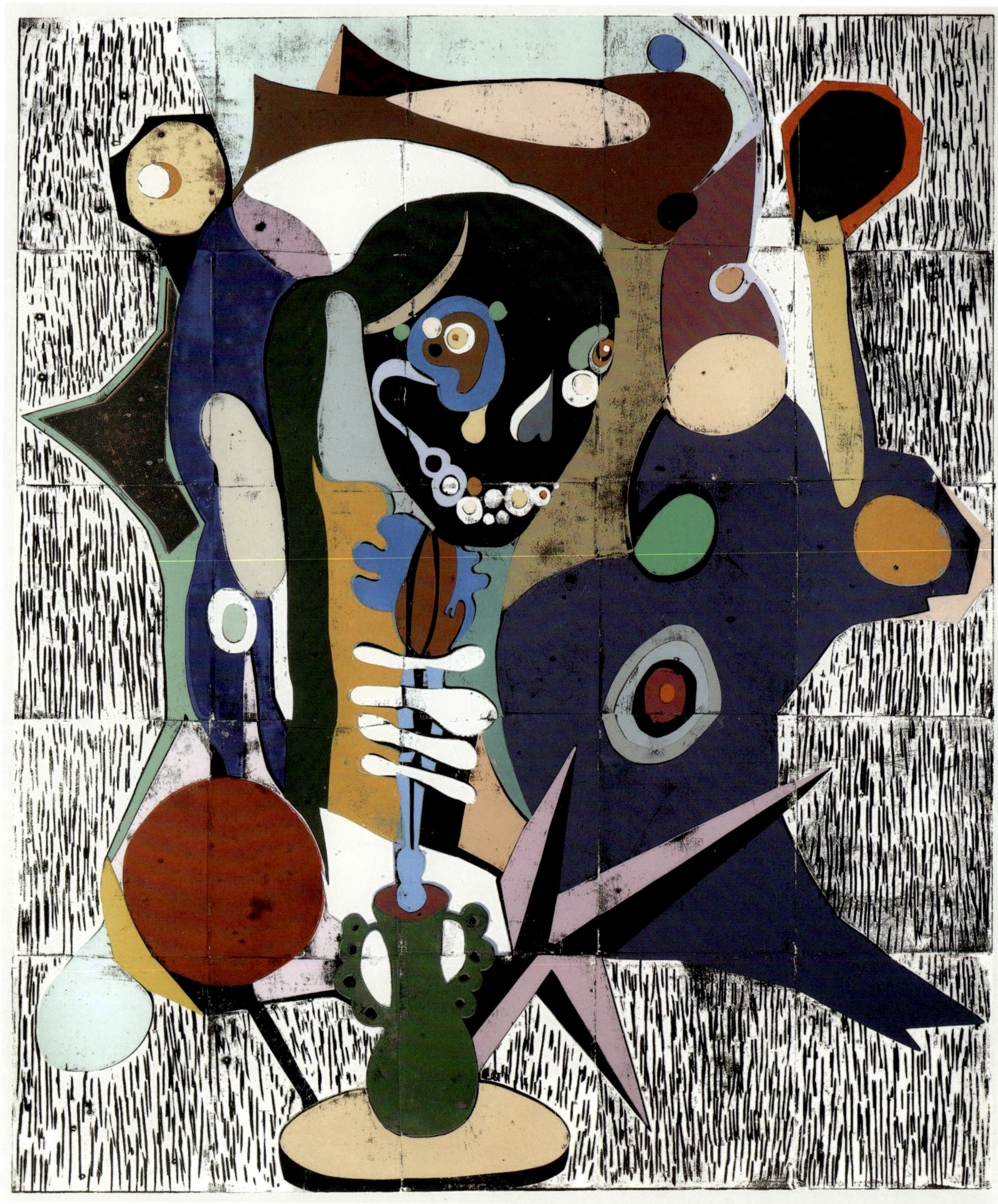

GERT AND UWE TOBIAS
Untitled 2005
Acrylic, crayon and woodcut on paper
200 x 165 cm

previous page:
Untitled 2007
Coloured woodcut on paper mounted on canvas
268 x 401.7 cm

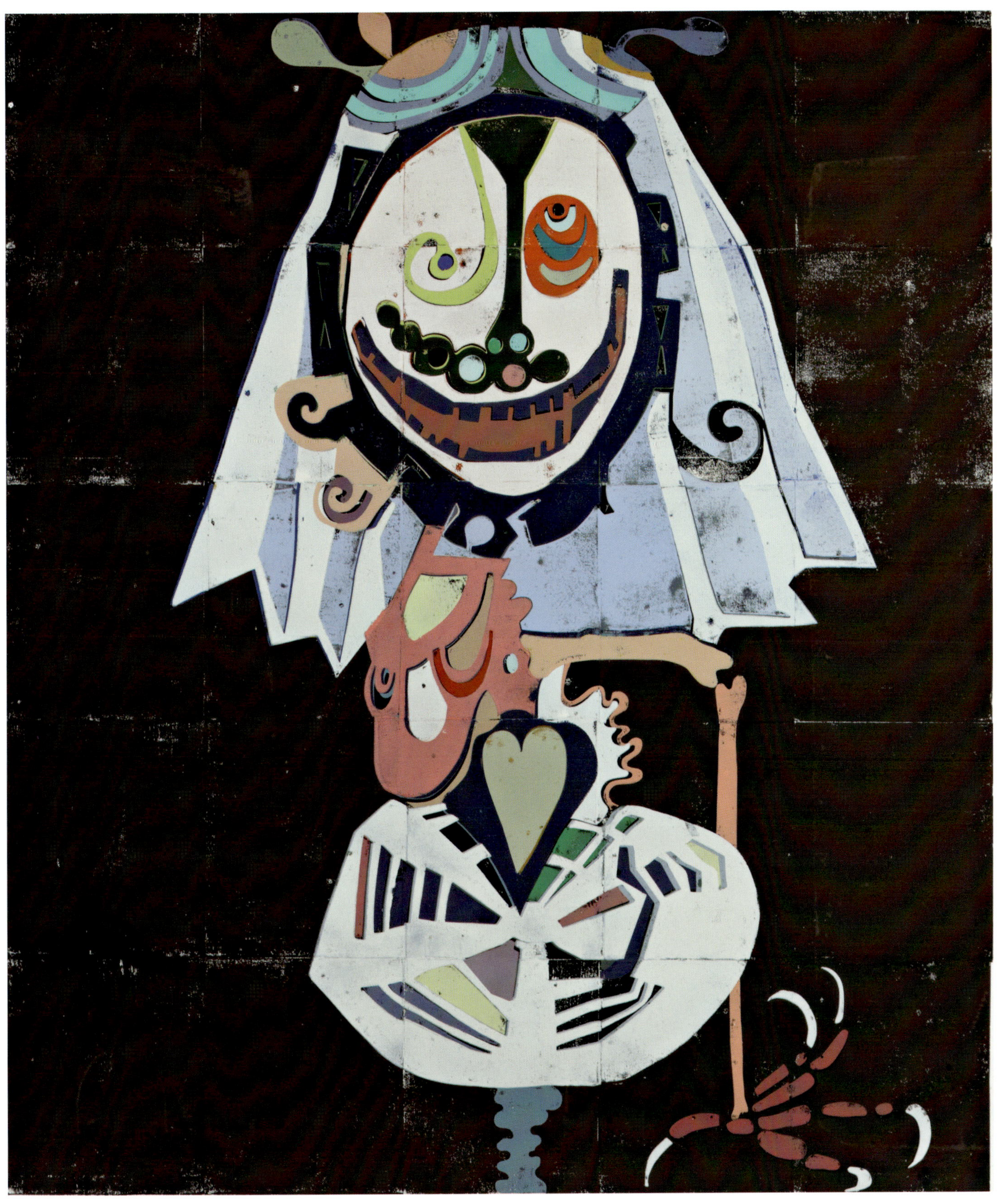

GERT AND UWE TOBIAS
Untitled 2005
Coloured woodcut on paper
211 x 177 cm

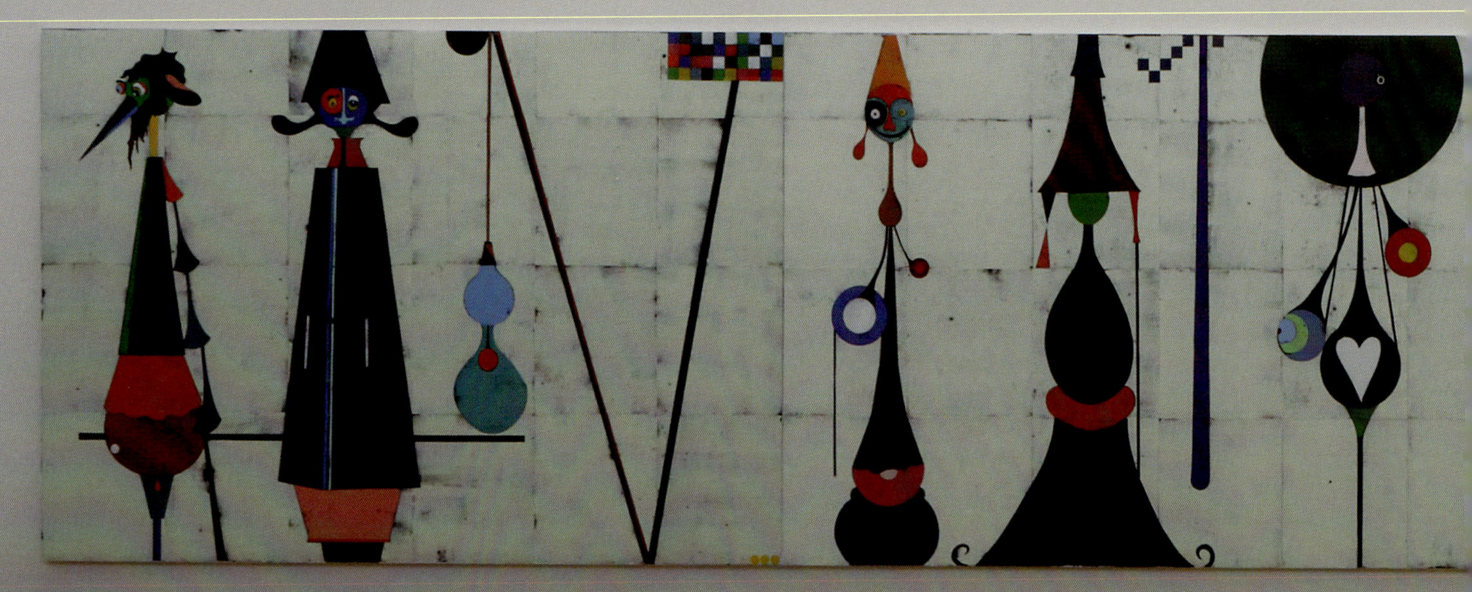

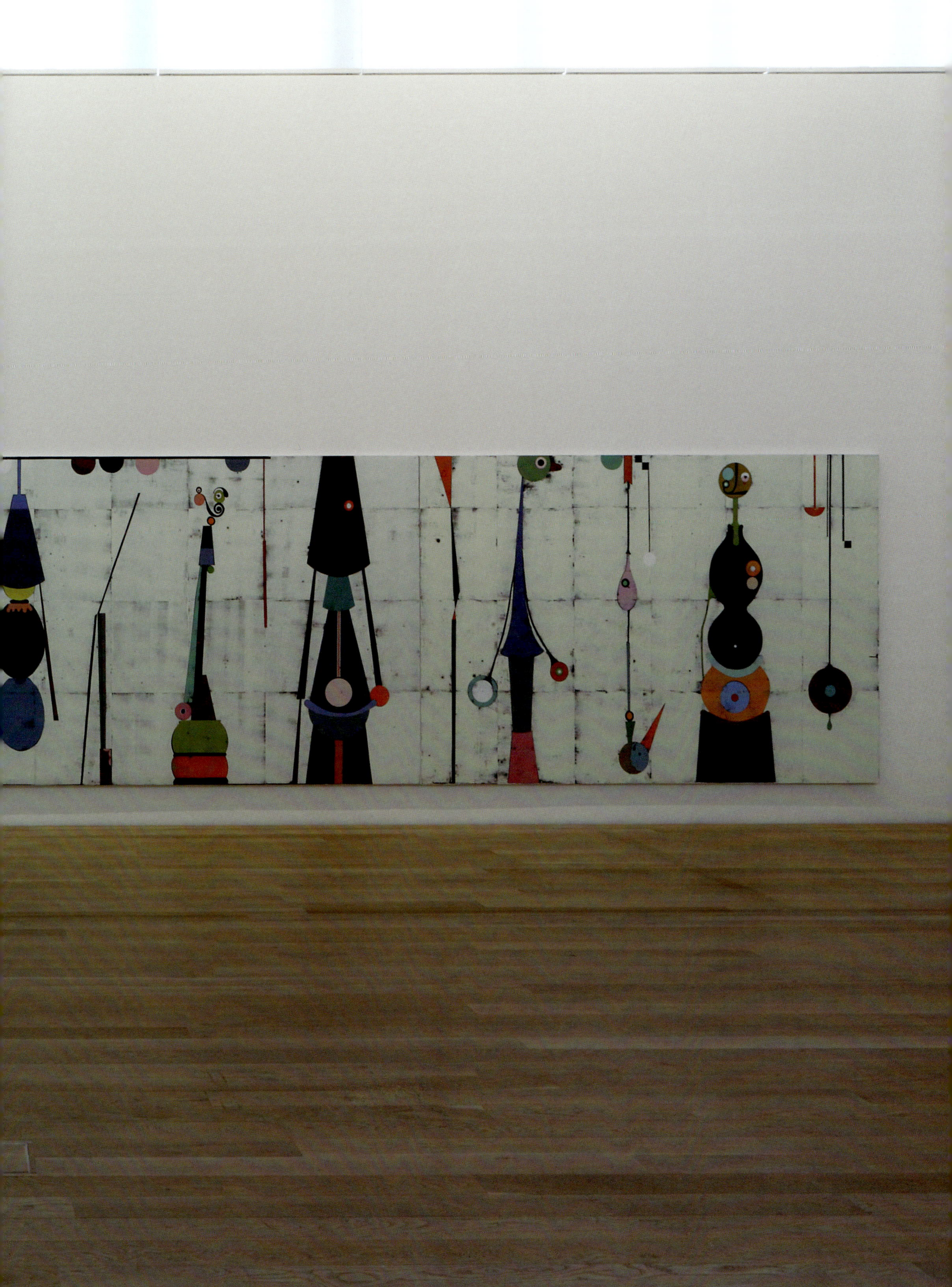

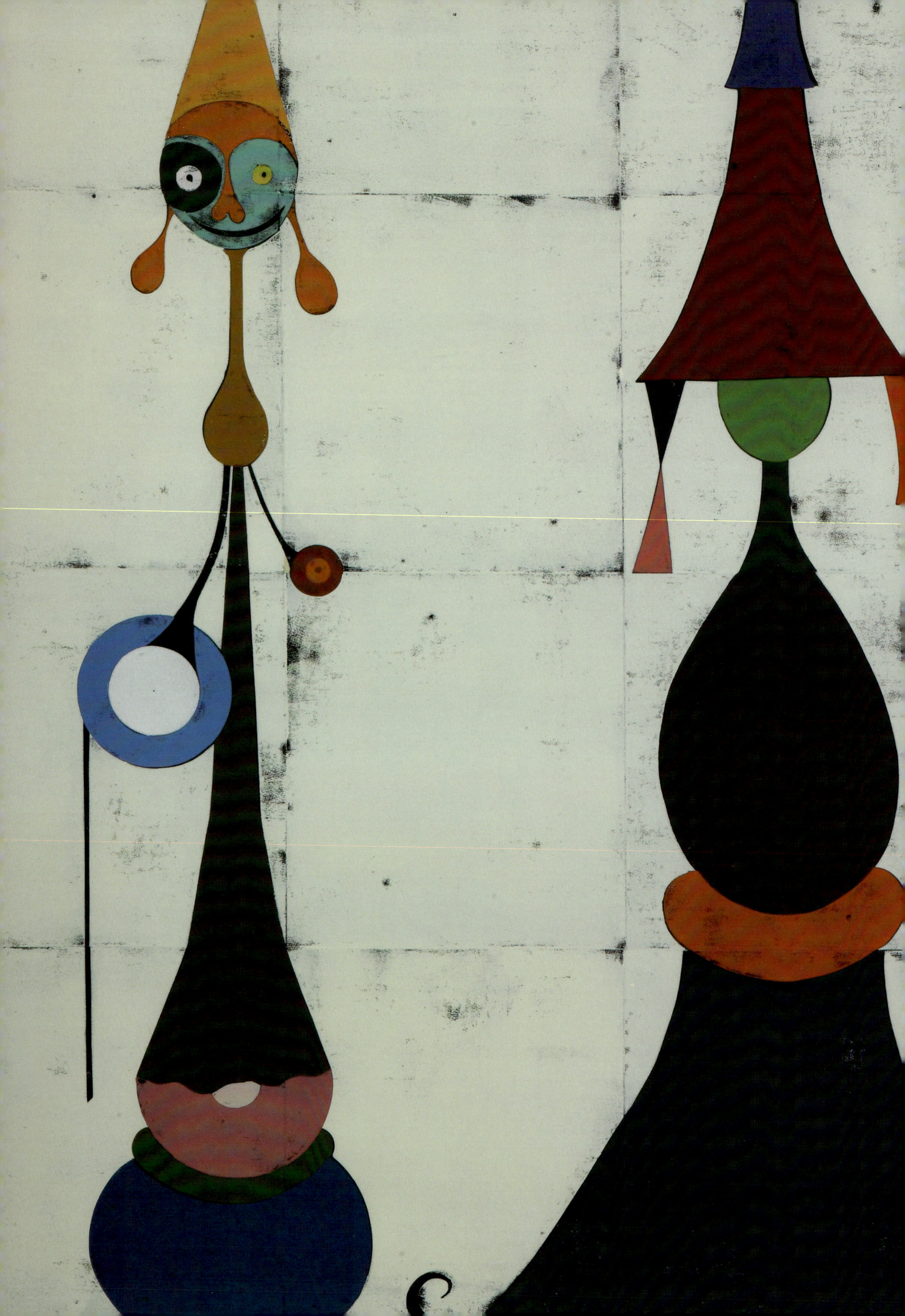

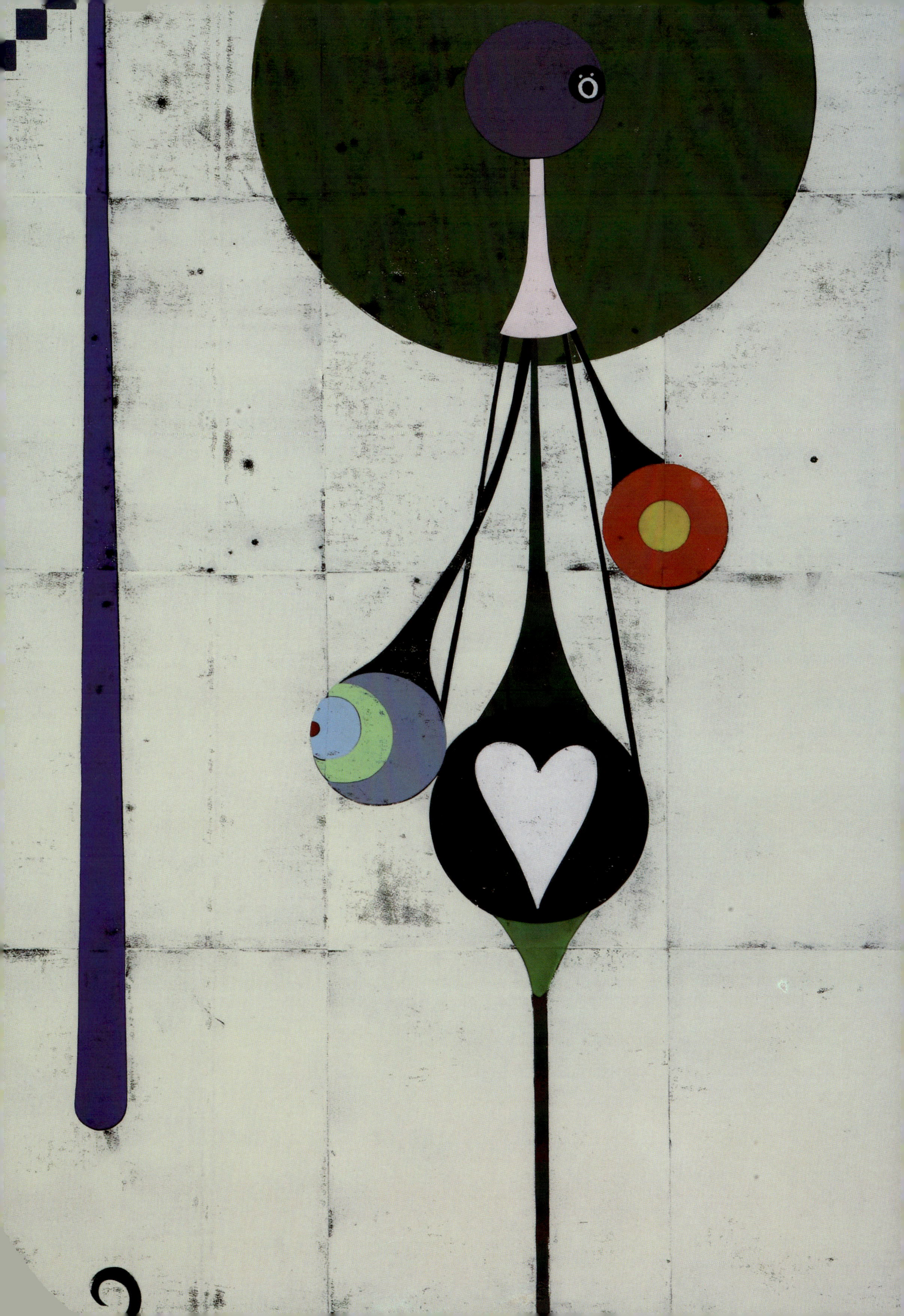

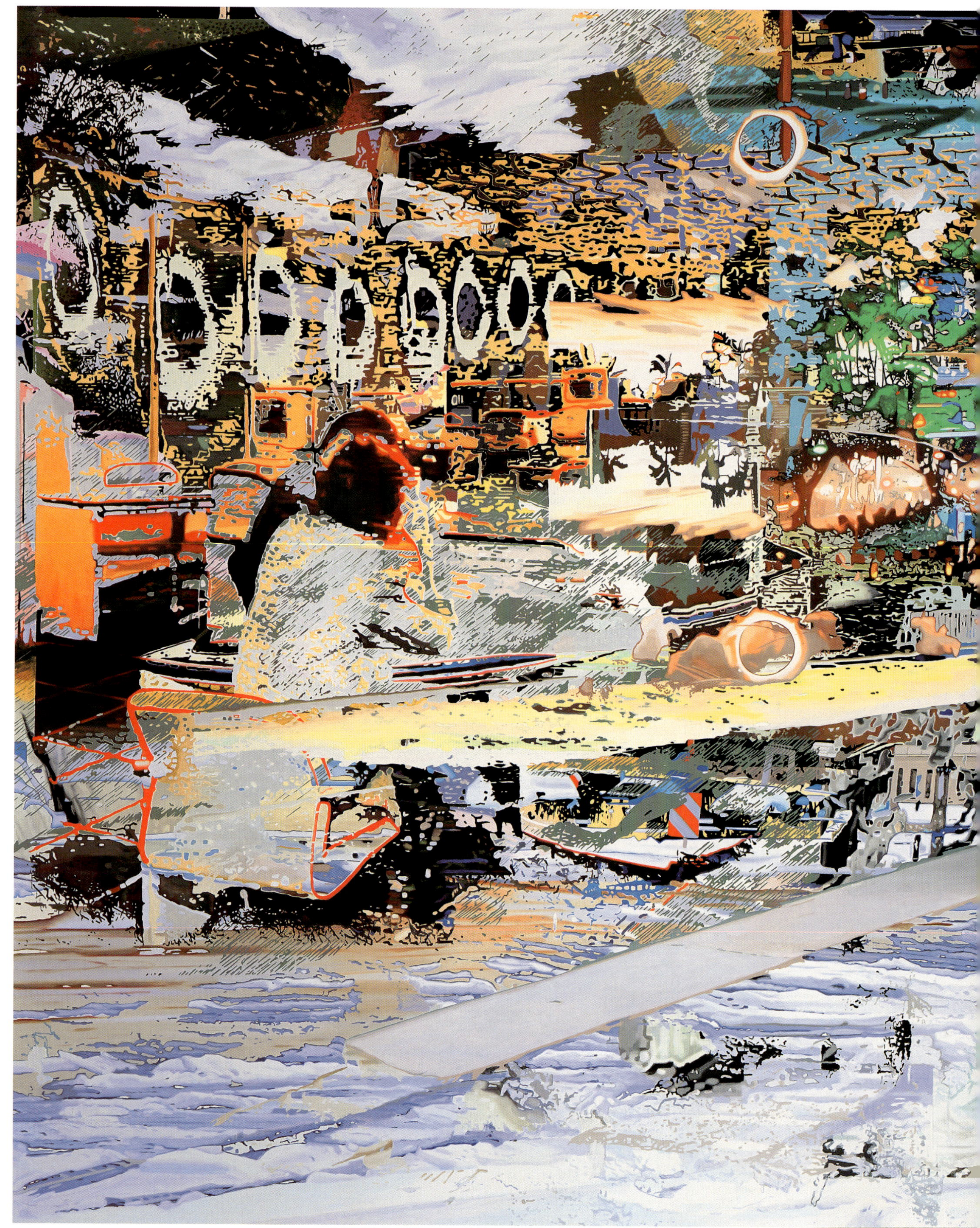

CORINNE WASMUHT
Siempre Es Hoy 2008
Oil on wood
261 x 434 cm

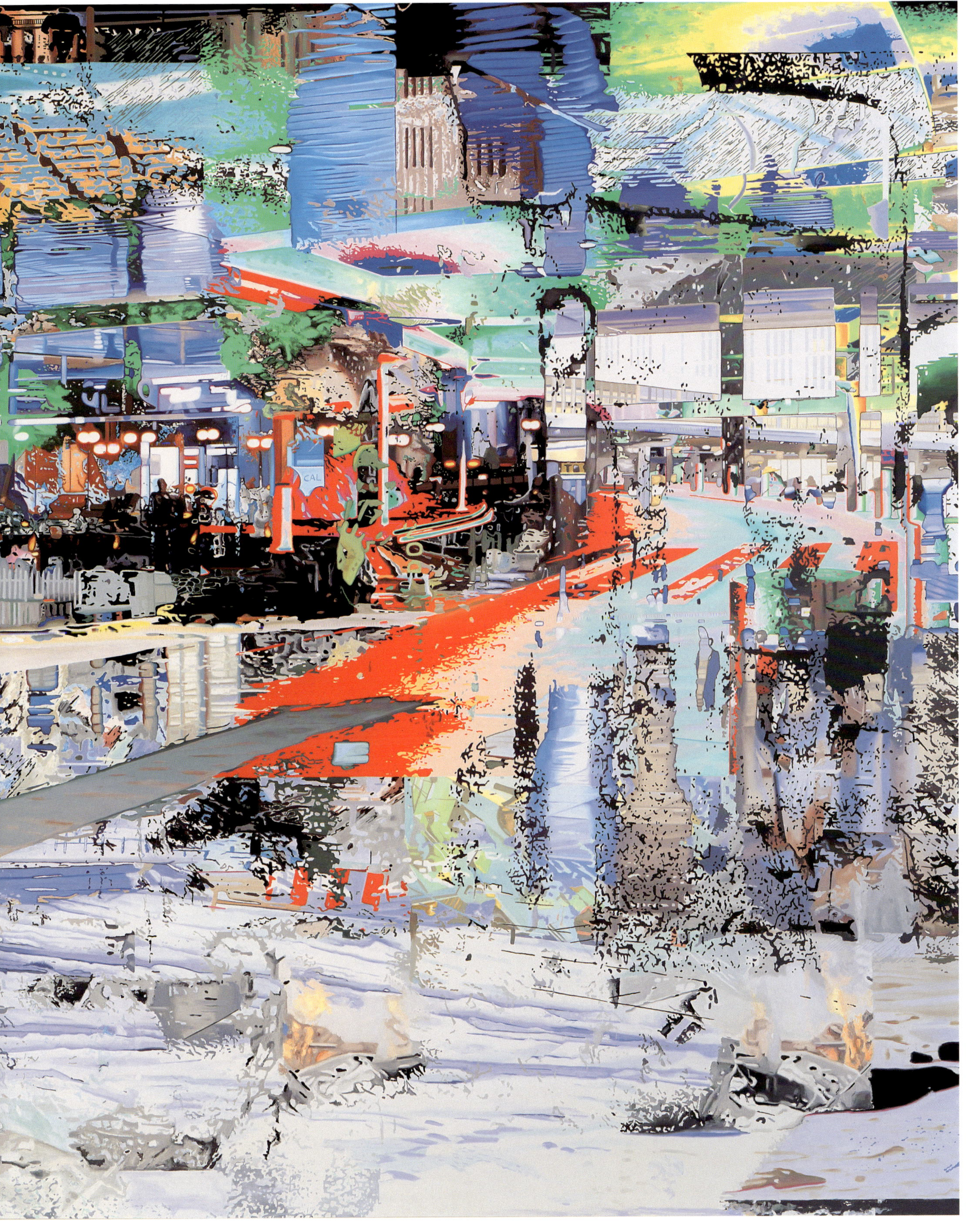

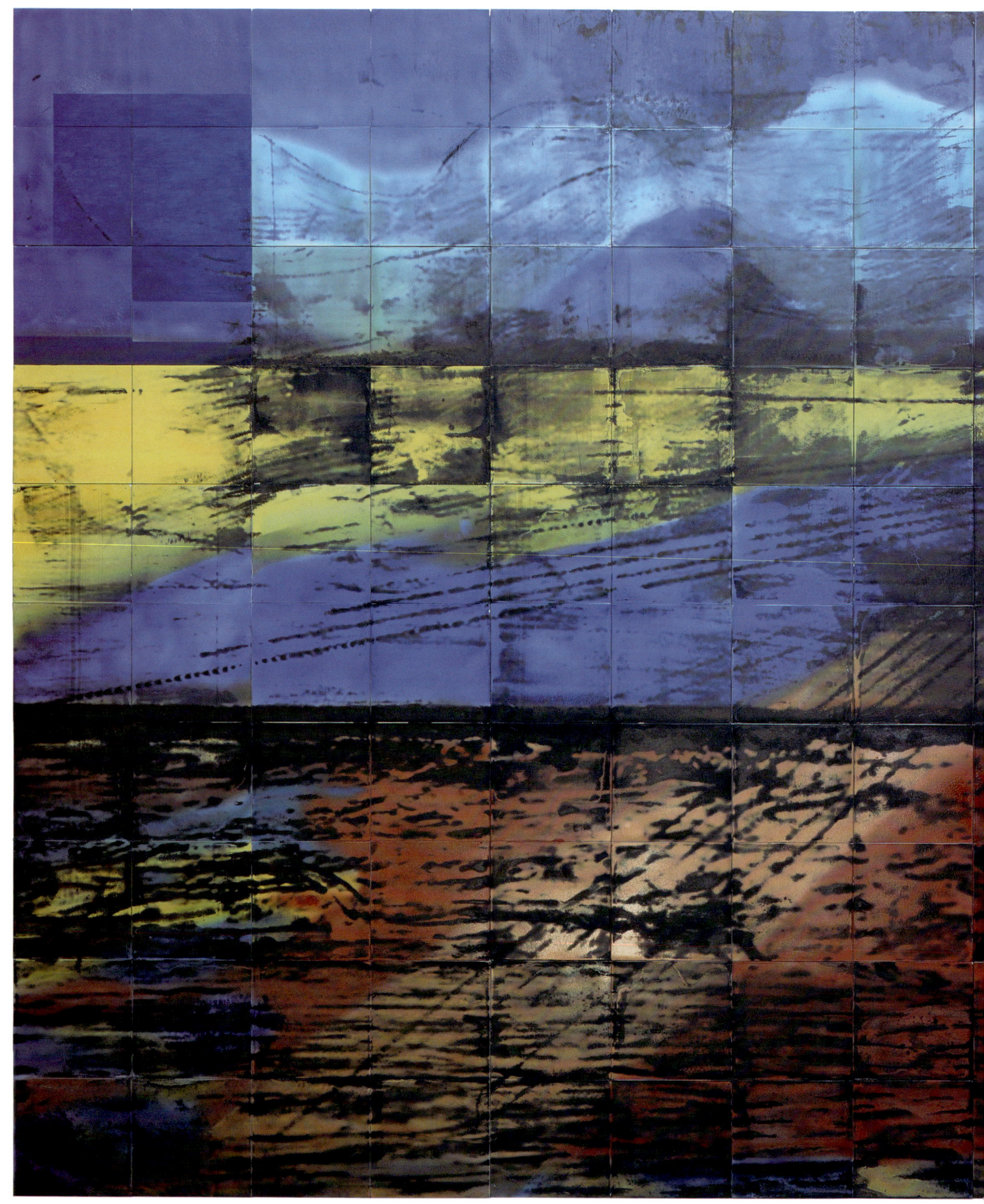

ANDRO WEKUA
Sunset 2008
Installation of 170 glazed ceramic panels, metal framework, steel scaffolding
500 x 800 x 82 cm

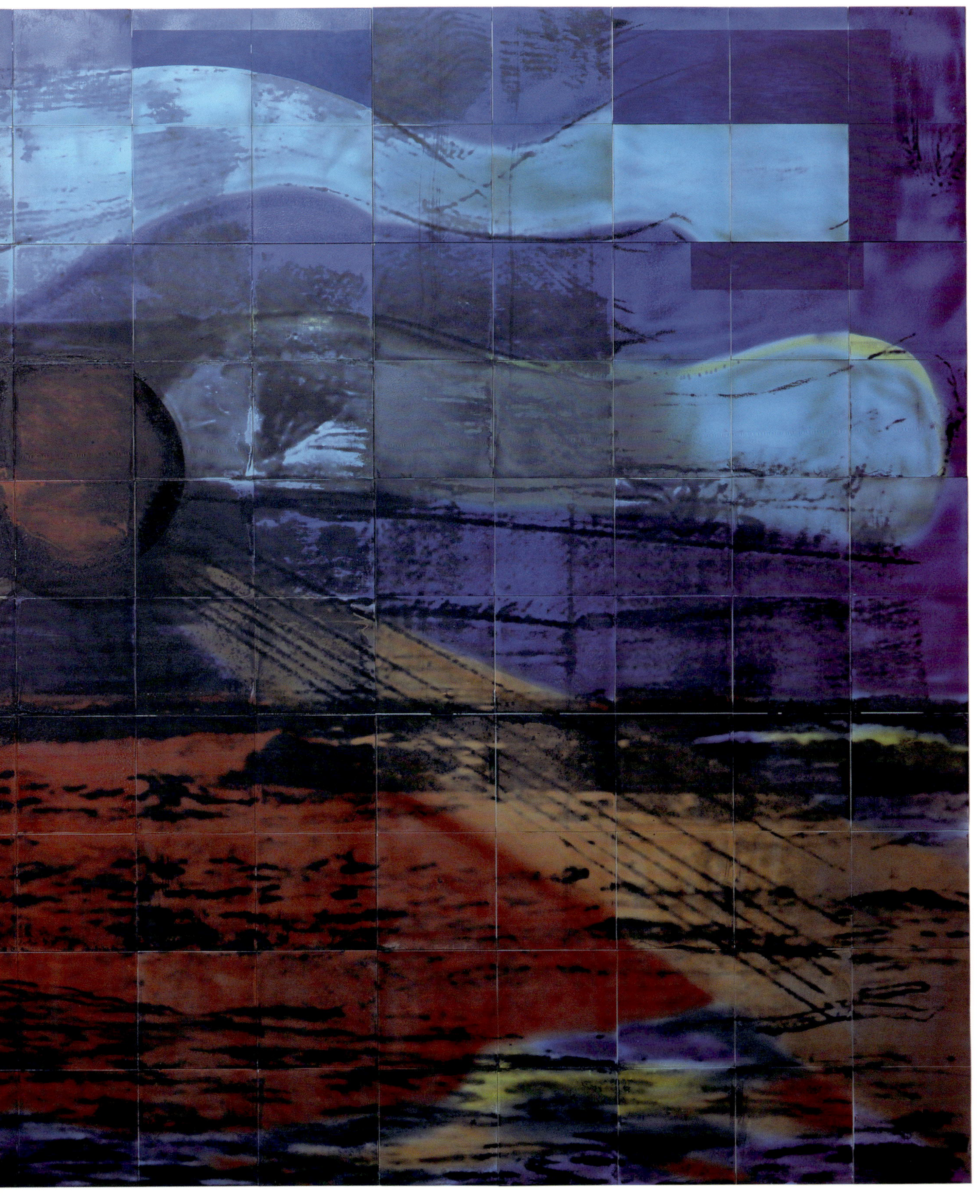

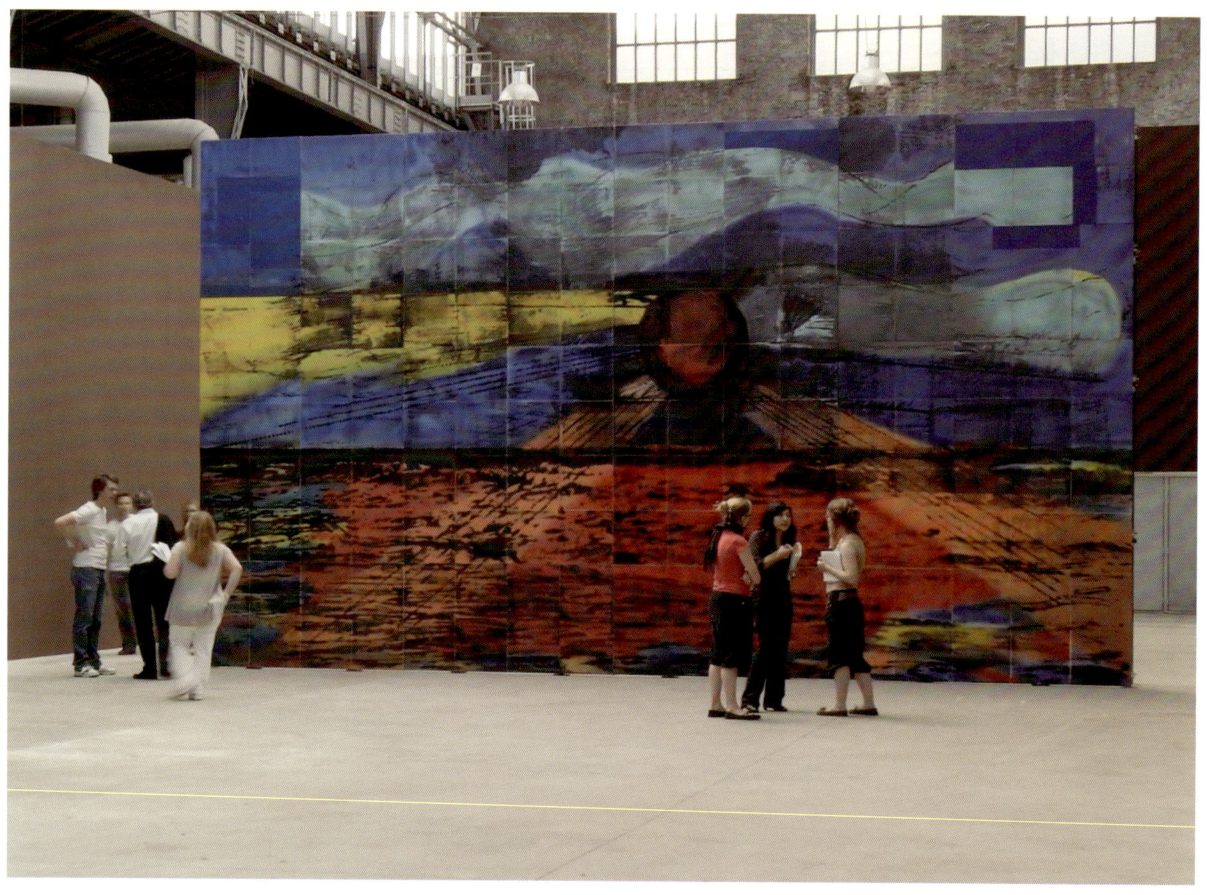

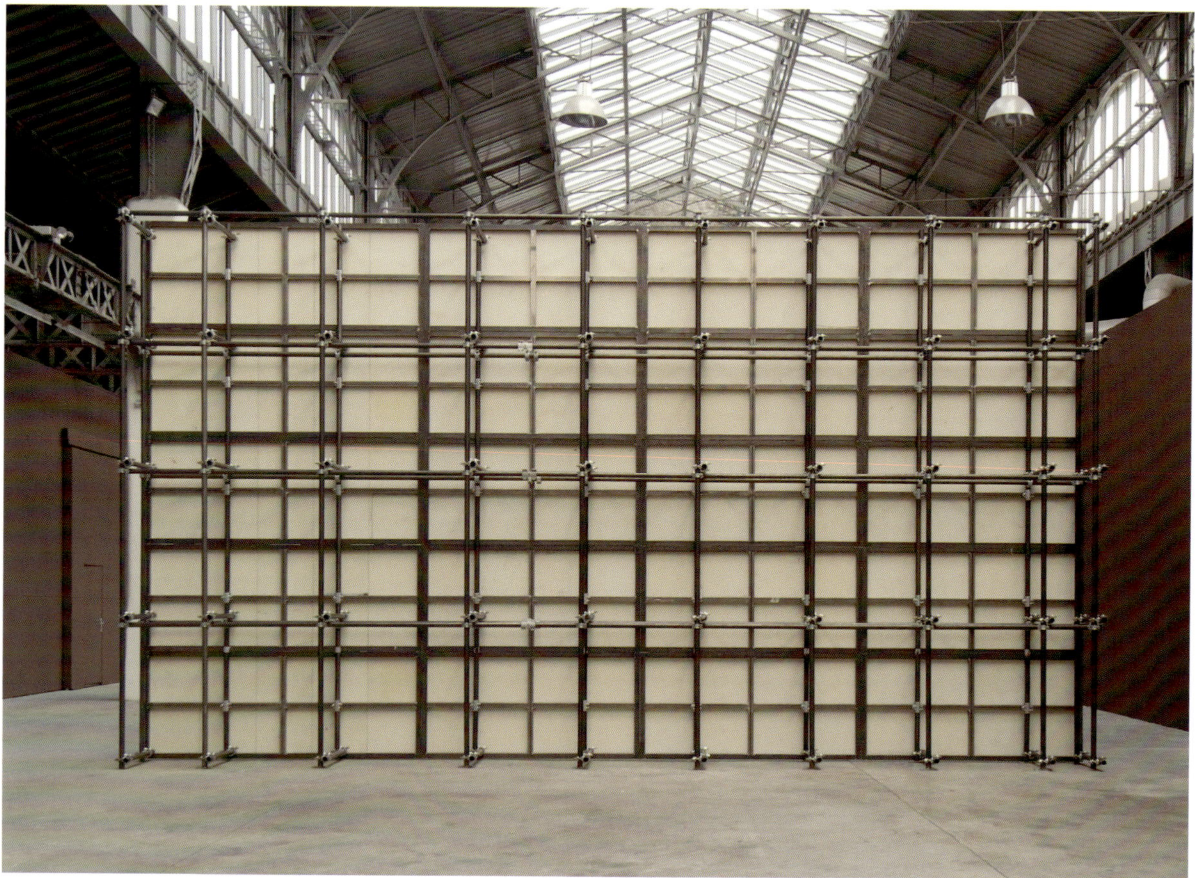

ANDRO WEKUA
above top and above, rear view:
Sunset 2008
Installation of 170 glazed ceramic panels, metal framework, steel scaffolding
500 x 800 x 82 cm

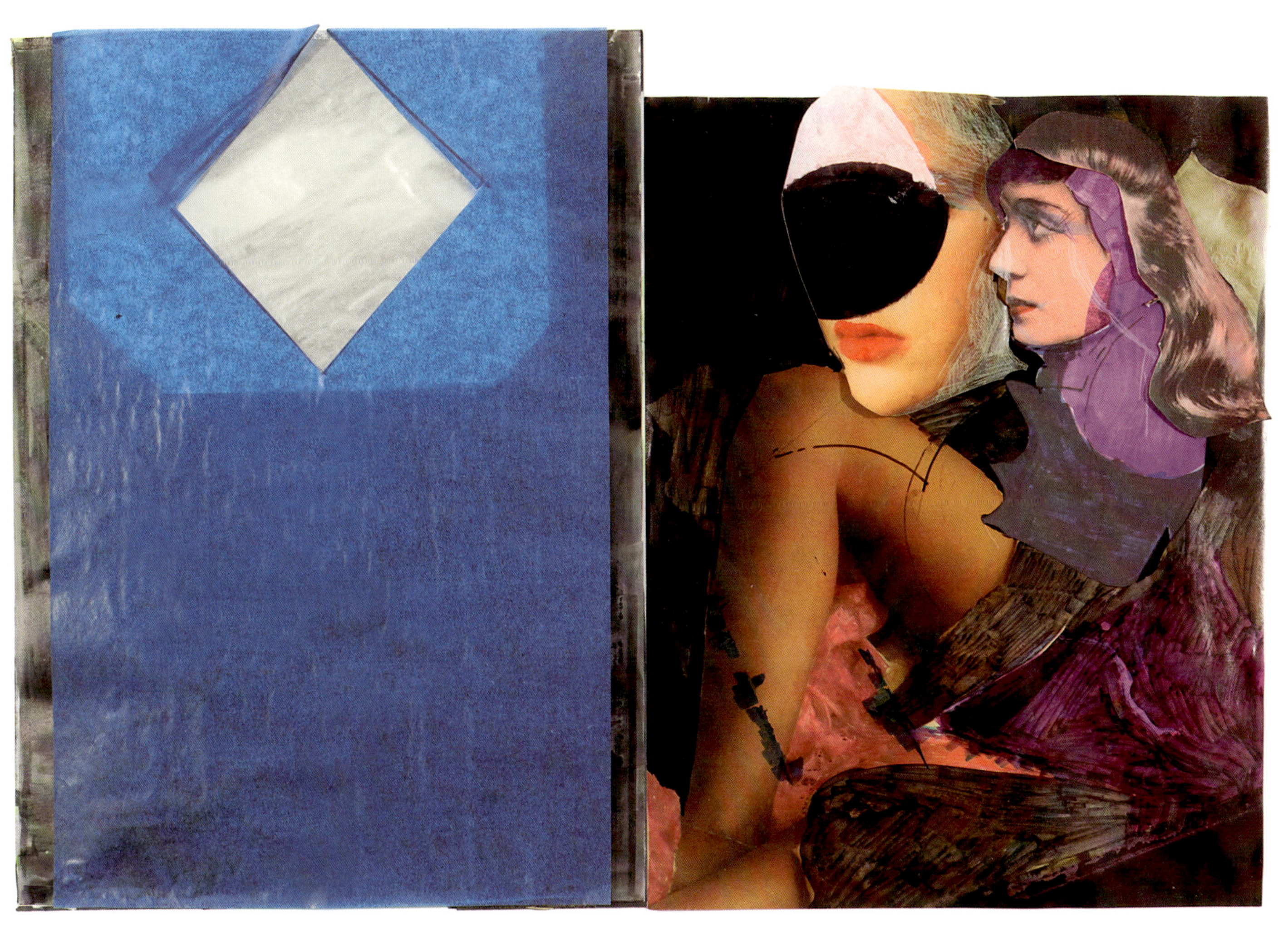

ANDRO WEKUA
Covered 2006
Collage, silver foil, tissue paper, colour pencil and felt pen on illustration
36.6 x 48.2 cm

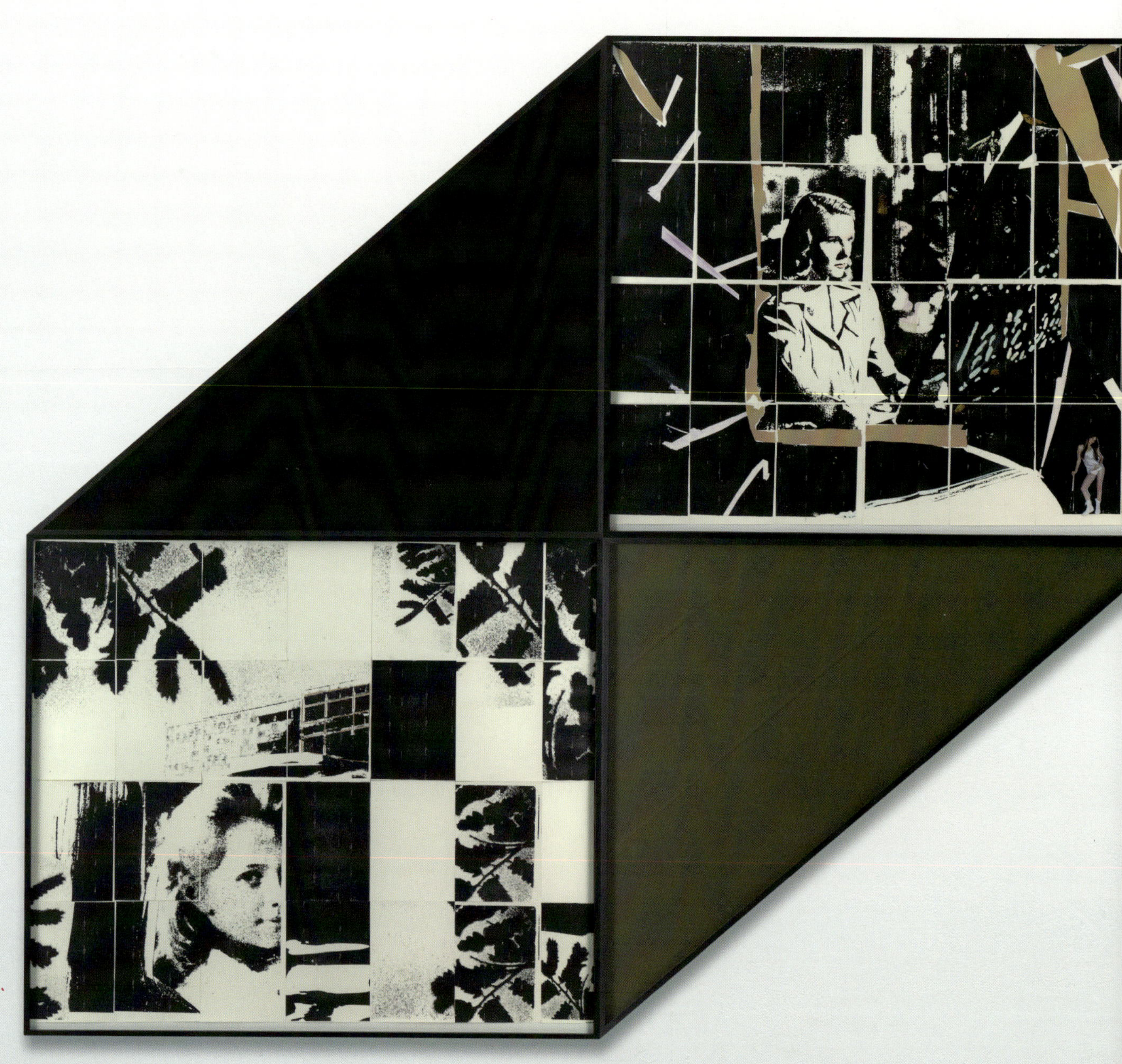

ANDRO WEKUA
Black Sea Surfer 2004
Installation in 7 parts with 3 collages, colour pencil, pencil and felt pen on paper, four fabrics (velours)
175 x 200 x 265 (Overall 3.5 x 8m)

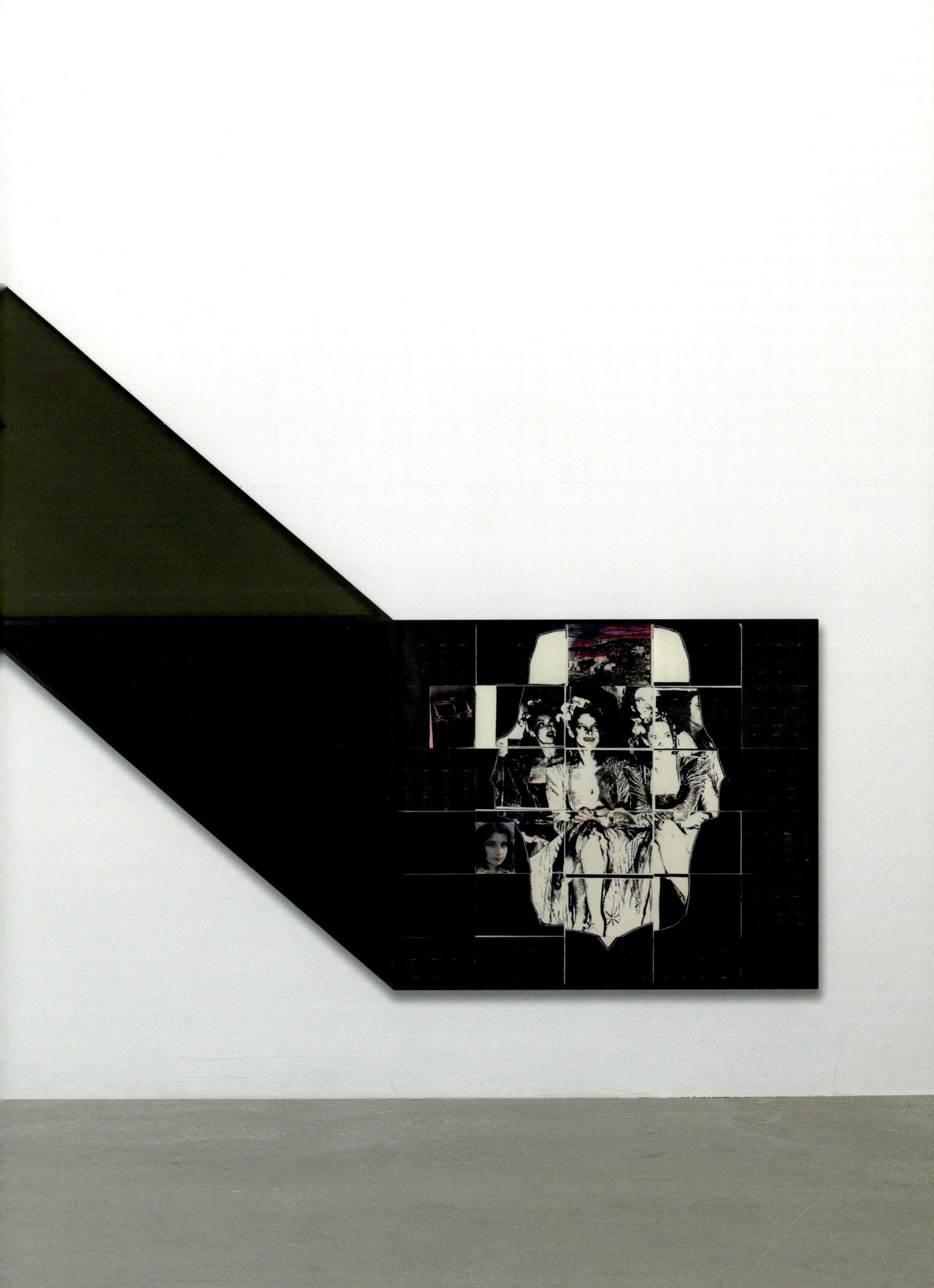

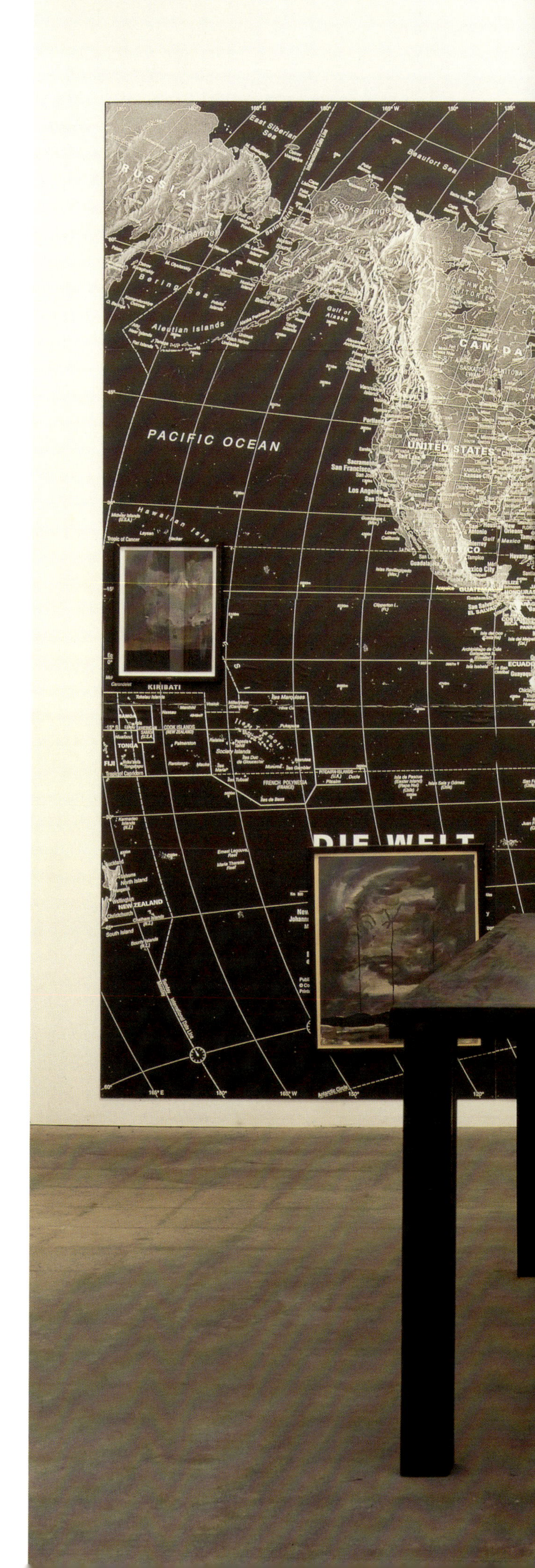

THOMAS ZIPP
World Kantzler Office 2004
Mixed media
300 x 400 x 250 cm

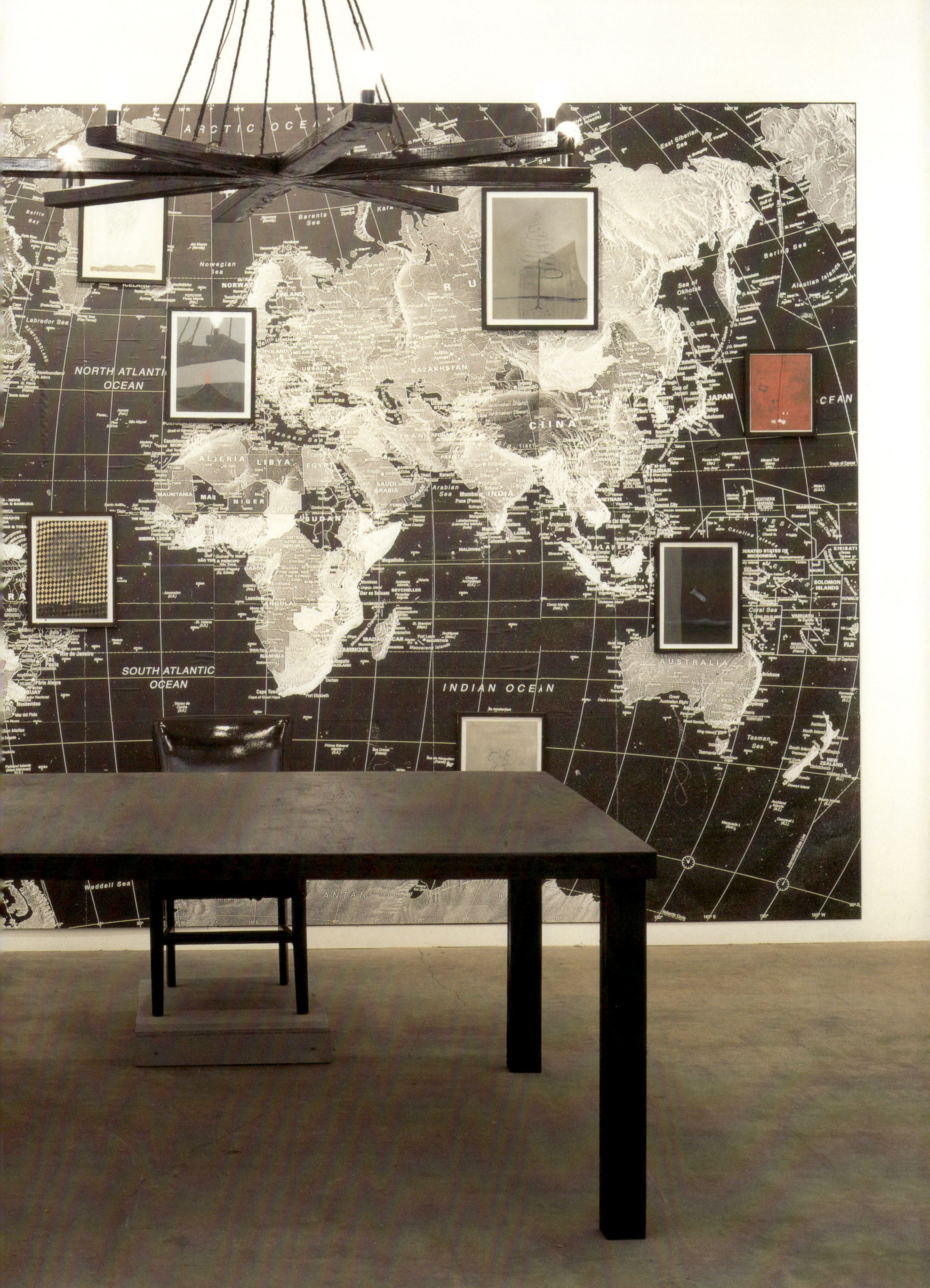

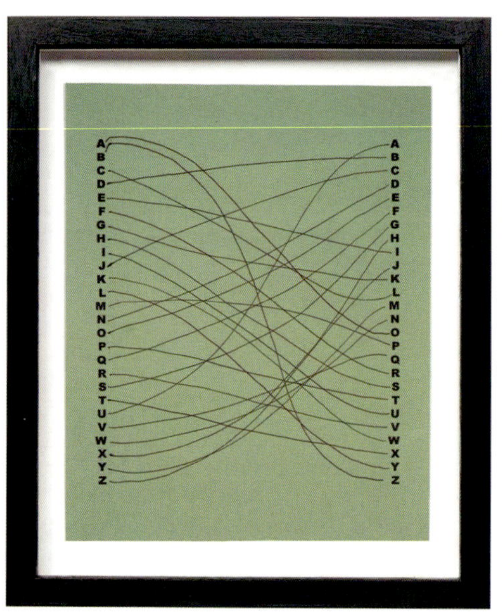

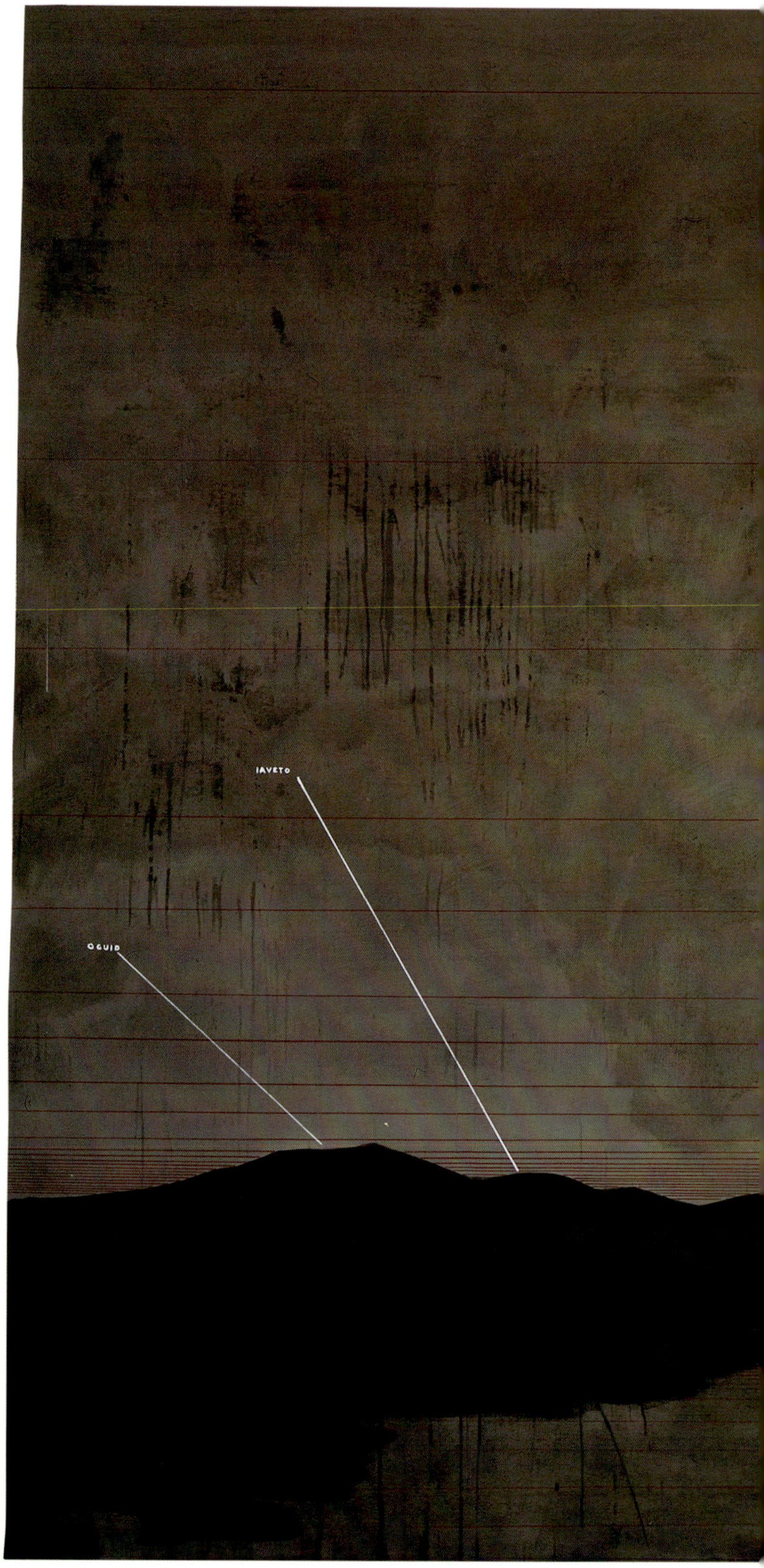

THOMAS ZIPP
A.B.:H.G.:B.16. 2005
Acrylic and oil on canvas, mixed media
Two parts: 280 x 400 cm / 42 x 32 cm

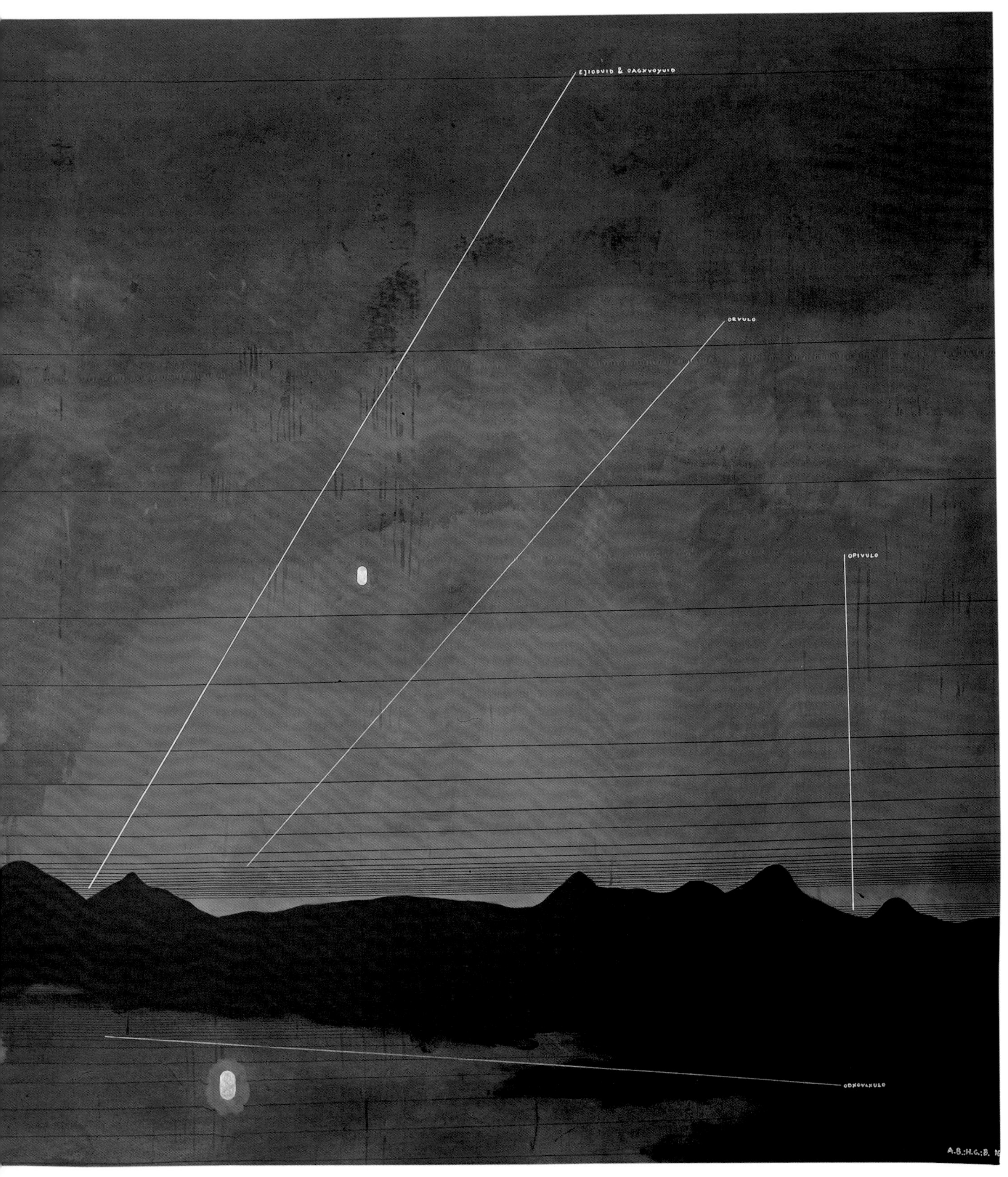
EJIODVID & DAGKVOYUID
ORVULO
OPIVULO
ODKOVAKULO
A.B.:H.G.:B.

THOMAS ZIPP
Der Schlaf IV (Y-Drops) 2006
Acrylic and oil on muslin, mixed media, chandelier
Three parts: 250 x 340 cm / 32 x 27 cm / 166 x 155 cm

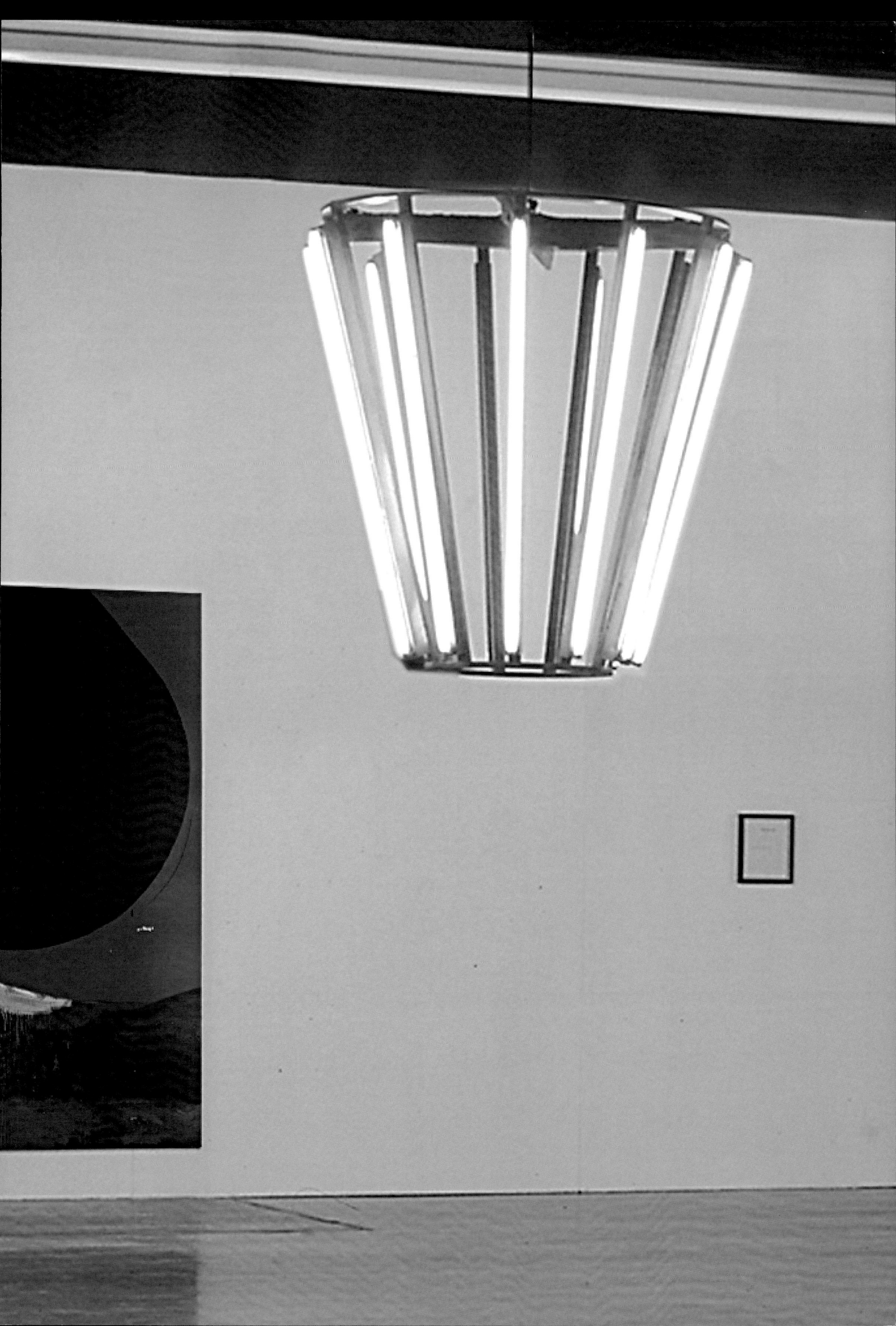

THOMAS ZIPP
E-Licht 2006
Acrylic and oil on canvas, mixed media
Three parts: 250 x 340 cm / 160 x 200 cm / 32 x 27 cm

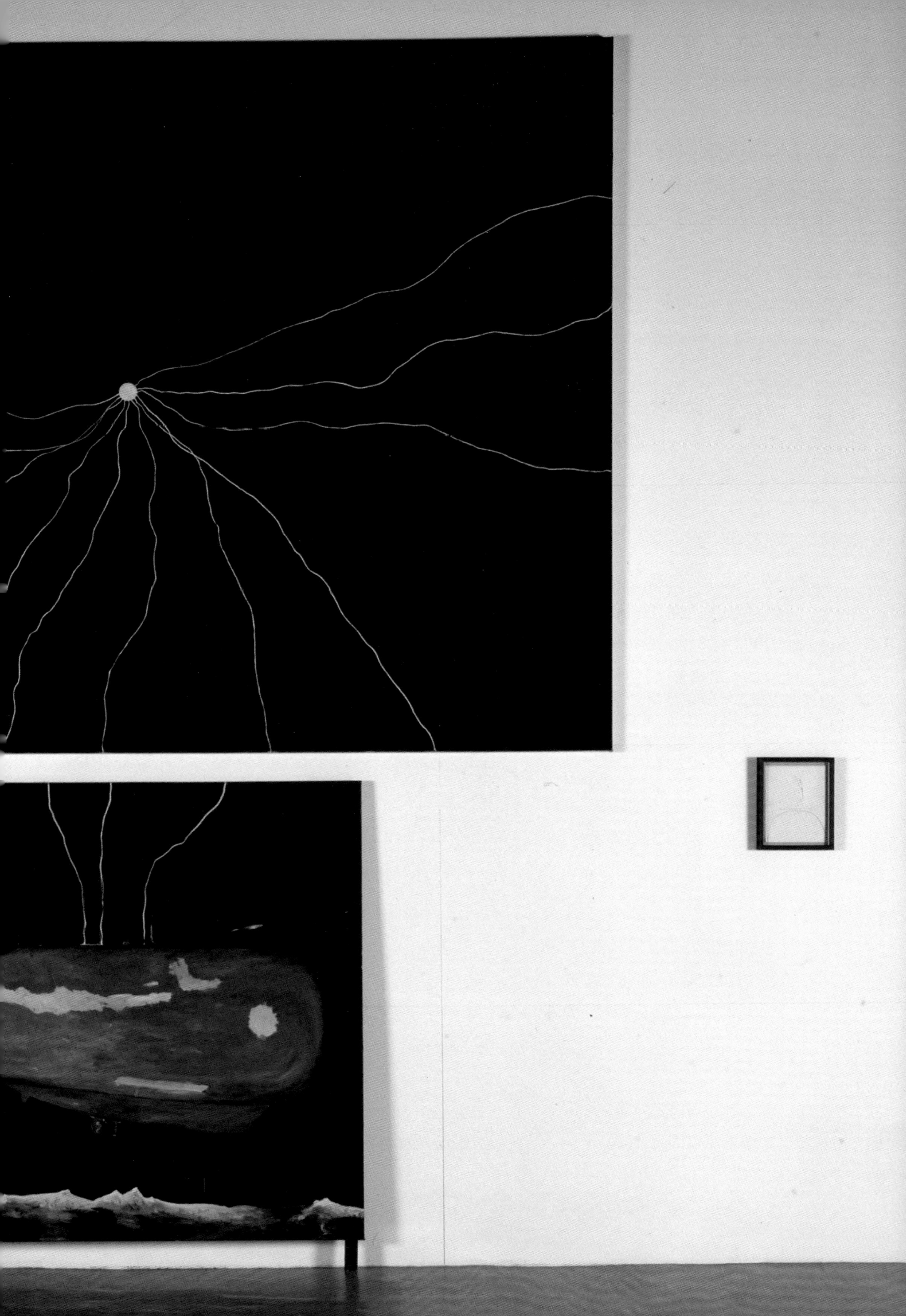

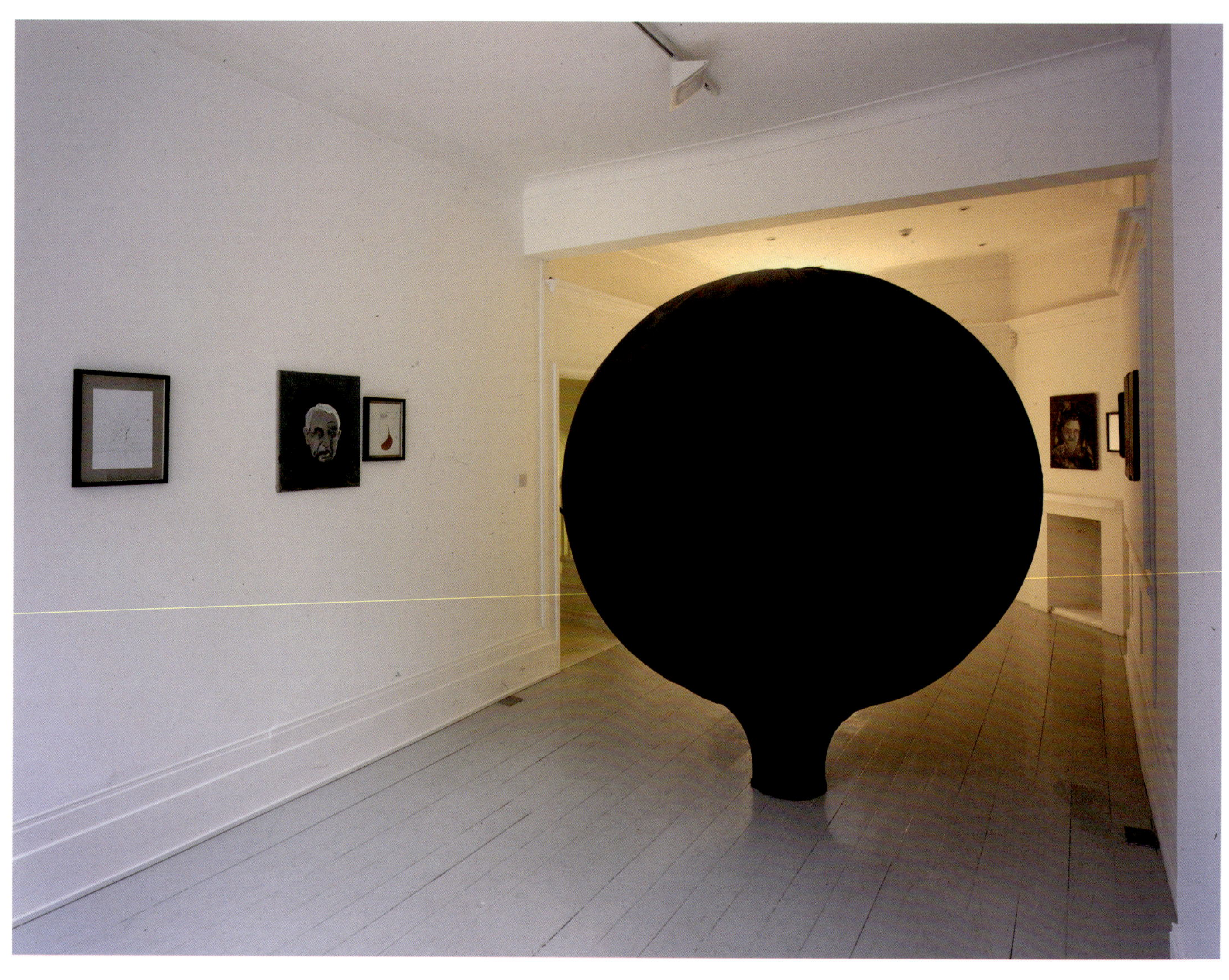

THOMAS ZIPP
above and right:
Schwarze Ballons (1. down, 2. up, 3. S.K., 4a. tumb…tumb…,
4b.ABCE, 5. little U-light, 6. L.E.M., 7. O.E., 8. Elektrizitait) 2005
Installation in nine parts, mixed media
Dimensions variable

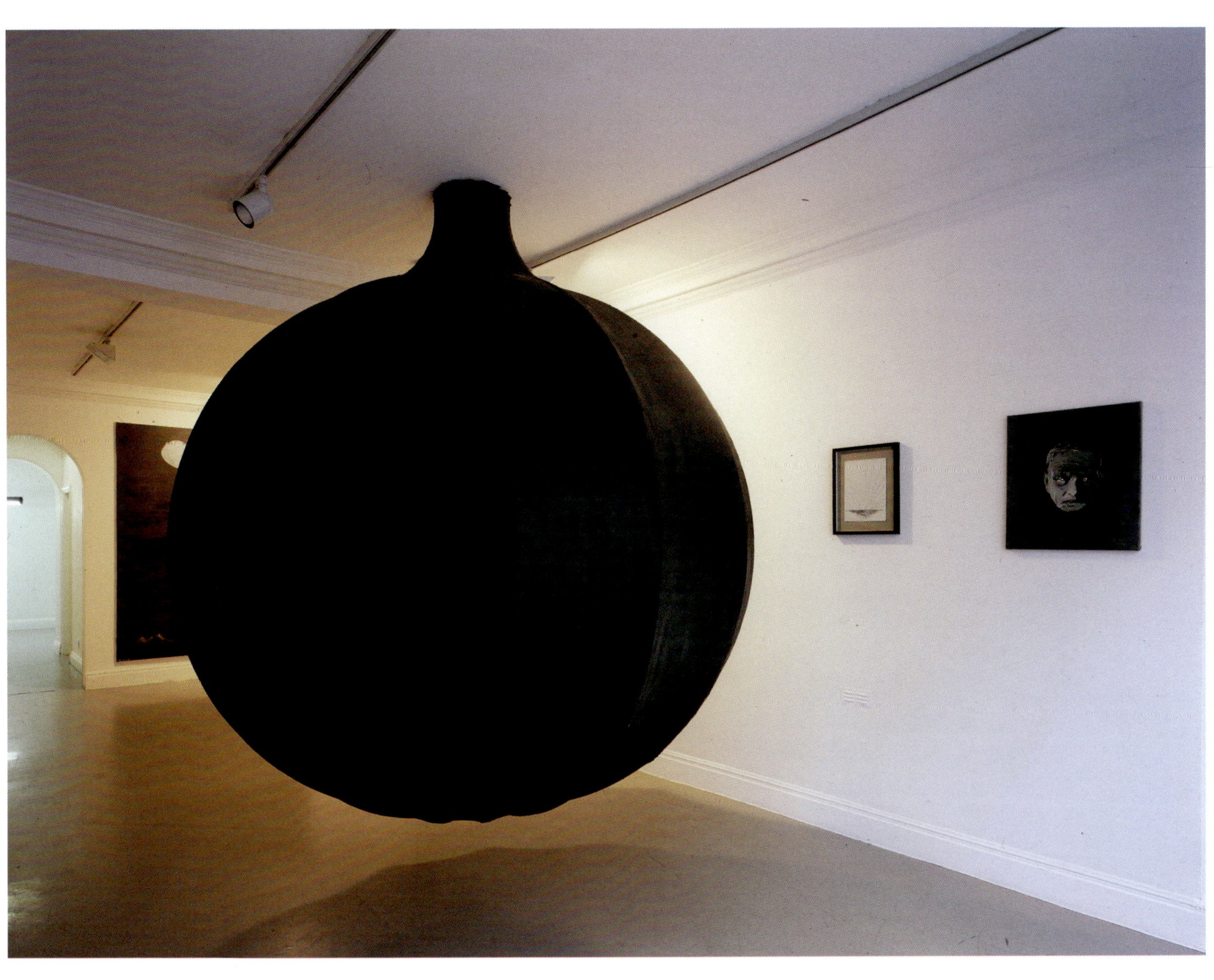

DIRK BELL

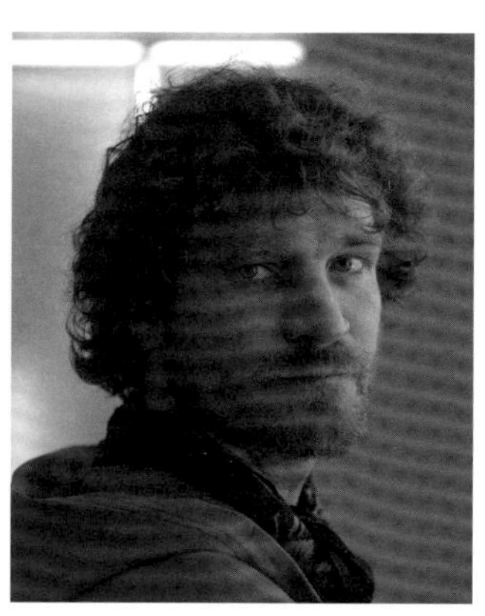

Dirk Bell was born in Munich in 1969. Over the last decade he has had solo shows at Sadie Coles HQ, London, The Modern Institute, Glasgow, Gavin Brown's enterprise, New York, and most recently at the Pinakothek der Moderne in Munich. He lives in Berlin.

Dirk Bell's intimate figurative drawings and paintings unveil a new way of depicting and perceiving sensuality, like an evanescent but still present memory. In works such as the delicate *Rabbit's Moon* (2007), with its illusion of a watery craquelure all over its surface, and the darker, more violently rendered *Wolf Hamlet Madonna Elmex* (2006), the artist revisits traditional genres and compositions – the *memento mori* still life, the symbolic representation of the human figure – filtering and compressing art historical references with a contemporary sense of dismantlement and disintegration.

The pictures within the frame of *Rabbit's Moon*, depicting posing figures, illustrations in books, and other less easily identifiable shapes, are on the same illusory plane as the skull, glass of wine, bottle and ashtray next to which they stand, and contain the same visually hallucinogenic power.

In the limb-plagued *Wolf Hamlet Madonna Elmex*, two figures, one holding the other, are set against a background full of multiple marks suggesting motion. The exact meaning of the work, which is more explicit viscerally than *Rabbit's Moon,* is as impenetrable as similarly gestural prehistoric cave paintings.

Nowhere is Bell's embracing call for a new kind of ungraspable but overpowering figurative sensuality proposed more clearly than in *Abgrund (Abyss)* (2008). A naked figure, painted in soft brushwork and installed under a neon light, is partly revealed by a half-drawn lace curtain. A ledge running along the bottom of the frame holds broken mirror shards and charred pieces of bone. A certain frustration hovers over the work. *Abyss*, Bell explains, 'marks a point of no return… The mirror shards can be used to look into fragments of the future, whereas the past as well as memory are spread out before one's eyes and can be looked at… The cindered bones are relics of a picnic at the roadside…The whole scenery can be veiled by the curtain.'

ALEXANDRA BIRCKEN

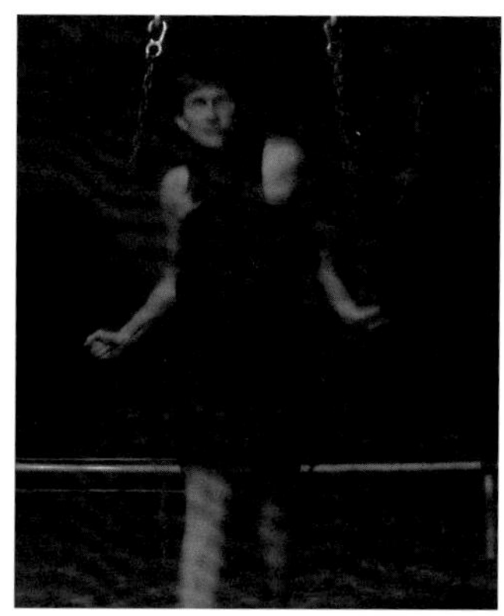

Alexandra Bircken was born in Cologne in 1967. Since graduating from Central Saint Martin's College of Art and Design, London, she has had solo shows at Herald Street, London, BQ, Cologne, BQ, Berlin, Gladstone Gallery, New York, and the Stedelijk Museum, Amsterdam. Her work was presented by Herald Street at Art Basel's Art Statements in 2007. She lives in Cologne.

Alexandra Bircken's unmonumental stretcher frame sculptures are informed by her background in fashion design and interest in the radical aspects of handmade culture. A fragmentary array of irregular objects and organic shapes, often coloured by the artist, is hung and displayed on strings and aluminium rods.

Embedded and held aloft as if on a weaver's loom, lowly materials such as found tree trunks, slices of Styrofoam, building offcuts and thin cloth swatches (seen in *Unit 1*, *Unit 3* and *Unit 4*, all 2008) are reincarnated as a new kind of artwork, twisting traditional painting and sculpture into icons of vernacular art and craft.

Drape (2007) weaves coloured rags in and out of twigs and uneven cut branches creating a precarious stretcher. Although the wooden structure appears fairly random in its design, the ends have been carefully sealed with red wax as if to point to a purposeful intention. This imperfection and unpolished uniqueness is the very source of its beauty.

The detritus, wool, reedy trunks and rags that find their way into Bircken's grids are reminiscent of the temporary architectures and all-incorporating make-do of alternative communities on the margins of mainstream society. The weaving and crafting involved in her method additionally brings to mind 1960s and '70s feminist art politics.

When shown together, her works can appear as a radical lifestyle *Gesamtkunstwerk*. 'I am interested in dismantling prevailing hierarchies of value regarding these objects and materials by way of connecting them, thus putting them in a new context to each other. It's an alternative system or cycle.'

ANDRÉ BUTZER

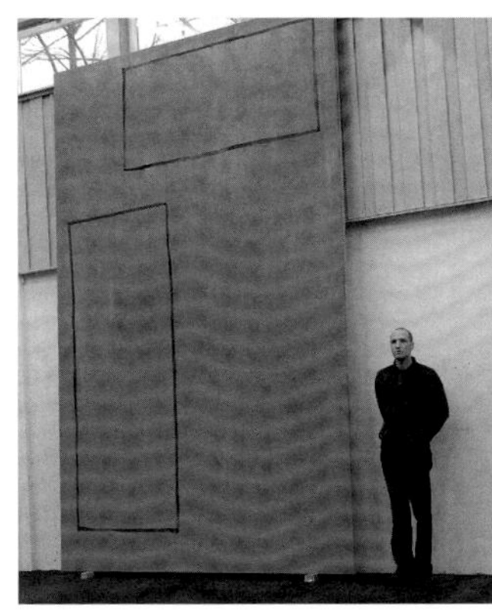

André Butzer was born in Stuttgart in 1973. He has had solo shows at Metro Pictures, New York, Alison Jacques, London, Galerie Christine Mayer, Munich, Galerie Max Hetzler, Berlin and Guido W Baudach, Berlin. In 2009 he had a mid-career survey at Kunsthalle Nürnberg. He was one of a group of Hamburg artists who founded the art school Akademie Isotrop in Hamburg in 1996. He lives in Rangsdorf, near Berlin.

André Butzer's mural-like canvases are a compression of painting's recent history in all its totality, animated by the artist's trademark anarchic visual codes. *Ahnenbild 2411* (2006) is overrun with a roughly executed, psychedelic use of colour and the frantic repetition of a hollow-eyed mask, at turns grinning like early twentieth-century cartoons or expressing ugliness and terror à la Munch's *Scream* or de Kooning's *Woman* paintings.

The whole composition brings to mind the rambunctious street art references in Basquiat's abstractions and the dark symbolism of James Ensor's grotesque carnival of covered faces. The juxtaposition of American pop art gestures and German Expressionism conveys an angst and horror at the consumerism and globalisation of post-war and contemporary culture. That the painting's title means 'ancestral portrait' is also a clue to the work's subtext, a jaw-dropping, unstoppable regurgitation of the modalities of its medium.

The repetition of the same exaggerated, anxious faces and unmasked pleasure in the physical act of painting appears in two works named *Untitled* (both 2007). A sense of urgent immediacy is articulated through their high impasto technique and vivid, almost neon-toned colours. Butzer doodles wildly over dark or light backgrounds in separated, unblended clusters, reminiscent of Joan Mitchell's abstract expressionist canvases. His embrace of an unapologetically bright and varied paint box is conceptual: 'Colour is basically about history. To animate colour is historic in the way that the image will tell us about the future and the past.'

Three other *Untitled* works (all 2007), which also combine abstraction with figuration, explore similar ideas but through a much more restrained, almost greyscale palette. Their pared-down unfilled faux naïve geometric shapes recall surrealist compositions and Cy Twombly's accumulated mark-making. Equally romantic and nihilistic, the artist has described these works as 'the kind of things Donald Duck would do when he paints'.

ZHIVAGO DUNCAN

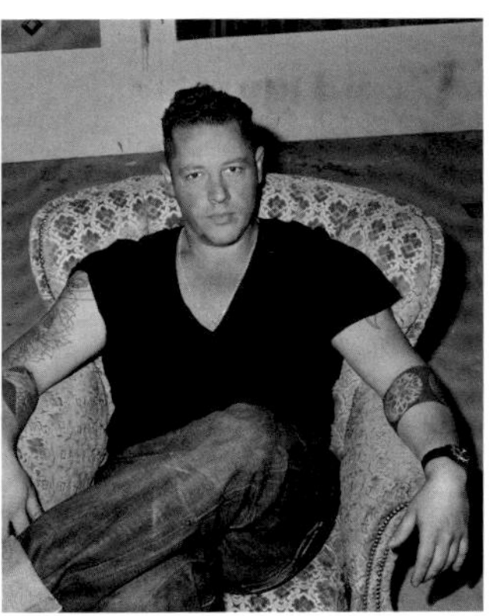

Zhivago Duncan was born in Terre Haute, Indiana, US in 1980. Since graduating in 2007 from the Chelsea College of Art and Design, London, he has had solo shows at CFA, Berlin, Cruise & Callas, Berlin, Teapot, Cologne, and Private Loft of Shelley von Strunckel, London. He lives in Berlin.

Through his sprawling, messy multimedia artworks, Zhivago Duncan comments on the state of contemporary culture and its obsessions, crassly quoted and re-created from an irreversibly apocalyptic future point of view. The work shown here was part of a recent exhibition entitled 'Dick Flash's Souvenirs of Thought' in which viewers were taken on a journey into the meaning of the senseless remains that might fill a time to come.

The artist explains: '*Pretentious Crap* (2010-2011) is the result of the imaginary journey of Dick Flash, the world's sole survivor of the apocalypse according to him and his legacy. Semi-amnesiac, Dick Flash roams the converted world digging up the fruitful remains of his debauched ancestors. Without any recollection of his personal past, Dick Flash does, however, experience moments of epiphany, in which abstract notions of the origin of self, a collective memory, and the accumulated trials and tribulations of humanity are vaguely delineated, as revealed to him in prophetic visions.'

This work is one of Dick Flash's relics from his journey, a cabinet in which former art objects are reinterpreted as mysterious ruins. It's as if Flash is re-writing the history of culture through his chaotic assemblages, starting from scratch, like an artist, taking on an *Übermensch* persona.

'With no memory of his former life, Dick Flash naturally rediscovers his affinity for physics, kinetic energy, and his predisposition for philosophical reflection. By repurposing found scraps of metal and steel, the skeletons of automobiles and locomotives that have somehow withstood civilization's destruction, and random matter once considered waste that has ironically survived its very creator, Dick Flash fabricates a new iconography, commemorating his interpretation of an extinct empire and its tragically flawed constituents.'

IDA EKBLAD

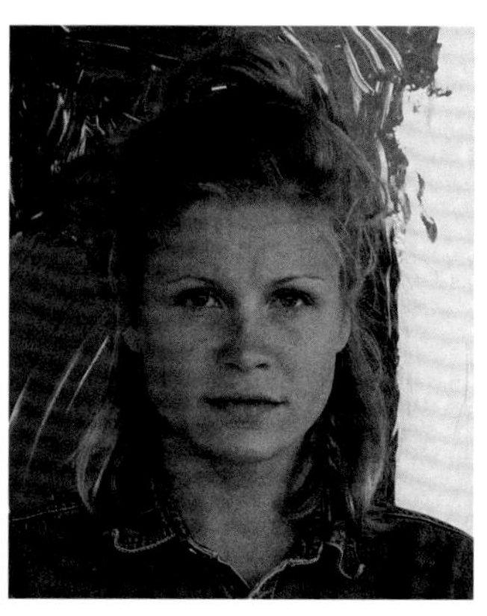

Ida Ekblad was born in Oslo in 1980 and studied at Central Saint Martin's, London, the National Academy of Art, Oslo and the Mountain School of Art, Los Angeles. She has had solo shows at Herald Street, London, Bonniers Konsthall, Stockholm, Galerie Giti Nourbakhsch, Berlin, and has an upcoming solo show at Greene Naftali, New York. Her work was featured in ILLUMInations at the 54th Venice Biennale, 2011. She lives in Oslo and Berlin.

Ida Ekblad's chance-based art practice is a literal reflection of her peripatetic methodology, a special kind of no-holds-barred urban folk art. The production of her sculptures, paintings, music and poetry revolves around 'drifts' taken around the cities in which she will be making the work. Like a scavenger on a mission to extract essential, survival sustenance out of the discarded remains of contemporary culture, Ekblad collects materials on her walks, sifting through piles of rubble from demolished buildings and industrial heaps of metal.

Her resulting works are exquisitely vibrant, free-associative compositions pairing dissonance with visual inventiveness. She displays a prodigious and playful imagination, referencing the visual language of fellow 'drifters', the Situationists or the expressionism of CoBrA painters such as Asger Jorn.

Some of her works, such as *Banging, Dubbed, The L, The LL, The Lapis Lazuli, Night Ocean Return Without and Without Hesitate* (all 2010), could almost be called concrete poems – collected refuse objects have been literally embedded into wet panels of the material, finished with an inscription of the artist's initials at the bottom, nodding to mark-making on actual street art. Similarly, in her sculpture *Loops* (2010) discarded scraps of metal have been planted in a concrete pedestal. The heaviness of these pieces contrasts with the delicacy and refined balance of *Figurine with Horns*, *Tennessee Hills* and *Organ Invention* (all 2010), abstract shapes that somehow find completion in the artist's ambiguous titles.

There is something sci-fi and post-apocalyptic about Ekblad's embrace and presentation of what is essentially humanity's waste. Equally, there's an explosive sense of future-retro abstract centripetal release, seen for example in *Stalk Gills And Caps Of Goodbye* (2009), *Dusty Dry On The Tongue Swallowed Some* and *To Drink a Glass of Melted Snow* (both 2010). 'Painting to me combines expressions of rhythm, poetry, scent, emotion… It offers ways to articulate the spaces between words, and I cannot be concerned with its death, when working at it makes me feel so alive.'

MAX FRISINGER

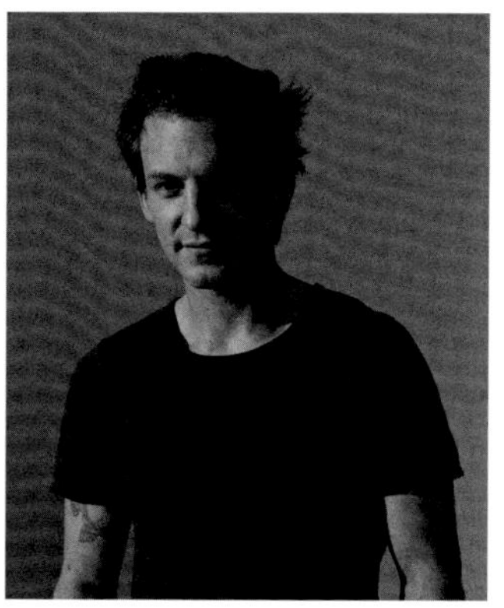

Max Frisinger was born in Bremen in 1980 and studied at the University of Fine Arts, Hamburg. He has had solo shows at CFA, Berlin, and Galerie Katharina Bittel, Hamburg, and has been presented by CFA, Berlin at Art Basel in Miami Beach, Frieze, London, FIAC, Paris and Art Forum, Berlin. He lives in Hamburg.

Max Frisinger's raised glass cases – assemblages crammed with found material – are witty visual paradoxes, governed by a dual sense of cacophony and order. They demand careful observation, with each side like an entry point, revealing a different topography made up of found scraps – metal, wood, tubing, table legs, plastic tubs, offcuts and other broken designs – all random-looking but somehow perfectly framed around each other and their spatial limitations.

Frisinger's works juxtapose apparent chaos with a careful sense of arrangement, and flirt with an art historical understanding of perspective, representation and abstraction. Depending on the viewer's point of view, the objects within these three-dimensional boxes may appear to be independent from each other, or unified and flattened, like abstract paintings.

Noah's Ark (CocoRosie) (2010), a vitrine chock full of mismatched shapes, is striking for the complex imagery that rises out of its superimposed objects and the gaps left between them. *Rising (Yoko Ono)* (2010) shows a somewhat axial arrangement suggesting kineticism despite its crammed, unquestionably static nature.

When asked about his works and the development of his practice, Frisinger simply states: *'inveni, vidi, vici'* ('I found, I saw, I conquered'). His assemblages can be seen to be making reference to the tradition of refuse-based art, recycling detritus to comment on the society of excess. Looming over Frisinger's new time-capsules of the everyday are the ghosts of found-object sculptures by Marcel Duchamp and Jean Tinguely, Arman's 'accumulations' and Daniel Spoerri's 'snare pictures', as well as a poetic playfulness, somewhere between Joseph Cornell and the musical, performative improvisation of Fluxus.

But Frisinger's boxes, like portable, flat-pack dumpsters, contain not just a nod to the past, but an up-to-date comment on our current culture of waste and excess in society in general but perhaps also within the art world.

ISA GENZKEN

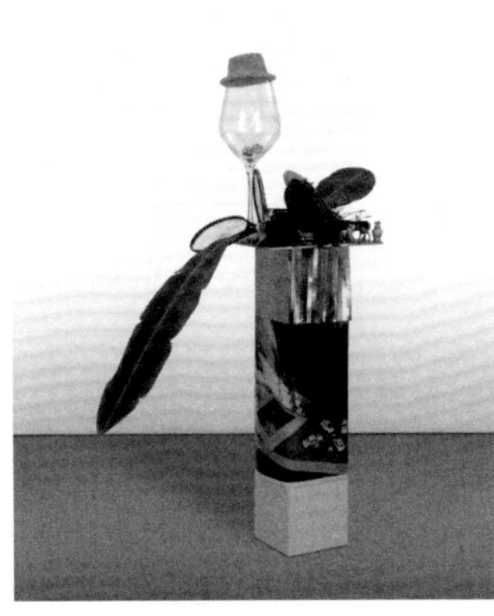

Isa Genzken was born in Bad Oldesloe, Germany in 1948. Her most recent solo shows have been with Hauser & Wirth, London, Galerie Daniel Buchholz, Berlin, Galerie Chantal Crousel, Paris and David Zwirner, New York. She has had museum shows at the Whitechapel Art Gallery, London and Museum Ludwig Köln. She represented Germany at the 2007 Venice Biennale. She lives in Berlin.

Isa Genzken's totemic sculptures, colourful mirrored panels and lacquered paintings articulate the artist's mysterious method. Harvesting, fusing and re-constructing references from myriad sources, she takes an anything-goes approach to the materials she uses to convey multiple meanings in unexpected ways.

Her practice is mostly three-dimensional but it also embraces photography, video, film and collage, the latter finding its way into her sculptures as well as wall-based works, as part of her investigation of the way we create and read images and objects.

In *Kinder Filmen* (2005) mirrored panels, covered in a chaotic collage of adhesive tape, magazine and book pages, lacquer and spray paint, create an illusion of space, drawing attention to the power of art to subvert our preconceptions. They are suggestive of architectural façades and the information overload of urban experience.

Genzken's *MLR* painting series (1992), which the artist has said references the work of the nineteenth-century artist Hilda of Klimt, depicts gymnast's rings frozen moments after their release in mid-air. The images invite the viewer to ponder the symbolic, allegorical act of letting go.

The oversized fake leaves and giant wine glass dominate *Urlaub* (2004), inviting a surrealist-tinged, free-associative interpretation. *Bouquet* (2004) is a comically uptight version of a beautiful, excessive still life as well as a memorial to modernist form. The combine plinth of *Mutter Mit Kind* (2004) creates an almost sacred altar-like space, bringing together religious and minimalist symbols. *Geschwister* and *Untitled* (both 2004) juxtapose found objects into, respectively, a recognisable shape and a non-utilitarian re-purposing to provoke questions around given material meaning. Built around traditional notions of narrative and form, these works suggest a crudeness and frailty behind what has been human-made.

It is for these kinds of assemblages exploring the tension between open and precise meaning that Genzken is best known. As she says, 'There is nothing worse in art than, "you see it and you know it"… That's a certainty I don't like.'

FELIX GMELIN

Felix Gmelin was born in Heidelberg in 1962. Since graduating from the Royal University College of Fine Art, Stockholm in 1988 he has had solo shows at Portikus, Frankfurt, Gasworks, London and Malmö Konstmuseum, Malmö. He has participated twice in the Venice Biennale in 2007 and 2003, in the October Salon, Belgrade, and the Berlin Biennial, both in 2006. He lives in Stockholm.

Pablo Picasso once said, 'for me, an image is the sum of destructions.' Felix Gmelin, an artist based in Stockholm and Berlin, explores this defining idea from a rather literal angle – in a series of works he made for an exhibition entitled 'Art Vandals' which focus on the creative energy latent within acts of revolutionary destruction. Gmelin reproduces artworks that have literally been destroyed in public spaces, including galleries and museums, in order to examine and question traditional notions of history versus what actually constitutes historical truth.

In his painting *Kill Lies All After Pablo Picasso (1937) and Tony Shafrazi (1974)* (1996), Gmelin reminds viewers of a famous example of art vandalism – the defacement of Picasso's *Guernica* by an angry young artist, Tony Shafrazi, now a famous New York art dealer, who spray painted 'Kill Lies All' over it in red.

'I wanted to bring the art absolutely up to date, to retrieve it from art history and give it life. Maybe that's why the *Guernica* action remains so difficult to deal with. I tried to trespass beyond that invisible barrier that no one is allowed to cross,' Shafrazi has explained. The ravages of war depicted in the painting serve as the background for his indicting statement on the contingency of history as it is constructed.

Perhaps Picasso, who once painted over works by Modigliani, would agree with Shafrazi's point of view, but the art historical establishment certainly doesn't – the Museum of Modern Art staff quickly removed all the damage from *Guernica*, essentially updating the act of iconoclasm over another artist's work themselves. 'By turning Picasso's *Guernica* into a masterpiece', Gmelin explains, 'the museum helps to make the picture historic, thereby rendering it invisible in the present.'

JEPPE HEIN

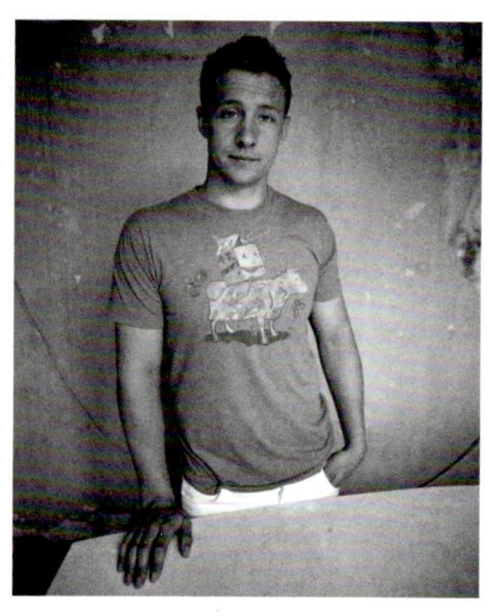

Jeppe Hein was born in Copenhagen in 1974. Since studying at the Royal Danish Academy of Arts, Copenhagen and the Städel Hochschule für Bildende Künste, Frankfurt, he has had solo shows at Johann König, Berlin, 303 Gallery, New York and the Museum Nürnberg. He has an upcoming solo show at the 21st Century Museum of Contemporary Art, Kanazawa. He lives in Copenhagen and Berlin.

Imbuing technology with an element of surprise and humour, Jeppe Hein's interactive works playfully remind viewers of their vital part in activating art's communicative potential. At first glance Hein's sculptures appear to be uncomplicated, formally simple affairs possibly nodding to 1970s conceptual art and minimalism, but something happens as they are approached: they react to human presence.

Shaking Cube (2004), an aluminium box placed directly on the floor, starts to vibrate when a visitor goes near it, stopping after a few seconds only to begin trembling again if the invisible field of motion sensors around it is entered again. We know it's not alive, but it makes us take another look. Its sudden frantic movement and noise have a somewhat slapstick quality – think wind-up chattering teeth – but its animation is also disquieting, automaton-like, as if expressing alarm, a warning about something we cannot understand.

Something similar happens when visitors get close to *Mirror Wall* (2010). What at first appears to be a large but straightforward mirror begins to move slightly when approached. Viewing one's vibrating reflection in it and the accompanying distorted backdrop of the gallery space creates a sense of dizziness and a strange feeling of separation from the familiar. It prompts us instinctively to re-calibrate our spatial awareness and our relationship to what we see and where we are.

Hein's experiential, perceptual magic tricks are his vehicle for raising engagement between art and its audience. He makes work that can only be experienced through participation, expanding our notion of what art is or could be. 'For me, the concept of sculpture is closely linked with communication… By challenging the physical attention of the viewer, an active dialogue between artwork, surrounding and other visitors is established that lends the sculpture a social quality.'

THOMAS HELBIG

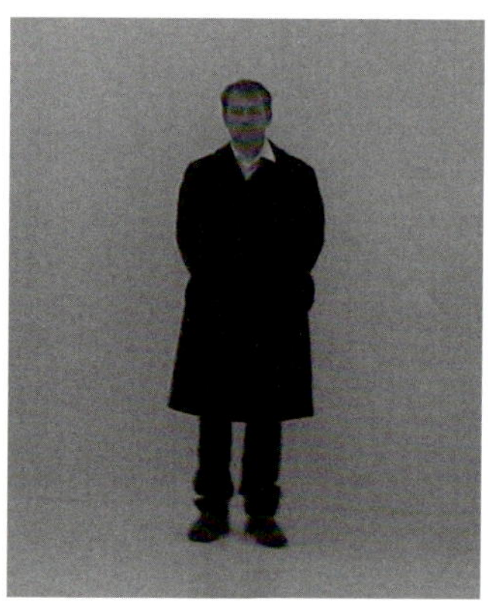

Thomas Helbig was born in Rosenheim, Germany in 1967. He attended the Royal Academy of Fine Arts, Munich and Goldsmiths, University of London. He has had solo shows at Galerie Guido W. Baudach, Berlin, Vilma Gold, London, China Art Projects, Los Angeles, Jiri Swestka, Prague, Galerie Rüdiger Schöttle, Munich and Bortolami Gallery, New York. He lives in Berlin.

Thomas Helbig's precisely composed, semi-abstract paintings provoke a feeling of confusion and fascination in the viewer. The soft, muted geometric shapes and colours that stretch and blur over the surface of his wooden panels look slightly adrift, as if in the process of emerging from a backdrop of uncertainty, rife with possibility.

Helbig has said that his paintings 'are about reduction to an unrecognisable state from which something new can then evolve. Concealing in order to reveal something, encrypting in order to make something visible.' His ethereal brushwork, gauzy tones and subdued palette oscillate between hiding and unveiling familiar forms. Some of his paintings are rooted in teach-yourself art manuals, yet instead of focusing on precise copying he leaves the works unfinished, in a state of engagement with abstraction and a sort of larger-than-life open-endedness.

The real tension in Helbig's paintings is that nothing is simply what it first appears to be. Though anchored around portraits, landscapes or art historical subjects, his compositions suggest an eerie, remote intangibility. *Wilde Mit Spiegel* (2004) echoes a traditional mirror-facing vanitas, but here it has been fleshed out through an abject model whose monstrosity seems to be disintegrating and shifting before our very eyes.

Maschine (2005) also deliberately plays with half-articulated meaning, as if delighting in teasing us with the idea of transition and *pareidolia* – the recognition of accidental anthropomorphic shapes in abstraction. Helbig's subversion of the viewer's expectations extends to his handmade frames, which are intentionally imperfect and lead us to contemplate further the undefined and uncertain nature of what it is we are looking at.

Helbig also makes sculptures which rest on plinths crafted by the artist. At first *Jungfrau* and *Vater* look like objects from an alien or ancient world. In fact they are strange, contorted hybrids made out of everyday junk, which has been reassembled to create these abstractions, both primitive and futuristic in their sensibility.

GEORG HEROLD

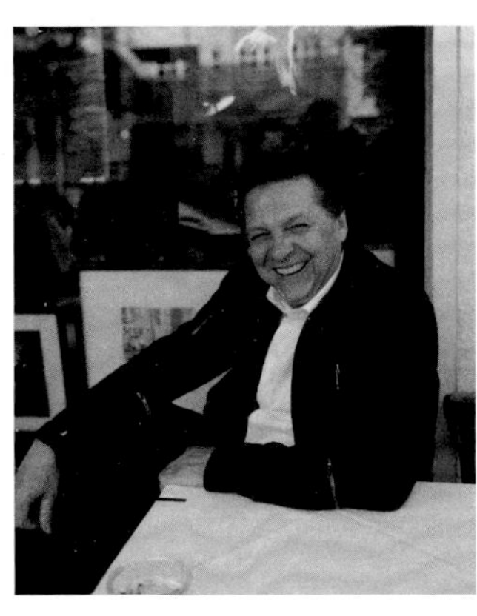

Georg Herold was born in Iena, East Germany in 1947. He studied at the Academy of Fine Art, Munich and at the Academy of Fine Art, Hamburg. He has had solo shows at Museum Brandhorst, Munich, Sadie Coles, London, CFA, Berlin, Friedrich Petzel Gallery, New York, The Modern Institute, Glasgow, SMAK, Gent, and Galerie Max Hetzler, Berlin. He lives in Cologne.

Georg Herold's arching and stretching anthropomorphic sculptures from 2010 suggest an ambiguous, self-aware state of tension. The crude stick figure minimalism of the two reclining bodies contrasts with the visceral nature of their poses. There is something fetishistic about these figures: one looks like it's being dragged along the ground with its hands tied up; the other exaggeratedly bends its back in an overtly sexualised and gendered stance. The viewer is left to take in the weird conceptual paradox they embody: the objectifying dehumanisation they point to and the very human artifice of their construction — they are made out of roof battens, canvas, lacquer thread and screws, materials which the artist has been working with for decades.

In the late 1970s Herold studied with Sigmar Polke and soon after became associated with a wave of radical young German artists including Albert Oehlen and Martin Kippenberger. His work reflected an anti-bourgeois rebelliousness and appropriated building materials and caviar alike as the vehicles for his artistic expression. The lack of a single unifying principle, material or interpretative, is one of the consistent aspects of Herold's work. Whether presenting a simple plank of wood on a wall or an abstract portrait made out of numbered fish eggs, he prefers to leave the viewer to ponder on his mysterious visual propositions, their meaning half-familiar, half-alien.

Herold's work plays with our expectations of what it is we are seeing, what art is, or should be, and with the artist's role in making meaning and challenging the viewer. 'I intend to reach a state that is ambiguous and allows all sorts of interpretations', he has declared. The artist's ironic, pop-tinged humour is an irresistible part of the process.

VOLKER HUELLER

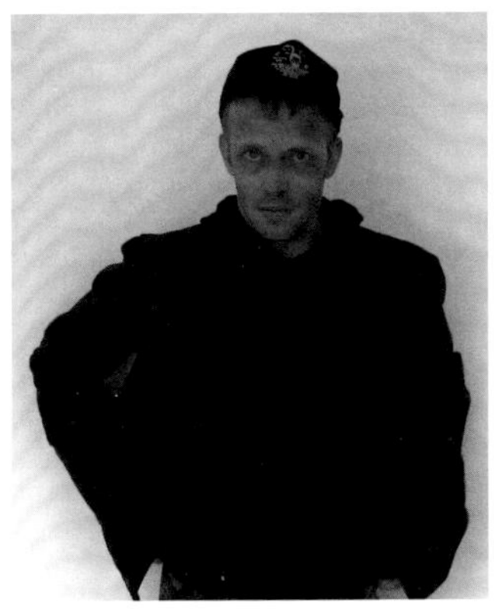

Volker Hueller was born in Forchheim, Germany in 1976. He studied at the Academy of Fine Arts, Hamburg and the GSO, Nürnberg. His most recent solo shows have been at Eleven Rivington, New York, Timothy Taylor Gallery, London, Produzentengalerie, Hamburg and Grimm Fine Art, Amsterdam. He lives in Berlin.

Volker Hueller's large-format collaged canvases and smaller hand-coloured etchings engulf the viewer in a world where shapes and meaning arc fragmented and interconnected to present an eerily abstract sense of portraiture. The monochromatic patchwork of textures in *Sie Sind Unter Uns XII* and the washed out tones of *Drei Halunken Und Ein Halleluja's* geometric figuration (both 2009) articulate a strange tension: figuration is created and sustained by the abstract patterned shards cutting through the visual ground.

Stylised silhouettes of heads in profile taken from 1930s advertisements inhabit *Drei Halunken Und Ein Halleluja* with its angular and curved lines and soft, transparent hues. The overall pattern can be re-interpreted as something more than coolly assigned decorative motif: it seems to be a necessary spatially symbolic graphic which anchors the figurative elements, a sort of *sine qua non* in Hueller's world. The whole composition is like a modernist-aware yin and yang, where each component in these pairings — darkness and light, figuration and non-representation — is part of the other.

Portraiture, and the symbolic geometry of the face and head, is one of Hueller's central preoccupations. *My Portrait In The Year 2080* (2007) is both whimsical and dark with its nebulous combination of filled in and empty spaces, its squiggly hairs and wrinkles, blackened teeth and nervous crosshatching. Its ostensive self-caricature sets up a dialogue with the imperfection and intimacy of outsider and avant-garde paper-based art. This visual thread is continued in the raw doodling and associative, prism-like compositions of *Puppetmaster, Wohin-Sehen, Rauch Im Aug, Elegy,* and *Untitled (Haupt)* (all 2009).

Art history informs Hueller's works, whether it might be echoes of Paul Klee's fanciful abstractions, Antonin Artaud's hallucinogenic, shamanistic ink drawings, Miró's early surrealist works or Picasso's harlequins and greyscale compositions, which in Hueller's hands all coalesce into something new.

THOMAS KIESEWETTER

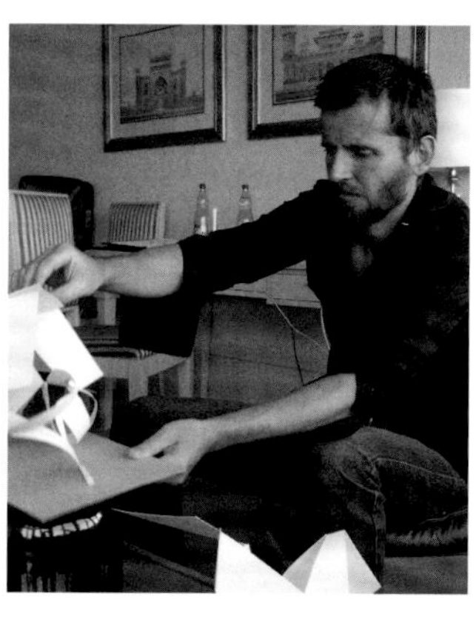

Thomas Kiesewetter was born in Kassel in 1963. He has had solo shows at CFA, Berlin, Sies + Höke Galerie, Düsseldorf, Galerie Almine Rech, Paris, Roberts & Tilton, Los Angeles and Jack Tilton Gallery, New York. He lives in Berlin.

Thomas Kiesewetter makes elegant abstract sculptures in which an industrial material, sheet metal, is playfully bent, folded and imbued with organic, almost human characteristics. Bolted together and painted in bold colours, his sculptures are reminiscent of modernist architectural shapes, as much as they make us conscious of the solidity of their single material. These angular works, unified by their material and their colour, look as if they have been frozen in action, caught mid-stride in their slightly neurotic articulation.

'What strikes me with metal as a material is its resistance. Metal seems to me like a stubborn interlocutor and the attempt to change it by pushing and bending involves a certain energy and power. The material demands patience, as it needs to be persuaded into acquiescence while it rigidly proclaims itself as unalterable. When the metal is bent physically, the energy of bending remains apparent.'

Matisse Blau and *Barriere* (both 2010) rest on plinths and are far sturdier than the more precarious shapes of his previous works. 'The earlier sculptures such as *Untitled* (2004) are static and resemble figures. There is a constant notion of a singular unity that continues throughout the working process.'

The newer works push the material and formal qualities of metal further, collapsing what look like architectonic quotations and modernist atelier icons, and at the same time ironically redefining the connotations of his material – from rigid hardness, strength and industrial alienation, to something more pliable, harmless and life-like. '*Matisse Blau* and *Barriere* have more of a flow and momentum. In these sculptures I tried to capture something of the lightness of Henri Matisse's paper cut-outs against the heaviness of the metal.'

JUTTA KOETHER

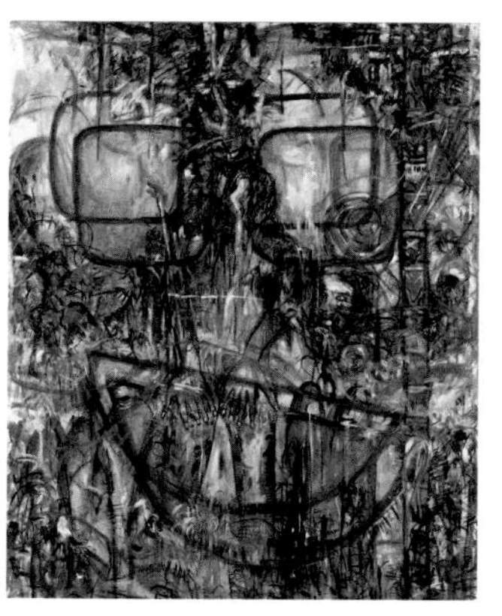

Jutta Koether was born in Cologne in 1958. She has had solo shows at Galerie Daniel Buchholz, Cologne, Reena Spaulings Fine Art, New York, Bergen Kunsthall, Norway, Sutton Lane, Paris, Galerie Francesca Pia, Zürich and Susanne Vielmetter, Los Angeles. She lives in New York.

Jutta Koether's abstract paintings, with their translucent interconnected web patterns, fragments of texts and songs, are like a portrait of the artist in our times. She is a painter, but not only that. Interweaving soft, sinuous brushwork and delicate colouring with bold cartoon-style figuration and graffiti-making is just part of a bigger whole – an interdisciplinary artistic practice overlapping performance, music, writing and other activities, and reflecting her strong, feminist, punk/pop-influenced engagement with contemporary theory and culture.

Koether used to edit the German culture and music publication *Spex* and has been based in New York since the 1990s. In her vibrant paintings she shows a fascination with the German 'bad painting' of Martin Kippenberger and Albert Oehlen, while taking unabashed pleasure in the physical, handicraft of art-making and its associations with traditional women's work. Her lush style is reminiscent of the fluid nature of street art, DIY and self-published comic books, and shares a similar disregard for received ideas about technique.

Gesturing hands, legs and a face float amidst the sketchy greens of *Mède* (1992). Multiple embedded elements are fused into a swirling, magnetic whole whose stormy, messy layering includes a strangely pop 'smiley face' over the whole work. *Frontage (Well, Show Me Nothing)* (1994) features an exploding cartoon bubble at its centre, from which contradicting lines, figurative elements and letters radiate and intersect in thinned pastel shades. The lines recalling railway maps, a hand holding dollar bills in the upper right-hand corner and an open one at the centre of the canvas suggest multiple possible narratives in the sweeping abstract composition.

Leibhaftige Malerei (2007), an elegant large-scale painting, harnesses abstract abandonment into a dark forest scene depicting figures performing a mysterious act in the foreground. The painting fuses Koether's interest in experimental technique with the primal, raw power of self-consciously primitivistic imagery.

FRIEDRICH KUNATH

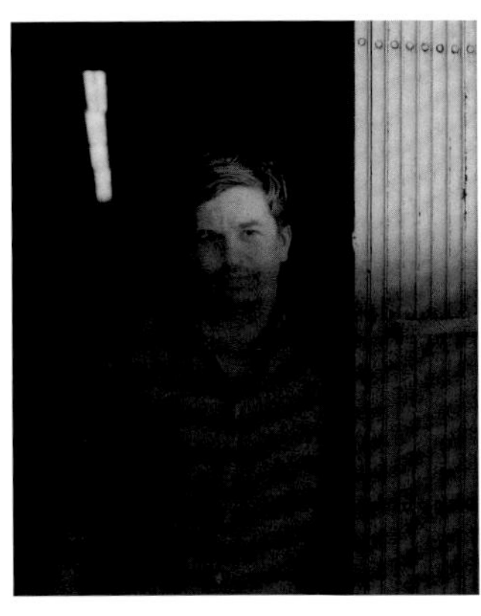

Friedrich Kunath was born in Chemniz, Germany in 1974. He has had solo shows at the Schinkel Pavillion and BQ, Berlin, White Cube, London, Andrea Rosen Gallery, New York, Kaikai Kiki, Tokyo, Kunstalle Baden-Baden, Kunstverein Hannover, Hammer Museum of Art and Blum & Poe, Los Angeles. He lives in Los Angeles.

Friedrich Kunath uses a wide range of ubiquitous media to explore themes around the melancholy, existential nature of everyday experience. His drawings, photos, prints and sculptures have an immediate yet quizzical charge, raising questions about the obvious. Kunath has the ability to imbue approachable, ordinary materials with conceptual heft, always lacing his treatment of quotidian pathos with a jester-like humour.

Untitled (2007) builds up an exaggerated, vaudeville-style mask of sadness through parts that make it whole: a bird on a branch, a knotted rainbow, snowy windows, an inverted statue at dusk, branches blowing in the wind, a black giant poodle hanging its head. A symbolic single perfect tear and a lengthy staircase fall from the eyes of this tragicomic blonde harlequin, whose diamonds have been transposed onto his cheeks.

The seven colour photographs comprising *First Life Takes Time Then Time Takes Life* (2010) show seven frames almost repeating the same still-life composition: a piece of toast leaning on a pineapple-shaped white vase. Gravitas and the art-historical *memento mori* are referenced and made lighter by the gag inherent in Kunath's visual pun – the 'time' alluded to in the title is illustrated through the noticeable change from frame to frame, showing the slice of bread being 'overexposed' and toasted to a cinder.

In the sculpture *Untitled* (2007), Kunath teases out ideas of existential anxiety shedding literal light over an appropriated *New Yorker* cartoon of shipwrecks hiding from their rescuers. The platform on which the scene is being examined is completed by kitschy figurines, including the classical Pierrot. Summing up Kunath's sad clown approach to art-making are his thoughts on becoming an artist: 'I can only refer to Werner Herzog, who said that the only artists left are those working in the circus.'

STEFAN KÜRTEN

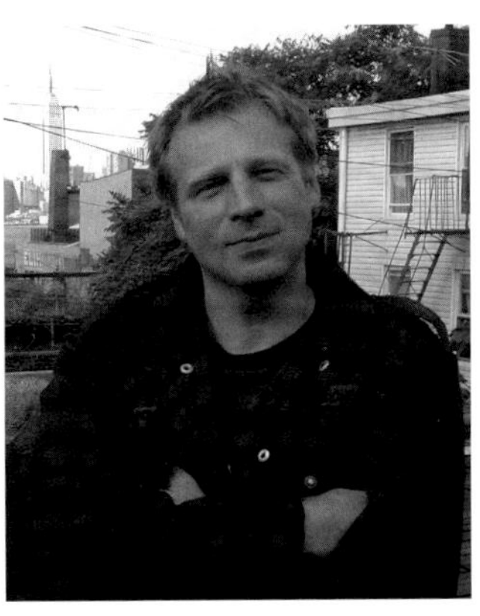

Stefan Kürten was born in Düsseldorf in 1963. He studied at the Heinrich Heine University, Düsseldorf, Kunstakademie in Düsseldorf, and the Art Institute, San Francisco. He has had solo shows at Thomas Dane Gallery, London, Hosfelt Gallery, San Francisco, Galerie Ute Parduhn, Düsseldorf and Alexander and Bonin, New York. He lives in Düsseldorf and New York.

Stefan Kürten's architecture-based compositions propose a new Germany growing over abandoned constructs and aspirations of a fading past, where memories are broken down and allowed to mutate into dizzying pattern and abstraction – and, notably, where man-made structures and nature are seen to coalesce.

Decorativeness and ornament permeate his oil paintings. The surfeit of roots, branches, foliage and flowers looming over interior objects and neat brick walls is almost impossible to take in all at once. The subjects in the mid-century art collector chic of *Ultramarine II* (2004), the busy pattern and soft furnishings of *Long Time Now* (2002) and the backyard vertigo of flora and collapsed modernist housing of *The Handsome Family* (2004) and *Heartbeat* (2004-2005) share a slightly aggressive sense of wild, untamed beauty perhaps most disquieting in the overgrown brutalism of *Silence* (2001). Rich metallic tones imbue his motifs with an unreal, oneiric aura, displacing them from their usual context, as if referencing the look and connotation of religious illuminations.

Kürten's catalogue of imagery merges the impersonal with an intimate sense of presence, creating a weird domestic geography that's both comforting in its familiarity and asphyxiating in its excessive detail. As the artist puts it, 'the paintings are differing versions of an idyll, or rather stages of disappearing idylls. They seem to find a last refuge in all sorts and styles of picturesque houses with manicured lawns and cosy living rooms, or tamed and domesticated versions of nature, the gardens and parks of our communal recreation, counter-images and escapes from the quotidian and its purposeful rationality. Like faded images from a long expired dream, their very lack of authenticity makes them true.'

JOSEPHINE MECKSEPER

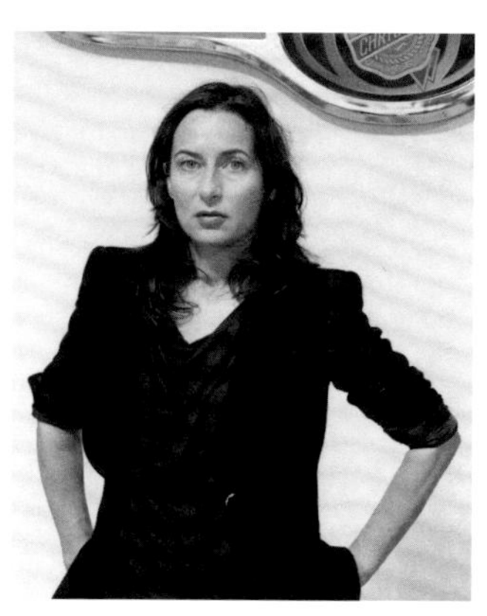

Josephine Meckseper was born in Lilienthal, Germany in 1964. She studied at the California Institute of the Arts and Berlin's Hochschule der Künste. She has exhibited widely including at Elizabeth Dee Gallery, the Whitney Biennial and MoMA, New York, Arndt, Berlin and Migros Museum für Gegenwartskunst, Zurich. She lives in New York.

Josephine Meckseper makes collages and installations that reconstruct the worlds of contemporary advertising and fashion in the context of the gallery, as a way of critiquing the political implications of the iconography of consumer culture.

In her display cases and photographs we see people and things re-objectified, symbolically removed from their original, all too familiar mediated contexts, and rearranged into self-consciously mirrored window dressing. 'Yes, the mirror and chrome sculptures, glass-and-steel vitrines, and mirror slatwalls are not affirmations or glorifications of consumerism,' Meckseper says. 'Their shiny surfaces are meant as provocations for destruction. They are designed to be targets, like high-end shop windows being smashed during riots and protests. These works mimic retail aesthetics in order to activate the commercial zone into a political one.'

In *Untitled* (2005) a naked mannequin stands in front of a terrorist biography, wearing a hoodie and scarf, both menacing and politically charged items as well as emblems of 'radical chic'. Issues around power, class, nationalism and gender are raised through the fetishised, cropped poses of underwear models and anthropomorphic props in *Blow Up (Michelli)* (2006), *Untitled (End Democracy)* (2005) and the Godardian liquidation sale of *Tout Va Bien* (2005).

Ubi Pedes Ibi. Patria (Where the feet are, there is the fatherland) (2006) provokes free-associative thoughts of sweatshop labour, bargain basement desperation, social homogeneity and images of shoe piles from the Holocaust. A witty take on cultural consumption, *The Complete History of Postcontemporary Art* (2005) is redolent with 1990s art allusions, while in *Pyromaniac 2* (2003) lifestyle ideals merge with revolutionary violence in a female model on the brink of self-combustion.

Meckseper's politically engaged works highlight ongoing problems of corporate corruption, status anxiety, social privilege and representations of women. They are also a chilling reminder of the excesses and distortions of capitalism, which has created a world in which, she would argue, there is no separation between materialism and political ideology: we are what we buy.

KIRSTINE ROEPSTORFF

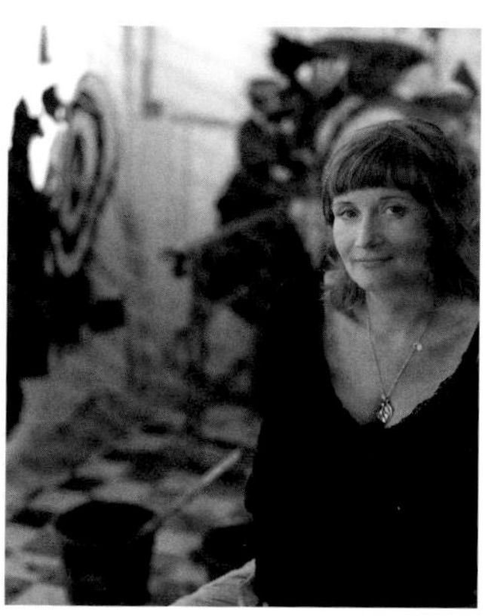

Kirstine Roepstorff was born in Copenhagen in 1972. She studied at the Royal Academy of Fine Arts, Copenhagen, and at Mason School of Fine Art, Rutgers University, US. She has had solo shows at Peres Projects, Berlin and LA, Galerie Mullerdechiara, Berlin, Galleri Christina Wilson, Copenhagen, Patricia Low, Gstaad and RH Gallery, New York. She lives in Berlin and Copenhagen.

Kirstine Roepstorff's mounted collages combine paper, pearls, sequins and paint to create new worlds in which found imagery and associations are re-created, deconstructed and given a glittery agit-prop urgency. She collects material in a variety of media and transposes it onto found political and advertising photography, through a technique which she has called 'appropriarranging': using the method of collage to appropriate and rearrange reality.

Her images question the ideas behind cultural cliché, nodding to the politically subversive cut-and-paste tactics of Hannah Höch's Dadaist collages, the Situationists, the crammed visual seduction of Peter Blake's pop art, and the photo-based work of Sigmar Polke and Gerhard Richter. Humorous visual puns and wordplay permeate Roepstorff's paper tapestries. 'I'm attracted to forms, mostly because of the space they generate in between. I'm interested in how, on the one hand, forms are very concrete and, on the other hand, subject to abstractions and mental manipulations.'

Roepstorff builds up to a big picture of social critique through her combination of shock and 1970s-style kitsch. *You Are Being Lied to* (2002) posits a vision of a world dominated by middle-class white men, engaged in a variety of archetypal, if socially constructed, activities – the scene is littered with motorbikes, boats, fighter jets, sports and barbeque paraphernalia.

In *Hidden Truth* (2002) sci-fi housing nestles within mountains which frame a paradisical landscape of green rolling hills, perfect autumnal trees and, at the centre of it all, a sun-like cluster, floating and dazzling in the explosion of its material riches.

All Possible Experiences (2006) uses a central radiating image too, this time surrounded by a vast constellation of newsreel snaps representing a recent past and exposing the enigmatic spectacle of twentieth-century culture.

JULIAN ROSEFELDT

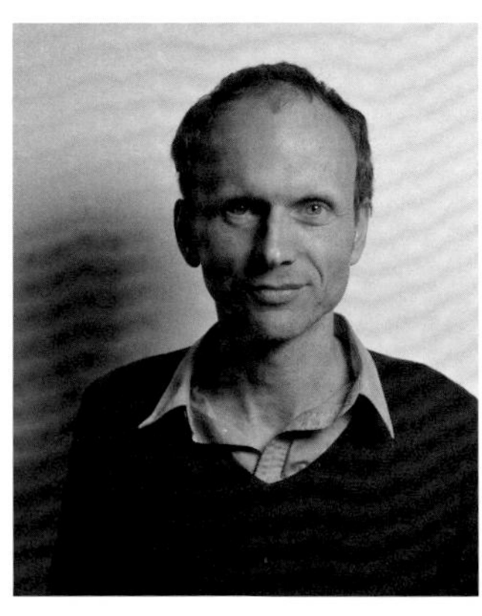

Julian Rosefeldt has exhibited internationally since 1997 at the Bienal de São Paulo, Athens Biennal, PS1, New York, Kunst-Werke Berlin e.V. – Institute for Contemporary Art, Royal Academy of Arts and BFI, London, Centre Pompidou, Paris, Galerie Arndt, Berlin, Max Wigram, London and the Kunstmuseum Bonn. He lives in Berlin.

Julian Rosefeldt's work reflects the artist's fascination with day-to-day reality, and the stereotypes, clichés and mindless repetitions that suffuse popular culture. Since the mid-1990s Roseteldt has been producing complex film and video installations, as well as photographs, through which we can observe from a cool, detached perspective the formulaic imagery and content that is generated by contemporary media.

Global Soap (2000-2001) was made by sifting through a massive collection of headshot stills taken from a source as contemporary and ubiquitous as reality shows: televised soap operas from around the world. The melodramatic expressions of the performers are ordered according to type, then sampled and re-edited into grid arrangements that form a kind of iconographic study of emotional codes, half real and half illusory, of our time. Rosefeldt's analysis of the repetitive gestures, facial expressions and situations appearing again and again in the soaps points to the genre's universal vocabulary and opera-like pace and choreography.

Rosefeldt has argued that 'soaps have taken over the function of the church' and, making an implicit reference to the work of German art historian Aby Warburg and his systematic study of the iconography of religious painting, he terms his distilled arrangements 'icons of the media age'.

In soaps, roles are polarised into familiar oppositions – the goodies and the baddies, innocence and guilt, victim and perpetrator – which override and overlook specific characteristics of ethnic and national identity. Warburg's types and formats, his 'formulas of pathos', are re-contextualised into the modern age through Rosefeldt's contemporary imagery, despite its highly contrived context.

MARKUS SELG

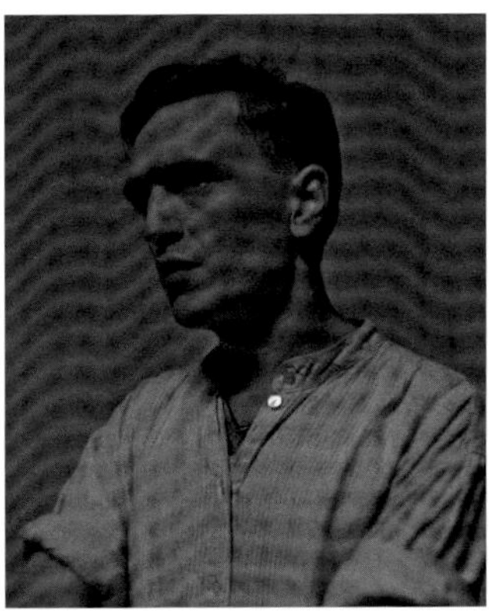

Markus Selg was born in Singen, Germany in 1974. From 1996 to 2000 he was part of the Akademie Isotrop, Hamburg, of which he was a founding member, and co-editor of Isotrop magazine. He has had solo shows at Galerie Guido W. Baudach, Berlin, SVIT, Prague, MeetFactory Gallery, Prague, Vilma Gold, London, Galerie Christine Mayer, Munich and Daniel Hug, Los Angeles. He lives in Berlin.

Markus Selg's myth-based work dares the viewer to reconsider contemporary art as all-encompassing, immersive and universal. His printmaking, sculpture and video-based practice is infused with recurring themes from world art history, and merges traditional craft and technology to re-spiritualise the role of the artist within a contemporary context.

Selg works in unusual self-isolation, quite literally: the artist has retreated into the woods in order to work, donning the role of the traditional craftsman and exploring the idea of self-sufficiency that accompanies it. At the same time, Selg takes advantage of the latest computer technology to produce multi-layered images like the dreamlike *Vorahnung (Premonition)* and the colour-saturated *Angelus* (both 2010), recalling the imagery and symbolism of earlier visual traditions of the German Romantics and Expressionists.

Thematically, night, nature, sex, life and death fill works such as the quasi-Biblical *Traum der Sarazenin* (2007) and the Gauguin-esque *Searching for Ruwenzori* (2010). Similar ideas around the life cycle, human loneliness and other allegorical states haunt his dramatically posed figures made out of plaster, jute, metal and wood. *Mild und Leise Wie Er Lächelt* (2008), which looks like a Buddhist icon, is more intricately ornamented and polished than more recent works from 2010 based on drawings, which free the figure with a more essentialised representation. *Trauernde (Mourner), Betender, Eva, Anima* and *Abgrund (Abyss)* show the artist continuing a three-dimensional shedding process and a tendency towards rustication, seen in the roughly-hewn *Bench (Tiger)* and *Chair (Hanush)* (all 2010).

The imagery in the works shown here is inspired by life and creation. When asked about the imperfections embedded in them, Selg refers to the sense of almost spiritual, single wholeness permeating his practice. 'All of The Creation is perfect…The less you care about form and the more you are able to follow your intuition, the closer you can get to a truth, which is not only following the outer world. The cardinal example of a *Gesamtkunstwerk* is life itself.'

GERT AND UWE TOBIAS

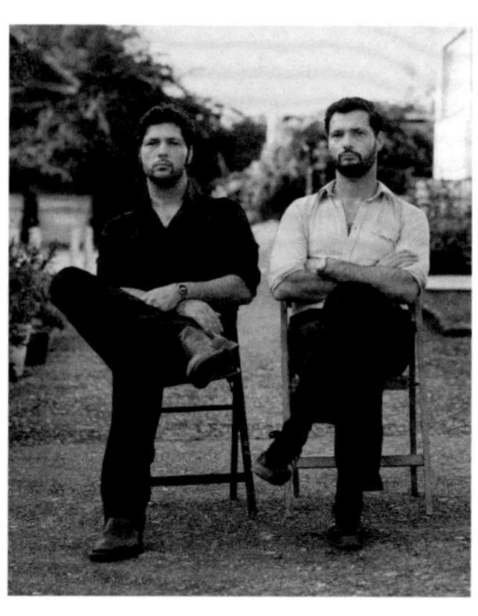

Gert and Uwe Tobias are twin brothers and were born in Brasov, Romania in 1973. They have exhibited their work widely including at the The Breeder, Athens, Galerie Rodolphe Janssen, Brussels, Team Gallery and MoMA, New York, Kunstmuseum Bonn, Hammer Museum of Art, Los Angeles, Nottingham Contemporary, UK and Gemeentemuseum, The Hague. They live in Cologne.

In Gert and Uwe Tobias's large-scale, carnivalesque panels we see an uncommon merging and subversion of techniques and traditions. The twin brothers, who have worked together since 2001, have created a world of their own out of reviving a diverse range of craft-based arts — wood-cuts, lace, embroidery and the national costume of their native Transylvania all find their way into their works.

In their engravings and collages traditional folk image-making skills, such as carving and hand printing, are given a twist, alchemically put through the filter of the twentieth and twenty-first century. Their exaggerated imagery, at turns abstract, geometric, fantastic and eerily animistic, carries remnants of the people in Breughel paintings, Russian Constructivism, and of Oskar Schlemmer's stereometric figuration (as in *Untitled*, 2009).

Gert and Uwe Tobias manage to fuse the monochrome backgrounds of Yves Tanguy's surrealist landscapes and the macabre faces of traditional apotropaeic amulets with the lightness of cartoons, worn down graffiti and schoolyard murals. There is something flayed about their figures — as if they have been peeled of their individuality, made into universal puppets or still lives.

Untitled (2007), composed of coloured woodcuts on papers mounted on canvas stretching over four metres in width, confronts the viewer with what look like heads precariously balanced on geometric poles that are weighed down by pulley-like arrangements. The modernist, Bauhaus-style mechanisation of the composition, dominated by primary shapes and graphic symbols — hearts, bull's eyes — becomes animated by perverse, half-toothed grins, horns, hair and cassocks and robotic pop-out eyes. Two large works named *Untitled* (2005) riff on traditional genres of still life and portraiture, bursting with whimsical abstraction, colouring and graphic boldness as well as a darker, gothic element — those grim-reaper smiles, a veiled countenance, skeleton bones, and menacing claws.

CORINNE WASMUHT

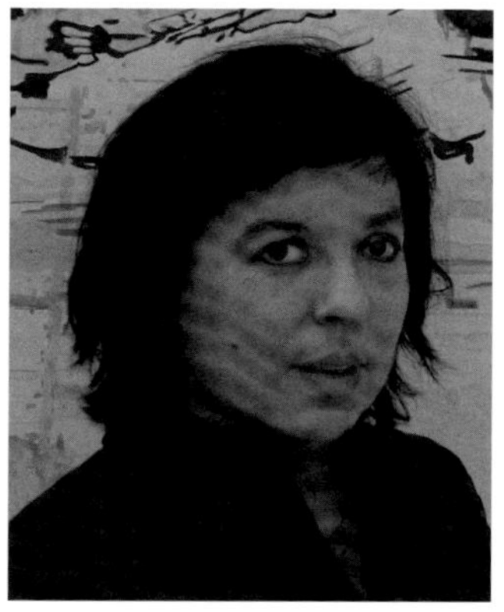

Corinne Wasmuht was born in Dortmund, Germany in 1964. She has had solo shows at Meyer Riegger Galerie, Berlin, Kunstraum Innsbruck, Kunsthalle Nürnberg, and Friedrich Petzel Gallery, New York. Her work was featured in ILLUMInations at the 54th Venice Biennale, 2011. She lives in Berlin.

Somewhere between the digital and the analogue, Corinne Wasmuht's mural-sized paintings stun the viewer with their enveloping perspectival composition and jagged explosion of colour. Wasmuht's work finds its origins in imagery sourced from the Internet which she collects, re-arranges, and then paints onto wooden panels in multiple layers, whose detail is apparent only when the viewer comes closer to the work. Layer upon layer of varnish adds a brightness to her colours, suggestive of the backlighting of HD televisions and computer monitors.

Wasmuht's paintings create a unique kind of illusory space, both abstract and fixed in recognisable form, and somehow almost tangible. Repeated shapes and colours in her paintings hint at a sense of *mise en abyme*, of infinitely multiplying mirrored images, reflecting the vastness of networked culture and a never-ending insatiable yearning for images and information.

Siempre Es Hoy (2010), a monumental oil painting on wood over four metres wide, is like a cinematic projection, larger than life in dimensions and overwhelming to the viewer with the collected data it contains. Dominating the left-hand area is an ambiguous shape that could be a seated human figure, gazing over an infinitely unfolding could-be cyberworld in whose imaginary planes this being is embedded. Wasmuht has spoken of wanting to step into these spaces, 'to live inside as in a real landscape… The painting is all around me; it encircles me completely.'

Dissolving spatial boundaries, her work invites the viewer to reconsider our relationships with all kinds of spaces, from urban panoramas to natural landscapes, to absorb a sublime sense of everythingness all at once.

ANDRO WEKUA

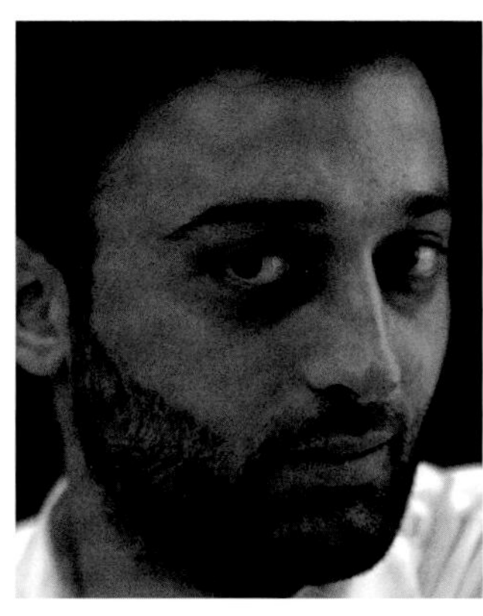

Andro Wekua was born in Sochumi, Georgia in 1977, and studied at the National Art School, Sochumi and at the Visual Art School, Basel. He has had solo shows at Gladstone Gallery, New York, Camden Art Centre, London, Galerie Peter Kilchmann, Zurich, Castello di Rivoli, Turin and the Kunsthalle Wien in Austria. His work was featured in ILLUMInations at the 54th Venice Biennale, 2011. He lives in Zurich and Berlin.

Andro Wekua's photographs and painted sculptural installations channel fragments from his own memories of childhood into mosaic-like narratives, conveying a very real but always remote sense of place. In his work, which often features an element of tiled form, it is as if broken images are being put back together, like a seductive but ultimately unsolvable puzzle.

Sunset (2008), an eight-metre wide installation composed of 170 glazed ceramic panels supported by metal scaffolding, is an abstract composition which is also reminiscent of a landscape with softly billowing clouds and a central red and black circle representing the sun falling over a darkening ground.

Primary colours dominate the work, whose painted areas are suggestive of strong but incomplete recollections typical of a dream or a long-ago experience, the details of which have become hazy over time. The scale of the work and its fired tile composition make it appear like an ominous public pool mural from the Soviet era, or a larger-than-life backdrop from a Ballets Russes production.

Aspects of his pieces have a decidedly East European flavour. His use of geometry and his photographic montages, such as *Black Sea Surfer* (2004) and *Covered* (2006), seem to come from the visual culture of Communism, but they also feel completely embedded within a more universal underground cinema aesthetic.

Although Wekua uses representational elements in most of his works, his visual symbolism is often perplexing and self-contained. His practice develops elements inspired by both contemporary culture and by his background – he is originally from Soviet Georgia but left at the age of 15 and has since then been living in Germany and Switzerland. All that remains of his past are ruins, strangely juxtaposed with his present-day perspective.

THOMAS ZIPP

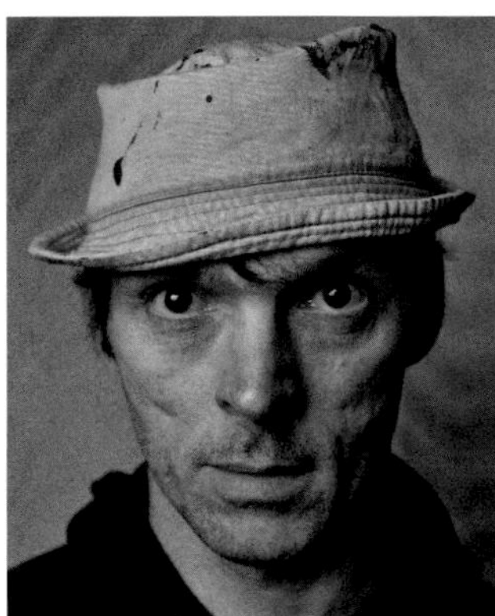

Thomas Zipp was born in Heppenheim, Germany in 1966. He studied at the Städelschule Frankfurt and the Slade School of Art in London, and has had solo shows at Galerie Guido W. Baudach, Berlin, Galerie Rüdiger Schöttle, Munich, Alison Jacques, London and Patrick Painter, Los Angeles. In 2010 he had a solo show at the Kunsthalle Fridericianum, Kassel. He lives in Berlin.

Thomas Zipp's installations appropriate the language of museum and scientific display to convey a madman-made, foreboding view of western civilisation's achievements. *Schwarze Ballons* (2005), a nine-part installation, includes among its components framed drawings that look like archival documentation, and roughly painted portraits of menacing individuals with brightly lit eyes, like undead gangsters. Two large black balloon-shaped sculptures, one suspended and one resting on the floor, fill the space with a sinister air. The work as a whole feels like a futuristic memorial, the result of an unfamiliar modern witchcraft.

Der Schlaf IV (y-drops) (2006) is an ominous installation in greyscale, consisting of a painting, a framed sheet with a crossed line and needle pricks, and chandeliers made out of fluorescent tubes. Sleep (the English translation of *Der Schlaf*) and the dark realm of the unconscious are referenced in the title and the mountain topped with sexually charged shapes painted in black. The framed sheet, with its unreadable message, points to indecipherable depths of dream logic and the impossibility of understanding even with the help of the bright lights overhead.

In Zipp's works, the free-association of the unconscious is an entry point into investigating collective guilt. *E-Licht* (2006), another museum-like display, juxtaposes two paintings – one of a flying zeppelin and the other a large, nervous abstraction – with a schematic drawing, like a minimalist condensation of idealist values from a previous era. *A.B.:H.G.:B.16.* (2005) and *World Kantzler Office* (2004) appropriate the codes of war-cabinet imagery to playfully question the way history is constructed.

Asked about his practice, Zipp responds with a brief history of lysergic acid diethylamine, aka LSD, and its early transition from medical hope to potential CIA tool for mind-control and chemical warfare. Each of Zipp's charismatic works aims to shed light on the quasi-fictional truths of post-Enlightenment so-called progress, conveying a sense of the real darkness lurking behind irrational, violent acts that are historically constructed as victories.

The Saatchi Gallery gratefully acknowledges the following who have contributed photographs of the artists and artworks:

Maja Bajevic, Maxime Ballesteros, Hans Bell, Thomas Brinkmann, Thor Brodreskift/Bergen Kunsthall, Ivo Corra, Anne Mie Dreves, Albrecht Fuchs, Olle Kirchmeier, Heinz Peter Knes, Jean Gid Lee, Jochen Littkemann, Roman März, Gunnar Meier, Benjamin Pritzkuleit, Stefan Ruiz, Fabian Schubert, Elfie Semotan, Karina Tengberg and Corinne Wasmuht

The Saatchi Gallery would also like to thank:
Alison Jacques Gallery, BQ Berlin, Contemporary Fine Arts Berlin, Eleven Rivington Gallery, Elizabeth Dee Gallery, Friedrich Petzel Gallery, Galerie Daniel Buchholz, Galerie Giti Nourbakhsch, Galerie Guido W. Baudach, Galerie Peter Kilchmann, Galerie Rüdiger Schöttle, Galleri Nicolai Wallner, Herald Street, Irena Hochman Fine Art, Josephine Meckseper Studio, Karma International Zürich, Max Wigram Gallery, Peres Projects, Thomas Dane Gallery, Timothy Taylor Gallery, Vilma Gold Gallery

Published by the Saatchi Gallery in 2011
© Saatchi Gallery 2011

Printed by ArtQuarters Press, London

Front cover: *Geschwister*, 2004 by Isa Genzken
Back cover: *Eva*, 2010 by Markus Selg

Lupe Núñez-Fernández is a writer and translator based in London and Madrid. She was formerly deputy editor of ArtReview, an editor at Phaidon Books and on the editorial staff at Modern Painters and LUX.

Designed by Georgina Marling of the Saatchi Gallery and Peter Gladwin of ArtQuarters Press